WAR CULTURE AND
THE **CONTEST** OF **IMAGES**

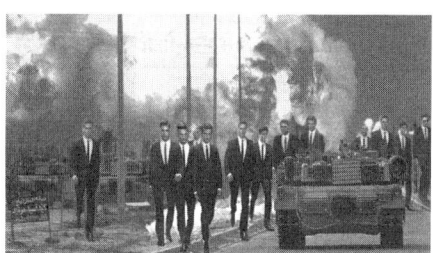

NEW DIRECTIONS IN INTERNATIONAL STUDIES

Patrice Petro, Series Editor

The New Directions in International Studies series focuses on transculturalism, technology, media, and representation, and features the innovative work of scholars who explore various components and consequences of globalization, such as the increasing flow of peoples, ideas, images, information, and capital across borders. Under the direction of Patrice Petro, the series is sponsored by the Center for International Education at the University of Wisconsin–Milwaukee. The center seeks to foster interdisciplinary and collaborative research that probes the political, economic, artistic, and social processes and practices of our time.

A. Aneesh, Lane Hall, and Patrice Petro, eds.
Beyond Globalization: Making New Worlds in Media, Art, and Social Practices

Dora Apel
War Culture and the Contest of Images

Daniel Leonard Bernardi, Pauline Hope Cheong, Chris Lundry, and Scott W. Ruston
Narrative Landmines: Rumors, Islamist Extremism, and the Struggle for Strategic Influence

Mark Philip Bradley and Patrice Petro, eds.
Truth Claims: Representation and Human Rights

Melissa A. Fitch
Side Dishes: Latina American Women, Sex, and Cultural Production

Elizabeth Swanson Goldberg
Beyond Terror: Gender, Narrative, Human Rights

Linda Krause and Patrice Petro, eds.
Global Cities: Cinema, Architecture, and Urbanism in a Digital Age

Andrew Martin and Patrice Petro, eds.
Rethinking Global Security: Media, Popular Culture, and the "War on Terror"

Tasha G. Oren and Patrice Petro, eds.
Global Currents: Media and Technology Now

Peter Paik and Marcus Bullock, eds.
Aftermaths: Exile, Migration, and Diaspora Reconsidered

Freya Schiwy
Indianizing Film: Decolonization, the Andes, and the Question of Technology

Cristina Venegas
Digital Dilemmas: The State, the Individual, and Digital Media in Cuba

WAR CULTURE AND THE CONTEST OF IMAGES

Dora Apel

RUTGERS UNIVERSITY PRESS
NEW BRUNSWICK, NEW JERSEY,
AND LONDON

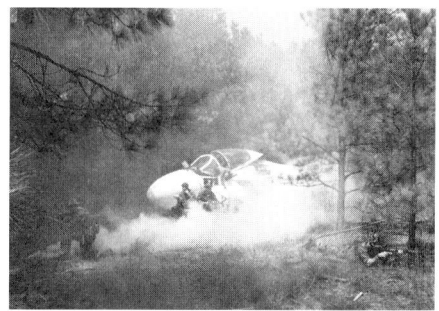

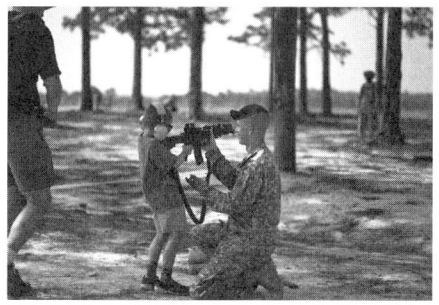

Library of Congress Cataloging-in-Publication Data
Apel, Dora, 1952–
  War culture and the contest of images / Dora Apel.
      pages cm — (New directions in international studies)
  Includes bibliographical references and index.
  ISBN 978-0-8135-5395-5 (hardcover : alk. paper) — ISBN 978-0-8135-5394-8 (pbk. : alk. paper) — ISBN 978-0-8135-5396-2 (e-book)
  1. Art and war. 2. War and society. 3. Art and society. I. Title.
  N8260.A64 2012
  701'.03—dc23
2011048990
A British Cataloging-in-Publication record for this book is available from the British Library.

Copyright © 2012 by Dora Apel
All rights reserved
No part of this book may be reproduced or utilized in any form or by any means, electronic or mechanical, or by any information storage and retrieval system, without written permission from the publisher. Please contact Rutgers University Press, 106 Somerset Street, New Brunswick, NJ 08901. The only exception to this prohibition is "fair use" as defined by U.S. copyright law.

Visit our website: http://rutgerspress.rutgers.edu

Manufactured in the United States of America

*In memory of my parents,
Samuel and Ethel Apel,*

and

for Rachel

CONTENTS

List of Illustrations ix
Acknowledgments xi

Introduction 1

PART I
THE ROMANCE OF WAR

1 Technologies of War, Media, and Dissent
 in the Post-9/11 Work of Krzysztof Wodiczko 17
2 Historical Reenactment: Romantic
 Amnesia or Counter-Memory? 47

PART II
THE BODY OF WAR

3 Abu Ghraib, Gender,
 and the Military 79
4 The Body as Political Corpus 112

PART III
THE LANDSCAPE OF WAR

5 Controlling the Frame: Photojournalism,
 Digital Technology, and "Modern Warfare" 151
6 Israel/Palestine and the Political Imaginary 183

Conclusion: On Human Rights 232

Notes 239
Selected Bibliography 255
Index 261

ILLUSTRATIONS

1. Krzysztof Wodiczko, *If You See Something...*, 2005   20
2. Krzysztof Wodiczko, *...OUT OF HERE: The Veterans Project*, 2009–2011   41
3. An-My Lê, *Rescue*, from series *Small Wars*, 1999–2002   67
4. Iraq Veterans against the War, *Operation First Casualty*, New York City, 29 May 2007   70
5. First lynching reenactment at Moore's Ford, Georgia, 2005   74
6. Coco Fusco, still from video *Operation Atropos*, interrogator and "detainee," 2006   98
7. Photo posted on Facebook by former Israeli soldier Eden Abergil, posing with Palestinian detainee, 2010   101
8. Regina José Galindo, *Confesión* (Confession), 2007   113
9. Guillermo Gómez-Peña and La Pocha Nostra, performance still of *Mapa Corpo 3* with Violeta Luna, Detroit Institute of Arts, 28 October 2008   119
10. "Iraqis chant anti-American slogans as charred bodies hang from a bridge over the Euphrates River in Fallujah," 31 March 2004   124
11. *Flat Daddy*, 2006   127
12. Nina Berman/NOOR, *Pfc. Alan Jermaine Lewis*, 2003, from series *Purple Hearts*   131
13. Timothy Greenfield-Sanders, *Dawn Halfaker, First Lt., U.S. Army*, 2006   133
14. Nina Berman/NOOR, *Marine Wedding*, 2006, from series *Marine Wedding*   137
15. Ewa Harabasz, *Untitled*, 2005–2006   140
16. Adi Nes, *Untitled*, 1996   141
17. Adi Nes, *Untitled*, 2003, from series *Prisoners*   144
18. Martha Rosler, *Invasion*, 2008   147
19. Geert van Kesteren, American soldiers raiding apartment in Baghdad, 2003–2004   157
20. Dying Iraqi doctor in bed at hospital. Photo sent via cell phone for *Baghdad Calling*, 2005–2007   158
21. Three bodies dumped in a lot. Photo sent via cell phone for *Baghdad Calling*, 2005–2007   160
22. Ashley Gilbertson/VII Network, "A marine slides down the marble handrail in Saddam's palace in Tikrit," 2003   166
23. Ashley Gilbertson/VII Network, "One of four Iraqis who surrendered to the marines and said they were students trying to avoid battle," 2004   168
24. Nina Berman/NOOR, *Human Target Practice, All America Day, Ft. Bragg, North Carolina*, 2006, from series *Homeland Insecurities*   171
25. David Tartakover, *Greeting Card*, 2006   192
26. Rana Bishara, *Homage to Palestine*, 1999   197

27. Mohammed al-Hawajri, *Cactus Borders*, 2010 197
28. Shai Kremer, *The Separation Wall, Jerusalem*, 2005, from series *Infected Landscape* 198
29. Shai Kremer, *Interior, Urban Warfare Training Center, Tze'elim*, 2007, from series *Infected Landscape* 199
30. Miki Kratsman, *Nablus #2*, 2003, from series *West Bank and Gaza Strip* (1986–2008) 201
31. Nir Kafri, *Balata Refugee Camp*, 2002 202
32. Gilad Ophir, *Untitled*, 1997 204
33. Miki Kratsman, *Road 443 #9*, 2001, from series *Panoramas of Occupation* (1999–2009) 207
34. Miki Kratsman, *Gilo 1*, 2001, from series *Panoramas of Occupation* (1999–2009) 208
35. Miki Kratsman, *Gilo 2*, 2001, from series *Panoramas of Occupation* (1999–2009) 209
36. Banksy, Palestine, 2005 211
37. Banksy, stenciled image of living room with view painted over 212
38. Artists without Walls, *Eastern Side/Abu Dis*, 2004 213
39. Miki Kratsman, *Abu Dis*, 2003, from series *Panoramas of Occupation* (1999–2009) 214
40. Miki Kratsman, *Territory 0201-2*, 2005, from series *Territory* 218
41. Gaston Zvi Ickowicz, *Untitled*, from series *Settlement*, 2006 219
42. Yael Bartana, still from *Zamach (Assassination)*, 2011 221
43. Tamy Ben-Tor, *Women Talk about Adolf Hitler*, still from video, 2004 224
44. Boaz Arad, *Marcel, Marcel*, still from video, 2000 225
45. Sigalit Landau, *Barbed Hula*, still from video, 2000 229

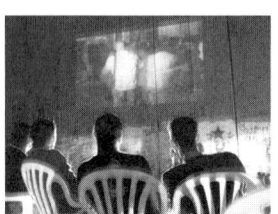

ACKNOWLEDGMENTS

For generous funding of this project I thank Wayne State University for the Research Enhancement Awards in the Arts and the Career Development Chair; Walter Edwards and the Humanities Center; the University Faculty Fellowship and the Dean's Creative/Research Award. I also thank my department chair, John Richardson, for his support, and Marie Persha, Terry Kerby, Ian Chapp, and Ted Duenas for their assistance. I thank my superb research assistant, Jonathan Salvati, and the students in my courses on Imagery of War from Goya to Iraq and the seminars Trauma, Memory, and Visual Culture, and Trauma, War, and Photography.

I thank all of the artists, and their galleries, who generously shared their work and images, as well as the director of exhibitions, Brian Wallis, at the International Center for Photography in New York and Director Raphie Etgar at the Museum on the Seam in Jerusalem for meeting with me to discuss exhibitions they sponsored and to share materials. I thank Ruth Weinstein for her warm hospitality while I conducted research in Israel/Palestine, and the artists who met with me there, including Rana Bishara, Yael Bartana, and Boaz Arad. I also thank David Cotterrell, Shai Kremer, An-My Lê, Krzysztof Wodiczko, Ewa Harabasz, Martha Rosler, Guillermo Gómez-Peña, and Violeta Luna for meeting with me in New York, Detroit, at Art Basel Miami, or elsewhere.

Many of the ideas in these chapters began as conference presentations. I thank all those who invited me to present my research on war images, including James Elkins and Maria-Pia di Bella, who organized the conference on "The Representation of Pain" at University College Cork in Ireland; Ewa Harabasz and Buzz Spector, who invited me to speak to the Department of Art at Cornell University; Lisa Langlois and Artswego at the State University of New York at Oswego, who invited me to speak to the Department of Art and the International Studies Program; Sally Schluter-Tardella and the Honor Society at Oakland University in Rochester, Michigan, who invited me to speak to the Honors College; Corinne Granof at the Block Museum of Art at Northwestern University who organized the symposium "Visual and Literary Culture in Germany between the Wars"; Eric J. Sundquist, who organized the conference on "Aesthetics after the Holocaust" for the UCLA/Mellon Program on the Holocaust in American and World Culture; Walter Edwards, who organized the Humanities Center conferences on "The Environment" and "Questioning Foundations and Methods in the Humanities and Arts" for Faculty Fellows at Wayne State University; Juergen Martschukat, Silvan Niedermeier, and

Michael Wildt, who organized the conference on "Violence and Visibility: Historical, Cultural, and Political Perspectives from the 19th Century to the Present" at Humboldt University in Berlin; and Sarah Rogers and Noah Simblest, who organized the session panel "Interdependent Identity: Paradigm and Paradox in Contemporary Israeli and Palestinian Art" at the College Art Association Conference in New York City. I also thank the colleagues and audiences before whom I presented these papers.

Chapter 1 on Krzysztof Wodiczko is an updated and extended version of an essay originally published in *Oxford Art Journal* 31:2 (July 2008), and reprinted in *Krzysztof Wodiczko*, edited by Duncan McCorquodale (Black Dog Publishing, 2011). Versions of the text on Martha Rosler's work *Invasion* (chapter 4), Wodiczko's work *Veteran Vehicle Project* (chapter 1), and the Iraq Veterans against the War project *Operation First Casualty* (chapter 2) were first published as "Iraq, Trauma and Dissent in Visual Culture," in *What Is Radical Politics Today?*, edited by Jonathan Pugh (Palgrave Macmillan, 2009).

At Rutgers University Press, I am grateful to the marvelous editor-in-chief, Leslie Mitchner, and series editor Patrice Petro. One couldn't ask for better or more supportive editors with whom to work. I thank all those associated with the press who helped shepherd this book to completion. I am also grateful to my friends, colleagues and family for their encouragement and support, which has greatly contributed to the writing of this book in ways large and small. Enormous gratitude is especially due my husband, Gregory Wittkopp, who is always on the lookout for research material, ever willing to read my drafts, and never holds back from pointing out their weaknesses. He has gamely shared my life through continuing research on lugubrious topics and never (hardly ever) complains about not having sabbaticals or summers for research and writing. I also thank my daughter, Rachel Apel Wittkopp, whose high sense of justice makes a mother proud. This book is dedicated to her.

**WAR CULTURE AND
THE CONTEST OF IMAGES**

INTRODUCTION

In modern warfare and the accompanying culture of war that capitalism produces as a permanent feature of modern society, the contest of images is as critical as the war on the ground. We might say that the contest of images is the continuation of war by other means, affecting not only our political understanding of the present, but also of the past, in ongoing battles for meaning that are fought out on the field of visual representation. At stake are the prevailing myths of national identity and the social and political policies of the state in relation to the lives and liberties of domestic populations as well as other peoples and nations. We begin from the understanding that the documentary image is always framed in order to control the visual and narrative dimensions of war and its ramifications. This framing is structured by the choices and conditions that are part of the image production, by what is included and what is excluded, and by the agencies, institutions, groups, and discourses that surround the circulation of the image. As Judith Butler has shown, the frame is not merely a passive device but must be understood as a structuring device that actively interprets what is real and what is not. Thus our critical attention must be focused on the conditions of the frame and how it limits or presents what may be seen and what may count as reality.[1] Yet even as the state solicits our complicity in the normalization of war and the destruction of targeted populations, the effects of war can never be fully contained by the frame; reality can never be fully controlled. In different contexts, the meanings of the same images may even contradict one another or contradict the original intentions of their producers, demonstrating the instability of the frame. Furthermore, the excluded or repressed excess to the frame provides "the potential resources for resistance." "In the destructiveness of war," writes Butler, "there is no way to restrict the trajectory of destruction to a single visualized aim. Invariably, the fantasy of controlled destruction undoes itself, but the frame is still there, as the controlling fantasy of the state, albeit marking its limit as well."[2] Examining how the controlling fantasy of the state "undoes itself" is one of the aims of this study.

The understanding that images are mediated in terms of both the production of the image itself and how the image is framed through context has been a given in photographic theory for two or three decades and has called into question the truth value of the documentary image while placing traditional documentary in a disputed and unstable position in relation to the field of artistic production. Yet the power of the documentary image is greater than ever, emerging during a period of social and political crises in the twenty-first century when the image can digitally travel the globe with unprecedented speed. Does the understanding that the photographic image is always framed undermine the potential of documentary practices today to function as weapons of radical critique? How do contemporary documentary practices make explicit the frame of meaning in ways that do not rely on tropes of universalism and transparency, which may be used to serve the cause of the state? How are contemporary documentary images used to construct counterhegemonic narratives and to call into place a public sphere, based on shared ways of seeing, that are critical of and outside the control of the state? How have critical documentary practices merged with artistic genres such as video, reenactment, performance, and conceptual art in new and dynamic relationships?

These are the overarching questions that govern my analysis of war culture and its oppositional responses; more specifically, I argue that documentary practices represent a visual culture of resistance engendered by the permanent culture of war in the United States and in the Middle Eastern zones of conflict in Iraq, Afghanistan, and Israel/Palestine (and growing globally). Recognizing that the disputed borders between documentary photography and politically engaged art have become increasingly permeable for technological, political, and cultural reasons, I believe this makes it all the more critical to examine the radical potential of documentary practices in relation to democratic ideals and social struggle and to focus on the conditions of making and discourses that surround contemporary documentary practice. Such practices have evolved to serve as weapons of critique against the perpetual militarization of society and to make visible the injustices done to those who may be recognized globally as fully deserving of democratic rights only in the public sphere that is called into place and constituted by these visual documentary practices.

Documentary and Democracy

Since the American Civil War, the aftermath of which was the first to be extensively photographed, war and related events are at least in part staged for the camera. This is as much a part of warfare as other strategic and tactical decisions, while every attempt is made to keep the staging, like all deceptions on which war is based, deliberately hidden from the camera. The U.S. government staged and documented a number of notorious "heroic" moments in the war on Iraq, such as the orchestrated toppling of the statue of Saddam Hussein in Baghdad by American troops following the city's occupation, or the simulated "Top Gun" landing of President George W. Bush on the USS *Lincoln* aircraft carrier in the embarrassingly and grossly premature "Mission Accomplished" publicity stunt.³ Other photographs, like those taken at Abu Ghraib prison and never meant to be made public, were taken by soldiers themselves, a practice that began in World War I, when war photos circulated by the thousands and were passed from hand to hand within like-minded communities of patriots and veterans, or among pacifists and antiwar activists.⁴ It is far more difficult today to keep the images made by soldiers hidden from the public. Since the introduction of popular Internet video-sharing sites and social networking sites such as YouTube and Facebook, tens of thousands of viewers have been able to watch videos of military operations, such as the torture and abuse of Iraqi prisoners by U.S. soldiers, or U.S. troops under attack in which soldiers are hit by snipers or armored Humvees are hit by roadside bombs as a camera records the action.

On one level, the uncontrolled explosion of imagery may be seen as feeding a desire for a "universal archive." Artist and curator Jorge Ribalta describes the universal archive as a dream or unconscious repository based on the belief that the unruly disorder of the world can be ordered and contained in "a rational-organized-industrialized system" that provides the basis for myths of both national identity and universal citizenship in the liberal public sphere.⁵ The idea of universal citizenship, by promoting a transnational global public sphere tied to the state, elides most forms of oppression and those excluded from political rights; the mythical universal citizen embodies the nation, which still depends on the paradigm of the white Western Christian heterosexual male. Militarism is justified as loyalty to and defense of the nation, and the universal archive comes to serve, in Ribalta's terms, "the legitimation of the modern romantic-colonial nation-state system."⁶ The Internet archive today becomes part of this machinery, which mobilizes and recruits the liberal public sphere of largely young male viewers for whom this imagery replaces the real with the representational and offers a romanticized narrative of sacrifice and heroism in service to the state.

All war experience is publicly understood only through representation. Even combatants, whose perceptions of a vast and complex war are limited to their own immediate experience and subject to the traumatic effects of that experience, produce and rely on photographs and videos so that they can remember what happened and legitimize their own experience through these images, often by posting them on the Internet as part of the "universal archive." These file-sharing sites generally have minimal captions and no apparent framing narratives, and this seeming lack of framing devices is a large part of their appeal, allowing viewers—again, usually young men—to focus on the excitement of individual experience, the "manliness" of combat, rather than on the historical specificity and ramifications of the events or the political significance of the larger conflict. The posting of imagery on the Internet has become such a pervasive global trend precisely because of the seemingly uncensored viewing it provides, allowing the viewer to insert the images into whatever narrative they "choose." Yet those political and social narratives are all too readily constructed by dominant patriotic discourses, and are in turn constituted and reinforced by these images.

Theorist John Tagg historicizes documentary as a practice that emerged during the New Deal era of the 1930s and served the interests of the liberal-corporate state during a period of severe crisis. This crisis was social and political as well as economic and threatened capitalist rule. Documentary practice, he argues, was a deliberate cultural strategy that the state instrumentalized for "social consensus, national cohesion, the displacement of radical explanations, and the restoration of a sense that policy could be grounded on shared recognitions of authentic experience." Programs were developed to employ artists in order to construct a national community based on a concept of social loyalty and responsibility, one which would "no longer be divided by the conflicts and contradictions of capitalist development" and which supported interventions by the state as a benevolent paternal body.[7] Documentary practices were thus part of a "machinery of capture" that had little to do with "the poor and dispossessed," the "*objects* of documentary," and more to do with the "recruitment of *subjects* as citizens, called to witness" at a time of crisis when national cohesion was needed.[8] Despite his brilliant analysis, Tagg takes on a despairing tone, which Ribalta regards as "melancholic defeatism" and associates with Tagg's decision to focus on hegemonic practices and discourses to the exclusion of any resistance or disruption.[9]

To demonstrate his thesis that even the most straightforward-seeming truth value of the documentary image can serve the state, Tagg uses the example of the 1992 Rodney King video, which was used by a jury to acquit the police who gratuitously beat a defenseless black man. Yet the broader public saw the King video differently and registered their outrage through massive rioting against the jury's new frame of meaning. Similarly, the Bush administration attempted to reframe the Abu Ghraib photographs as the work of a few "bad apples," but most of the world now sees these photographs as a direct consequence of American military policy, demonstrating that the state does not have a monopoly on constructing meaning.

The openings for social struggle generated by the contradictions of capitalism in the 1930s, as in our own era, also produced exemplary models of resistance. With the first large-scale expansion of the public sphere through the illustrated press in the 1920s, photography became central to modern visual culture and an important form of visual persuasion. Groups such as the American Photo League attempted to call into place a working-class public sphere, while internationally the 1930s produced emancipatory photographic representations in the form of the workers' photography movement promoted by the Communist International and circulated in magazines such as the *AIZ* and *Der Arbeiter Fotograf*. Through the new and expanded visual public sphere created by the illustrated press, documentary photography represented a new mass subject, which included the working class and the public. As Ribalta observes, "In the 1930s, the image of the everyday man, the rhetoric of the human and of the man in the street was the embodiment of the potential for revolutionary transformation and its spectres."[10] The documentary photography of the 1930s was plural in its effects and should not be reduced to an instrumentalist frame or mere appendage of the liberal state. Documentary was not destined to serve one master only. In the Cold War era following World War II, however, artistic innovators lost their connection to mass political movements and formed new relations with proliferating art world institutions that supported and were supported by the capitalist state; these institutions, such as MoMA, articulated a new formalist aesthetic that delegitimized social considerations in documentary photography. But the pendulum has swung back the other way.

Claiming the Frame for the Rightless

Framing always does some sort of violence to open-ended meaning, yet meaning never can be wholly contained or structured by the frame because there are too many parties to the production of meaning. While recognizing the history of photographic mobilization and recruitment for state-sanctioned war and violence, we must also recognize the myriad forms of resistance to that framing. Today renewed social struggles and digital technologies have galvanized new producers to create alternative frames outside state control. These alternative frames of meaning are able to produce new forms of social knowledge that may be mobilized to fight for democratic rights and new freedoms. This idea of documentary as emancipatory representation is premised on the Western ocularcentric paradigm that identifies knowledge with vision. This is why we cling to the claim of photographic realism. "Even if we know after Photoshop that realism is a construction," writes Ribalta, "I think we cannot simply abandon the claims of photographic realism. It continues to exist and to be necessary in the so-called digital era. If we want democracy to continue, we need some form or idea of documentary."[11] Moreover, we must recognize that the idea of documentary has revitalized the relationship between art and documentary practices.

Theorist and curator Ariella Azoulay analyzes documentary practices that do not support and are outside the control of the state. She remarks, "Photography's critics tend to forget that despite the fact that photography speaks falsely, it also speaks the truth," and amends Barthes's formulation that the photograph attests to "what was there" with the understanding that what was there "is never only what is visible in the photograph," but also reproduces a set of social relations that made the taking of the photograph possible.[12] Given the persistent public belief that the camera is an objective observer, despite ample evidence to the contrary, we must recognize that while the state frames meaning according to its own interests, it is also possible to frame alternative realities and to make the frame apparent, that is, it is possible both to expose the racist, antidemocratic, and class interests of the state and to strengthen the critical polemical power of the forces that oppose it. There exist today documentary practices that make no claim to universality and instead make apparent their critical stance in support of transformative politics. These are documentary practices that claim the frame. Oppositional documentary practices thus reject the pretense of "objectivity" by making their stance apparent; they make visible the social and political conditions that make the photograph possible, and this, in turn, strengthens the power of the documentary image as a tool of materialist analysis. In particular, they make visible the liminal political spaces where what we think of as "human rights" are seen to be precarious, unenforceable, or nonexistent.

Italian philosopher Giorgio Agamben has designated these spaces or conditions of precariousness as "zones of indistinction" that produce a "state of exception," and they demonstrate the ease with which governments can shift categories of people from those who have rights to those who do not. We may think of "human rights" as belonging to all people everywhere, but this is not the way it works. The contemporary understanding of human rights has been greatly influenced by Hannah Arendt's *The Origins of Totalitarianism* (1951) and Agamben's idea of "bare life" based on the exemplary figure of *homo sacer*, an obscure figure of Roman law who is stripped of citizenship and deprived of rights. Arendt addressed the condition of the refugee as a subject without rights and argued that an individual who is deprived of statehood or sociopolitical identity is made rightless. Human rights, then, are the rights of the citizen, but those most in need of rights—the refugee, the homeless, the political prisoner, the "unlawful" enemy combatant, the migrant laborer, the "ghost detainee," the internally displaced, the victim of torture, the asylum seeker—are beyond the law and have no recourse to it. This is the implicit shortcoming of modern liberal democracy, which cannot be trusted to ensure human rights. As British art historian Anthony Downey notes, "The 'rights of man' are a convenient fiction, in that they belong only to the citizen who is imbricated within a national, and therefore political, community."[13]

Agamben builds on Arendt to warn of a "coming community" of the rightless, to which we could all someday belong. Utilizing Michel Foucault's notion of "bio-politics," which is grounded in the meaning of life and the legal sanctity of the human, Agamben theorized the "zone of indistinction," in which the sovereign is always both inside and outside the law, the one who makes and therefore can declare a "state of exception" from the law, producing bare (or sacred, in the rarer sense of "set apart," and taking on the qualities of accursed, baleful, or abandoned) life, that is, biological life, in which a life may be seen as "devoid of value" and killed but not sacrificed in any religious or legal sense.[14] The most egregious examples of bare life are the Nazi concentration camps, but also internment camps and refugee camps, which are still rampant today. Zones of indistinction may include the holding cells of national airports as well as the torture cells and prisons where people languish outside the purview of any national or international law, exemplified by Abu Ghraib and Guantánamo Bay, and the ongoing statelessness of the Palestinians, who have no citizenship and, therefore, no rights.[15] The easy slide into a state of exception is exemplified by the Bush administration's use of the terms "terrorist" and "unlawful enemy combatants" to characterize people who are deemed to have forfeited all human rights and who are imprisoned indefinitely, or killed. Even an American citizen, the Islamic cleric Anwar al-Awlaki, was murdered by the Obama administration without legal charges or trial, based on a secret Justice Department memo that reinforced the shredding of civil liberties as a necessary component of the "war on terror," a "war without end against no readily definable enemy."[16] The "zones of indistinction" in which we find modern-day bare life are in urgent need of representation by contemporary documentary practices, which are capable of both reframing the reality of the visible and bringing into focus the invisible.

French theorist Jacques Rancière, however, argues against seeing these categories as too rigidly determined; he suggests that Agamben collapses the distinction between the political and the social, producing a "biopolitical trap" in which sovereign power and bare life appear "as a sort of ontological destiny: we are all, every single one of us, in the same situation as the refugee in a camp." Rancière suggests that this "radical suspension of politics" is a logical outcome of Arendt's position, which attempted to keep separate the political and the social or private, apolitical life. This leads to a "state of exception" from which there is no rescue other than an act of God, and avoids a specific political accounting, a view that is rooted in the unquestioning acceptance of the necessity of the world capitalist economy and its state focus on security.[17] Rancière argues that the United States did not start a war out of feelings of insecurity but rather that "the war was necessary to impose feelings of insecurity," in order to consolidate consensus through "the fear of a society grouped around the warrior state." The essence of the capitalist state, in its final form, is a police state, which integrates capitalist, state, military, and media powers, and must be opposed by what Rancière calls "dissensus"—whereby the distinctions between bare life and the political blur, and subjects act on the rights they do not have, thereby enacting those rights.[18]

Thus it is possible for the documentary image, like the subject who is represented in that image, whether citizen or disenfranchised, to either further the interests of the state or to critique and oppose sovereign power by claiming the frame for the rightless. The critically deployed contemporary documentary image does not demur at partisan positioning. This is in part a response to the thoroughgoing critique of the myth of universality and transparency launched in the 1970s and 1980s by theorists such as Martha Rosler, Allan Sekula, John Tagg, and others, so that documentary practices today assert a new combative political potential. Although documentary practices are still linked to the liberal-corporatist state, there are many documentary practitioners who assert the possibility of documentary practices that call into place a counterhegemonic public sphere based on a shared way of seeing that explicitly recognizes the political conditions that lead to a loss of rights and a need for dissent. These viewers are not necessarily sovereign citizens of any state, as in the case of the Palestinians, but they are, in Azoulay's terms, "citizens of the citizenry of photography," who utilize photography to support each other and to build an oppositional public sphere so that they may, ultimately, act on the rights they do not have and, by enacting those rights, bring them into being.

A Citizenry without Borders

My study builds upon a view of the public sphere that is both critical of the state and dependent on visual technologies. In *The Civil Contract of Photography*, Azoulay suggests that documentary photography can produce a "civil contract" that in turn produces a new kind "citizenship" based on a secular agreement among viewers that is not limited to conditions of the state but founded on "relations between the governed" and their sense of responsibility toward each other, including "the spectator's responsibility toward what is visible."[19] This is related to Judith Butler's elaboration of a Levinasian public sphere in which there is an ethical responsibility to respond to the appearance of others, especially to their "cry of suffering."[20] For Azoulay, too, the political sphere is a public democratic space shared by the governed whose duty is, above all, to each other, rather than to the state, but this shared public sphere is, crucially, established through photography and its public circulation. "Photography," she writes, "being in principle accessible to all, bestows universal citizenship on a new citizenry whose citizens produce, distribute, and look at images." The critical function of photography is to "contest injuries to citizenship" in the form of "photograph-complaints" that "would be worthless, however, if it were not for the citizenry of photography and its citizens who produce these photograph-complaints, as photographers or as spectators."[21] Photography thus forms a citizenry without borders, language, place, national or ethnic identity; indeed, it has no "means of exclusion." Citizenship, moreover, is not a passive status but an active condition produced by engaging in the civil contract of photography and the political responsibility it implies.

Azoulay also addresses the potential violence of photography in relation to the way it may exploit the vulnerability of the photographed. She asserts that this "threat of violation always hangs over the photographic act, and this is the precise moment in which the contract between photographer, photographed, and spectator is put to the test."[22] The threat of photography's exploitation is mitigated when photography serves as a mediating agent in social relations, i.e., as a source of protection or "civic refuge" for those robbed of citizenship, in which they may produce grievances and claims that otherwise would not be made visible. Their invisibility would therefore further an unwitting public consensus in support of the state against the oppressed.[23] The threat of violation that may revictimize those pictured is thus mitigated by the fact that the continuing oppression allowed by invisibility produces a far greater threat. Documentary practice therefore can become a kind of moral refuge for the oppressed. By making oppression visible, photography also demonstrates that anyone who threatens the social order simply does not have rights in a liberal order, and this ability to strip people of rights is a very useful ideological tool for imperialist expansion and the domination of other peoples.[24] Thus bare life is always already politicized, its purpose always larger than mere existence.

Documentary and Art

The language of documentary has increasingly become the predominant language in contemporary art, particularly in photography, video, and film, and it even may be argued that the dynamic polemical nature of the documentary image has revitalized photography. Nonetheless, there are those who argue against loosening the boundaries between artistic and documentary photography and who question the legitimacy of picturing suffering and violence.[25] This is the "aestheticization of violence" argument that suggests it is unseemly and in bad taste to represent social suffering, that this form of engagement, despite being associated with the politically radical Russian and German artistic avant garde of the 1920s, is not the proper province of artists. The logic of this argument is that the photograph should exist as a fine art object only. Against Michael Fried's advocacy of postwar formalism in photography in *Why Photography Matters as Art as Never Before*, Ribalta asserts that the relegation of photography to formal concerns and to the art market would represent a politically reactionary and antidemocratic turn. The photographic idea of documentary, though it may be used to displace dissent and to reaffirm the order of the liberal-paternal state, is nonetheless inextricably linked to the idea of democracy and can be used to mobilize and recruit a radicalized public sphere.[26] To erase photography's documentary power today would be to deny its potential link to emancipatory political struggles, rendering it a sterile academic enterprise.

Moreover, at this point in history the attempt to separate photography from documentary seems quite beside the point. Not only does this dichotomy maintain the arid disconnection between photography and social struggle, but it fails to recognize that such images are already globally pervasive and made by producers who reject the distinction between artistic autonomy and social engagement. Why, they may wonder, should we allow atrocities to remain off limits, shrouded in secrecy and public invisibility? Why should perpetrators remain unaccountable and victims remain unacknowledged? The issue is not one of aesthetics, of making suffering "beautiful" for the pleasure of the viewer, but ethical and political. Since no representation is without "aesthetics," resulting from the myriad choices made by the producer whose "style" is related to a set of values and conditions, the question is not whether aesthetics have been employed, which they certainly have, but what the images effectively accomplish and what is at stake in what they represent. The anomalous attempt by photographer Luc Delahaye to draw a distinction between his own "photojournalistic" and "fine art" photographs of the same subject (Northern Alliance troops in Afghanistan) do not hold up under close examination; his allegedly more detached and impartial fine art photographs are constituted by just another set of formal conventions whose meanings still depend on the conditions of production and circulation, and they are difficult to distinguish from his photojournalistic pictures.[27] At the same time, as Erina Duganne argues, there are indeed artistic practices that attempt to slow down the consumption of painful images in order to make the viewer more critically aware of how we see and what we cannot see, in works by artists such as Sally Mann, Andres Serrano, and Alfredo Jaar.[28]

Political scientist Mark Reinhardt argues that the image cannot be so horrific that we cannot look at it and therefore aesthetics make it possible to look. He rejects the anxiety of critique raised by commentators such as Susan Sontag, who is ambivalent and self-critical about looking, yet, like most of us, finds it important to look. In *Regarding the Pain of Others*, Sontag meditates on the tension between withholding and display and questions who has the right to look. She observes that "the photographer's intentions do not determine the meaning of the photograph, which will have its own career, blown by the whims and loyalties of the diverse communities that have use for it," and ultimately argues that the act of looking, and remembering, is an ethical act. She rejects the innocence that not looking may confer, concluding, "No one after a certain age has the right to this kind of innocence, of superficiality, to this degree of ignorance, or amnesia.... Let the atrocious images haunt us."[29] In response to the argument that to aestheticize—and all photographs aestheticize—is reactionary, Reinhardt argues that this kind of thinking simplistically reduces content to form. Instead, he asserts, aesthetic strategies deepen engagement with and understanding of suffering. John Taylor, citing John Keane, similarly suggests that the "public spheres" of death and disaster images "keep alive memories of times when terrible things were done to people; they heighten awareness of current cruelty; they canvass and circulate judgments about whether violence is justified; they encourage people to find remedies for savagery."[30]

In a global culture where everyone is a producer as well as a consumer of public imagery, the mastery of the polemical power of the image is crucial to any emancipatory and transformative program of social struggle. The accumulation of human, economic, and environmental disasters, including the attacks of September 11, the permanent state of war in the United States that has existed throughout the twentieth and early twenty-first centuries, and the massive revolts in countries across North Africa and elsewhere, have put global anticapitalism and systemic critique back on the table and opened a larger space for critical and oppositional visual practices. We must attend to the multiple forms of documentary practices so that we may hold the perpetrators of war and violence responsible for their deeds, acknowledge the grievances of their victims, expose the material conditions and political circumstances that are the underlying causes of their claims, and consider how the visual culture of war may help us to shape the future.

Chapters

Under the umbrella of war culture, I include in this book a wide variety of visual and documentary practices that examine the waging of war and the militarization of society. By placing artistic practice in dialogue with vernacular and photojournalistic images, we may better understand both the unique potential of contemporary visual art practices as well as their merging with documentary modes; indeed, a more comprehensive view of the overlapping practices of artists and photojournalists demonstrates the refusal of both to accept an artificial divide between artistic autonomy and political engagement. Not surprisingly, attempts to exhibit and theorize new rhetorical strategies about documentary imagery of war and violence have proliferated in recent years, constituting them as part of our cultural legacy.[31] Taken together, the works examined in this book demonstrate that war is not only about the usual war aims—the killing and maiming of people, grabbing of land, seizing control of resources, and exploiting populations—but also about the permanent militarization of the homeland, the demonizing of other cultures, the attempt to make suffering invisible and to silence dissent and opposition. The study of contemporary war culture is, in its largest sense, an examination of the social and visual construction of national identities through the mythologies that are mobilized to sustain them and to suppress other ways of seeing, and the subversion of that project through documentary practices that oppose the suppression of civil liberties and the oppressive rule of capital in a contest of images.

The first two chapters engage with the "romance" of war. In chapter 1, I examine Krzysztof Wodiczko's video projections and public works in response to 9/11 and the wars in Iraq and Afghanistan and their relationship to contemporary media technologies. Wodiczko explores the rhetoric of war, including the promise of manliness, patriotic gratification, and the protection of democratic freedoms at home and abroad, and the effects these discourses actually produce, such as ever more sophisticated surveillance technology, the increased militarization of domestic space, and the shattered domestic lives of U.S. war veterans and Iraqi civilians. Wodiczko incorporates the documentary mode, often employing people telling their own stories, but in ways that defy linear narrative and seek to implicate the viewer in what often feels like "zones of indistinction."

Chapter 2 focuses on the popular phenomenon of war reenactment in the United States and traces two trends: one that elides history by focusing on the romanticized mythology of individual experience and one that focuses on the political. Political reenactments that challenge the understanding of the past include the photography of Vietnamese-American artist An-My Lê, who participated in and documented reenactments of the Vietnam War, and the guerrilla theater of the American group Iraq Veterans against the War, which restaged raids by American troops against civilians in Iraq on the streets of American cities. An-My

Lê examines the way war reenactments romanticize and obfuscate the past, while the documentary-style street performances of Iraq Veterans against the War reframe a mythologized understanding of America's role in Iraq and Afghanistan by producing visual countermemories.

Chapters 3 and 4 focus on war experience in relation to gender and sexuality and the body. Chapter 3 considers the Abu Ghraib photos that went viral in 2004 and continue to provoke new artistic responses and scholarly analysis. I examine the sexualized use of American female soldiers in the tortures and humiliations of Arabs and Muslims at Abu Ghraib and Guantánamo Bay and the response to these issues in the video and performance work of Coco Fusco; the sexual abuse and discrimination against women within the U.S. military itself and how the reception of the Abu Ghraib photos was inflected by that; and the suppressed image of rape coupled with the appearance of Iraqi women raped by American soldiers on Internet pornographic sites. In addition, this chapter examines the cell phone technology and low-resolution "mediality" of the Abu Ghraib images as part of their documentary affect, and analyzes the debates over the public display of the Abu Ghraib photographs at the International Center of Photography and the Andy Warhol Museum.

Chapter 4 regards embodied experience as a metaphor for the sociopolitical corpus in the performance works of Guatemalan artist Regina Galindo, who submits herself to various forms of torture, and Mexican American performance artist Guillermo Gómez-Peña and his group La Pocha Nostra, which metaphorically colonizes the body with a variety of techniques and produces arresting *tableaux vivants* that recall documentary practice without literally reproducing it. I further consider photography by artists and photojournalists, including the controversial images of burned and mutilated American contractors hanged from a bridge in Fallujah; the photos and war diary of British artist David Cotterrell, who served as an observer at a field hospital in Afghanistan; photographs by American photographers Nina Berman and Timothy Greenfield-Sanders, who represent the body of the wounded U.S. veteran in very different ways; and staged photographs of the Israeli soldier by Israeli artist Adi Nes.

The last two chapters address the landscape of war. Chapter 5 analyzes the construction of war and its navigational technology in the form of video war games in relation to real military technology, which appropriates video war games for military recruitment and employs games technology in actual gunships, as revealed in the Wikileaks video of Americans who gunned down a group of men in Baghdad that included two Reuters employees. This chapter also considers the effects on photographers of being embedded, unembedded, and disembedded, as well as vernacular photographs by Iraqis that document a landscape of war far beyond the perspective of embedded foreign photographers. In addition, I examine the landscape of war in the United States in the work of Nina Berman and Christopher Sims, both photographers whose critical documentary practices resist being instrumentalized to serve the liberal state.

Chapter 6 explores the landscape of war in Israel/Palestine as both contested terrain and symbolic cultural identity in the work of primarily Israeli documentary photographers but also by Palestinian artists, as well as graffiti on the Barrier Wall around the West Bank by the British artist Banksy and other anonymous artists. In addition, I examine the Israeli political imaginary of the landscape as founded on a mythologized Holocaust narrative in the performance and video work of several Israeli artists and consider, overall, the ways in which Palestinian and Israeli identity are structured in terms of each other and the visual landscape.

If the images in this book haunt us, and I think they do, it is not, in most cases, because of the horror they show; rather, it is because of the vast experience of violence they gesture toward but cannot show. For the true horror of war can never be adequately represented; it is the silencing of voices and the largely unseen nature of violence and suffering that is more often represented. The politics of oppression in the contest of images is the true subject of these visual practices, and how well they succeed is the subject explored in this book.

PART I

THE ROMANCE OF WAR

 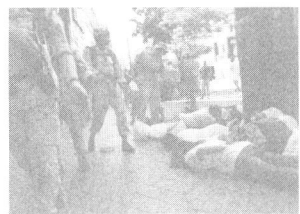 

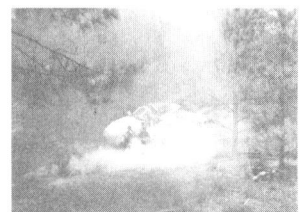  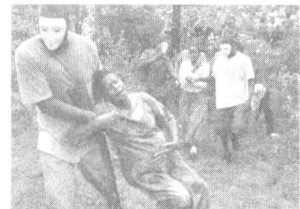

1

TECHNOLOGIES OF WAR, MEDIA, AND DISSENT IN THE POST-9/11 WORK OF KRZYSZTOF WODICZKO

In the U.S. war on Iraq and the elusive, euphemistic "global war on terrorism" manufactured in response to the events of September 11, video and surveillance have been used in radically diverse ways, eroding the line between public and private in the service of state control, political recruitment, terror, individual curiosity, and radical critique. These technologies have been used to scrutinize the body by government agencies, publicize beheadings by Iraqi insurgents, send global messages by Osama Bin Laden, and produce a recruitment tool by al-Qaeda now on the Internet.[1] Many independent agents have produced private videos that have found their way to a global audience via Internet sites such as YouTube, and, of course, the news media rely on video, subject to the pressures of state control. Artists, too, draw on the technologies of video, surveillance, and the media to produce critical works about the troubling and often invisible effects of war. I want to examine some of these effects, focusing on the work of Krzysztof Wodiczko and his post-9/11 video, sound, and vehicle projects, which mobilize war and media technologies in order to perform a radical critique of the war on terror, particularly the political repression it has unleashed against immigrants in American society and the frightening impulses and enduring damage it has effected on soldiers who function as both perpetrators and cannon fodder in this imperialist adventure.

Surveillance technology is everywhere in evidence today, from puffers, chemical scanners, and biometrics devices being installed in airports to radio-frequency chips being inserted into passports, and "machine-gun toting robots" being developed for deployment in Iraq to the thousands of video surveillance cameras in public spaces. One report notes, "If face-recognition software is linked to the cameras, police can effectively compile dossiers on Americans' movements whenever they're in public places."[2] And yet, despite ramping up public surveillance, it seems to have no effect on "security" according to official U.S. intelligence assessments between 2000 and 2007, causing the *New York Times* to note, "We live in a continuous Code Orange, despite thousands of lives lost and uncounted billions of dollars spent in the battle the White House now calls 'the long war.'"[3] The invidious practice of surveilling the body to contain and control the population promotes the illusion of safety through fear of the pervasive potential of terror without actually providing greater protection. But this surveillance serves as a signal example of the erosion of the line between public and private, civilian and soldier, or, put another way, between the peaceable domestic sphere and the perpetual militarization of domestic space.

Video media such as television also exemplifies the increased blurring of the line between private and public. When television entered the home in the 1950s, it transformed the home from sanctuary and retreat from the threat of the outside world into a zone into which war could enter at any time.[4] By the 1960s, however, television also had become a dynamic force for radical critique as well as a powerful state and corporate instrument. Artists such as Nam June Paik subverted the corporate and state-run hegemony of television by appropriating its real-time capabilities as a medium for democratic potential, which was critical for the turn to social and political issues in the radical art movements of the 1960s and 1970s. Radical video artists questioned the ideological monopoly of television by changing our relationship to video and television from a passive to an active one.[5] Feminists, in particular, used video to interrogate conceptions of private and public, and responded to the way the mass media positioned the mass audience.[6]

If television allowed war to enter the home in the twentieth century, the Internet now allows the home dweller to interactively explore the world of war. The Internet user blurs the line between private and public by his or her ability to participate in the global blogosphere of the Internet community while nonetheless sitting at home alone, even preserving the ability to remain anonymous. Thus video and media technologies have been instrumental for dissolving the divide between public and private for both conservative and radical purposes, that is, for state and corporate influence and control, and for radical critique of those hegemonic institutions. As a form of dissent in the era of permanent warfare, video and mass media have been crucial players in the public sphere, which I define here in Peter van der Veer's terms as "the spaces, sites, and technologies available for public discourse that is critical of the state" and galvanized by images.[7]

Even conservative commentators have noted the sense of perpetual war produced on the domestic front. Historian Andrew Bacevich observes that for Americans most of the twentieth century was "an age during which war, actual as well as metaphorical, was a constant, either as ongoing reality or frightening prospect," producing "a relentless process of militarization."[8] Right-wing pundit George Will bluntly notes in the aftermath of 9/11, "For Americans, there are only two kinds of years: the war years and the interwar years."[9] The new "global struggle" may be seen as a deliberate attempt to cast the open-ended war on terror as a successor to the Cold War following World War II, continuing the constant threat of war that state power requires.[10]

In this context, attempts to control mainstream media technology have been increasingly tightened. If Vietnam was the first televised war, the Persian Gulf War of 1991, which acquired the reputation of being the first to be broadcast in real time through satellite communication, was also the first to control the movement of journalists through selective pools, to subject all copy, photographs, and video to strict censorship, and to force journalists to rely on military briefings where they could be fed false information. Most infamously, the Persian Gulf War disappeared all evidence of dead bodies, an unknowable number on the Iraqi side, substituting instead the antiseptic "eye" of the smart bomb and effectively blacking out coverage of American atrocities. Today, the excess production and circulation of images beyond government control is crucial in revealing atrocities such as the tortures at Abu Ghraib and the senseless slaughters of Iraqi civilians. Other more private and domestic traumatic effects are made visible through artistic intervention and deployed against the logic of the endless war and militarized homefront.

Documenting Trauma: Immigrants and the War on Terror

Krzysztof Wodiczko's 2005 project *If You See Something . . .* suggests that the technologies of artistic, military, and media culture are integrally related in ways that define our post-9/11 historical moment. The work consists of a quartet of video projections on walls in a darkened room in which indistinct life-size figures are seen as if through frosted glass windows, acting out private dramas of pain.[11] The figures are immigrants who are alone or talk to others present or on cell phones about their desperate situations, including deportation proceedings, political harassment, physical humiliations. We hear phrases such as "detainees," "happened to me," "American citizen," "everything I have," "no one wants to play with him," "crying." Sometimes police lights flash in the distance. Some figures wear business suits, some pace as if in a cage; a man holds up a newspaper to the window, like a desperate message in a bottle whose urgent meaning is difficult to read.

Though staged for the video camera, the stories are true and the voices that narrate them are those of the afflicted. The scenes convey the anxious and casual moments in which appeals are made or confidences revealed—a woman to a coworker during a cigarette break, a man to his lawyer, one prisoner to another, a father to a school principal. How do those strangers understand the racial, ethnic, gendered, and class nature of the traumatic experience? The potential dilemmas for the overt listeners in the video installation are simultaneously presented for the viewers positioned as covert observers.

Fearful of the long arm of the government, the speakers convey a growing, inexorable sense of helplessness and hopelessness. The overlapping islands of sound as one moves about, projected through small speakers placed in relation to the projected windows, heighten the sense of disconnection and fragmentation, of stories, of lives, just as the figures themselves fade in and out of visibility. They perform their own anxieties and reenact their own lives as the viewer watches in the darkness and listens through a veil of light and sound. The work turns the interior of the art gallery, as art historian Raphael Cuir writes, "into an expression of the interiority of the individual" so that viewers might "project themselves into the projection" and empathically find themselves on the other side of the milky glass.[12] Art critic John Haber suggests that the artist "let[s] the message take shape and intensify in the listener's ear, while also insisting on the distance between the overheard and the understood."[13]

Wodiczko is known for projects such as *Voices of Krakow City Hall Projection* (1996), in which victims of domestic abuse tell their stories; *Bunker Hill Monument Projection* (1998), in which the mothers and brothers of young men who were victims of a repeating cycle of urban violence speak their grief and attempt to break the "code of silence" of the street gangs;[14] and *Hiroshima Projection* (1999), in which A-bomb survivors and their children recount their experiences. Whether in public projections that mobilize the spectacular power of humanly animated civic architecture or through Wodiczko's specially designed technologi-

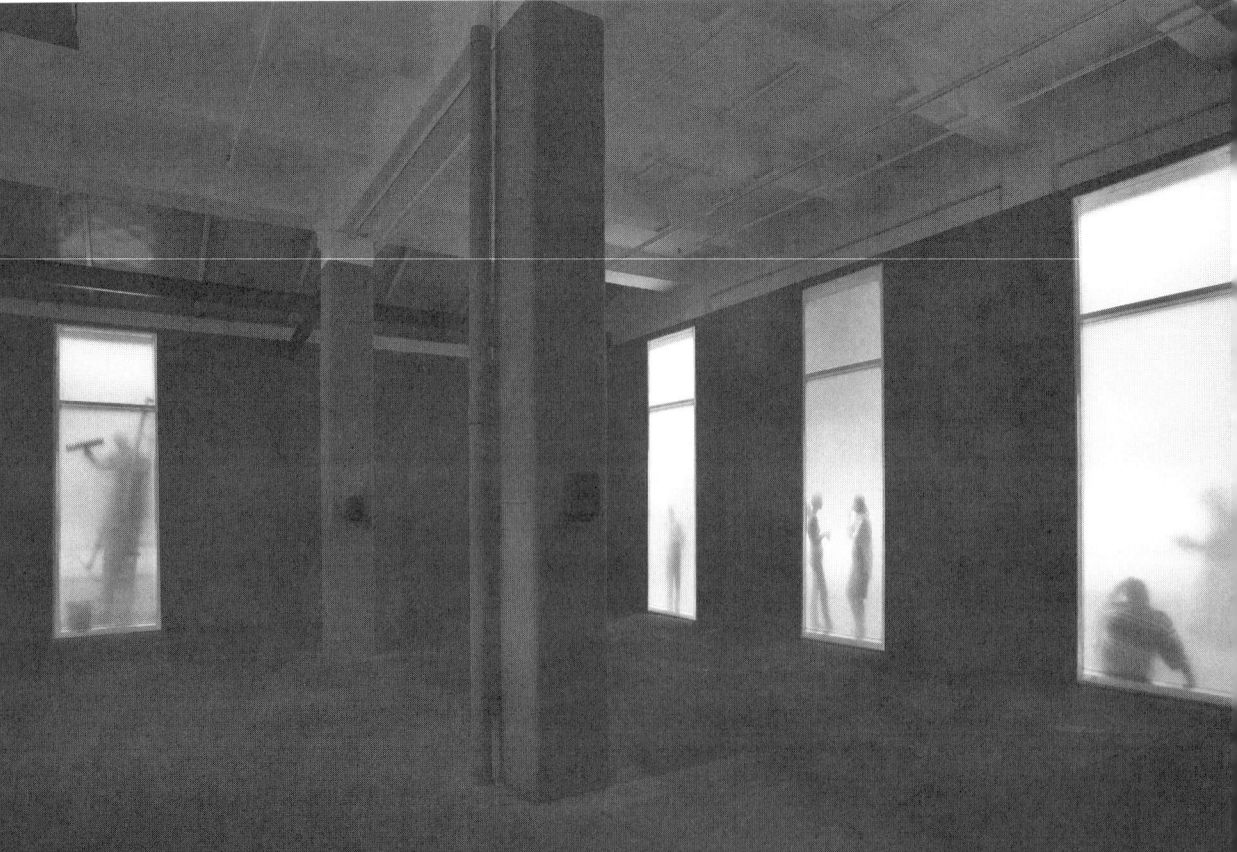

Figure 1. Krzysztof Wodiczko, *If You See Something . . .*, 2005. Installation view at Galerie Lelong, 2005. (© Krzysztof Wodiczko. Courtesy Galerie Lelong, New York.)

cal instruments, which empower individuals to speak in public spaces, the power of the word depends upon the means that enable and deliver it. Each project allows the individual body and voice to function as the body politic of the marginalized and dispossessed in order to effect a process of traumatic recovery and to penetrate and disturb public complacency.[15]

Though perhaps more difficult to accomplish in the rarefied art world atmosphere of a gallery or museum than in the vast projections on public buildings Wodiczko more commonly produces, *If You See Something . . .* nonetheless constructs a highly charged space through the creation of a series of vignettes constructed as "windows" onto private worlds. The installation is a video collage of simulated surveillance fragments that confront the viewer with pressing issues in America: immigrant rights, racist reaction, and the assault on civil liberties carried out in the name of the war on terror.

The projected windows bring into closer focus the life on the street that middle-class viewers usually hurry past, deliberately oblivious, not wanting to hear those voices, those stories, pressing the viewer into what may be uncomfortable voyeuristic positions. In one episode, for example, two men speak in Punjabi, although we recognize a few words of English: "deportation," "9/11," "Pakistan," and "Muslim." The first man stands in obvious distress with his arms extended, recalling the iconic image of the Hooded Man of Abu Ghraib. The second man tries to comfort him as his plaintive voice intensifies, and then, unexpectedly, he weeps. He weeps and we watch. We understand that his loss is profound and there is no comfort to be offered, except our willingness to witness.

The ability of the viewer to shift focus among the four projected windows, each with a series of stories, defies linear narrative and reproduces both the street and the open, interchangeable space of the media—newspaper columns, television split screens, the multiple windows of a computer screen—employing what Beatriz Colomina calls "the logic of the mass media." These are spaces that can be rearranged and moved through by the viewer/reader, offering an array of information through which the reader navigates at will, superficially or fully.[16] In addition to its formal entwining with media technology, the multiple environments of Wodiczko's installation demonstrate the infiltration of war technology through the trope of surveillance. Conceptually, the project addresses the effects of contemporary war culture and the incursion of the heightened power of the state into every kind of domestic or homeland space, creating a perpetual state of hypervigilance in which the "homeland" is always already mobilized for war. If military technology can be domesticated, the domestic also becomes militarized.

Wodiczko earlier employed the logic of the media in his *Xenology* project, on "the art and science of the stranger," in which he invented communicative instruments and interrogative devices meant to empower and protect the alien or foreigner. The project consists of a series of portable and wearable video instruments such as *Alien Staff* (1992), *Porte-Parole* (The Mouthpiece) (1993), *Aegis: Equipment for a City of Strangers* (1998), and *Dis-Armor* (1999), which employ video technology to produce greater visibility for the immigrant. *Porte-Parole*, for example, positions a video monitor directly in front of the mouth, displaying huge distorted images of the lips in order to "spread the communicable (contagious) process of the exploration of one's own strangeness."[17] *Aegis* includes a pair of screens rising from the wearer's back that project multiple pre-recorded images of his or her face. Like a strange winged creature, the foreigner transforms the process of surreptitious stares and covert surveillance into a deliberate civic display of a technologically "angelic" presence. Through such self-surveillance instruments, the normally voiceless and invisibly marginalized enter the public sphere through new media invented specifically for them, projecting not only their presence, but also their anxieties in an unwelcoming environment.[18]

Similarly, *If You See Something* . . . simultaneously figures and subverts the technology of surveillance, commandeering and appropriating its effects. The milky glass in the projected windows functions as a screen through which the invisible video camera records private conversations and solitary moments, recalling the relentless spying represented in the film *The Lives of Others* by Florian Henckel von Donnersmarck. Von Donnersmarck's 2007 drama about the round-the-clock monitoring of East German citizens by the Stasi inevitably evokes the secretive and paranoid political culture of the U.S. government, which functionally constructed the trappings of its own police state through the unprecedented concentration of power in the hands of the executive branch under the Bush/Cheney administration. And like the Stasi officer who ultimately finds himself in sympathy with his subject, we, the viewers, are also meant to empathize with the projected subjects, to recognize the peril of the individual in relation to the state.

Only one moment in the video projection breaks the illusion of an unwitting subject under the surveillance of an unseen eye. This occurs when the man presses a folded newspaper against the milky glass, openly addressing the unseen viewer. The newspaper seems like an offered appeal. We "read" its import through the gesture, which activates a sense of daily awareness of the media and its role in militarizing domestic culture. Like the milky glass that filters the text, we have been denied the full extent of the effects of the "war on terror" on the lives of thousands of ordinary innocent people, some brief, piercing examples of which are provided here in the projected windows. By producing an imaginative living archive through the projection of the performative, Wodiczko's project does what the mainstream media, embodied in the offered newspaper, cannot do. Though both the media and the video project may be seen as practicing some form of "documentary realism," Wodiczko's project enters the public sphere to challenge the anti-immigrant atmosphere of fear and suspicion that the mainstream media has helped to create by uncritically reproducing government rhetoric in support of the erosion of democratic rights in the name of "homeland security."

It may be argued that the environment of the museum or gallery space is a kind of neutral space, resonating with the ideals of high modernism following World War II. The International Style, which offered a promise of universal comfort, economy, and clean design as a route to personal contentment and social improvement, produced the massive glass and steel skyscrapers of the corporate city centers, recycling the techniques and materials developed for the military. The World Trade Center, described by its architect Minoru Yamasaki as "a living symbol of man's dedication to world peace,"[19] came to embody the bureaucratic state as the twin colossi of finance capital, which made them such appealing targets (first attacked in 1993). They exemplify both the logic and the failure of this style. The proportions of the projected windows in Wodiczko's project, which were videotaped through the actual front windows of Galerie Lelong, evoke the shape of the towers so that the architectural space of the projected windows and the actual gallery space are mobilized both to invoke and redirect the trauma of 9/11 through the discourse it has produced. Redeployed by the artist, the multiplied modernist towers and the suffering they embody reanimate the implicit emancipatory demand for social freedoms in a democratic state.

The Transit Campaign and Government Spying

If You See Something . . . also addresses an ongoing media campaign in New York City's mass transit system, begun in 2002 by the Metropolitan Transit Authority (MTA). The MTA plastered the city with posters enjoining citizens who "see something" to "say something" and made public announcements on city transit that exhorted listeners, "If you see something, say something. Don't keep it to yourself." In the wake of the 11 March 2004 Madrid train bombing and the 7 July 2005 London train and bus bombings, San Francisco transit officials also unveiled a program called "See Something? Say Something!" for bridges, ferries, and buses in November 2005, and the program spread to mass transit in Chicago and Boston; the Washington Metro deployed a "See it? Say it!" campaign; and the Ohio Department of Homeland Security adopted it.

London and Australia have their own versions as Western countries become increasingly preoccupied with their Muslim communities.[20]

Wodiczko's work responds to the injunction to spy on behalf of the state by standing it on its head. Our putative protectors are easily understood not as benevolent Big Brothers but as the potential enemy, while those from whom they would "protect" us—neighbors, coworkers, strangers—emerge as the aggrieved and the harmed, the latest victims in an American history overfull with such victims: immigrants, black people, workers, Latinos, gays, women, leftists. The morally and legally questionable activities of the Bush administration, inherited and in some cases continued and even extended by the Obama administration, are by now well known: condemning people to torture through "extreme rendition," the hellhole of Guantánamo, Abu Ghraib, and other prisons, and the secret detention camps into which even U.S. citizens declared "enemy combatants" can be thrown without recourse and held indefinitely, harking back to the incarceration of 120,000 Americans of Japanese descent who were interned in American concentration camps until the end of World War II.[21]

By inverting the sense of the MTA slogan, Wodiczko evokes a history of informers and accusers in other persecutory and repressive campaigns, from the Salem witch trials of the late seventeenth century to the Sedition Act of 1918, which forbade Americans to use "disloyal, profane, scurrilous, or abusive language" about the United States; from the McCarthyite witch-hunts of the 1950s to the FBI COINTELPRO (counterintelligence program) operations used to repress political dissent from 1956 to 1971, which led to the government murder of thirty-eight Black Panthers; from Bush administration press spokesman Ari Fleischer's public warning, in response to the comment of a talk show host following 9/11 about the "courage" of the suicide bombers, that people should "watch what they say, watch what they do," to former attorney general Alberto Gonzales's blatant attempt to threaten freedom of the press and intimidate journalists who published classified information, much of which was illegally classified and hidden from the oversight of Congress in the first place, by suggesting they might be prosecuted for performing a criminal act. As Geoffrey Stone, a lawyer on the faculty of the University of Chicago Law School, notes in a letter to the Intelligence Committee in the House of Representatives, "In this category of secrets, government officials are attempting to shield from public scrutiny their own misjudgments, incompetence, misconduct, venality, cupidity, corruption, or criminality. In a self-governing society, it is vital that such secrets must be exposed. What makes this difficult is that government officials attempting to maintain such secrets may invoke the claim of national security as a cover."[22]

A Latina video and performance collective, Fulana, also responded to the MTA campaign, noting in a poster of their own, "If You Fear Something, You'll See Something," because "the news and the MTA are drilling fear into your head nonstop, and this could activate prejudices you didn't even know you had."[23] The group produced their poster in English and Spanish on its website and invited visitors to download the flyers and post them around the city to counter the MTA campaign. A blogger posted a photo showing the addition of a *New York Post* editorial headlined "Fight Terror, Speak English" over the Spanish version of the MTA ad. The Post editorial calls for making English the official language of the United States, a law which specifically denies any right of government agencies or officials to provide information or services in other languages in all spheres of public life, including bilingual education. The blogger ironically notes, "If you see something, say something, but in English."[24] The American Civil Liberties Union responded with information on "What to do if you are stopped or questioned on the subway or bus" by transit police as a result of the MTA campaign, asserting in a counterslogan, "If you endure something, do something."[25]

The dystopian visions of George Orwell's *1984* and Ray Bradbury's *Fahrenheit 451* seemed to grow in significance as the Bush/Cheney administration, in its own version of "newspeak" and "doublethink," redefined torture in order to declare that the United States did not practice it. With ample evidence of flagrant violations of the constitution, the appeal to "see" what cannot be seen in the upheld newspaper may be understood as the stories suppressed or not yet written. While the MTA campaign encourages seeing the imagined criminal intent of our neighbors, who may, for example, have Spanish or Saudi accents, Wodiczko's *If You See Something . . .* encourages us to "see" the mushrooming effects of a growing anti-immigrant hysteria—while leaving ambiguous, however, the political form of the "tell."

Immigrants as Workers

Immigrants from Mexico and Central America are at the center of the American debate on immigration, and are included in Wodiczko's project in the form of an exchange in which a man from Guatemala laments to another Central American of uncertain origin about the injustice of the 1996 anti-immigrant law following the Oklahoma City bombing by Timothy McVeigh:

MAN B: . . . The law is not made for you; it is made for them. You understand what I am saying? This law. All right, look at this stuff; remember when Timothy McVeigh blew up the Federal Building?

MAN A: Uh huh.
MAN B: That's when the '96 law came in.
MAN A: OK.
MAN B: The '96 law was made for terrorists. You understand?
MAN A: So we are terrorists (laughs).
MAN B: But look at it. The person who blew up the building is American; he is not an immigrant. He is American. But he is still, they are gonna make a '96 law against immigrants. He's American, he's not an immigrant.[26]

McVeigh is an impossible anomaly for those Americans who find it uncomfortable to consider the fact of white, homegrown right-wing terrorists, just as Londoners felt uncomfortable with the fact that the subway and bus bombers were native Britons from Beeston in Leeds, or that the majority of those arrested for plotting to blow up trans-Atlantic airplanes with liquid explosives were British born, living in High Wycombe and East London. It is even more difficult for the state, which seeks through the "war on terror" to call into being a patriotic citizenry in order to evoke a sense of national unity and community. Homegrown right-wing bombers disrupt the construction of a civic-minded and responsible citizenry through the use of government surveillance and intrusion into the domestic sphere, and are quickly dispatched as anomalies. The laws that come about as a result of their actions are aimed not at them but at those who are more easily constructed as threats to the national imaginary—foreigners, immigrants, and those who openly dissent to government policies.

Guatemalans in particular have been caught in the American anti-immigrant net. A great many leave their native country, finding it too difficult to repay loans for land or to farm the soil, and because the schools have no books and there are no health clinics. The rural poverty, landlessness, and lack of social services still common in Guatemala, especially for the Maya groups who make up about half of the population, drive many to migrate north through Mexico to the United States, along with poor Mexicans.[27]

Since 1993 more than thirty-five hundred Mexican and Central American immigrants seeking some means of livelihood have died trying to cross into the United States through the desert in Arizona, more than were killed on 9/11. As a result of the 1994 imposition of NAFTA in Mexico, millions of Mexicans were forced out of the countryside into the swelling ranks of poverty in the cities, creating the mass migrations of desperate immigrants looking for work in the United States. It is estimated that 10 percent of the Mexican population now lives in the United

States, including one of every seven Mexican workers, and the twenty billion dollars they send home annually is Mexico's third-largest source of income.[28] Recent studies show that immigrants do not "steal" jobs from Americans since these are jobs that Americans do not want to do. Where cheap labor power in the form of immigrant labor is available, employers use it instead of turning to machines.[29] Only the desire to continue the massive exploitation of the millions of "illegals" that do the dirtiest, lowest-paid, and most difficult labor in the United States, with no citizenship rights, has prevented the legal integration of Mexican labor into the American economy.

It was Democrat Bill Clinton's 1996 immigration "reform" law that first renewed militarization of the U.S./Mexican border, resulting in increased deaths, in addition to deporting immigrants with green cards for infractions that had occurred decades earlier. As the United States continues to step up the technological militarization of the border, with support of both Republicans and Democrats, it has done nothing to change the annual mounting death toll, while the monstrous proposal of a nearly four-hundred-mile wall, similar to that built by the Israeli state in the West Bank, along with five hundred miles of vehicle barriers, provoked massive outrage in Mexico.

With an estimated twelve million illegal immigrants in the United States, immigrants from South America and other regions of the world function as sources of cheap labor for modern capitalism only to find themselves the most expendable elements of the labor force during times of economic contraction.[30] *If You See Something* . . . presents the concrete effects of anti-Arab hostility by employers in the lament of an American woman. She describes how the unrelenting harassment of her Lebanese husband and the unwillingness of employers to hire him drove him to return to Lebanon and forsake the marriage. The construction of Muslims and Arabs as alien elements to be driven from the nation or inferior peoples to be subdued in a "clash of civilizations" is the basis for the culture of fear and the strategy of permanent war even as it fails to account for the global interpenetration of peoples or to recognize the transnational public sphere. It further fails to understand that terrorism is "a tactic and not an enemy" and that terrorist groups are stateless, originating in the despair of the impoverished and oppressed.[31]

From a safe distance of privilege and security, the onlookers who survey the actors performing their own stories in Wodiczko's project must realize that "we" do not exist apart from "them." Even if we do not trace our immediate family history to recent immigration, there is no "we" in America beyond the small ruling elite that is safe from surveillance and the abrogation of civil rights under the rules of the U.S. Patriot Act, quietly renewed by the Obama administration in 2010 (or in the U.K. under the Prevention of Terrorism Act). Middle Eastern immigrants and dark-skinned foreigners are the most harassed only in the first instance, followed by blacks, leftists, workers, environmentalists, and dissenters of all kinds. What is remarkable about the torture chambers, rendition, and domestic spying is that such police state powers in support of an imperial presidency were no longer covert but openly and aggressively justified, and acceded to by Democrats and Republicans alike.

In one projected window, two window washers speak to each other in Polish about immigration issues, then a dog sniffs and licks at the window. Raphael Cuir writes, "The dog sniffing the olfactory traces of his kind before leaving his own [trace] is as concerned with the concept of territory as the immigration police who obsess on it. Much less trivial than it seems, here the animal serves as a metaphor for Giorgio Agamben's observation that 'there are certain thresholds in the surveillance and manipulation of the body that cannot be crossed without entering a new biopolitical era . . . the gradual animalization of mankind carried out through the most sophisticated means.'"[32] Intimate forms of bodily scrutiny are part of the logic of state-imposed domination, expanding as new forms of sophisticated technology are developed, such as the iris recognition scanner, which will have the ability to "scan the iris of the eye without the knowledge or consent of the person being scanned."[33] The dog is a figure with which many poor immigrants register an ironic identification, a nomadic creature that sees the world from below and is poorly treated while attempting to stake a claim to a patch of territory. From another perspective, the dog also figures terror and surveillance in the form of human/canine border patrol agents, drug-sniffing police dogs, and as weapons used to terrify and attack foreign prisoners held by Americans.

The task of window washing in the projected window also reminds us that immigrants are workers; indeed, it suggests the vast army of immigrant workers who do the lowest-paid and often most dangerous manual labor that supports the immense edifice of corporate America. The milky windows, produced by gluing a screen to the glass, separate the corporate sphere from the unwelcome world outside by veiling the teeming multitudes, including the actual teams of immigrant window washers in the city who remain visibly indistinct as well as socially invisible, thereby maintaining the separation between classes on either side of the windows.[34]

Although only implied by Wodiczko's project, the fact that immigrants come to the United States first and foremost to enter the *working class* bears some emphasis. As Slavoj Žižek astutely observes, "Typically, in today's critical and political discourse, the term 'worker' has disappeared, substituted and/or obliterated by 'immigrants [immigrant workers: Algerians in France, Turks in Germany, Mexicans in the USA]'—in this way, the class problematic of workers' exploitation is transformed into the multiculturalist problematic of the 'intolerance of Otherness,' and so on, and multiculturalist liberals' excessive investment in protecting immigrants' ethnic rights clearly draws its energy from the 'repressed' class dimension."[35] More precisely, many immigrants face a double oppression in the United States, both as threatening or suspect because of their perceived foreignness, an attitude that is sharpened with every real or imagined "terrorist plot" publicized in the media, and as largely invisible but deeply exploited workers.

The seemingly fruitless effects of the window washers' labors on the frosted glass induce a sense of stalled social mobility and unending burden, evoking the labors of the critical artist himself whose work attempts to illuminate what the rhetoric of the state seeks to obscure. At the same time, it brings to mind the need for an organized, radical, and politically coherent response that raises the call for no deportations and full citizenship rights for immigrants, the immediate freeing of all detainees in Guantánamo and other "black sites," and the immediate withdrawal of American troops from Iraq and Afghanistan.

John Haber, while finding Wodiczko's project representative of a deepening anger, and a more complex response than many projects produced in the wake of September 11, nonetheless criticized it as yet another expression of Wodiczko's long-standing critique of the abuse of power: "For a good thirty years, Wodiczko has invoked a police state, and his postmodern devices have had a way of staying on message a little too long for their own good."[36] Haber seems to imply that the message has become worn out, or overly didactic, the police state deployed as a generic device, perhaps derived from the artist's own experience of Stalinism in his native Poland. Haber seems to question the reality of a society perpetually militarized and mobilized for war, "the war years and interwar years." Far from being a figment of Wodiczko's imagination, however, the "war on terror" has brought us closer to a police state than at any point since the McCarthy era. The project uses the technology of war and the media to bring the private terrors of the persecuted into the public domain, politicizing domesticated technology as a clear form of dissent. The glimpses into the torments of the persecuted constitute a form of public testimony, a strategy Wodiczko has successfully employed in his previous projects. The prosthetic eye of Wodiczko's camera transforms the instrument of surveillance and repression into history's witness.

Wodiczko's appropriation of the technology of the media and of surveillance thus transforms the condition of "seeing" into a rather more complex moral dilemma. If we are not to be the eyes and ears of the state's repressive apparatus, what is our relation to its hapless victims? Are we passive bystanders or active witnesses? Wodiczko's project becomes more than an exposé of an arrogant and repressive government, more than troubling glimpses into its terrors and abuses. The project also becomes a vehicle for the persecuted to speak and to find some sense of communal recognition among the project's viewers, that is, the project attempts to create a radically democratic public sphere through representation, a public sphere with a shared way of looking that is critical of the state and the perpetual militarization of society. It invites the spectator to consider the fragility of the liberties we take for granted and the need to defend every shred of democratic rights. *If You See Something...* creates a collective space that counters the construction of the subject (the viewer) by the ideology of the state with the authentic testimony of its victims, who demonstrate the political results of the ideology of war and the perpetual militarization of civil society.

Although not a community project in any usual sense, the work is rooted in an ethos that attempts to reformulate the concept of "community" on an ethical basis oriented toward the public sphere. Wodiczko worked with individuals and organizations such as the American-Arab Anti-Discrimination Committee, the Asylum Project, Immigrant Rights Program, Bellevue/NYU Program for Survivors of Torture, National Immigration Project, and Physicians for Human Rights. Thus the project utilizes a local "community" of immigrants that is not a community at all in order to conceive "community" in a larger global way.[37] This is consistent with Wodiczko's long-standing artistic practice of seeking to effect social awareness through the psychological and emotional impact of the work both on its participants as individuals in the process of producing the work and on its audiences, who are called into being as antihegemonic witnesses with a shared way of seeing.

Speaking Flames

Wodiczko employs different technology in his 2005 installation, *Speaking Flames*, composed of three artificial candles (with real flames) on pedestals with soundtracks that seem to emanate from each candle. The tiny gusts of air that affect the flames are generated by the vibration of sound from unseen speakers through thin air tubes concealed by the shafts of the candles. Despite the lack of any visible agency, the flickering flames respond, in uncanny fashion, to the expulsive breath of the voices one hears, producing a chilling effect of embodied awareness that makes the viewer conscious of his or her own breathing. With sound that seems to come from everywhere and nowhere, the work creates a new kind of rhetorical space, a metaphorical space in which one might lose track of the surroundings and find oneself conceptually in a vast darkness, wanting solace in the presence of these incorporeal voices.[38]

Two of the flames contain indistinct fragments of soldiers' interactions in the course of combat in Afghanistan and Iraq, privately recorded snippets that convey the adrenaline-fueled context in which soldiers feed each other's frenzied drive to kill or that exhibit the intense stress of being under attack. In one instance, while interviewing two soldiers on leave, Wodiczko watched and recorded the audio of a video they had made from their armored vehicle while in Iraq that captured a suicide attack; in the other he recorded the audio of a video on the Internet showing the killing of people from a helicopter at night in Afghanistan.

The switch from the visual mode to the aural adds to a sense of disorientation in the installation of "speaking flames." The principal and only clearly articulated voice among the three candles is fixed on the center flame, where an American officer conveys in his halting monologue a profound uneasiness about his experience as a self-described killer. He begins by declaring his ambivalence, followed by the justification for his actions: "Umm . . . again, very strong feeling of ambivalence, because through my actions and my unit's actions umm, I'm convinced that we were, that we were able to . . . save American lives. Um . . . which I believe is a good thing. . . . Uh . . . there was an instance where umm, there were, uh, enemy inserted forces who were firing rockets and missiles at our various bases, umm, in and around the Syrian border. . . . We returned fire and, and, and we, we killed those enemy operatives. And it was, it was perfect and we were, we were happy about it. Um, I was happy about it. I was the one who had given the order to fire. . . ."

But his satisfaction with a successful mission is undermined by later doubts and a desire to distance himself from the killing: "Um, it's only in retrospect, looking back, that I see, um, that I have grown uncomfortable with the idea of being happy about having killed other people. Even though, I didn't directly pull the trigger, um, there's a, there's a sort of psychological displacement there. I didn't directly kill anyone, but I was, ya know, as the officer in charge, the person who gave the order to fire, I . . . I . . . I am responsible for what happened." He did not "pull the trigger" but knows he cannot evade his role. Then he becomes uncomfortable with the word "killing" itself and the unbearable responsibility for the deaths he ordered: "Um, and, and so it's hard to tell, the more I think about it, um, the more I, the more I wonder should I have been glad uh, to have, to have, um . . . removed these individuals? Um, should I be happy over their deaths? . . . as time progresses, and I get further and further away from the events, I, uh, wonder more and more about it and it leads to a greater feeling of ambiguity." Finally, he faces the moral dilemma: "I, I, I suppose, I suppose what troubles me most is that um, I felt happy to have killed other people, which by extension means that I was happy to be, to be a killer. And killer has such a negative connotation to it, even though it is true and precisely what it was that I was at that time."[39]

The trauma here is conveyed by the impossibility of holding two different and mutually exclusive conceptions of the self simultaneously, one as an honorable man, of which one can be proud, and therefore an upstanding member of one's community, and the other as a killer, which is intolerable and insupportable within civil life and therefore induces a crushing sense of shame. Shame arises when an individual feels he has violated the social codes of the community and acted in morally unacceptable ways. The soldier's dilemma rests on the mutually exclusive imperatives of two communities that are in conflict here: the military and the civil. The soldier, moreover, is repulsed at discovering in himself the joy of killing, a feeling cultivated by the military but impossible to reconcile with the expectations of civilian life. This, in part, is what renders many returning veterans hopelessly alienated from their friends, families, and civil society, unable even to articulate their dilemma, unlike the soldier above. Through the unexpected voice of a veteran, *Speaking Flames* constitutes a critique of American militarist bellicosity by juxtaposing it with the psychic damage it has produced in relation to expectations of the domestic sphere.

"Democracy Assassinated the Family That Was Here"

Almost five thousand U.S. soldiers have died in Iraq and more than one thousand in Afghanistan, figures that are not yet commensurate with the estimated one hundred thousand-plus Iraqis or more than thirty thousand Afghan civilians who have been killed. A UN-issued report in September 2006 stated that Iraqi civilian casualties have been significantly underreported; some estimates calculate casualties as over six hundred thousand.[40] As Seymour Hersh and others have shown, the tortures and murders at Abu Ghraib and Haditha in Iraq were not aberrations but the result of conscious policies designed to secure the occupation of Iraq, like the 1968 My Lai massacre of some five hundred villagers in Vietnam, and the massacre of some four hundred Korean civilians at No Gun Ri during the Korean War in 1950. Government documents made public in recent years show that top U.S. military officers and Korean officials sanctioned the killing of civilians who fled the fighting that led to the massacre at No Gun Ri; at My Lai, General Samuel Koster, the division commander in overall charge of the troops, watched the killings from the air and radioed orders to Lieutenant William Calley, who led the massacre in the village.⁴¹ In Haditha, where U.S. soldiers on a rampage killed twenty-four unarmed civilians, the *Washington Post*, on 27 May 2007, noted a line of graffiti on one of the houses of the murdered: "Democracy assassinated the family that was here." "Democracy," American-style, has become code for criminal occupation, wanton murder, and massive destruction.

Wodiczko's sentient candles evoke eternal flames in the tombs of unknown soldiers and commemorations of genocides, but also act as surrogate figures both for the tens of thousands of unnamed dead and injured in Iraq and Afghanistan, whose public mourning has been prevented in the United States by keeping their deaths anonymous and uncounted, and for the American and allied dead and injured, most of whom have been thrown into the rapacious maw of destruction for reasons they little understand. For the living on all sides, the implications for altered lives, fractured families, cultural destruction, and the larger burdens on society have only begun to become broadly visible. By giving voice to the memorial flames, Wodiczko shifts their function from the elegiac to the provocative and disturbing, undermining the possibility of a transcendent and redemptive narrative. The transmutation of body into voice becomes a metaphor for the invisibility of pain.

The conjuncture of confession and candles also evokes the rituals of the Catholic Church, without, however, offering the solace of faith. Instead, it conveys a failure of absolution for the disillusioned soldier. Implicit is the soldier's sense of betrayal by the government in whose name and in whose defense he and others like him carried out their acts of terror and violence, a recognition of that government's inability to compensate for the effects of conscience. The speaking flames draw on the opposition between terrorist and citizen, the former a transnational actor, the latter an embodiment of the nation, as an opposition that is easily lost or confused in the context of war.

Manuel Delgado defines the anthropology of war as the settling of an "accumulated volume of debt," which in this case might be regarded as the "unfinished business" of the Gulf War initiated by George Bush Sr. Writes Delgado, "Violence and warfare are not the outcome of opposed parties having given up on their ability to communicate, but of them having decided to intensify the efficacy of their messages to the maximum. Contrary to what is usually thought, armed conflicts are not a consequence of the 'failure of dialogue,' but of its exacerbation."⁴² Dick Cheney and Donald Rumsfeld et al. sought to intensify the efficacy of their message through a "shock and awe" bombing campaign that might be said to rival the blitzkrieg of the German Luftwaffe over Guernica during the Spanish Civil War. While Picasso's painting famously evoked the print media coverage of that event in French newspapers, Wodiczko's work employs contemporary war and media technology to produce a new kind of performative, living memorial for the twenty-first century. Like *If You See Something...*, *Speaking Flames* contemplates the continuing and devastating implications of war in the domestic sphere.

As Mieke Bal asserts, "Suffering requires witnessing," for "without witness, the sufferer is irremediably alone, deprived of a social environment and all but dehumanized."[43] Wodiczko's project is again one of witnessing. It conveys the trauma that many perpetrators cannot escape and that they transmit to others, evoking the creation of a new generation of veterans suffering from posttraumatic stress disorder with its social dysfunction, violence, and suicides, who are inadequately cared for, if not largely abandoned, by the state, and who leave their traumatic effects on those around them in waves that ripple outward.

The disarticulation of voice and body, however, also has the important effect of preventing the soldier's narrative from being reduced merely to the personal experience of an individual. It allows the listener to embody the disembodied voice, to experience not only intellectually but affectively, through heteropathic identification, the easy slide into complicity with violence. To be sure, this is a troubled, unsettled identification that does not allow the wholesale pleasure of vicarious identification, which cancels out the difference between self and other. The listener is left in a deliberately uneasy position, in which the pain of the other cannot be ignored as the viewer embodies the deep disillusionment with the romance of war and registers the hollow euphemisms as vocabulary leaks away.

The work also may be read as a metonym for the damaging actions of the state. The tension between the psychological and the political, or between the individual and society, in Wodiczko's post-9/11 project points to what may be regarded as the key problematic in liberal sensibility, in which individual experience stands for the whole so that individual healing equates to national healing. Robert Hariman and John Lucaites define this as "the fundamental dilemma of liberalism: by making the individual's experience the primary source of meaning, internal transformations can suffice for action in the world." In this sense, the political is elided in favor of the individual. "The fundamental tension in political life," they note, "is between the individual and society, and once the individual is protected, other political possibilities are likely to be deferred to the more immediate engagements of private life," so that "public life becomes a dead zone."[44] In *Speaking Flames*, the indistinct cacophony produced by the other two candles suggests that the task of healing the individual is vastly insufficient.

War Veterans Vehicle Projects

In his *Veterans Vehicle Project*, premiered in the week before and during the 2008 Democratic National Convention in Denver, Wodiczko appropriated the trappings of war technology to produce another critical intervention about the effects of war on returning veterans. A "new media sculpture" that transforms a military Humvee into a traveling media and sound projection vehicle, the *Veterans Vehicle Project* makes public the stories of Denver homeless veterans in their own words and voices. Left to assimilate as best they can without adequate federal social support, there is an unprecedented incidence of homelessness among veterans, who are damaged and traumatized through repeated tours of duty in ways that make their reintegration into civil society and into their own families a daunting task.

Creating an electrifying three-dimensional sound with four-horned speakers, like a battlefield under bombardment, the Humvee-mounted projector, the most powerful of its kind, shoots out words that seemingly explode toward the viewer when projected on a wall, with each speech act ending in a repeated phrase to the sound of rapid gunfire, "to really blast home the message," as one observer noted.[45] Difficult to recognize out of context, the sound script is taken from electronic war games on the Internet in which all the details of gun operation from the reloading mechanism to shells falling on the ground can be heard, a level of sophistication more convincing than sound used in the movies.[46]

The video text was culled from collaborative sessions over the course of seven months with more than forty Denver-based veterans. In short narratives, the work offers intimate portraits of the veterans' experiences through audio and text projected onto the wall of the Aromor building in a central part of Denver that was undergoing renovation by Mercy Housing Colorado as permanent supportive housing for homeless veterans. The project was presented at dusk from 22 August through 26 August, and included a one-night projection on a wall of the Performing Arts Center next to the convention center. Proceeds from a private VIP event went to the nonprofit organizations America's Road Home and their Denver partner, Denver's Road Home, which focus on ending family homelessness.

Wodiczko's project therapeutically addresses traumatic injury and healing by attempting to construct a radically democratic space that reconnects the individual with his or her community. In her landmark study, *Trauma and Recovery*, Judith Herman established the central dialectic of psychological trauma as the conflict between the will to deny terrible events and the need to proclaim them and have them heard. The truth of trauma, once spoken aloud and witnessed, is the first step toward repair and recovery; thus it is imperative for the larger society in which the trauma resides, and in which secondary trauma ripples outward through the families of victims, to act as civic witness and take responsibility for acknowledging and addressing the effects of trauma on its citizens.[47] During World War I, the medical establishment considered traumatized soldiers weaklings or cowards, hysterics or moral invalids. Although in World War II "shell shock" was recognized as a psychological injury that could happen to any man in combat, especially if exposure was intense and prolonged, it was not until Vietnam that the diagnosis of PTSD (posttraumatic stress disorder) gained legitimacy and was later extended by theorists such as Herman to include other traumatized groups, such as the victims of sexual abuse and rape.

One goal of the veterans who participated in Wodiczko's project was the desire to dispel the fantasies of heroic deeds, the imprimatur of manliness that war experience allegedly produces, and the promise of a better life propagated by military recruiters. As one veteran comments in the video, "Recruiters lie; if his mouth is moving he's lying." The *Veterans Vehicle Project* thus becomes a critical examination of the rhetoric that constructs patriotism.

Wodiczko also emphasizes the lack of awareness regarding secondary trauma. "Veterans often destroy family life to protect their families from themselves," he observes. "They refuse help because they are 'warriors,' until they are picked up by ambulances." One moving outcome of the project was the response of a son to the plea of his veteran father who had walked away from his family nine years earlier. The appeal from the father to his son (just before the son's eighteenth birthday) asks for forgiveness and implores the son to break his long refusal "to have anything to do with me." The sound clip from the video featuring the father's plea was aired on the local NPR station, and Wodiczko independently called the son and left a message inviting him to the projection as part of his routine telephone invitations and announcements made to the families of the homeless veterans. After the first projection night, the father called Wodiczko and tearfully announced that his son had called and was planning to attend the next night's projection. "But," warns Wodiczko, "one problem will be replaced by ten."[48] Many social and cultural support projects are needed to respond to the crises in which veterans find themselves.

In a similar project in Liverpool, England, in September 2009, Wodiczko interviewed British veterans and projected the image and sound of their speech from projector-mounted British army trucks. Driven by veterans, these roving units transmit their testimonies onto the façades of major buildings and monuments in the city, "disturbing the peace" of silence and complacency and making visible the ongoing domestic effects of war trauma. The projected testimonies include stutters and repetitions of words, followed by reiterations of key phrases punctuated by gunfire.

Two examples serve to illustrate expressions of disillusionment with the romance of war experienced by veterans who found enlistment very different from what they had imagined:

> As you say war is not just we go there we fly the flag we shoot a few things and win and walk away which has been propaganda since the first world war if not before or before or before that.
> SINCE THE FIRST WORLD WAR/IF NOT BEFORE OR BEFORE OR BEFORE THAT

> It's about how you're trained to be aggressive you're trained to use the adrenaline and do things at speed and use your aggression to get you through certain events and the problem being when you come back you don't switch the aggression off like a light it's it's everything you do afterwards is done with aggression.
> YOU'RE TRAINED TO BE AGGRESSIVE

The most common targets of that aggression are soldiers' wives, yet another invisible group whose voices rarely reach the public sphere. Studies show that whether service members' experience psychological or neurological trauma, it tends to spread to their intimate partners,[49] and more than a third of military wives show symptoms of secondary traumatic stress requiring treatment.[50] Domestic partners are hidden casualties in other ways, too. Journalist and army wife Stacy Bannerman observes, "Veterans with PTSD are two-to-three times more likely to commit intimate partner violence than veterans without the disorder, according to the Veterans Administration. What remains unspoken is that spouses and girlfriends of male veterans with post-traumatic stress disorder are two-to-three times more likely to be victims of domestic violence than women involved with male veterans who do not have the disorder."[51]

Two other examples from the Liverpool project represent the traumatic stress and fear of domestic violence voiced by the wives of veterans:

> I just couldn't believe I'm saying the way he was talking to me the looks he was giving me I was like oh my god I think he could kill me I think he could actually kill me now could put his hands around my throat and strangle me you know and I mean it wasn't nasty I'd just say do you want a cup of tea but the look in his eyes and I thought I can't I can't do

this it was just he could have killed me even now he does it to me and looks at me as if I'm shite.

I THINK HE COULD KILL ME/EVEN NOW HE DOES IT TO ME AND LOOKS AT ME AS IF I'M SHITE

I know now I'll never get my Rob back who I met and I fell in love with and I've got this other Rob that when he's he's there he's brilliant like Homer Simpson everybody loves him you know the kids honestly and yet when he goes on those downers it's like it's just like it's just like ice and darkness.

I'VE GOT THIS OTHER ROB/ICE AND DARKNESS

Bannerman notes that in addition to the uncounted hundreds or thousands of wives and girlfriends who have been beaten or terrorized, "dozens of military wives have been strangled, shot, decapitated, dismembered, or otherwise murdered when their husbands brought the war on terror home. These women are as much casualties of war as are the thousands of troops who killed themselves after combat."[52]

Another project on war veterans was designed in collaboration with Theodore Spyropoulos (and still under production as of this writing). *War Veteran Vehicle Project* is a vehicle with mechanical wings that serve as "communicative shields" equipped with video screens and speakers for transmission of the veterans' memories and images of war. It includes special containers and display components attached to the inside sections of the vehicle wings, and a screen and speakers attached to the top of the vehicle to allow for transmission of the face and voice of the veteran without direct exposure of his or her actual face.[53] The vehicle addresses the war trauma that is deepened and extended through the unprecedented multiple redeployments of older soldiers from the military reserves and National Guard, many of whom have new families. Wodiczko notes that "each returning-from-war soldier retraumatizes seven to nine people, children, spouses, and parents among them... one third of the U.S. population is already a victim of primary and secondary war trauma.... In this way, the spread of war trauma reaches the epidemic level."[54]

Through the use of the vehicle's "communicative shields," the proposed vehicle would both assist a war veteran in "acknowledging in the open the presence of his or her emotional defensive war 'armament,' while inspiring the veteran to 'disarm' himself or herself by publicly sharing war and postwar experience." However, the process of exposure can be carefully controlled. "When it becomes emotionally necessary," writes Wodiczko, "the vehicle will allow the veteran to seek refuge behind the closed-again vehicle shields, opening them and closing them again and again as often as needed."[55] Physically manifesting the desensitizing and numbing emotional shields necessarily developed by veterans, the vehicle operates as a metaphor for the difficult and lengthy process of dismantling the emotional armor which must first be recognized and acknowledged by the veterans themselves, their families, friends and the larger public.

With the "post Sept. 11 brave-new-world of surveillance," as Susan Buck-Morss has dubbed it,[56] which includes tapping phones and snooping through computer sites, library accounts, and bank accounts, the space of the home as a protective sanctuary has shrunk considerably, narrowing down private space to absurd proportions in portable and nomadic technologies, such as the gas masks Israelis wore in their homes in 1991 as Saddam Hussein sent Scud missiles into Israel, or the plastic sheets, wind-up radios, and duct tape advertised in the United States following 9/11.[57] Like them, the war veterans' vehicle narrows down private space to the chair in which the veteran sits.

Wodiczko produced several forms of protective nomadic technology prior to the *War Veterans Vehicle Project*. His 1988–1989 *Homeless Vehicle* and 1991 *Poliscar*, designed for the displaced and dispossessed, simultaneously offer a supportive technology for daily living while underscoring the inability of the capitalist state to support its own population through full employment and housing, making the need for a beautifully designed homeless vehicle painfully ironic.[58] Just as the homeless vehicle projects are not a permanent solution to the problem of homelessness, the *War Veterans Vehicle Project* is not a permanent solution to war trauma; both are a kind of "transitory artifice."[59] Such vehicles allow the marginalized to develop a civic voice in the public sphere through technology, externalizing the interiority of trauma by making what is functionally private and effectively invisible into something highly public, and demonstrating, in the case of the *War Veterans Vehicle Project*, the social militarization of domestic space and the drastic shrinking of that space for the victims of war trauma and homelessness alike. The war veteran vehicle projects, in all their forms, are meant to pierce the silence of the media and of the returning soldiers themselves, most of whom will never speak publicly, and to create a public sphere of viewers with a shared way of seeing the devastating effects of war on this visually repressed segment of the domestic population.

. . . OUT OF HERE: The Veterans Project

In November 2009, the Institute of Contemporary Art in Boston premiered a new work by Wodiczko that combined sound and video projection to produce an immersive experience unlike any of his previous works.... *OUT OF HERE: The Veterans Project* is set in a large dark space that simulates the "interior of a warehouse or an old military base," as wall text at the entrance provided by Wodiczko informs the viewer. Grids of windows are projected near the ceiling on three sides of the room so that we look upward and at first see nothing but blue sky and clouds. There are seven of these high dirty windows, each divided into three sections, each section with eight panes of glass. Before long, events begin that we can discern and imagine only through the layered sounds we hear as if through a thick concrete wall.

To our left is the voice of Barack Obama on a radio or television; to the right a man singing in Arabic, perhaps an imam chanting. There is other street noise, perhaps a nearby open market. Obama is quoting Thomas Jefferson: "Our wisdom will grow with our power. We must use diplomacy to solve our problems whenever possible." Then we hear a report that "a senior Hamas official has told Al Jazeera that this is a Martin Luther King moment," underscoring the hope—and its failure so far—that Obama will change conditions for Muslim and Arab peoples. We are somewhere in Iraq, perhaps Baghdad. We hear children's rising voices in play and the kicking of a soccer ball, which flies aloft and briefly appears in the windows on the left. Iraqi women and children are talking and laughing. Then the ball hits a window pane and it cracks. Like an ominous foreshadowing, it produces a small jolt of dread, as if to remind us of the vast field of violence we cannot see and have been prevented from seeing.

We hear the whir of a chopper before we see its silhouette on the right; it descends, hovers, and moves out of sight. There is a deep mechanical portentous sound that is hard to place; then vehicles arrive.

"We were here before. Remember that?" a man says.

"What's going on?" another voice crackles over a radio.

"Get the kids out of here," says a third.

"Stop!" We realize by now that we are listening to an American military patrol. "Look at that pile of trash."

"What's going on up there?" the voice over the radio asks again.

Black smoke billows upward, then a boom, the scream of a child, gunfire. "On the balcony!" shouts one of the soldiers.

We hear an explosion and some of the window panes are blown inward. A couple of holes are blown into the wall, toward us, we who are now psychologically hunkering down in the dark. We do not know how many shooters there are or where they are or who they are. There is more automatic gunfire, an Iraqi man shouting, gunshots through the glass panes. We are bombarded by sound from all sides, trying to take it all in.

Figure 2. Krzysztof Wodiczko, . . . OUT OF HERE: The Veterans Project, 2009–2011, seven-channel color video with sound. Installation view at Galerie Lelong, 2011. Photo by Michael Bodycomb. (© Krzysztof Wodiczko. Courtesy Galerie Lelong, New York.)

The U.S. soldiers curse. "Miller's down!"

"Back me up!"

One seems to have spotted a shooter: "12 o'clock!"

A dog barks. "Shut that dog up!" followed by a gunshot and a yelp.

There is a continuous exchange of gunfire. The Americans decide to leave.

"Take the kid!"

"Forget the kid!"

"The kid's hit!"

"*Leave* the kid!"

"Let's get out of here! Get Miller in here!"

"Sergeant, let's *go*!"

The soldiers drive off, having made their choice between saving the child and, as they see it, saving themselves. There is a pause. Then two Iraqi women shout in distress and call out. "Yasmin! Yasmin!" The loop ends with their plaintive voices rising in a heartrending lament for the dead or dying child. We have rapidly shifted our attention from the children to the soldiers to the dog to the mothers.

Moments of silence pass and the bullet holes in the broken glass panes slowly heal themselves. We are back where we began; the laughing children return and the cycle of violence begins again.

"I find it interesting," notes Jim O'Neill, a thirty-eight-year old army vet who was deployed to Iraq for the 2003 invasion, "that it's on a loop, so it just keeps going over and over and over and I think vets can relate to that." O'Neill worked with Wodiczko on the project, checking facts and advising on the authenticity of the sound experience.[60]

Constrained by the unwillingness of more Iraqi civilians in the United States to participate in the work out of fear of the persecution or kidnapping of their family members in Iraq for ransom or revenge, and by the use of mainstream production crews used to working with scripted narratives, Wodiczko collected a variety of stories, employed a script, and produced a more narrative work than in his previous projects, although . . . *OUT OF HERE* nonetheless refuses a closed narrative. As we gaze through the clerestory of windows, never able to see a human figure, sight becomes subordinated to sound perception, disrupting ordinary consciousness and drawing the viewer into the sensory familiarity with horror and chaos experienced on a daily basis by sequestered civilians during wartime. Immersed in a dark cavernous space with not a lot to see, . . . *OUT OF HERE* takes the viewer/listener inside subjective experience, which is made more stressful and haunting by its ambiguity. We unwittingly become part of a war experience reenactment, simultaneously aware of being inside and outside the experience.

But who are we? Are we playing the role of Americans or Iraqis? The ambiguity expands our empathy in all directions. We identify with everyone—the laughing children, the ambushed soldiers, the civilians under fire, the murdered dog, the dying child who is left behind, the anguished mothers. There is no separating war and life. Subjected to the terrors and traumas beyond the wall, experiencing something of the confusion and uncertainty of those who are trapped or hiding, not knowing where to look first, we experience anxiety and terror, however briefly and imperfectly, for the duration of this seven-minute loop. Perhaps we begin to employ coping mechanisms such as dissociation, fixating on the shapes made in the broken glass by the bullets: it looks like a mushroom; it looks like a star. Watching and listening, we know that we cannot know what is really happening "outside," that many things are happening simultaneously, that we hear and see only fragments, that our allegiance to one side may block or distort our understanding of the other. "I believe that if there is any truth," writes Wodiczko in the gallery brochure, "it lies in realizing the impossibility of gaining full access to the truth of such an experience."

The title suggests as much: . . . *OUT OF HERE* is a panicked shout, a dangling emergency phrase, part imperative command ("Let's get out of here!"), part desperate desire ("How do we get out of here?"). The ellipse also suggests the political quagmire from which the U.S. occupying power seems unable to extract itself ("We can't get out of here!"). There are too many stories that come "out of here," too many effects that will flow through lives and across generations, long after the violent moments in which they occurred have ended. They will not be encompassed by any single narrative retelling. The narrative shatters into fragments, a series of moments that embody the alert, benumbed, traumatized, or haphazard apprehensions of a largely unseen experience. Wodiczko's work calls into being not merely a shared way of "seeing," but a shared way of "being." We become ersatz survivors, as this brings to shared public visibility the vast community of real survivors.

The project may be seen as an imaginative form of documentary practice. The events are a composite based on firsthand accounts of war experience culled from workshops and conversations with soldiers who have returned from combat as well as Middle Eastern residents in the United States. They act as advisers, consultants, and actors. Michael Anthony, a Boston native and former army medic who wrote *Mass Casualties: A Young Medic's True Story of Death, Deception, and Dishonor in Iraq*, suggested dialog, made diagrams, and collected stories and live combat footage from fellow veterans for the project. Tala Khudairi, an Iraqi American with family and friends still in Iraq and an academic dean at Roxbury College, served as one of the voices of the wailing mothers.[61]

Inside a shifting soundscape with our vision largely blocked, the work compels viewers to repeat viewings in an attempt to "master" the events, to hear and see what was missed before, which only heightens our recognition of the limitations of perception and the stress of traumatic experience. The immersive experience is facilitated by surround sound, producing a sound collage or sound sculpture in which sound travels across space through hidden speakers. The darkened interior doubles as the space of inner experience—like the relived memories, or nightmares, inside the head of a soldier back from the war or an Iraqi child hiding in a basement. The wall serves as a metaphor for all that separates us from the experience of those who really are at war halfway across the world, or locked inside their interior traumas. Breaking through the wall to the "outside" is impossible, yet the attempt do so is the imperative of Wodiczko's installation, which attempts to decrease the distance between viewers and those on the other side of the wall.

By creating a physically and psychologically three-dimensional environment, this sense of being both outside and inside events at the same time distinguishes... *OUT OF HERE* from Hollywood films about the war. As Greg Cook, art critic for the *Boston Phoenix* observes, "Rather than have someone recount a memory, Wodiczko involves us in a visual and audio experience that becomes our memory."[62]... *OUT OF HERE* reframes our understanding of the war in Iraq, in which civilian experience in particular remains almost wholly invisible to most Americans. By keeping the violence unseen, it becomes all the more emotionally palpable, while the ambiguity of subjectivity makes nationalist identification impossible.

The U.S. government, on the other hand, keeps the violence from public view because of its incompatibility with the high-minded "helping" role it has adopted to legitimize the invasion and occupation of Iraq and Afghanistan. Keeping the violence invisible also allows the government to deflect criticism, evade accountability, play down the traumatic effects on soldiers sent to do its dirty work, and, of course, to abandon those whose societies, cultures, homes, and families are destroyed. The years of war since 2003 in Iraq follow on the heels of twelve years of economic sanctions against Iraq. More than two million Iraqis have been displaced inside Iraq while another two million or more have become refugees in Syria, Jordan, Egypt, Iran, Lebanon, and Turkey. The infrastructure of the country remains largely destroyed, electricity works only a few hours a day, unemployment is astronomical, and explosions are a daily fact of life. Traumatic effects are far greater than those suffered by American soldiers, which are also greater than ever before. In 2007, a study published in the *Archives of Internal Medicine* reported that one-third of returning U.S. veterans were diagnosed with mental illness or a psychosocial disorder, such as homelessness and marital problems, including domestic violence. More than half had more than one disorder, the most common combination being PTSD and depression. In 2008 the U.S. Army reported that the rate of suicide among soldiers for the previous year was the highest since the army started keeping records in 1980.[63]

Iraqi deaths among police and military personnel is several times higher than American deaths and the "tour of duty" for the average Iraqi civilian is now seven years and running. If the rate of PTSD among Iraqi civilians, which remains uncalculated, merely parallels that of American soldiers at about one-third, this means at least five million Iraqis are suffering from it.[64] In addition, according to Iraqbodycount.org, there have been more than 100,000 civilian deaths in Iraq, with hundreds of children killed each year (although some sources place the civilian death count much higher). NPR reports: "Iraqi children also have been the victims of kidnapping, torture, and rape." Hundreds more children, as young as nine, are held in prison. The rate of PTSD is impossible to gauge among

Iraqi children since many parents refuse to seek help for what is seen as a humiliating stigma, especially for girls, but the number is thought to be "hundreds of thousands." In 2008 Iraq opened its first clinic dealing with PTSD among children.[65]

Though the situations represented in . . . *OUT OF HERE* are typical of Iraq, they also resonate with the trauma experienced by civilians and soldiers in other wars. Wodiczko himself is a war veteran, both civilian and military. Born in Poland in 1943 and living in hiding in non-Jewish Warsaw with his Jewish mother under false papers during the Warsaw ghetto uprising, Wodiczko experienced war as an infant and child as well as its devastating aftermath, in which his mother lost her entire family. The family moved a number of times to cities such as Lodz, Lublin, and Krakow before moving back to Warsaw. Though Krzysztof and his mother survived, there were no support systems in place for them. In his early teens, his mother and Protestant father, an orchestra conductor, divorced. Later Wodiczko served in the Polish army, training as part of the special military service required of university students. While at the Music Academy and Academy of Fine Arts (Studium Wojskowe), Wodiczko trained in bouts of "merciless" three-week periods at a military facility just outside Warsaw, where the Studium Wojskowe officers' cruelty toward students was legendary, culminating in three months of service in a regular military unit where Wodiczko was trained as an officer. His unit was called up for various lengths of service for military "maneuvers" and poised for emergency military situations, such as the Cuban Missile Crisis and the Russian invasion of Czechoslovakia. He had seven soldiers under his command, all of whom were weapons specialists, and likely saved them from trauma, injury, or death when he convinced them not to sign up for service in Vietnam by persuading them that they would need to clean their weapons excessively and repair them constantly because of the tropical humid climate. The soldiers had been told they would serve far behind the front lines, which Wodiczko was convinced was a lie, though he would have risked prison had he argued the point openly and told them straight out not to go. He ended his training with the rank of lieutenant of the motorized infantry.[66]

The trauma of childhood war experience, military service, and state repression under Stalinized rule thus informs an artistic practice that seeks to offer those whose rights have been trampled or denied access to speech and visibility, to utilize "the spaces, sites, and technologies available for public discourse that is critical of the state." Wodiczko's works give public voice to the politically disenfranchised because "it's the least visible who always have the most to say."[67] "The kind of work I make," says Wodiczko, "which is on the side of those who have less access to rights than others, is for me a way to contribute to democracy. Because you don't find democracy, you make it."[68] For those deprived of rights through political invisibility, access to visibility in the public sphere through the artistic license of imaginative documentary practice creates new social knowledge and counters the state's derealization of war's terrible effects.

Ultimately, the darkened space seems to externalize a zone of indistinction, where we do not know if we have rights or not. Law scholar John T. Parry points out that only the state can create the conditions, that is, citizenship, in which rights can be successfully claimed and that these rights are as much about restricting the individual as liberating him or her; at the same time, they create an "abstract autonomous individual or citizen." While defined as equal in formal terms, this condition of abstract equality depends on participation in a particular set of social structures and conventions. Those who do not share these structures and conventions are excluded from the group of equal rights-holders, but the state assumes a paternalistic stance toward those it deems incapable of having equal rights, and may dominate such people to the point of violence in order to turn them into individuals who have rights. Such logic underwrites colonial rule and supports the open-ended domination of peoples by state powers. Thus the very idea of liberal rights has developed in conjunction with and depends upon colonialism, imperialism, and modern systems of production and trade, and serves the interests of the modern state.[69]

Taken together, Wodiczko's post-9/11 projects expose the criminal and repressive effects of imperial power in its less visible aspects. *If You See Something . . .* speaks to the ways in which xenophobic nationalism and the reification of stereotypes are utilized to promote a pervasive domestic atmosphere of suspicion. In the interests of permanent warfare, such suspicion is always designed to paralyze political will, suppress dissent, and justify the onslaught against basic democratic rights and civil liberties. *Speaking Flames* and the various war veteran vehicle projects examine the effects of the wars in Iraq and Afghanistan on the injured and traumatized soldiers who tend to be forgotten and marginalized once they have returned from war, and *. . . OUT OF HERE* extends our view of war experience to civilians in the war zone, for whom the damage and destruction of American bellicosity will resonate for generations.

2

HISTORICAL REENACTMENT: ROMANTIC AMNESIA OR COUNTER-MEMORY?

War reenactors and "living history" groups (who perform for the public only while reenactors perform both publicly and privately) have grown from a small phenomenon when reenacting began to a startling array of contemporary groups and events. In the United States alone, war reenactments draw thousands of participants and spectators each year; in 1998 as many as twenty-five thousand "troops" took part in a huge re-creation of the 1863 Battle of Gettysburg. Reenactment has grown to encompass nearly every war that has been prosecuted. Who reenacts? What is the appeal? Are all reenactment projects more or less the same in conception and effect? Is the drive to reenact a traumatic compulsion, a passion for history, or a desire to participate in a grand imagined narrative? How does reenactment intersect with contemporary culture, politics, and society? Although many historians have contempt for the idea of traditionally mounted historical reenactments that re-create what they regard as a mythologized history, a growing number of political reenactments as well as international art exhibitions that have taken political reenactment as their central theme in recent years seek to reframe the past in critical and provocative ways.[1] This suggests that reenactment should be seriously considered both as an important aspect of the hegemonic culture of war and as a potentially subversive practice that makes visible forms of violence otherwise historically occluded or forgotten. While some popular reenactments construct, rather than re-create, historic events according to patriotic and romanticized myths, other forms of reenactment bring a violent past into the present in order to call into place a public sphere that not only recognizes those who have become historically invisible but also reckons with the continuing effects of that political repression.

In this chapter I want to outline some of the apparent motivations for war reenactment in order to argue that there are two general trends in reenactment: one which aspires to recapture an imagined nostalgic past that focuses on individual experience while affirming dominant historical assumptions, and one that seeks to question entrenched hegemonic narratives by evoking new ways of understanding the past, by keeping alive moments of resistance, or by again making visible what has been publicly forgotten. Many of these forms of progressive reenactment take place in the art world.

American studies scholar Jenny Thompson, who spent seven years attending war reenactments and getting to know reenactors, observes in her book *War Games: Inside the World of 20th-Century War Reenactment* that war reenactors vary widely in income, education, and profession. They come from all walks of life, including "factory assemblers, computer programmers, construction workers, lawyers, waiters, advertising copywriters, doctors, teachers, bricklayers, and bank tellers; and no single occupation or job type dominates among them." One of the appeals of reenacting is precisely a disregard for distinctions in class and profession in the democratic forum of reenactment, which "levels the playing field" among participants. Significantly, however, reenactors are overwhelmingly white and male. Of the 3 percent of women who participate, they either play peripheral roles, such as war correspondents, or they reenact as men; blacks are even scarcer. Reenactors range in age from young to old; but most start "the hobby" in their twenties and the average age is thirty-eight. About half admit to being either conservative or Republican; only 20 percent describe themselves as liberal.[2]

Whether college students, firefighters, or doctors, reenactors fall into three categories: "farbs"—those who spend little time or money in maintaining "authenticity" and might wear modern shoes or smoke a modern cigarette (this is a term used derisively by hard-core reenactors); "mainstream" reenactors who fall between farbs and authentic—they look outwardly authentic but might not wear period underwear or might use modern items after hours; and "hard core," "authenticity Nazis," or, as they like to be called, "progressives." They seek an immersive experience in which, for example, not only is the food authentic but seasonal and regionally appropriate; inside seams are sewn in period-appropriate manner; and they never come out of character.[3] The authentic clothing and gear has become big business, and "sutlers" often sell period gear at reenactments. The reproduction clothing and gear needed to reenact is expensive, and estimates of the cost of getting started in the hobby are about fifteen hundred dollars, though one can spend much more.[4] The hobby requires months of preparation and is widely understood as addictive. Average reenactors attend four or five events a year and may do the same or different "impressions" or soldier personas; more hard-core reenactors may include "five World War II events, two World War I events, two Vietnam events, and usually at least two public events," according to Thompson. Some do more. Many spend time at flea markets, militaria, and gun shows, collecting for their kits or accumulating large collections. Perhaps not surprisingly, they marry less frequently than the national average and divorce more often. At the extreme are reenactors for whom the hobby becomes the consuming passion of their lives; they lose the ability to distinguish reality from fantasy and overidentify with their impressions, turning off even other reenactors.[5]

Small groups of Civil War reenactors began dressing up as Union and Confederate soldiers in the 1950s, but the hobby gained traction with Civil War centennial memorials in which major battles were reenacted beginning in 1961. World War I and World War II reenacting grew out of Civil War reenacting in the later 1960s and 1970s and these in turn produced more events, including Korean and Vietnam War reenacting. Groups formed to reenact the French and Indian War, the English Civil War, the War of 1812, and especially the American Revolution. Other kinds of historical events are reenacted, too. In Saginaw, Michigan, for example, fur trading with the French is reenacted on the Saginaw River. Nor is reenacting limited to the United States. Under "reenactment groups," *Wikipedia* lists official groups in thirty-one countries, including those in Western Europe, Eastern Europe, Scandinavia, Asian countries, North and South America. There are twenty-nine official World War II groups and no doubt many more unofficial ones; other national groups reenact Napoleonic wars, colonial wars, Viking, Saxon, Norman wars, ancient Greek wars, the War of the Roses, the Hundred Years War, the storming of the Bastille, and much more. Reenactors in each country reenact events from their own history, but the American Civil War is also reenacted in Europe and Australia.[6]

One reason reenacting became so popular in the United States in the decades following World War II is that the last veterans of the Civil War were dying off, creating nostalgia for a past that would no longer remain in living memory, which was officially enshrined in the Civil War memorial reenactments of the early 1960s. But it is no accident that the fifties also began the era of civil rights activism that produced greater freedoms for blacks, or that the sixties and seventies were the era of the anti-Vietnam War movement and the gay rights, women's rights, and Black Power movements. Reenacting war can be seen as a reaction to the political protests and the more general antiestablishment ethos of those decades, the community-building camaraderie, bawdiness, and male bonding of war reenactment groups as a counterpart to the civil rights marches in the South, the love-in at Woodstock, and the antiwar demonstrations in Washington, D.C. The rise of Civil War reenactments may be seen as a form of symbolic defiance against the era of affirmative action and the challenge to the white patriarchy. Many reenacting groups were on the right-wing fringe and shared a white supremacist agenda.[7]

War reenactments are loosely scripted or unscripted, in order to keep them open ended and free flowing. This allows the event to remain unpredictable, exciting, and centered on personal embodied experience and choice, even when it contradicts historical facts. Curator Robert Blackson notes, "The degree to which performers empower themselves through layers of authenticity is secondary to their willingness to allow personal interpretation rather than verisimilitude to influence their actions."[8] This is what distinguishes war reenactment from repetition, simulation, or reproduction, which minimize personal agency, and makes it possible for a battle known to have been won by the Germans to be won, in reenacted form, by the British. Despite the emphasis on period authenticity, reenactors focus not on the historical detail of battle events, but rather on individual experience, valorizing it over historical and political meaning. The reenactor-soldier allegorically embodies the uniform he wears, and the reenactment experience gives him access to the quality of manliness—consisting of virtue, courage, and the sublimation of personal needs to a higher purpose, forged in the "steel bath" of battle.[9] The intensity and intimacy of male bonding during real shooting wars also is a central feature of war reenacting, where homoerotic camaraderie and humor thrives without threatening a sense of manliness in the acutely masculine world that reenactors create.

Interestingly, there is a favorite among soldier impressions: the Nazi SS. Many consider the German uniforms and equipment the best looking and most striking, with their high boots, helmets, and well-cut tunics. While a few reenactors refuse to do a German impression because of its political implications, far more find it irresistible, succumbing to its fascination. Most reenactors feel that all soldiers are the same and it does not matter what uniform they put on because, for them, war is ultimately about male bonding. As one reenactor explains, "It doesn't come down to your flag or your country or your politics. It's the men in your platoon. The men in your company. That's who you're fighting for. You're not fighting for any glorious cause or whatever. What it comes down to is you're fighting for the twelve guys that you happen to be in combat with."[10] Reenactors who buy the clothing and gear, drive hundreds of miles to events, and spend days participating in military skirmishes and mock battles revere the idea of the soldier and see the soldier-male as universal. Hence the focus on details of period clothing and equipment, verified by old photos, rather than on the historical events themselves; hence, too, the insistence of most reenactment groups that they are apolitical, which in turn underscores their refusal to contextualize and interpret history. This refusal is the most serious critique of war reenactment by scholars.

In his book on conservation heritage and display, *The Representation of the Past*, Kevin Walsh proposes that modern and postmodern life serves to distance people from the economic, cultural, and political processes that affect and even control their lives, often inducing "an uncritical patriotism which numbs our ability to understand and communicate with other nations." Analyzing the heritage boom in Britain in the 1970s and 1980s, he suggests that artificial heritage museums regard the past as isolated and complete, obscuring the contingency of the past on the present. He dismisses historical reenactments as "nothing but mere titillation, meaningless amateur dramatics promoting the postmodern simulacrum, a hazy image of a manipulated and trivialized past." These simulacra, moreover, contribute to actual historical amnesia.[11] Similarly, the recent rise in reenactment during an era of economic decline may be seen as nostalgia for an imagined heroic past just as "living history" or "heritage" museums—John D. Rockefeller's Colonial Williamsburg (founded 1926), Henry Ford's Greenfield Village (founded 1929), and Plimouth Plantation (founded 1947)—erected during the intensification of industrialization in the case of the former two and expansion of black equality during World War II in the latter, represented a nostalgic longing for the preindustrial and colonialist past. Reenacting can be distinguished from video war games that also draw the player into an immersive experience that creates the illusion of acting within a field. Reenacting is not only physically embodied but also offers the possibility of collapsing time and producing the "period rush" that occurs when the present seems to merge with the past and the reenactor feels, for a moment, that the experience is real and not merely fantasmatic. These moments are treasured by reenactors.

Because reenactors are aware that historians often see their hobby as trivializing history or that others scoff at reenacting as obsessively militaristic, many reenactors justify their hobby as educating the public and keeping history alive while honoring the sacrifices and memory of past soldiers. They often scorn Americans for being ignorant about and dismissive of military history. Yet, as Thompson observes, their own obsession was bred within a thriving American war culture, which has militarized domestic society, inflated the rhetoric of patriotism, and lured tens of thousands of America's youth to sign up for real wars in foreign lands. Over 80 percent of reenactors have relatives who served in the wars they reenact. This is significant, not because those relatives have necessarily romanticized the wars in which they were involved, but, on the contrary, because they have transmitted their trauma, even if they are unable or unwilling to reveal much about their experience. The act of participating in a battle meant to simulate events in Germany or Vietnam for the children or grandchildren of war veterans is a way of connecting to that experience and to the fathers or grandfathers who have not talked much about it, who remain distant, silent, or inaccessible. It might be older brothers, uncles, or the father of a friend, because the trauma ripples outward through the families, neighborhoods, and communities in which the veterans live. Their efforts to bury the past tend to fail no matter how hard they try or, perhaps, precisely because they try. Reenacting, then, also becomes a way of trying to understand the past in order to better understand the effects of war on veteran families. As historian George Mosse observes, "Part of the impulse to re-enact seems to be a desire to control war's legacy by owning it."[12]

Most reenactors are romanticists who grew up immersed in war movies, television war programs, war games, GI Joe, and toy soldiers; they read war histories, fictions, and memoirs, and collected war memorabilia. They were members of the Boy Scouts of America, which was modeled on the idea of the soldier and emulated the ideals of sacrifice, heroism, discipline, and courage. If they were unable to break through to their own silent veteran fathers, reenactors had a wealth of other sources and "came of age consuming war."[13] This consumption relied primarily on visual representations for the production of memory and meaning. But there is more to the story. Why does the obsession with trying to connect to that taboo experience so often induce war enthusiasm? Many, perhaps most, reenactors love the violence, the imagined blood and gore, the opportunity to act out a sanctioned form of brutality in a safe environment. Writing of public and private reenactments, Thompson observes, "Unlike their attempts to control violence in public, in private they are willingly and mercilessly violent. Not only do they freely and repeatedly kill each other as well as die themselves many times in a single event, but they also inevitably enact a variety of war crimes and executions."[14] In private, reenactors are unrestrained in committing simulated atrocities. Perhaps this is a form of compensation for having missed the real thing, a chance to prove their manliness and to measure up to their forefathers—but perhaps it is also a submission to simple fantasy bloodlust.

In most of the war stories that filled the heads of reenactors as they grew up, the "Americans" were the heroes, and they often recite lines from war films. Thompson heard the films *Kelly's Heroes* and *Cross of Iron* endlessly quoted during World War II events. Stanley Kubrick's film *Paths of Glory* is a favorite among World War I reenactors who like to quote the line, "Ready to kill some Germans today, soldier?" Vietnam reenactments, however, are the most influenced by movies, with lines such as "I want every swinging dick in the field" from *Platoon* and others from *Full Metal Jacket* often quoted.[15]

Crossing the Line into Fantasy

Peggy Phelan offers a thoughtful analysis of the relation between film and reenactment in the shooting of Ronald Reagan by John Hinckley in 1981. Hinckley had seen the film *Taxi Driver* sixteen times, and his reenactment of Travis Bickle was the basis of the case his lawyers made that he was innocent by reason of insanity. "Hinckley's trial," writes Phelan, "was about the consequences of merging reality and representation, not in order to demonstrate their seamlessness as postmodern theory often suggests, but rather as an illustration of the robust desire to use representation as a way to transform reality." If film can reenact life, life can reenact film. Moreover, reenactment can be seen as a way to both discover and induce feelings about the event being reenacted and to transform reality. This is one of the functions it seems to serve for war reenactors. Hinckley, however, was judged insane, his lawyers successfully arguing that he could not distinguish reality from his own fantasies.[16]

Phelan points to a similar tendency in the remarkable comments by an aide in George W. Bush's administration to journalist and political reporter Ron Suskind about the "reality-based" community. Writes Suskind,

> The aide said that guys like me were "in what we call the reality-based community," which he defined as people who "believe that solutions emerge from your judicious study of discernible reality." I nodded and murmured something about enlightenment principles and empiricism. He cut me off, "That's not the way the world really works anymore," he continued. "We're an empire now, and when we act, we create our own reality. And while you're studying that reality—judiciously, as you will—we'll act again, creating other new realities, which you can study too, and that's how things will sort out. We're history's actors . . . and you, all of you, will be left to just study what we do."[17]

This is not only breathtakingly arrogant but an extreme statement of subjective idealism. The Bush team seemed to believe that they were operating in a vacuum in which nothing happened unless they dreamed and desired it, that only their aims and intentions mattered, while entirely ignoring not only the materialist and dialectical nature of reality that produces constant change but the fact that the aims of politicians clash and things happen that no one intends, desires, or foresees. Those who are convinced they can create their own reality, like Hinckley, the Bush administration, and reenactors who have become pathologically addicted to their obsession, have crossed the line into fantasy.

There is another dimension to reenacting for those who enjoy the long periods of waiting, freezing in the winter or boiling in the summer, and continuing even when they are exhausted. They find pleasure in their suffering and luxuriate in their isolation and misery. These tests of endurance are another pathway to manliness and self-esteem, reinforcing the characteristics of strength, aggressiveness, and stoicism among those who identify with the soldier not only as history's hero but also as history's long-suffering victim, the tarnished and underappreciated public servant, the pawn of governments, the cannon fodder of war that is forgotten when war comes to an end.[18]

Although one of the charms of war reenactment is violence itself, such violence is of course a fantasized and fetishized form of violence, not the real experience of violence. In a *New York Times* article on World War II reenactment, Brett Sokol describes how a son, who had drawn his war veteran father into reenacting, then enlisted for the real thing. At age twenty-seven, he was shipped out to the battlefields of Iraq with his Pennsylvania National Guard unit to the consternation of his father, who said, "I cannot dictate to my kids. But I kept drilling into him, it's not going to be the same." In an email message sent from the western outskirts of Baghdad where the son, Brian Cessna, was a staff sergeant on a Stryker assault vehicle, he quickly came to the same conclusion: "You might get the romantic side of things," he wrote. But when it came to real bullets and battle conditions, "You're cursing and praying to God at the same time, wondering if your wife is awake yet, realizing that the difference between making someone live or die is your trigger finger."[19] Clearly he had not quite realized this on the reenactment battlefields.

The appeal of reenactment is the appeal of war without the imminent threat of death, although some reenactors conflate the two. As one asserts, "the only difference between us and the real veterans is that we don't stay in the rain as long as they did or in the cold or run out of food or try to dodge real, live bullets."[20] He says this as if not having to dodge "real, live bullets" were a quantitative and not a qualitative difference, like not running out of food. The reenacted battles may be safely circumscribed—the dead will rise again and rejoin their comrades—but the young men who enlist tend not to think about death; they have glorified American militarism with Boy Scout idealism and feel invulnerable. Perhaps, however, war itself is a form of reenactment on the part of soldiers, a delusional acting out of a romantic idea of selfless bravery, a fight for national glory and honor based on the ideals of war learned through cultural representation regarded as documentary truth. Horror and loss are usually shown occurring only on the enemy side and thus are insufficient deterrents for those who want to connect to the past, to those experiences borne by their fathers and forefathers, and to the patriotic ideal of the manly and heroic soldier. Many of those who enthusiastically enlist in the armed forces are no doubt driven by the desire to reenact the past.

Even a painful past holds the promise of satisfaction and a holiday atmosphere when reenacted. A *New York Times* article headlined "Weekend at War" on the front page of the "Escapes" section observed, "It's winter 2009, but for hundreds of re-enactors, it's December 1944 at the Battle of the Bulge." A photo shows couples in World War II uniforms dancing to a Glenn Miller–style big band and having a grand time. More than fifteen hundred World War II reenactors attend the Battle of the Bulge Living History Commemoration every January at the Fort Indiantown Gap military base in Annville, Pennsylvania. They live in a cluster of barracks built as temporary housing in 1941 and little modified since. Twenty or so actual veterans are invited as guests of honor for an extended weekend of activities, sometimes causing unexpected flashbacks in those veterans who experience the reenactments for the first time since the real war ended.[21]

As might be expected, war veterans in general are not driven to reenact or eager to reconnect to that traumatic experience. Thompson asserts that most reenactors are civilians with no desire to experience real war: "Most re-enactors stress that they do not want to be in the military nor do they want to experience real war. They want to re-enact."[22] With reenactment comes the chance to get as close as possible to war experience without going to war, to immerse oneself in "danger" and shared experience, where everyone is just a soldier, every event is different, and bloodlust can be vented without any sense of guilt or responsibility for its consequences. Nevertheless, the fantasy of war can never approximate the real thing, and the obsession with details and factoids of authenticity comes at the expense of critical engagement with history and the meaning of the issues behind the events reenacted.

Recruiting for the National Guard

The blurring of reenactment and real war experience becomes evident in a recruiting film for the National Guard shown in movie theaters along with previews of coming films in 2008–2009 (and on YouTube). The three-and-a-half-minute film short explicitly trades on the fantasy of connecting to a heroic past. The story line follows a NASCAR race driver (played by Dale Earnhardt Jr.) who gets called up to National Guard service. With the band 3 Doors Down performing their song "Citizen Soldier," the video employs rapid editing cuts and includes the band playing, making it look like a normal music video.[23] The image of modern-day soldiers is intercut with documentary-style clips of American soldiers of the Revolutionary War running through the woods with muskets while avoiding cannon-ball blasts. The scene alludes to the Guards' roots in the colonial militia and fuses present-day militarism with the fight for American national independence. The line of text "I fired the shot that started a nation" is superimposed on the screen. The running soldiers are romantic figures in a picturesque landscape, possibly even war reenactors, whose services the TV and film industry often calls upon.²⁴ Other lines of text appear as the video progresses, such as, "I am an expert and a professional," "I comfort my neighbors," "I will never accept defeat," and "I will never quit." As scenes of Americans storming the beach at Normandy during World War II appear onscreen, the text "I stormed the beach at Normandy" makes it clear that the modern soldier is a universal soldier who has fought in all wars past. The video concludes as the soldier delivers a young boy found in a destroyed shelter to the grateful arms of his mother and the word "brave" is emblazoned on the screen.

Mapping the gallant present onto a valiant past, the film appeals to a sense of idealistic nationalism founded on the rhetoric of freedom against tyranny that served as the foundation of previous wars. The target audience of working-class young men, NASCAR and rock-video fans, is meant to be inspired by the idealized figure of the soldier, the humanitarian nature of his job, and the gratitude with which his brave efforts are rewarded. Merging together pure fiction, reenactment, and the romance of war, the recruiting film does not suggest the real desert conditions of Iraq and Afghanistan, where soldiers will not be running freely through deciduous forests. It is meant to draw youths with bleak economic futures into a dream of universal admiration, self-respect, and national pride and to appeal to those who long to connect to the heroically mythologized traditions of their forefathers as the ultimate incubator of manliness and strength.

The recruitment literature of the National Guard focuses primarily on stateside good works in pastoral settings. In a June 2009 mailing, the National Guard appealed to youthful concerns about ecology, the environment, and the "greening" of America. The envelope pictured young men and women dressed in jeans and T-shirts and working together in a sunny meadow to pick up litter. What could be more apolitical or unobjectionable than the beautification of the American landscape, itself a romantic symbol of an innocent and idealized nation? The slogan printed in green on the envelope is "Benefits for You and the Environment." "Eco-friendly" T-shirts, bags, and notebooks are advertised on the back of the large envelope and the inside literature is labeled "Guard the Environment" and specifies activities such as "nurturing wolf cubs." It lists programs and efforts made by the National Guard for various states, for example, "Texas: Creating sustainable buildings with energy efficiency, water conservation, and use of green products," or "Mississippi: Acquired 17,000 acre tract of rural, undeveloped land, protecting it from development." Yet the use of green products or the acquisition of undeveloped land does not exactly require the sustained services of recruits to the National Guard.

The Guard also offers money for college, career skills, academic credits for college, part-time service, and extra cash during Basic Training and Advanced Individual Training, appealing in particular to the economically battered working and middle classes. Only in the phrase "Defend Freedom and the Environment," listed at the bottom of the page, is there even a hint that any other kind of service might be demanded. One must extrapolate from that innocuous phrase, "Defend freedom," that a more gruesome and life-threatening commitment may be involved than "nurturing wolf cubs." The idea that one might be signing up for a tour of duty in Iraq or Afghanistan cannot be deduced from these materials. In fact, tens of thousands of National Guardsmen have been sent to Iraq, so depleting the manpower and equipment needed to deal with natural disasters such as hurricanes, floods, and fires that state governors from both political parties complained to the Bush administration.[25]

A further irony is the false idea of the warrior hero as the embodiment of manliness. In reality, military training is about "breaking" and "rebuilding" recruits to serve with absolute and unquestioning submission so that the soldier does not resist when sent into the maws of destruction and death. As one scholar observes, "We encourage the soldier's delusion of masculine virility and call him a hero—in order to lure him into becoming a sacrificial victim."[26]

Race and Reenactment

It is no accident that there are very few black reenactors, and this is especially significant for Civil War reenactment, raising questions about the assertion that reenactment simply "keeps history alive " and "honors the sacrifices of soldiers" as many reenactors contend. Tony Horwitz's *Confederates in the Attic*, which explores the meaning of the Civil War in the modern South and the popularity of reenacting it, points out that attitudes toward the Civil War divide along racial lines, with too many whites fondly mythologizing the war and rejecting its real historical implications.[27] In 2003, for example, the Beauregard-Vernon NAACP chapter in DeRidder, Louisiana, formally denounced a planned Civil War reenactment, citing as their reasons "racism and hatred." The *Lake Charles American Press* reported the group's opposition to "The Battle of Hickory Creek," which was described as a fictional Civil War battle "loosely based on the massive overland invasion of western Louisiana in the fall of 1863." The local NAACP group's position was consistent with that of the national NAACP, which opposes display of the Confederate flag and is against Civil War reenactments nationwide.[28] We can understand why. There are white supremacists across the country that still display the flag today, one hundred and fifty years after the Civil War began, making it one of the most inflammatory symbols of racial violence and hatred in America.

The Confederate flag became an embattled symbol in the 1990s, when it flew underneath the U.S. and South Carolina flags on a pole atop the State House dome in Columbia, igniting a national media controversy. Supporters of the flag defended the values it represented while critics pointed out that those values included racism and a defense of slavery. A compromise was eventually reached and in June 2000, in a solemn ceremony, the flag was removed from the State House dome, where it had waved since the 1960s, and placed on a pole behind the Confederate Soldier Monument on the north grounds of the State House. "There it waves today," writes historian James Farmer, "more visible than before, illuminated at night but nonetheless vulnerable to opponents whose nocturnal raids require that a supply of replacements be kept on hand."[29] Farmer argues that Confederate reenactors, by reenacting the Civil War, see their role as counterattacking those whom they regard as insulting their ancestors by opposing the symbols of the Confederacy.

Local organizers and participants of the DeRidder reenactment claimed they were preserving their historical heritage, an odd claim indeed since this is a fictional battle. Plans were made to bus in schoolchildren from around the area to educate them about the "glory days" of the Old South. One member of the NAACP, Charles Butler, lost his job with the City of DeRidder's Public Works Department for opposing the reenactment, which was held in February, during Black History Month. Such an annual reenactment can only be seen as constructing and sanctioning an exclusionary white community, and demonstrates that the archetype and patriarchal ideal of the warrior-hero in America is always white.[30]

Folklorist Rory Turner, another observer/participant of Civil War reenactments, writes, "Saturday evening at Gettysburg in 1988, in the Confederate camp, I stumbled across the end of a reenacted minstrel show. A large rowdy crowd was gathered in the darkness. In the middle several performers mimicked 'negroes' with scatological routines. Dancing and singing, they really had their crowd in stitches about old Bo who believed that 'the blue mass' would cure constipation. When the skit was over they passed the hat and everyone sang 'Dixie.'"[31] Reenactment of the Civil War never seems to challenge the racism on which it is based; on the contrary, it thrives on it.

For many, the Civil War was not primarily about slavery at all, as the Republican governor of Virginia, Robert McDonnell, proclaimed in 2010 when he issued a state proclamation celebrating April as Confederate History Month. When asked to explain why there was no mention of slavery in his declaration honoring "the sacrifices of the Confederate leaders, soldiers and citizens," he acknowledged that slavery was one of "any number of aspects" of the war but explained that he had focused on issues "I thought were most significant for Virginia." For the black residents of Virginia—one fifth of the state's population—slavery was quite significant, and when they objected, along with many others, McDonnell finally backed down and apologized. But McDonnell's efforts continue a long tradition of Civil War revisionism that attempts to erase slavery from the war narrative and to reimagine the Civil War and the lost Southern cause as a noble battle for states' rights against an oppressive federal government. This view is held by the conservative white Tea Party movement that has developed since the 2008 election of Barack Obama, and by the white supremacist militia movements, whose opposition to the federal government spurred Timothy McVeigh's bombing of a federal building in Oklahoma City in 1995, killing 168 people.

It is no accident that McDonnell "forgot" his black constituents since the image of the black soldier does not fit the "archetype" of the warrior hero. John Howard and Laura Prividera assert that the warrior is tied to the patriarchal ideal, but not all masculine figures are entitled to be the warrior. "The symbolic power of the U.S. military lies in the ease with which it ties the archetypal and patriarchal role of protector (warrior) to the state (motherland)." They describe the warrior hero as "an archetypal icon that relies on and glorifies (hyper)masculinity, whiteness, heterosexuality, moral and national superiority, and violence—all of which are sanctioned during times of war. Thus, not all masculine figures are entitled to be the warrior. As manifest in the United States, his signification of national identity is almost exclusively white. Consequently, men of color can be the combatants but are denied legitimacy as a warrior representing the U.S. state. Moreover, the warrior hero is the antithesis of that which is feminine."[32]

Reenactors of later wars often accept the racist and sexist segregation of troops on the grounds that to do otherwise would be inauthentic. "History," as one reenactor asserted, "absolutely precludes from allowing any women or blacks into the unit." Other reenactors resist such discrimination and exclusion, but they have had little impact on the hobby.[33] As an example of an exception to this unwritten rule, Rory Turner reproduces a 1988 image of a black reenactor who re-created the role of a slave to one of the Confederate generals at Gettysburg. Writes Turner, "I was told that his role as the general's slave was an authentic re-creation, but this does not explain why he was supporting a past struggle to continue the subjugation of his people. He spent a lot of his time incoherently preaching about 'obeying the master,' and suffering for the sins of others."[34] Clearly the psychological stability of this black reenactor is open to question.

How far can one reasonably take the argument for "authenticity"? Should unit recruiting efforts be limited to those areas where units were actually raised, so that reenactors from other states are turned away? Should overweight reenactors be excluded if the troops were known to be hungry and thin? Should spectators, whose presence inevitably changes the experience but who were not present at Civil War battles, be allowed to attend? Is it authentic if a World War II battle that occurred in France is reenacted on American soil? Vanessa Agnew points to similar questions that were raised in regard to the BBCs reenactment of Captain Cook's first voyage, filmed as *The Ship* and set in the eighteenth century, for which Agnew was a consultant participant: "Were antimalarials and sunscreen crimes against history? Did safety harnesses lessen the terror that was necessary to our experience of the past? Should we have been flogged?" As Agnew suggests, "Such debates show that reenactment has appropriated the language of relativism—each reenactor offers his or her own version of the past—but not its lessons about the constructedness of history."[35] History is created by those who selectively shape and mold a story by choosing what to make visible and what to exclude, what to privilege or deemphasize, in order to construct interpretive frames.

Moreover, can even the visceral experience of the "period rush" be trusted as the authentic experience of soldiers in a different historical moment? Is it possible to experience what a soldier thirty or fifty or ninety or one hundred and fifty years ago would have experienced in the same way, without the knowledge and experience of the modern world shaping that experience in the reenactor? How can the modern-day reenactor escape the conscious awareness of the significance of the event, which makes it worth reenacting in the first place? Moreover, reenactors approach the hobby with a form of competitive aggression. One anecdote relates that "at a reenactment of a battle on World War II's Eastern Front, the competition got pretty rough—not between the Germans and the Russians, but between the authentics and the super-authentics. The latter group included a West Point professor who awed his associates by producing, at the appropriate moment, a packet of Nazi toilet paper."[36]

Discussing investigative historical reenactments filmed for television (such as *The Ship*), historian Alexander Cook asserts that even with weeks or months of immersion, "*We* can never be *Them*." While the mechanism of sympathy forces reenactors and audiences to engage with a different historical perspective and counteracts the "condescension of posterity," this sympathy exists in tension with the critical distance necessary for historical analysis. "In practice, moreover," writes Cook, "it is extremely difficult to employ sympathy as a universal mode of engagement with the past. The clash of forces and interests in history is such that a sympathetic identification with one group of people almost inevitably entails taking a critical distance from the perspective of some other group."[37] Thus it is no surprise that Civil War reenactors have little sympathy, if not outright antipathy, toward both Union troops and African Americans since the historical actors with whom they identify opposed the cause of free labor and the end of slavery. Indeed, the persistent practice of Civil War reenactment reinforces, over and over, a racist historical perspective with a pervasive and destructive impact on Southern culture, institutions, and political life.

Yet reenactment as a form of historical investigation holds great appeal for both reenactors and audiences. Can something beneficial and enlightening come out of it? Alexander Cook effectively summarizes the three primary problems with reenactment: (1) the idea that we can know the past by analogy, that is, that the subjective experience of modern reenactors can be mapped onto the past; (2) filmed observational reenactments want to tell two conflicting stories: one story about a group of modern individuals thrown into unfamiliar adversity, which chronicles their unscripted struggles to adapt and control the experience of psychological destabilization; and another story about a particular historical period, which demands a scripted narrative arc; (3) the visceral, subjective engagement of the reenactor comes into conflict with the critical distance needed for historical investigation. "The real question is not whether the experience of reenactment allows us to simulate the mentalities of the past," writes Cook, "it is whether the exercise can help *improve* our understanding of a different world and of the behavior of its inhabitants," by better understanding the conditions of existence in which those inhabitants acted through a "denaturalization of the present."[38] As Cook points out, these issues are problems that historians must grapple with more broadly in any construction of history. Perhaps most significant for understanding reenactment, however, is the discovery by the developers of reenactment projects that "a substantial disjunction" is almost always found between the responses of reenactors and the attitudes of those in the original situation that can be found in the historical record.

This can perhaps be more clearly understood in relation to the practice of "playing Indian," a hobby most popular in the United States but historically well represented in England and Germany, and to a lesser extent in Russia, Poland, France, and Italy. Like playing soldier, playing Indian allows one to escape from the conventional and restrictive boundaries of normative cultural identities and to give vent to the imaginary "savagery" ascribed to a cultural other, in the case of the Indian, or the suspension of civilian order, in the case of the soldier. Thus when colonists outraged by new taxes on tea in 1775 expressed their displeasure by dumping tea into Boston Harbor in what became known as the Boston Tea Party, they dressed as Mohawk Indians. The popularity of playing cowboys and Indians and the Indian mascots and team logos adopted by organized sport teams in the 1920s and 1930s, and surviving to date, reify the use of the Indian for a ritualized reenacted battle replete with paraphernalia and clothing as well as the war-whoops of victory, victory dances, and other imagined Indian behaviors. Such rituals pay no attention to real Indians, to tribal distinctions, or to American history; on the contrary, they depend on the invisibility of real Indians and repression of Indian experience.[39]

But the common experience of a "denaturalization of the present" that occurs with prolonged immersion in a different lifeworld can pave the way to critical social inquiry about both past and present. Key to productive reenactment is the foregrounding of self-reflexivity: participants must see themselves as modern researchers engaging with a historical imaginary, not as empty vessels embodying a knowable past. In addition to historians such as Cook, art theorists such as Sven Lütticken and Robert Blackson see new possibilities for reenactment. Lütticken notes that while historical reenactment and living history "are fatally implicated in the current conservative climate," they may "provide impulses that go beyond its limits" and even offer emancipatory potential. Blackson takes this further: "This liberating trait of reenactment is its signature quality and is what draws both practitioners and audiences to it again and again."[40] As historical reenactment becomes more and more popular, so does the belief among scholars and artists that we must pay closer attention and explore its potential. However contemptuous of reenactment academics may be, living history "affords us a particularly rich source for the study of our own biases."[41] Artists are especially attuned to investigating these possibilities, and the reenactment projects discussed below can be seen as self-reflexive and creative acts of interpretation critically engaging the contemporary understanding of the past and raising questions about the way the past has been mediated through documentary representation.

Producing Counter-Memory

Collective memory may be understood as official memory, the memory encoded in the public archive of representations. Such representations, reproduced over and over, come to codify the experience of an event for audiences who were not present or even alive at the original event, and even those who were find it difficult to take in the whole of an enormous and complex event beyond their own immediate circumstances and awareness. Such awareness in turn may be shaped or diminished by the traumatic effects of the event. Official memory is thus shaped by those who control the images and reports, while evidence to the contrary often becomes invisible to larger public view. Counter-memory, then, is the production of new memory that challenges official memory, which may be skewed, distorted, partial, or deliberately false. Counter-memory is a way of envisioning that which has been invisible, producing an alternate reality, a new and shared way of seeing. It re-creates the past in the present in order to reframe that past from the perspective of those who were silenced or obscured, or whose interests were repressed during the construction of official memory by the agencies, institutions, and discourses of the state.

An example of the production of such counter-memory may be seen in a work about Iraq produced by British artist Jeremy Deller. Best known for his reenactment project *The Battle of Orgreave*, which in 2001 reenacted the climactic clash between picketing miners and riot police in England in 1983 and was shown on national British television, Deller's Iraq project produces a multiplicity of perspectives and meanings that may be seen as a form of "relational aesthetics,"[42] described by French critic and curator Nicolas Borriaud as "an art taking as its theoretical horizon the realm of human interactions and its social context, rather than the assertion of an independent and *private* symbolic space."[43] Setting up a tension between spontaneity and unpredictability, on the one hand, and control by the artist who has given the impetus to the event on the other, Deller's 2008 work, *It Is What It Is: Conversations about Iraq*, was an effort to summon participatory audiences and encourage conversation about a contested political arena. Commissioned by the New Museum and Creative Time, the traveling installation presented the current circumstances in Iraq in the form of a revolving cast of participants including veterans, journalists, scholars, and Iraqi nationals who have expertise in a particular aspect of the region and/or firsthand experience of Iraq. They were invited to take up residence in the various gallery spaces in which the work was presented with the express purpose of encouraging discussion with visitors. This conceptual work was designed to produce conversation that filled the "information gap" between the American public's understanding of the Iraq war and the history of Iraq and called on museum goers to engage in discussions with the selected participants over the duration of the show.

To facilitate this dialog, Deller designed a conversation zone consisting of a few futon couches, some chairs, and a coffee table, framed by a monumental blue banner with the stitched saying It Is What It Is in both English and Arabic by artist Ed Hall. A large outline map of America and a smaller one of Iraq, with Baghdad exchanged for Manhattan, adorned another wall. Most significant among the objects on display,

Deller imported the twisted rusted hulk of a car destroyed in an explosion that killed thirty people in March 2007 on Al-Mutanabbi, a book-market street and intellectual hub of Baghdad. The car both alludes to and conceals the human loss of the war. Deller observed, "Whenever you watch the news and there's been a bombing, you don't see the bodies. You see a car. It becomes a replacement for the body."[44] From New York, Deller took his show on the road in a trailer that towed the car wreck, for a three-week cross-country tour through American cities and towns.

Deller's project brought together those who are geographically, economically, and politically distanced and created a site for politicized discussion through the "living history" narration of events by those with firsthand experience, allowing the audience to participate in this narration as ethical witnesses.[45] The work offered an opportunity for reframing the motivations and effects of the American war in Iraq and the construction of political and historical counter-memory, providing new knowledge and perspectives in contrast to the memories produced by much American press coverage of the war. Deller was keenly aware of the effects of the Iraq war on individual as well as national consciousness: "If you're fourteen or fifteen now, half of your life has been lived with the war in the background—on the TV screens, and in arguments and so on. So it's had a massive effect on individuals as well as the country."[46] By reframing events of the past in ways that Americans have never heard about, Deller's project is meant to connect that past to the present and change perspectives on the future.

Similarly, it is possible to use reenactment to connect with the past in order to deconstruct an official view, to represent the repressed, to make visible the effects of that repression and its implications in the present, and to study our own biases. These forms of reenactment seek to avoid the romance of war and violence or nostalgia for a mythologized past and instead challenge received wisdom or attend to the forgotten experience of ordinary persecuted people that has become invisible to history. Replacing the passion plays or historical pageants of earlier times, the reenactment of events from the wars in Vietnam and Iraq reexamine traumatic histories and myths that shape contemporary social and political realities. Unlike historical war reenactment, which sacrifices broader interpretive questions about the memory and meaning of historical events in order to privilege intensified personal experience, reenactment that reframes official histories to produce counter-memories aspires to investigate the political over the self and to utilize the intensified personal experience of participants and witnesses to support a more critical political awareness of the past and its effects on the present.[47]

Reenactment also can be seen as an attempt to reinforce the symbolic liberating effects of a political event. The Storming of the Bastille at the beginning of the French Revolution on 14 July 1789, for example, is widely celebrated with reenactments in France, as well as in London and Philadelphia. The Storming of the Winter Palace in Petrograd was first reenacted in 1920, just three years after the original event during the Russian Revolution and in the middle of a civil war while the city was under siege and suffering food shortages. The eight thousand participants were witnessed by an audience of one hundred thousand, a quarter of Petrograd, and the event was coordinated by army officers, artists, musicians, and directors. As Sven Lütticken notes, it was meant "to be a continuation of the revolution, activating the masses and giving history a forward impulse."[48]

Vietnam in Virginia: An-My Lê

Nearly every war in which the United States has been involved is reenacted, but perhaps the most surprising, because it was not a "good" war in the way that others have been mythologized, is the reenactment of the Vietnam War. In the United States, Vietnam units are now established in Kentucky, Texas, Virginia, and North Carolina. Others exist in Belgium, Poland, and France.[49]

These are not mass events that draw thousands; in fact, they are closed to spectators, discarding the need for showmanship and allowing for a more immersive experience. The action is never scripted, but each side might "choreograph" their event in the form of tactical mapping out and timing the routes their patrols will take. Leaders of both sides might work together to stage ambushes, while keeping the other reenactors unaware of their plans so they are free to react as they see fit. This allows maximum opportunity for experiencing the intensity of war and the possibility of "period rush."

Though private and wary of outsiders, a group of Vietnam War reenactors in Virginia whom she found via the Internet agreed to allow Vietnamese American artist An-My Lê to photograph them on the condition that she also join them as a participant. By integrating her into the group rather than allowing her the distance of an outsider, they no doubt hoped to win her sympathy, while she hoped to win their trust. Lê got to know the reenactors, whom she describes as "straightforward, conservative men," and participated at weekend events in the forests of Virginia for four summers, often playing a North Vietnamese army soldier or Vietcong guerrilla fitted out in loose black pajamas and sandals, unlike the heavy combat boots and clothing worn by American soldiers that was so unsuited to the hot, humid climate and terrain in Vietnam. She also played a "Kit Carson" scout, a North Vietnamese informer for the Americans. Lê's ethnicity added to the "authenticity" of the reenactments, and the unit would often construct elaborate scenarios around her character, which Lê describes: "I have played the sniper girl (my favorite—it felt perversely empowering to control something that I never had any say in). I have been the lone guerrilla left over in a booby-trapped village to spring out of a hut and ambush the GI platoon. I have played the captured prisoner."[50]

Reenactors, Lê asserts, would never restage an event like the My Lai massacre because there is "no glory in it, only pain." She notes that no actual Vietnam veterans reenacted with her unit (neither did other Vietnamese Americans). The reenactors were men who were not there but wished they had been, those who had a need to connect to the enormity of that experience, and those who had family members in the war. One had lost a brother; the fathers of two others had fought in the war. Sometimes, said Lê, reenactors pretended to have fought in Vietnam when they had not.[51]

Lê's participation also allowed her to both discover and induce feelings about the events being reenacted. She found that they reawakened her memories of night explosions and screams that she had experienced as a child living in Saigon with her parents, both college professors. She recalled the trauma of waking up in the morning to find dead bodies in the streets. Her desire to interrogate that experience must be seen as part of her desire to photograph and reenact the Vietnam War, even while demonstrating that no amount of period authenticity could produce anything but dreamlike inventions as memory substitutes. In speaking about her earlier series *Viêt Nam* (1994–1997), produced when Lê returned to Vietnam after an absence of twenty years, she said, "I began making photographs that use the real to ground the imaginary."[52] The same could be said of her series on war reenactments in Virginia titled *Small Wars* (1999–2002).

Much of Lê's understanding of the war, like most Americans', depends on representation: history books, movies, newspapers, magazines, the stories of friends and relatives. Born in Vietnam in 1960, she came to the United States as a fifteen-year old political refugee in 1975 after she was airlifted out with her family. Her exploration of the war through photography and de facto reenactment is also a way to question, in her words, "the Vietnam of the mind" and the way that the accumulation of representation constructs memory and imagination of the war after the fact.[53] *Small Wars* has been shown at PS1/MoMA Contemporary Art Center in Long Island City, New York, the San Francisco Museum of Modern Art, the Museum of Contemporary Photography in Chicago, and the Contemporary Arts Center Cincinnati, among other venues.

HISTORICAL REENACTMENT 67

The photographs in *Small Wars* are black-and-white landscapes in which events and figures are seen from a distance; soldiers may appear tensely poised before a downed chopper in the forest, as in *Rescue*. These are very different from the war photography of photojournalists such as Larry Burrows, Robert Capa, James Nachtwey, Gilles Peress, or Tyler Hicks. Lê's photos do not focus on violence or chaos, or immediately implore the viewer toward a moral stance; on the contrary, they are quiet, lush, beautifully printed silver gelatin prints, produced with a large-format camera and tripod like the kind that was used for Civil War photographs made by Alexander Gardner and Timothy O'Sullivan for the studio of Matthew Brady. Lê's photos, exhibiting a nineteenth-century landscape sensibility, convey a respectful ambiguity, resulting from the political ambivalence of a former Saigon native who saw the Americans as defending her country from the communists and not merely despoiling it. "We lived through many political coups," says Lê, "years of fear and uncertainty, as the Viet Cong would shell the city randomly every night. War became a routine, something we accepted as part of our lives.... We returned to Saigon [from Paris] in 1973, only to see the country fall to the Communists in 1975. We were fortunate to be evacuated by the Americans that April."[54]

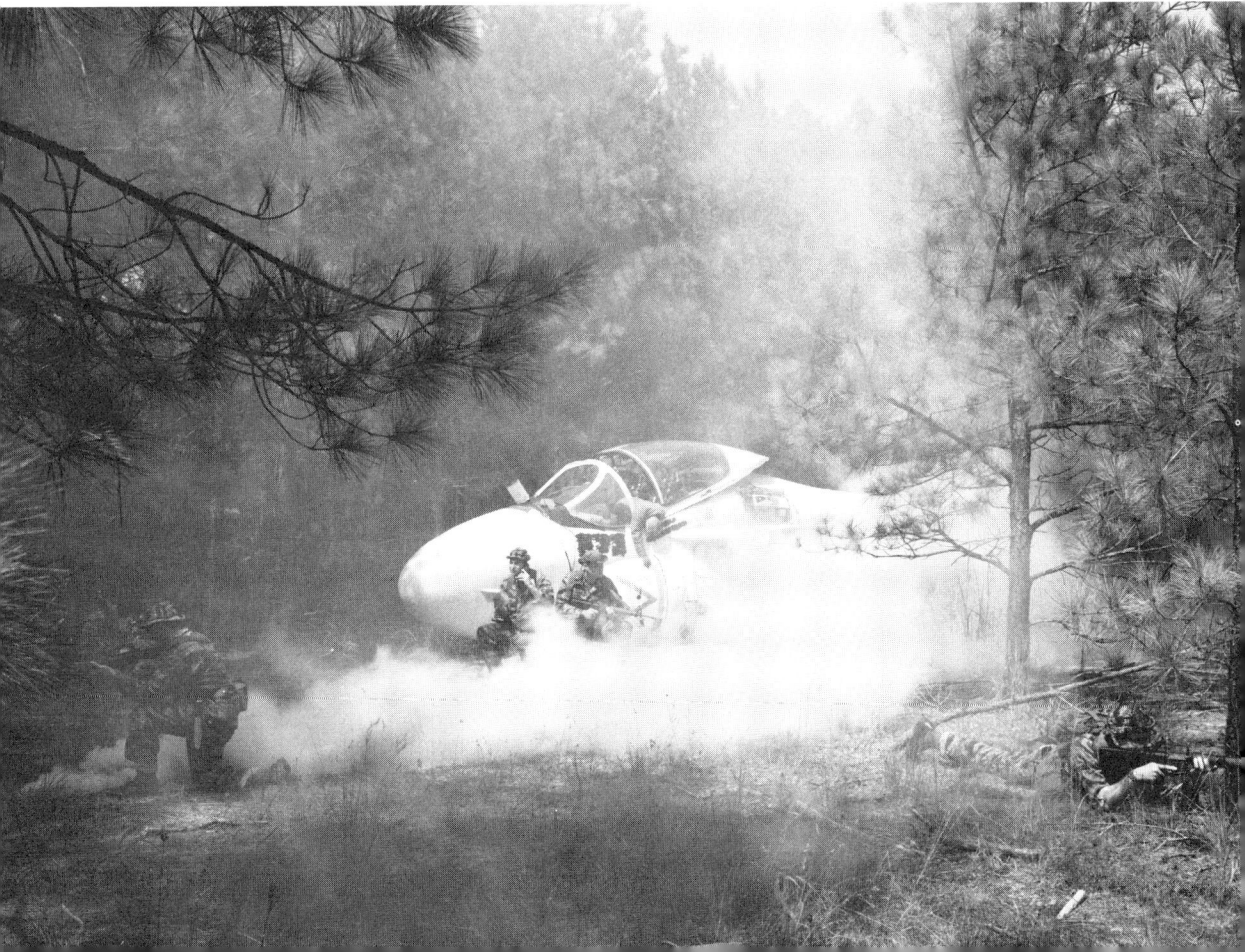

Figure 3. An-My Lê, *Rescue*, from series *Small Wars*, 1999–2002. (© An-My Lê. Courtesy Murray Guy Gallery, New York.)

In her desire not to mock the reenactors, whose complicated motivations she came to respect, Lê edited out of the final series some of her most heavily theatrical images.[55] By doing so, she concentrates on moments of anticipation or reflection, such as two soldiers taking a break to write letters or read the newspaper (*Stars and Stripes*), resting in the grass (*GI*), a misty forest opening with the blurred movement of soldiers (*Ambush I*), or the trails of sparks captured with a slow shutter speed of an explosion in the forest (*Explosion*). The quietude of the scenes is underscored by the middle-gray scale of the photos that downplays the dramatic, instead shifting the focus to the immersion in the landscape, which takes on a mythic quality and becomes a character in the scenarios, almost overshadowing the dwarfed soldiers in frozen tableaux.

The elaborate gear included authentic airplanes and tents, but the pine and oak forest of Virginia is nothing like the dense, tropical jungle that covers much of Vietnam. This obvious disjunction highlights the artificiality of the reenactments. There is no pretense such as still exists about iconic images such as Robert Capa's 1936 *Falling Republican Soldier*, which many believe was a reenactment. Instead, the still moments Lê captures seem like projections of a reverie of war, impossible to reconcile with the memories of her urban childhood or the media images of rice paddies, rivers, palm trees, and jungles that have shaped collective American memory, yet still tapping into a longed-for connection to that experience.

Lê followed up *Small Wars* with another war project, this time a series on the Marine Air Ground Combat Center in the Mojave Desert in 29 Palms, California, where parts of it are meant to simulate areas in Iraq and Afghanistan. Marines train here before going overseas. Distressed by the start of another war, Lê moved from photographing imaginary reenactments of the past to imaginary reenactments of the future. Lê was struck by the magnitude of the fire power, "from artillery weapons to mortars, C-4 explosives, and air-delivered bombs—and its destructive potential" and the way it was "muted and transformed... in the middle of a tranquil desert."[56] Concerned about the devastating physical and psychic effects of an unjustified war, Lê saw this project as a plea to reconsider. The photos in the series *29 Palms* (2003–present) are often taken from a distance but convey the absurdity of pretending that California is Iraq or Afghanistan. Slogans painted on "enemy" homes, such as "Down USA," "Good Saddam," "Free Saddam," "Go Away," "Go Home GI," and "Kill Bush," designed to pump up and motivate the troops, demonstrate the hapless and superficial level of these war games.

Like *Small Wars*, *29 Palms* is shot in black and white with a large-format view camera. The five-by-seven negatives allow for great clarity while the lack of color produces images that seem, in Lê's words, "one step removed from reality."[57] At the same time, they echo the print and media images from which we draw our memories of war. Removed from the horror of war itself and focusing instead on "the precursor to war and its psychic aftermath," the coolness, distance and even the staged quality of Lê's projects are meant to evoke not gut reaction but more reasoned reflection on the unseen wars to which they allude, the devastation they have wrought or are about to unleash.[58] Lê's works also address the blurring of fact and fiction in war, the fantasy and romance of fighting "the enemy" that weaves its web both after the fact as well as before, and the artifice of war as events staged for the media that have little if anything to do with the real effects of war.

Iraq Veterans against the War

Perhaps the most searing examples of reenactments designed to produce counter-memories are the events staged by the group Iraq Veterans against the War (IVAW), founded in 2004 by and for active-duty service people and veterans against the war in Iraq. Among its other activities, IVAW offers a form of radical reenactment of the American presence in Iraq through its guerrilla theater squads that swoop into public spaces and perform the kinds of brutal raids and arrests that American soldiers perpetrate against Iraqi civilians. The organization includes veterans from Iraq and Afghanistan, active-duty servicemen and women from all branches of military service, and National Guard members and reservists who have served since 9/11, all of whom are opposed to the U.S. occupation of Iraq. The organization supports war resisters, including conscientious objectors, and advocates three radical demands: (1) the immediate withdrawal of all occupying forces in Iraq, (2) full benefits, more health-care benefits (including mental health), and other support for returning servicemen and women, and (3) reparations to the Iraq people (see ivaw.org).

In Washington, D.C., in March 2008, a group of twelve men and one woman from IVAW performed sweeps and raids in camouflage to mark the fourth anniversary of the war in Iraq. They crept down streets in formation, "detained" suspected hostile individuals (played by volunteers), and generally shocked and frightened tourists and office workers, who were delighted once they realized it was performative and antiwar.[59] The *Washington Post* website, which includes a video clip, reports that the marines are investigating two reservists for participating in the event.[60]

Similar performances took place in Denver, first on July Fourth and again during the Democratic National Convention in August 2008, with fully uniformed veterans in camouflage who mimed holding guns while stopping and subduing "suspects" face down on the pavement with cuffs

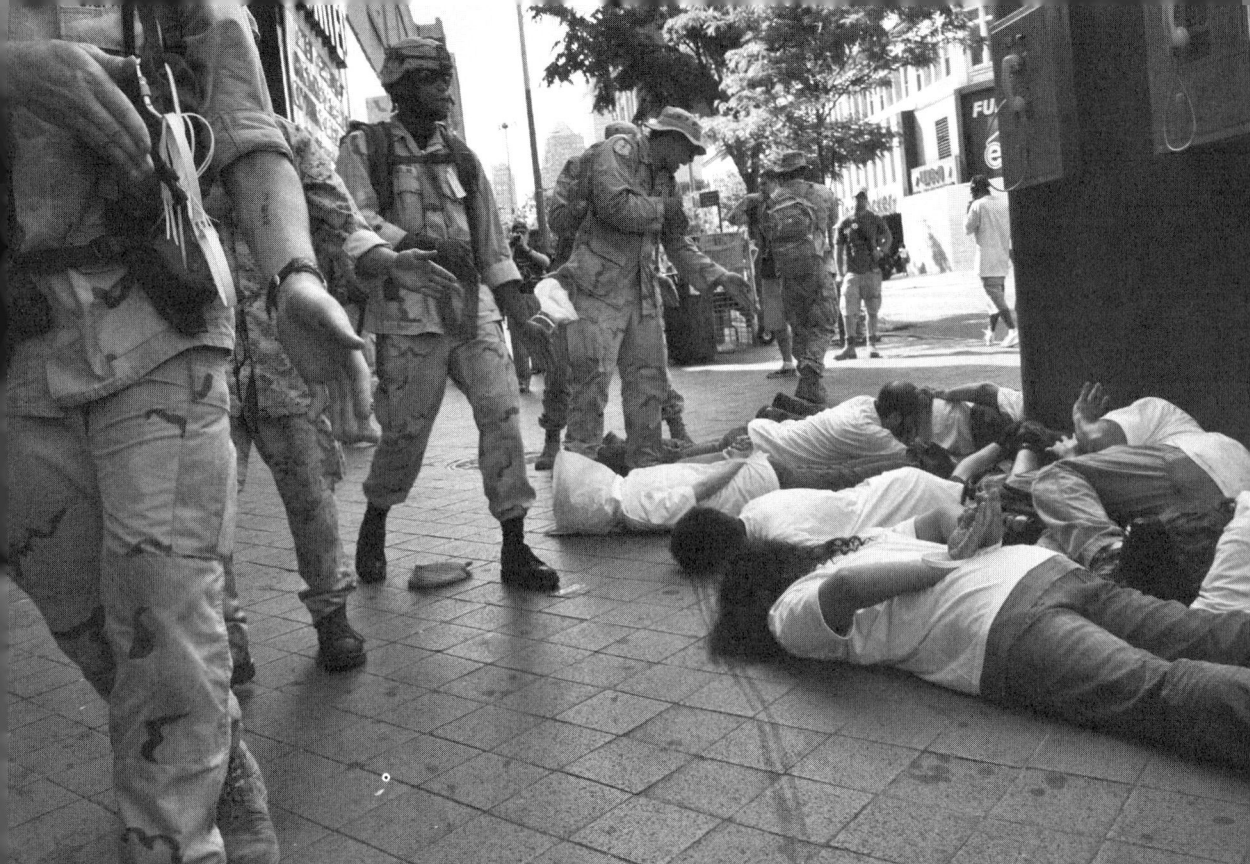

Figure 4. Iraq Veterans against the War, *Operation First Casualty*, New York City, 29 May 2007. Photo by Lovella Calica.

and hoods. Participant Geoff Milliard explained, "We're performing our guerrilla street theater called 'Operation First Casualty,' or OFC, because the first casualty in war is truth, and we're going to bring some of that truth here to Denver for the delegates to see."[61] Lasting about two hours, the veterans effectively re-created an atmosphere of trauma and terror (videos are available online at YouTube). The IVAW street theater is modeled after a Vietnam-era protest action, Operation Rapid American Withdrawal, which took place in Pennsylvania in the summer of 1970.

The IVAW protest performances were perhaps most shocking on the busy urban streets of New York City during Memorial Day. IVAW members performed searches, detentions, squad patrol, and crowd control operations in locations that included Central Park, Times Square, Union Square, and Grand Army Plaza. Described by James David on the Groundswell Blog as "alarming and powerful," he advised viewers to beware of the "shock value" of the online video he posted, in which the simulated military operations involved much shouting by soldiers and distress among witnessing bystanders. Another observer described the scene: "Out of nowhere and without provocation, nine soldiers in full-desert fatigues appeared and screamed at the group in white to 'get on the fucking ground.' The soldiers pinned people to the pavement and began 'bagging and tagging,' using zip-ties on their wrist and stuffing bags over their heads. People ran to get out of the way. The crowd pushed back to create a wall of wide eyes and open mouths around the soldiers."[62] In Iraq, a truck would have pulled up to haul people off to detention centers. Instead, IVAW members in black T-shirts distribute flyers after performances.

IVAW offers a form of reenacted violence that has not been visualized through the media and reframes the role of American soldiers in Iraq. The media tends to focus on the effects of car bombs, showing the aftermath of violence produced by factions within Iraq, but it does not begin to convey the experience of traumatic violence produced by the American presence. As terrifying as they are, it is safe to assume that IVAW reenactments offer only a glimpse of the daily abuses and dehumanizing experiences of Iraqi civilians, whose deaths in the tens of thousands remain officially uncounted, whose injuries are unattended by the mainstream Western media, and whose broken lives after years of war exist on an unimaginable scale of chaos, fear, and deprivation. The attempts of IVAW to raise public consciousness by reenacting terror raids on the streets of American cities produce a powerful reenactment that collapses the distance between the real and the imagined for the bystanders/witnesses whom it engages. The reenactment is not meant to produce a vicarious thrill or frisson of fear, but a measured dose of the real. What is most disturbing about this envisioning of the repressed is the realization that an occupying power has the ability to enact a shift in the status of the ordinary citizen from a member of a political community with rights to a state of exception and the sudden loss of rights with no recourse to state or legal authority.

The power of performative protest works such as IVAW reenactments and the videos that result from it should not be underestimated in an era of image wars. We can see the threat they represent in the contest of images as measured by the attempts of the U.S. government to harass and persecute members of IVAW and more generally to limit, censor, and ban images, such as pictures of the American war dead returning in coffins or the photos of Abu Ghraib. The street theater of IVAW performs valuable radical interventions into public consciousness, which can stimulate political thinking toward socially transformative effects. As Martha Rosler notes, "Social change depends on social movements, and all that artists can do is be a partner to a kind of concentrator of ideological currents."[63] IVAW reenacts war experience in order to make visible to the American public what remains invisible and the power of their street actions resides not only in their ability to trouble, disturb, outrage, and shock, but also their ability to produce a critique of the Iraq war through the materialization of bare life in ways that are terrifying and visceral.[64] This extreme form of engagement counters the imagery of military recruitment that romanticizes and idealizes war as an apolitical world that builds masculine identity.

Moore's Ford Quadruple Lynching Reenactment

Has the Civil War been completed? One of the most painful examples of a counter-memory event, in the struggle to make visible what has been publicly forgotten, is the quadruple lynching reenactment that has become an annual event in Moore's Ford, Georgia. The first reenactment took place in 2005 at Moore's Ford Bridge over the Apalachee River near Monroe in Walton County, Georgia. No one has ever been prosecuted for the lynching of four African Americans, two men and two women, one of whom was seven months pregnant, which took place more than sixty years ago on 25 July 1946. The killings are still under investigation by the FBI and the Georgia Bureau of Investigation despite FBI interviews with twenty-eight hundred people following the event and an FBI report that named fifty-five suspects.[65] The coroner's verdict, as usual in such killings, was "Death at the hands of persons unknown," demonstrating the political stranglehold of the perpetrators who, as was usually true, were leading members of the community. Their crimes depended on secrecy, intimidation of the local population, and an inviolate code of silence.

Just months after former Klansman Edgar Ray Killen was convicted of the 1964 killings of the three civil rights workers Michael Schwerner, James Chaney, and Andrew Goodman, the Moore's Ford lynching reenactment was organized by the Georgia Association of Black Elected Officials. Their goal was to keep the atrocity of this multiple lynching before the eyes of the public and to push for indictments against those responsible who were still living. They hoped to break the code of silence that had protected the perpetrators for decades, even after their deaths, and to encourage long-intimidated witnesses to come forward to identify those involved. The first reenactment took place on the fifty-ninth anniversary of the lynchings and captured the attention of the national news media, including the *New York Times*, CNN, and MSNBC. The previous month, one thousand members of the Georgia Association of Black Elected Officials passed a unanimous resolution urging prosecutors to bring charges in the case,[66] which was reopened in 2007 by the U.S. Justice Department.

The two African American couples who were murdered, George and Mae Murray Dorsey and Dorothy and Roger Malcolm, were sharecroppers lynched by a mob of local citizens following an altercation in which Roger Malcolm stabbed the son of the white farmer for whom he worked in the belief that he had been making sexual advances toward his wife, and also following a rumored disagreement over a crop settlement between George Dorsey and the white farmer for whom he worked. George Dorsey was a decorated veteran who had fought with American forces overseas during World War II, which was no doubt a further irritation to the white supremacist farmers. In the postwar period, demands for equality and the enforcement of voting rights by returning black veterans were deeply threatening to white supremacists, who were further inflamed by the incendiary racist rhetoric of the 1946 gubernatorial candidate in Georgia, Eugene Talmadge. Bold national civil rights initiatives in the following year led rebellious Southerners to form their own States' Rights Party, known as the Dixiecrats, which denounced civil rights, race mixing, and desegregation.[67]

For the first reenactment in 2005, echoing the long-standing intimidation of the white community, at the last minute the white men who had volunteered to play the Klan perpetrators backed out.[68] African American volunteers took their place, some of them wearing white plastic masks over their faces in a fraught heteropathic identification with the white supremacist killers. The masks ironically evoke the racist blackface minstrelsy once employed by whites to satirize African Americans, but there can be no equivalence between blackface and whiteface here. If blackface minstrelsy performance embodied a dialectic of "love and theft," as Eric Lott suggests, in which whiteness was defined against blackness while appropriating the very elements of blackness, usually tied to sexuality, that whites envied and feared, all in the name of entertainment, none of this holds true for the lynching reenactment.[69] In the hierarchy of American race relations in which whiteness always defines and supersedes blackness, the white masks do not suggest a premeditated race-change theatrical performance as a way of appropriating and domesticating the power of whiteness. On the contrary, the unexpected presence of the white masks deepens the chilling and alienating effects of the lynching reenactment by concentrating the lethal power of whiteness in a plastic facsimile. For many white viewers, who regard whiteness as the normative, unmarked condition of being, the white masks have the shocking effect of making the social construction of white identity visible.

African American organizers narrated events with a megaphone at every stop on the journey to Moore's Ford Bridge, from the farm where the stabbing took place to the jail where Roger Malcolm was held to the bridge where the two couples were driven by the white farmer Loy Harrison. Harrison bailed Malcolm out of jail but is widely believed to have been part of the setup that delivered the group to a Klan mob.[70] While it seems the mob at first intended to lynch only Roger Malcolm, the

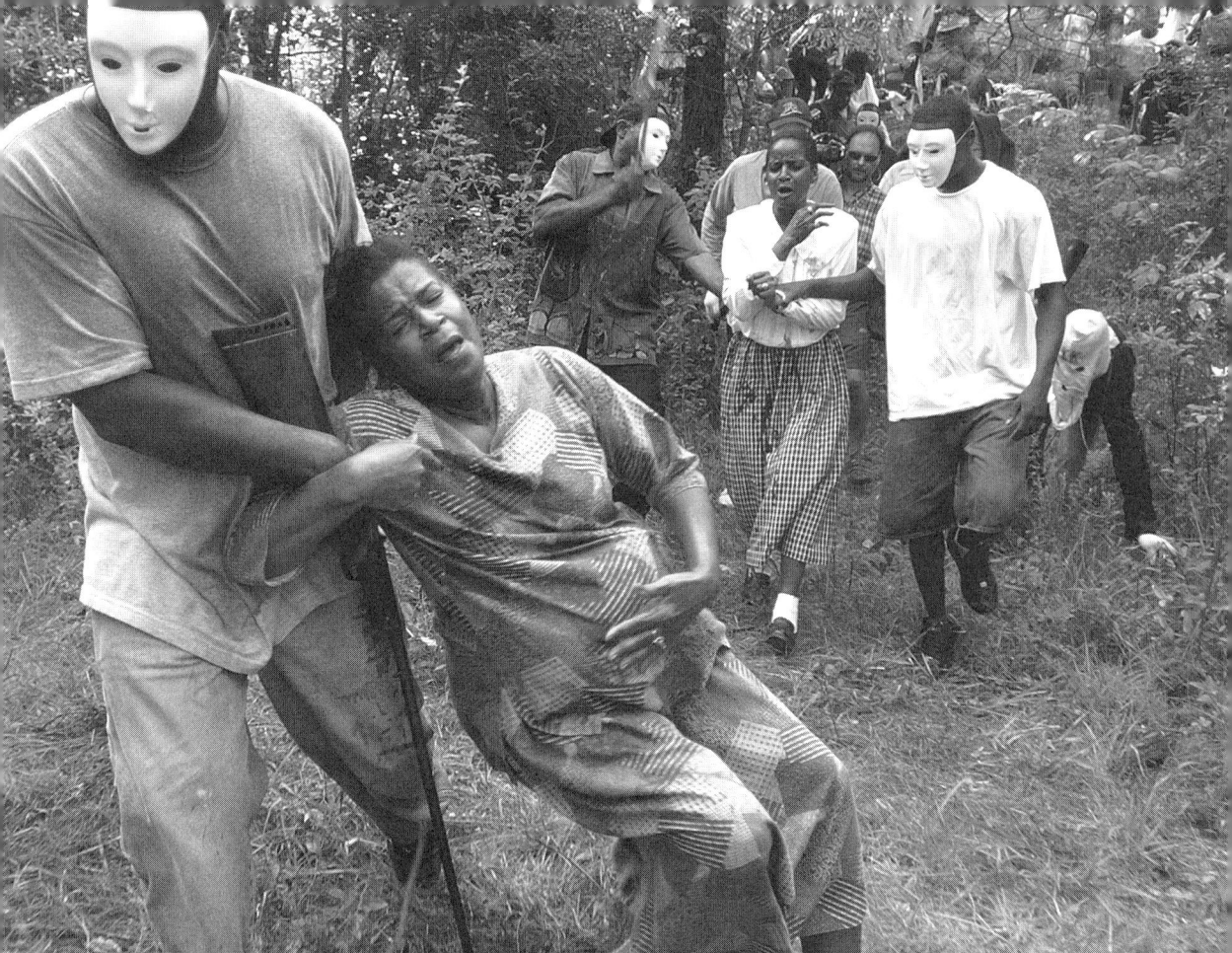

Figure 5. First lynching reenactment at Moore's Ford, Georgia, 2005. Photo by Eric S. Lesser.

momentum of the mob quickly grew to encompass both black men and then their wives, one of whom cursed a white man by name whom she recognized. Reenacting those events, the mob pulled the victims out of the car, "beat" them, dragged them down an embankment and "shot" them numerous times, using firecrackers but carrying real firearms, with fake blood poured over the prostrate victims' bodies. The reenactment concluded, as would every subsequent reenactment, with audience members comforting the reenactors in a tearful aftermath.[71]

In subsequent reenactments, whites from Atlanta, about forty miles west, played the roles of white supremacist perpetrators and supporters of Eugene Talmadge. The reenactments drew large African American audiences; however, few whites from Walton County attended (although the land on which the reenactments take place is owned by a white family). Some of these whites question the need for such a reenactment and suggest that it only fosters hatred and racial polarization. Reenactors and witnesses, however, understand that it is not the reenactment that is the cause of racial polarization, which has a long-standing history. Reenacting not only brings the unresolved past into the present, but also forms a bond between the victimized dead and the living.

The experience became so overwhelming and agonizing that in July 2010, none of the previous reenactors who played lynching victims was willing to do so again, requiring the hurried recruitment of four new volunteers from Atlanta.[72] Even some of the white men who played Klansmen began to have nightmares, and half a dozen refused to participate in the 2010 reenactment. One reenactor, who grew up not far from Moore's Ford and came to believe that his uncle might have been a perpetrator, explained that he could not recall the 2009 reenactment when it was over. "It's a horrible thing to do," he said. "I was not there. I'd say it's a fugue state. I'm still a little bit in shock. It's not somewhere that you want to inhabit."[73] This forced heteropathic identification with a subject position he abhorred was no doubt made all the more difficult by knowing it was likely occupied by one of his own relatives. Rather than imagine he could "go back in time" and feel what "it felt like then" in some empathic fantasy, this reenactor articulated a more painful truth, discovered by both white and black reenactors: the traumatic past "is not somewhere that you want to inhabit." Unlike popular and exclusionary reenactments that romanticize the past and reassert a racist order, the reenactment of the Moore's Ford lynching makes visible a buried past that its perpetrators and many of their descendants fervently hoped had been safely historicized and forgotten.

There is another possibility for the trauma produced by those involved in the reenactment, another reason that this troubled past "is not somewhere that you want to inhabit." Perhaps the traumatic response of the reenactors, especially the African Americans playing lynching victims but also those playing Klansmen, is related not only to the horror of those decades-old events, but also to larger implications in the present. The reenactments are powerful and wrenching emotional experiences, not because they return to the past, but, on the contrary, because they bring the past into the present. Rather than a period rush, the past rushes forward. As one black female reenactor said, "When I'm lying down there in the mud by the bridge, it's like no time has passed. This could happen to anyone, my brother, my son, my grandchildren. This thing, it happened then, but it's still happening."[74] The reenactment resonates with the disturbing facts of contemporary life, though it was produced in the wake of a number of prosecutions for civil rights era crimes. On one hand, those who came before are made to live on through memory and a kind of ritualized reenactment; on the other hand, to participate in the reenactment of a lynching is to reenact "bare life" in the "zone of exception" theorized by Giorgio Agamben, to vicariously embody *homo sacer*, the figure, taken from Roman history, who is stripped of citizenship and placed outside the law, a figure who loses all rights and may be killed without consequence.[75] The reenacted lynching becomes emblematic of all lynchings, evoking the infamous judgment of the 1857 Dred Scott decision in which the Supreme Court ruled that blacks, slave or free, were not citizens according to the Constitution and had "no rights which the white man was bound to respect," thus legally construing blacks as less than human. The reenactment of the Moore's Ford lynching brings into dramatic presence the continuing and permanent vulnerability of African Americans to the sudden loss of rights; indeed, it brings into focus the susceptibility of all of us to the same catastrophe.

As we have seen, Civil War reenactments reinforce racist mythologies, glorifying the archetype of the white warrior-soldier. By emphasizing personal experience over critical engagement with history, the role of African Americans and the issues of slavery and race violence are obscured. Yet counter-memory reenactments that value the political over the personal, such as the Moore's Ford lynching reenactment, lift the veil on a troubled past to reveal what many prefer not to see. They disturb a complacent present to make visible long-buried injustice and, through that shared experience of seeing, pave the way for social struggle. Perhaps what is most made visible by the ritualized violence and traumatized response to the lynching reenactments is the fact that the Civil War in America is not yet finished.

PART II

THE **BODY** OF **WAR**

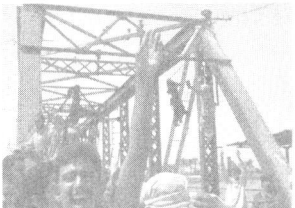

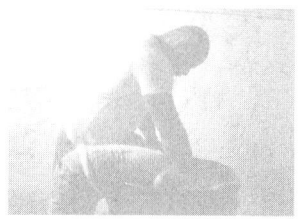  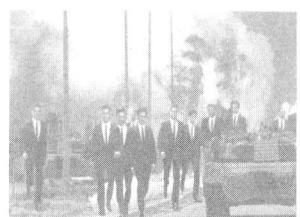

3

ABU GHRAIB, GENDER, AND THE MILITARY

The Abu Ghraib photographs join a genealogy of iconic war images despite the ever greater state efforts to control and contain images of war, an effort that fails in inverse proportion to the growth and availability of digital technology. After U.S. government censorship of photographs from World War II and Korea, photos such as the Saigon girl burned by napalm and the Communist guerrilla executed at point blank range in Vietnam as well as nightly videos of returning American dead in body bags had a shocking effect on the American public.[1] Similarly, the Abu Ghraib photos stand in stark contrast to the officially approved representations of the American presence in Iraq, the staged triumphal photographs or the abstracted images from the 1991 Gulf War. These sanitized representations are consistent with the government's refusal to report on Iraqi civilian casualties or its ban on photos of flag-draped coffins returning to the United States with the American dead. The Obama administration finally lifted the ban on coffins, in place since the Gulf War, in February 2009, after photos of flag-draped coffins had already been widely leaked in the media.

A lot has been written about the Abu Ghraib photographs, which are widely viewed as most emblematic of the American war in Iraq, the images that will be remembered when others have been forgotten. Many would argue that *the* iconic photo, first published in the *New Yorker*, is the Hooded Man, the figure who was told by Sabrina Harmon that he would be electrocuted if he fell off the box. According to the testimony of the victim, Abdou Hussain Saad Faleh, the wires were attached not only to his fingers but also his toes and penis.[2] The seeming familiarity and deep strangeness of the Hooded Man is part of its visual affect, which seems to ennoble the figure while withholding the face of suffering. Philip Gourevitch suggests that the very ambiguity of the photo symbolizes both what we know and what we cannot know about Abu Ghraib, the "carnival weirdness" of which "creates an original image of inhumanity that admits no immediately self-evident reading. Its fascination resides, in large part, in its mystery and inscrutability—in all that is concealed by all that is revealed."[3] W.J.T. Mitchell, in a sustained meditation on the Hooded Man, develops the idea that the photograph's familiarity has been premediated by Christological imagery, such as Christ as *imago mundi*, or microcosm of the world, and in images of the mockery of Christ. Mitchell goes further and argues that the Hooded Man updates and condenses all of Western religious imagery, including the iconography of Moses, with outstretched arms on the mountain, the passion of Jesus, and the veiled Mohammed; at the same time, the photograph twins or doubles the Hooded Man as "terror suspect and torture victim, criminal and martyr." In its direct address to the viewer, the image assumes the "theme of state" motif identified by art historian Meyer Schapiro, and becomes, finally, both the sovereign and its antithesis, the embodiment of the state and its abject enemy.[4]

We also may read the open-armed gesture, the same gesture a priest makes in the celebration of the Mass, as transforming the Hooded Man into the mock pope of Abu Ghraib, above all if we remember that the real pope covers for massive sins of the Church, including the pervasive and protected sexual abuse of minors. Elsewhere I have argued that the Abu Ghraib photos document events that were explicitly staged, in part, like spectacle lynchings, for the camera, and occurred, like lynchings, because both sets of perpetrators believed that their acts were sanctioned by a larger community and served the interests of that community; both sets of photographs reproduced visual protocols of domination and submission and instantiated political hegemony until they were released into the global public sphere and turned against themselves.[5] But recognizing the various forms of premediation in lynching and Christological imagery, or other images of conquest and submission from the history of art, while helping to explain the haunting quality of the images, does not explain everything.[6]

Religious readings tend to trump all others, but the emphasis on the religious and the sovereign, even as it ennobles the figure of the Hooded Man, also serves to abstract and distance us from the figure and the more immediate political implications of his plight. If we consider Walter Benjamin's observation that "the past flashes up at the instant when it can be recognized . . . by the present as one of its own concerns," we may recognize another possibility for understanding the Hooded Man's power as an image.[7] Perhaps what connects it so strongly to the present is that the Hooded Man embodies the *sui generis* condition of the "unlawful combatant," the state of exception invented by the U.S. government as a way of circumventing the Geneva Conventions and placing prisoners of war outside the law. As an outlaw, he evokes the rightless and stateless everywhere. He is *homo sacer*, the figure of bare life or sacred life, faceless and defenseless, bereft of citizenship and political community, to whom anything can be done. By seeming to appeal directly to the viewer, the figure implores us to recognize his suffering plight, and the ease with which a person defined as a terrorist by the liberal state becomes a person without rights. He incarnates the victims of state violence and repression in prisons, detention camps and black sites across the globe. Perhaps, then, it is the accursedness and abandonment, the condition of being set apart and counted out as "human," that makes this image so terrifying, the realization that there is neither spiritual nor earthly redemption available to him. If the Hooded Man as an image prefigured by the past is so troubling because he illuminates the most disturbing concerns of the present, that concern is the condition of the human being who can be deprived of all rights and killed with impunity, a condition which has become emblematic of modernity, while the creeping awareness grows that he could be any of us, that we are all susceptible to entering the state of exception where we may be stripped of rights.

The Hooded Man represents not only an image defeat for the Bush administration and its military aggression but also for the American archetype of the heroic warrior male, which has been resurrected, for example, in National Guard recruiting films that seek to revitalize the mythology of the warrior hero (see chapter 2). There is still more to learn from the Abu Ghraib photographs and the continuing investigations into questions raised by them. I would like to further examine the use and abuse of female sexuality in the military, the pornographic logic of torture and the suppressed image of rape, and the public display of atrocity photographs.

The Sex Line and the Class Line

Let us first recall the circumstances under which the photographs came to be made. Under the banner of "democracy," the American military arrested and imprisoned thousands of Arabs and Muslims, exempting them from the international laws of the Geneva Convention that govern the treatment of prisoners of war and torturing them in violation of those conventions. At the same time, the U.S. government claimed that it "does not torture" by calling it something else, by developing techniques, such as stress positions and waterboarding, that do not leave physical scars, and by outsourcing it. Torture has been covertly reconceived as not just physical, but moral and psychological, an alteration of the mind created through total isolation and sensory deprivation, which is even more destructive in that it is designed to engineer the collapse of personality.[8] New orders of bare life, such as "illegal aliens," "enemy combatants," "unlawful combatants," "detainees," and especially "ghost detainees" become lives that do not count as citizens, that can be incarcerated, punished, and eliminated without due process or trial. "Ghost" detainees in Iraq were hidden from Red Cross inspectors and officially consigned to a liminal space outside the law. A subject outside the law and depersonalized, as Judith Butler observes, "is neither alive nor dead, neither fully constituted as a subject nor fully deconstituted in death."[9] The most notorious case was that of Manadel al-Jamadi, the Iraqi prisoner beaten to death at Abu Ghraib whose name became known only because of the photos of his corpse packed in ice and accompanied by Sabrina Harmon and Charles Graner, each grinning and offering a "thumbs-up" gesture.[10]

At least some of the photos were meant as a form of blackmail against the prisoners, threatening to shame them in front of their families and community if they did not become informants for the United States. Yet it seems that most of the photos were trophy photos for the soldiers themselves. Once military officials became aware of them, they set out to contain and control them; it was the photographs, not the acts they represented, that were regarded as criminal as well as stupid. Donald Rumsfeld was furious that the photos had gotten out and immediately, if uselessly, banned the taking of photos and videos.[11] A memo on standards of conduct sent in January 2004 to all military personnel at the prison included this unusual item specifically targeted to Abu Ghraib, buried among the generic boilerplate about possession of alcohol and controlled substances: "Pursuant to Geneva Convention directives, personnel will neither create nor possess photographs, videotapes, digital videos, CD/DVDs, computer files/folders, movies or any other medium containing images of any criminal or security detainee currently or formerly interned at Baghdad central Correctional Facility, located at FOB Abu Ghraib, Iraq."[12]

It is not the illegal practices of torture and abuse that is being banned here, but only their visual documentation, because the military well understood the power of documentary. The memo further invited anyone in possession of such images to get rid of them "without penalty or legal consequence" during a forty-eight-hour amnesty period after which soldiers could be prosecuted. This was a blatant appeal, combined with a threat, to destroy evidence of prisoner torture and abuse. The photographs themselves were part of the abuse, but they were never meant to be seen by public audiences. It was only the *threat* of visibility that was the *official* impetus for the Abu Ghraib photos. The pattern of suppression of the photos that began with the Bush administration continues with the Obama administration, to the surprise of many liberals.

The twenty or so photos that went viral in 2004 were a deliberate selection by the news media that left out images of rape and naked Iraqi women.[13] What is the political effect of suppressing images of rape? At the same time, we might wonder why the photographs that became most well known contain so many images of American female soldiers. What is it about the pictured women soldiers that contributed to the notoriety of the images? How does the presence and behavior of the women soldiers color our understanding of the torture and abuse at Abu Ghraib? There are at least two key issues here: (1) the role of women in the American military and their relationship to power, and (2) the attempt by the U.S.

government to instrumentalize the publicized images to defend itself while suppressing and distorting the real nature and extent of the abuse.

Women (like gays and minorities) are in the contradictory position of being both discriminated against and complicit with the institution of the military. Although women have been subject to egregious discrimination because of their sex, they are still part of the military and must be held accountable for the abuse of Arab and Muslim prisoners. The gender discrimination against women in the military has allowed them to be scapegoated in significant ways, but this scapegoating should not divert our attention from understanding that they have chosen to join an institution whose primary function is to serve as the armed fist of the state. On the other hand, neither should the repressive role of the military that women have chosen to join serve as an excuse for the deliberate abuse of military women as women. The performance work of Coco Fusco provides a useful lens onto the issue of women in the military.

Fusco is part of the generation of antiwar protesters that came of age during the Vietnam War era who have been dismayed by the easy mobilization of war support through jingoist rhetoric following the events of 9/11. She writes: "The explosion of patriotic fervor after 9/11—the televised concerts from Washington DC just after the attack that were such obvious, crypto-fascistic rallying cries for war; the knee-jerk embrace of racial profiling of Arabs just after the practice had been publicly acknowledged as wrong and harmful to other minorities, the lumpen entrepreneurs on street corners making a fast buck peddling American flags; the obsequious stickers that soon appeared on cabs and gas station windows that said 'Proud to be Muslim and American'—all made me feel as though I had woken up inside a nightmarish cross between the Cold War and the Crusades."[14]

The militarization of campus life after recruiters were driven off campuses in the 1970s, the conservative watchdog groups on campuses that harass left-leaning professors, and other restrictions on civil liberties that especially target dissenters and minority groups via the Patriot Act have been largely embraced by younger generations who have been kept at a comfortable distance from the realities of war on the one hand while bombarded with patriotic rhetoric and efforts to chill dissent on the other. In addition, as Fusco observes, the gains of feminism have led to more women in the military than ever before and more women in positions of power who support the war, including two-thirds of the women in Congress who voted to invade Iraq and former secretary of state Condoleezza Rice, not to mention high-ranking military women such as Barbara Fast, in charge of intelligence in Iraq, and Janis Karpinski, in charge of Abu Ghraib prison.

This underscores the Marxist understanding that while women are indeed oppressed on the basis of their sex, the fundamental political dividing line is ultimately not between the sexes but between the classes. Working-class women are doubly oppressed, as workers and women, and black or Arabic or Latina working-class women are triply oppressed. Women who are part of the ruling class, however, or who serve in institutions that protect the interests of the ruling class, identify first and foremost with those political class interests, not with the interests of women as a whole. This is not new—women have always been split in their support for war, including the early women's organizations that formed during World War I and fought for the vote while simultaneously supporting their own bourgeoisie's nationalist war aims. Fusco paints this as the dark side of feminism but, without a class analysis, we are left without an adequate explanation for it.

Fusco makes the important point that the Abu Ghraib images selected for publication were not accidentally chosen. She suggests that the most notorious photos, in which women "direct their looks" to the camera, were chosen because they looked far less threatening and intimidating than military men and seemed to minimize the implications of torture and abuse as the work of weaker and softer, if not ineffectual, females. It allowed the government to claim that these fairly harmless looking white women were young and naïve and victims of their circumstances—as indeed, some of them were. It took the focus off the far more disturbing pictures of male soldiers urinating on, raping, and sodomizing boys and female prisoners or forcing prisoners, such as a father and son, to commit sexual acts with each other. It also took the focus off the fact that such abuse was widespread throughout the prisons under American control and was part of military thinking at the top. Lynndie England, Sabrina Harmon, and the other low-level soldiers at Abu Ghraib were court-martialed as "bad apples" and that was the end of accountability. Fusco writes, "Gender was the key to the interpretation of the events depicted and to diverting public attention away from the pervasiveness of prisoner abuse by engendering public sympathy for the handful of underlings who bore the brunt of the punishment."[15]

Revelations followed about female interrogators at Guantánamo who used sexuality as part of their interrogation techniques, including such practices as giving detainees hand jobs, lap dances, and reaching their hands into their own pants and smearing fake menstrual blood on the faces of detainees. This demonstrates that torture by female interrogators was a deliberate military tactic that specifically relied on female sexuality to exploit cultural taboos and shows that women in the military willingly embraced these tactics. It also highlights the fact that there are no photos of what actually goes on in military interrogation rooms. Although such images may exist, they are not available to the public or have been "classified, destroyed, lost or censored in the interests of national security," as Fusco notes. Thus sexual harassment by female interrogators is a category that is difficult to fully imagine by a public that tends to see women as victims rather than victimizers. Fusco argues that the public is encouraged to see sexual violence as something lesser than torture since it is being performed by the "weaker sex."[16]

Before we explore the issue of sexual violence and the image of rape further, let us examine a key photo of the Abu Ghraib scandal and the issues it raises about the genuine subordination and harassment of women in the American military, even though we do not defend the military itself. This is the photo of twenty-one-year-old Lynndie England holding a leash attached to the neck of a naked crawling prisoner, known to guards as "Gus," which was first published in the *Washington Post* on 21 May 2004. England was a reservist and administrative clerk who frequented Abu Ghraib prison in order to be with her boyfriend, Charles Graner, her superior in rank and fourteen years her senior. Her presence at Abu Ghraib serves as an example of the systemic problems in the military, which include understaffing, ambiguous command, and insufficient training. Despite attempts by the media to assign complete agency for the abuses to England, she denied such agency and claimed she was told to pose for the infamous photo by Graner. Graner was the local leader of the abuse, choreographed the events, and insisted on the photographs. In interviews conducted with soldiers at Abu Ghraib by Errol Morris, Graner emerges as a manipulative and depraved figure. On *Dateline* England explained: "And he wanted me in the picture, and I was like, 'no way.' And . . . Graner kept being persistent, 'Oh, come on, just take the picture, take the picture.'"[17] In her interviews with Morris, England described the circumstances slightly differently. Graner told England and Megan Ambuhl to follow him while he went to extract an uncooperative prisoner from a cell. Graner brought a tie-down strap and his camera. England explained:

> We went downstairs. When he opened the door Gus was in there. He was naked. He wouldn't come out of the cell. He was laying down on the floor. He didn't want to stand up. So that's why he brought the tie-down strap. Graner went in there and he put the strap around his neck. He was going to make him crawl out. Then Gus was crawling out of the cell. When he was about halfway out of the doorway, Graner turned around and handed me the strap and said, "Hold this." So I did. I just grabbed it, and he went over and he took a picture. . . . I'm just kind of

holding the tie-down strap. You can see the slack on it. I know people said that I dragged him, but I never did. After Graner was done taking the pictures, he put the camera back in his cargo pocket, walked over, took the strap from me, and I guess Gus wanted to cooperate then, so he took it off of his neck, and he dragged him up, and he took him to his cell. That was the end of that event.[18]

Though accounts such as England's are likely to be self-serving, it is clear in this account that the incident was staged for a photograph. Graner went to the cell with a tie-down strap with the apparent intention of using it, and his sole reason for extracting the prisoner from his cell with the strap around his neck was to photograph England holding the other end. Immediately after taking these photographs (there were three), Graner returned the prisoner to his cell. While we may speculate on Graner's desire to implicate England and exert some power over her, there is no denying that this photograph, more than any other, led to England's court martial.

We can indeed see the slack on the line, and there is no denying that Graner had a dark and violent side, which also was made apparent by his ex-wife, who said Graner had "threatened to kill her." She was sufficiently frightened to obtain "three protection orders against him since 1997."[19] Graner told his fellow soldier, Joseph Darby, who ultimately slipped a disc of the photos to authorities, that when he discovered his wife was unfaithful, "he had sat across the street from his wife's house with a rifle, waiting on her to come out."[20] England's discomfiture is palpable as she looks away from the camera toward the human being at the end of the leash she holds. We can easily believe that England is trapped in a descending spiral of victimization produced by the pressure to conform to the demands exerted by her domineering boyfriend and to be "one of the guys" in a male-dominated military culture. By handing her the strap and impelling her to appear complicit in an appalling act of humiliation and then visually documenting her complicity, Graner paved the way for England's future acquiescence and collusion in further acts of humiliation and abuse. As Gourevitch writes, "As far as she was concerned, it wasn't a snapshot of her relationship to Gus, because she had none; it was a snapshot of her relationship with Graner. 'It's showing that he has power over me, and he wanted to demonstrate that power,' she said. 'Anything he asked, he knew that I would do it.'"[21]

Communications scholars John Howard and Laura Prividera also argue that it was easy for the media to seize on England as the emblem of the abuse because she was a petite female incongruent with the archetype of the warrior hero. The media defined her as a morally, professionally, and sexually "fallen" white woman, who became pregnant by Graner and had a baby out of wedlock (for which she was blamed while he was not). The fallen woman archetypal rendering shifted responsibility from the military onto England while preserving the military's patriarchal ethos and subordination of women.[22]

England became the scapegoat for officials who not only used her status as a female but also blamed what happened at Abu Ghraib on "recycled hillbillies." Gender theorist Carol Mason terms this the "hillbilly defense," which she defines as "an effort to deflect criticism of lethal American force and to deny that American extremism is systemic by directing public attention to hillbillies, those mountain folks who are beyond the control of authorities because they are presumably beyond the reach of modernity's civilizing influence."[23] As the "violent" and "sexually wild" hillbilly woman, England represented the flip side of the rural white woman who was "pure" and "noble in poverty," a role filled by Jessica Lynch, who was pretty and blond. Lynch was an army supply clerk injured near Nasiriyah in the early days of the war when her convoy strayed off course and was ambushed. Iraqi doctors saved her life and tried to return her to the Americans, who fired on the ambulance. Instead, American forces staged a videotaped "rescue" and attempted to turn her into a heroine, describing her as a "female Rambo" who fired at the enemy until she ran out of ammunition, then used her knife to fend off Iraqi fighters. At the same time, the media suggested that this female Rambo was still a helpless female by reporting that she had been sexually violated in the Iraqi hospital, simultaneously raising the specter of a blond white women preyed upon by dark men. When Lynch herself rejected these fabrications, pointing out that she had never even fired her gun and had been treated kindly in the Iraqi hospital, her story was transformed into a rescue story of an injured damsel in distress. Both Jessica Lynch and Lynndie England were forced into the virgin/whore dichotomy of American white womanhood.[24] The construction of England as the center of the abuse at Abu Ghraib was key to the official "bad apples" defense and ignored Graner as the commanding photographer and director of the scenario, which would not have existed if he had not set it up for the camera. For the Arab world, the picture of a naked Arab man held on a leash by an American military woman was outrageously humiliating and emblematic of anti-Arab contempt harbored by Americans.[25]

It has become clear that in many ways both Lynndie England and Sabrina Harmon were also victims of Abu Ghraib. In interviews conducted by Errol Morris, Harmon suggests that the photographs were not quite what they appeared to be, that her smiles and thumbs up were a rote response, a way of fitting into the abusive culture in the prison while attempting to document it. Evidence in the form of letters home to her girlfriend Kelly demonstrate that Harmon was disturbed by the events at Abu Ghraib, in which she took no part, and that she took photographs as documentary evidence: "I took more pictures now to record what's going on. Not many people know this shit goes on. The only reason I want to be here now is to get the pictures to prove the U.S. is not what they think."[26] In another letter, after being advised by a fellow soldier in her unit to delete any photographs she had taken at the prison, Harmon wrote: "We might be under investigation. I'm not sure, there's talk about it. Yes they do beat the prisoners up and ive written this to you before. I just don't think its right and never have that's why I take the pictures to prove the story I tell people. No one would ever believe the shit that goes on. No one. The dead guy didn't bother me, I even took a picture with him doing the thumbs up . . . they said the autopsy came back 'heart attack.' It's a lie. The whole military is nothing but lies. They cover up too much . . . if I want to keep taking pictures of these events—I even have short films—I have to fake a smile every time."[27]

In addition to the inexperience and subordination by gender, Harmon's lesbianism was another deviation from the warrior ideal that made it easier to marginalize her. Similarly, racial difference is a deviation from the warrior ideal, signifying another level of oppression for the working-class black female soldier. Thus it is not surprising that the story of Shoshana Johnson was largely excluded from the media fanfare. Johnson was ambushed and wounded along with Jessica Lynch and held captive for twenty-two days until she was rescued along with several of her comrades by U.S. Marines. She was the first African American prisoner of war in U.S. history. Not only was she denied the celebrity status of Lynch but she was also given a much lower disability benefit for her injuries, which she fought until it was raised.[28]

In September 2005, Lynndie England and ten other soldiers were court-martialed and convicted in the Abu Ghraib scandal. Charles Graner received a ten-year sentence. Other U.S. military personnel were investigated and reprimanded for their role in the scandal; however, no senior officers in the U.S. military were ever put on trial nor did they receive widespread media attention. But Graner, as the one who orchestrated the photos and insisted England appear in them, was displaced from the center of the media narrative, which instead focused on the sex, morals, and poor working-class origins of England, who was infantilized as the "poster girl" or "poster child" for the scandal, shifting responsibility away from the culpability of the military, reifying the masculine ideal of the soldier, and letting the Bush administration off the hook. The photographs and their galvanizing effects nonetheless demonstrate that for atrocities and their implications to be made visible, public acknowledgment and continuing discourse is critical.

The Suppressed Image of Rape

Although we know there are images of rape, no such image has publicly appeared, or else has been quickly denounced as fake. The issue of gender and sexuality has been addressed to some extent in protest art, but the issue of rape and sexual torture has not been adequately addressed even though evidence of soldiers engaging in various sex acts with prisoners and among themselves was reported following the three-hour, closed-door session on 12 May 2004, during which members of Congress were shown over eighteen hundred photographs and videos. Images included forced sodomy, Lynndie England having sex with other U.S. soldiers in front of prisoners, prisoners cowering in front of attack dogs, Iraqi women being forced to expose their breasts, naked prisoners tied up together, prisoners forced to masturbate, and a prisoner repeatedly smashing his head against a wall.[29] One thing that is unambiguously revealed by the photos is the privileged look of the American soldiers and military police over their Arab and Muslim victims, who were often shrouded, not only dehumanizing them but also preventing them from discomfiting their torturers who did not want to be looked at and know themselves to be seen. The compact discs, videos, and computer files of digital images codified the right of the soldiers to "look" at the nude and brutalized bodies of their victims, even to pose with their nude bodies and corpses, while effacing the look of the prisoners through hooding and other forms of degradation.

As testimony from Abu Ghraib prisoners demonstrates, the photographs were meant to add to the sexual violence, humiliation, and shaming of the prisoners, as well as provide souvenirs and evidence of the soldiers' time at the prison.[30] That the photographs and videos of sexualized violence were interspersed with images of American soldiers having sex with each other testifies to their powerful erotic effect on the soldiers that no doubt stemmed from the political act of coercive power and domination. These tactics were prescribed by neoconservatives in Washington who used cultural anthropologist Raphael Patai's racist 1973 book, *The Arab Mind*, to justify the sexual violence as a way to "break" Arab and Muslim prisoners thought to be particularly vulnerable to this form of shaming and humiliation. As gender studies scholar Jasbir Puar observes, sexual torture is not an exceptional practice in any case: "The sexual is already part and parcel of the histories of colonial domination and empire building; conquest is innately corporeal."[31] The pleasure in the sexual degradation of others relies on a process of colonial dehumanization that depends in large part on constructing Arabs and Muslims as an undifferentiated mass of "terrorists," making them far easier to humiliate, torture, sexually exploit, and kill. Likewise, the derisive term "hajis" creates emotional distance and dehumanizes the other, just as the Vietnamese were called "gooks."

Photographs showing the rape of women, which first appeared in the *Boston Globe*, were later withdrawn from public view on the grounds that an authoritative source had examined the pictures and found them to be faked. This authoritative source traced their origin to the pornographic Internet site iraqbabes.com, which in turn took them from the Hungarian "Sex in War" site. This effectively ended discussion of the photos and the website was closed down by the American government. Ariella Azoulay questions the self-interested judgment of fakery and its easy acceptance by the public; she also questions the larger distinction, articulated by Donald Rumsfeld, between "torture" and "abuse." This distinction relegated rape and sexual violence to the status of a lesser crime, making sexual abuse and violence less serious than torture. Susan Sontag, in her essay on the Abu Ghraib photographs in the *New York Times Magazine*, did not mention the photos of rape but argued, against Rumsfeld, that the photos and the actions they depicted represented torture and not abuse. Azoulay suggests that Sontag and Rumsfeld, despite their differences, shared an implicit assumption that torture is more serious than sexual abuse and therefore evidence of sexual injury does not generate any "real urgency" or necessarily turn into "an emergency claim." Images of the rape of women then disappeared and only the sexual humiliation of men was left visible.[32]

Both Leonard Downie Jr., executive editor of the *Washington Post*, and Seymour Hersh, who broke the Abu Ghraib story in the *New Yorker*, justified decisions not to publish photographs of the rape of boys and women prisoners in their respective publications in the interests of "good taste." As Sontag remarks, pleading "good taste" is "always a repressive standard when invoked by institutions."[33] When the issue did not become public in other ways, however, as Hersh expected it would, he gave general descriptions of rape videos in public interviews, including a father and son forced to perform sex acts with each other.[34] The Obama administration in May 2009, despite a court order to release two thousand Abu Ghraib photographs, maintained the Bush policy of secrecy and suppression, despite Obama's claim that "they are not particularly sensational" and his earlier campaign promise to allow them to be published, a decision that civil liberties and human rights advocates deplored.[35] Obama's reasoning that the images would inflame anti-American feeling in Iraq and Afghanistan and further imperil U.S. troops belies the suggestions that the images are not "particularly sensational" and continues the policy of nonaccountability that permits the continued use of torture. The photos, whose existence was confirmed by Antonio Taguba in *The Taguba Report*, reportedly show an American soldier raping a female prisoner, a male translator raping a male detainee, and other sexual assaults on prisoners with truncheons, wire, and a phosphorescent tube.[36] Taguba published testimony from some of these victims in his 2004 report, who confirmed that photos were taken while they were sexually assaulted.

What is really at stake in this debate is the potential of the images not only to heighten and inflame opposition to the war among Iraqis and Afghanis, who need no further incitements, but *at home*. Obama, no less than Donald Rumsfeld, understands the power of images to construct national identity itself, as when Rumsfeld claimed that publishing the photos of torture and rape would allow them "to define us as Americans," that is, as a nation capable of committing sexual atrocities and rape. As Judith Butler notes, the government seeks to regulate those images "that might galvanize political opposition to a war" and this is central to their attempt to control what is representable and what may not be pictured. From the sexual abuse that occurs in interrogation rooms to the sexual abuse in prisons, "we cannot understand the field of representability simply by examining its explicit contents, since it is constituted fundamentally by what is left out, maintained outside the frame within which representations appear." The frame, as an exercise of state power, actively rules out and excludes "without any visible sign of its operation." It leaves the public to assume only one view of reality.[37]

Azoulay argues that the condition of the missing images of rape in visual culture more broadly occurs because "above images of rape looms a taboo that prevents turning the horror of rape into a common reference, which is a condition for mustering agreement on the need to prevent and stop it. This state of affairs attests to the fact that casualties of rape are not really full citizens—the imprint of their being excepted to the rule continues to shape the way in which sexual injury to them is treated and managed."[38] Thus it is no surprise that the rapes of Iraqi prisoners have not been prosecuted; indeed, even the rapes of American women in the military by their male comrades have not been prosecuted, underscoring Azoulay's assertion that the "casualties of rape are not really full citizens." In 2008, the Pentagon released a report saying that one out of three women in the military reported experiencing sexual assault, and they were at far greater risk for sexual assault in combat zones such as Iraq and Afghanistan. The Pentagon received 2,923 reports of sexual assault across the military in the twelve months ending 30 September 2008, a 9 percent increase over the previous year but only a fraction of the real number. The Pentagon estimates that only 10 to 20 percent of rapes are reported. Women are discouraged from reporting for a variety of reasons, including the fact that the military is still regarded as a masculine domain, is steeped in antiwoman bias, and most cases never go to military courts for prosecution.[39] One out of three women raped in the military is twice the number of rapes in the general population, which is one out of six, and even this rate is considered to be epidemic proportions. The absence of rape images in a culture that depends so heavily on images is therefore a political imperative, one that prevents the scandalous prevalence of rape "from being recognized as a state of emergency," in Azoulay's words, "a mass disaster on a worldwide scale that urgently needs to be dealt with."[40] It prevents the casualties of rape from being considered as and treated as full citizens. In the contest of images, the suppression of the image of rape allows the actual rising incidence of rape to continue unabated.

We must ask, with Azoulay, why were the photos of Iraqi women being raped so easily accepted as fakes that were produced for the legitimate sake of pornography? Redefined as pornography, such photos are clearly meant not to be taken seriously, while the photos of sexual assaults on Iraqi men were defined as mimicking pornography but not real pornography. Instead, they were understood as scenarios of torture and humiliation brought about by an abuse of power; the "pleasure" of these photos is not erotic but grounded in the exultant mastery of those who wield power over their victims, who represent a different cultural and political order. Such mastery is constituted by its ability to control the bodies of those it subordinates and to inflict sexual violence. This is most effective, in a political sense, by "feminizing" and sexually shaming the male members of the subordinated culture. The rape of its women is another matter, a taboo that evokes a level of barbarity ascribed to the Arab culture the Americans were sent to "liberate" and "civilize."

Azoulay asserts that the resemblance of the Abu Ghraib photos to pornography produced a kind of "porn industry in miniature" that fed a more sophisticated online porn industry which distributed rape images described as "real Iraqi women" raped by "real American soldiers" on the home page of the Iraq Babes website. Whether real or fake, the photos showed Iraqi women whose heads or bodies were forcibly held in place by U.S. soldiers as other soldiers penetrated their mouths or vaginas while the women cried or grimaced. The website was not shut down until Iraqi websites used the photos to substantiate the reports of rapes by Iraqi women.[41] Azoulay rightly observes that suppressing the image of rape leaves it to the realm of "ahistorical and apolitical fantasy" which avoids building widespread civic action against it. She concludes, "Breaking the taboo on showing images of rape will challenge the clear demarcation between images that are allowed to be shown and those that are not—the line of demarcation that distinguishes rape from the other horrors that afflict humanity and preserves women as the exceptions to the rule—and it will also challenge the division between the arenas in which they are allowed or forbidden to be shown, which leaves the visual treatment of rape, with the dramatic decisions that involves, to porn sites."[42]

The image of rape, long practiced but suppressed in the imagery of war, thus has been presented only on fugitive pornographic Internet sites where its status as a pornographic image is elevated while its indexical relationship to reality is denied, rendering moot the need to hold anyone accountable for a crime. The truth revealed in the controversial rape photos has little to do with their particular contents, however, but with the larger cultural attitudes and collective imagination that contribute to and are formed by these particular images. Indeed, incidents of the rape of Iraqi girls by American soldiers among the civilian population have episodically made their way into the news. In one example, two U.S. soldiers were convicted in September 2009 of gang-raping a fourteen-year-old Iraqi girl, Abeer Hamza, in 2006, then murdering her along with her six-year-old sister and her parents, and setting fire to Abeer's body, to destroy evidence, in a village near Al-Mahmudiyah, south of Baghdad. As of September 2009, three other soldiers had pled guilty and were awaiting trial. In another case, a woman named "Noor," who was raped and impregnated by a U.S. guard in Abu Ghraib, smuggled a letter out of the prison.[43] The shame and ostracism attached to having been raped is so egregious that most Iraqi women who have been released have difficulty discussing their experiences, but Iraqi women lawyers have begun to uncover the extent of rape and sexual violence against women across Iraq, many of whom are the wives or daughters of male suspects, arrested as a way of pressuring the men.[44] According to journalist Ernesto Cienfuegos, photographs were sent to his newspaper *La Voz de Aztlan* from confidential sources depicting the rapes of two Iraqi women by U.S. military personnel and private U.S. mercenaries in military fatigues in 2004. Cienfuegos wrote, "It is now known that hundreds of these photographs had been in circulation among the troops in Iraq. The graphic photos were being swapped between the soldiers like baseball cards."[45] This miniature porn industry, like the larger porn industry, creates a self-perpetuating loop between the perpetration of sexual violence against prisoners and its recycling as pornographic entertainment in photographs and videos. But violent porn, as the English scholars Carmine Sarracino and Kevin Scott note, was not the *cause* of the abuse, it was the *language* of the abuse, a political language with a long history of military usage.[46]

Sarracino and Scott argue that the language of violent pornography is the language of control, which turns the military figures, both male and female, into the dominant "male," and the prisoners, both male and female, into the submissive "female." They act out the assertion of will and domination of one nation over another. Military conquest has long produced the rape of the defeated nation's women by the soldiers of the conquering nation as a way of othering, subordinating, and psychologically distancing the vanquished from the more powerful nation while reinforcing the absolute authority and power of the conquerors. This is also what happens in violent porn narratives that establish male dominance and depend as much on pain and humiliation as on actual sex. Not only did the soldiers at Abu Ghraib integrate violent porn into their lives and jobs, but the violent porn of Abu Ghraib then became reflected in online websites, especially in violent porn subgenres of prison porn and military porn. What must be understood about violent porn, as distinct from other types of porn, is that it increasingly produces actual, not simulated, violence and humiliation, from real, not faked, kicking and smacking, to heads pushed down during fellatio scenes that induce gagging and vomiting, to women who are forced to drink bile, vomit, and the results of their own colonics. Feces are also increasingly present in humiliation porn, and were clearly present at Abu Ghraib, too, and documented in the photograph known as "shit boy," showing a man who was made to stand for hours smeared in feces as another means of rendering the other "repulsive." The sadistic pleasure derived from viewing such photographs is psychological, not sensual. "Violent porn," write Sarracino and Scott, "implicitly accepts power as the male trait. Further, it views male power in only one way: dominating others through sexual violence. This is precisely the dynamic on display at Abu Ghraib."[47] While violent porn is the language of abuse at Abu Ghraib, it is important to note that other kinds of porn are not at issue here because they do not depend on the visual pleasure of witnessing torture and suffering. As Butler asserts, there are many kinds of nonviolent and "vanilla" porn, "whose worst crime seems to be the failure to supply an innovative plot."[48]

The suppression of the images of rape also suppresses their grievances and emergency claims, which I define here in Azoulay's terms: "An emergency claim testifies to three facts: that a disaster exists; that it is an exception to the rule, one that necessitates immediate action in order to terminate it; and that there is someone who wants to assume the position that allows immediate action to be taken in order to terminate it."[49] Despite at least six Pentagon investigations into Abu Ghraib, no high-level U.S. official has been held accountable, leaving the ethics of this cruel and useless war still to be fully confronted.

Unsurprisingly, there were allegations of rape in recent conflicts such as the war in Libya, where psychologist Seham Sergewa in Benghazi identified at least 259 rape victims. The International Criminal Court said that evidence has emerged that Muammar el-Qaddafi had authorized his soldiers to rape Libyan women, although many of Sergewa's colleagues have criticized her for talking to the media or evinced skepticism about her report even as rebel officials said they discovered condoms and packets of Viagra in tanks and other vehicles captured from Qaddafi's soldiers and videos of rapes on the cell phones of killed or captured Qaddafi loyalists. Such videos have been quickly deleted, in part to protect the women, but one video of a woman assaulted by two men using a broom was broadcast by CNN, which also aired an interview with Iman al-Obeidi, a postgraduate law student who publicly accused Libyan forces of torturing and gang-raping her. This was a courageous act in a deeply conservative society where discussing sex crimes is taboo and women risk being shunned.[50]

Women's Capacity for Violence

In a series of performance works about the American "war on terror," Coco Fusco is concerned with the role of women as perpetrators. She critiques the expanding role of women in the military and examines female complicity with military power in her works *Bare Life Study #1* (2005), *A Room of One's Own: Women and Power in the New America* (2005), and *Operation Atropos* (2006). Fusco assumed the role of a military policewoman in *Bare Life Study #1*, and commanded fifty of her drama students, dressed in the orange jumpsuits of detainees, to clean the ground of a public space in São Paolo with toothbrushes, a frequent punishment in U.S. military prisons.[51] *A Room of One's Own* was a performance-lecture in which Fusco played a female interrogator justifying the use of military terror to a liberal audience using PowerPoint slides and video.[52] *Operation Atropos* is a fifty-nine-minute video that follows Fusco and six women who enrolled in a four-day interrogation training workshop led by Team Delta, a group of retired U.S. military interrogators, in Wilkes Barre, Pennsylvania. All three works grew out of the interrogation training course experience.[53]

Shocked by the systematic and highly sexualized deployment of women in Bush's global "war on terror," Fusco set out to better understand "the kind of person who sees her own internalization of the military's worldview and her success within its structure as feminist gains."[54] Fusco realized that female military interrogators assume fictional personas as part of their work and that this was quite analogous to performative practice. To get interrogation training in order to pursue this idea, she found a source of instruction through an Internet search, the Prisoner of War Interrogation Resistance Program run by Team Delta, a private concern organized by former members of the U.S. Intelligence Agency. The course was initially used to train elite soldiers to resist interrogation when captured, known as SERE (Survival, Evasion, Resistance, Escape), but was reconceived for private groups such as police officers, private security guards, and psychological researchers. During the four-day immersion program, participants play both captor and captive. Since the course is given only to groups, Fusco solicited volunteers and took a group of six young women with her to the course in Wilkes Barre during the summer of 2005, arranging to have the course videotaped by the artist Kambui Olujimi. Fusco's goal, ultimately, was to understand how feminine participation and visibility contributed to the acceptance and normalization of torture within American culture.

In *A Field Guide for Female Interrogators*, Fusco describes the forms of female sexual harassment that have been reported from several prisons, including sexual insults, baring their breasts, and threats of rape, as well smearing fake menstrual blood on detainees; sometimes teams of two or three women sexually harass the same prisoner, all under the unverified assumption that such procedures produce meaningful confessions or intelligence and not just humiliation and trauma. While making submission to sadistic female power a monstrous experience, it simultaneously renders American culture and values as grotesquely depraved, producing more anti-American feeling even as it fails to produce intelligence. Reports from prisoners show that many of them believe these female interrogators to be prostitutes. Why would a prisoner confess information—assuming he had anything to confess—to someone he believed to be a prostitute? Moreover, the use of women has mitigated and rationalized the use of sexual torture. The sexual violence perpetrated on Iraqi prisoners and the presence of women in the Abu Ghraib photos has served, Fusco argues, "to limit the understanding of sexual torture as a calculated practice" because the use of sexual aggression by female interrogators seems "milder and more acceptable than other forms of torture."[55]

Fusco's *Field Guide* includes a photocopy of a 2002 FBI memo that describes sexual aggression by a female interrogator as well as the performance text, "Our Feminist Future," that Fusco delivered in 2007 at the Museum of Modern Art at a symposium that coincided with the exhibitions *Wack! Art and the Feminist Revolution* at the Museum of Contemporary Art in Los Angeles, and *Global Feminisms* at the Brooklyn Museum, in which Fusco takes on the persona of a military woman who gloats about the military domestication and utilization of feminism. In the absence of manuals and photos accessible to the public, Fusco also creates her own "field guide" on tactics with a set of sixteen color illustrations by Dan Turner. They include humiliation through nudity, forced eating of pork, use of loud music, sleep deprivation, team harassment, terrorization through the use of dogs, sexual degradation, sexual contact, and direct sexual advances, concluding with the military tactic known as "Fear Up Harsh," in which a half-undressed female interrogator smears fake menstrual blood on a detainee who kneels before her.

Fusco focuses on women's capacity for violence in the military, rather than on their unfair treatment in the military and media, because for many feminists in the United States, the military mistreatment of women seems to occlude visibility of women's capacity for violence. Feminists, argues Fusco, focus on discrimination against women in the military but fail to critique the institution of the military per se and the aspirations of women to integrate themselves within it as such. We should not be surprised by this feminist approach, however, for this is integral to liberal feminism, which fails to see the intersection of the sex line and the class line, whereby women who align themselves with the ruling class will always betray their "sisters."

Fusco not only discovered a proliferation of interrogation courses on the Internet, but also that interrogators tend to be more educated than most in the military and that there are many Mormon interrogators because Mormon missionaries are required to learn foreign languages, making them better suited for intelligence work. Fusco also found that many of the illegal torture techniques, such as waterboarding, sleep deprivation, and extreme physical aggression, are taught to interrogators under the guise of teaching them "enemy" tactics. The Delta course instructor and his colleague who ran the course Fusco and her group signed up for were unfazed by the fact that she was a university professor, a demographic that turns out to constitute a sizable portion of their clients, as he informed her, and he easily agreed to allow Fusco to film the experience of her group.

After being driven to the camp, the group was given a mission, a code, and a contact number and their job was to refrain from divulging this information. The following day they began an immersive experience during which they were ambushed, captured, strip-searched (with their underwear on), and incarcerated in a mock POW camp, where they were subjected to four grueling interrogations over the course of the day. Afterward, their attempts at resistance were assessed by their instructors, and they spent two more days in classroom training and attempted to use their new knowledge about interrogation tactics in exercises with their instructors. The seven women understood that it was a simulation that could not duplicate the real experience, but the extreme verbal aggression, pressure, trickery, disorientation from hooding, fatigue, and fear that the interrogators managed to induce, with fake documents and stand-ins who took fake beatings, psychologically disarmed them with greater ease than they had anticipated. Four of the seven women broke under the stress and divulged their secret mission information. Some of them cried or lost their tempers. Only one managed to successfully fool them into thinking she was ill, hanging her head, crying, and moaning, "I don't know." She avoided two of the interrogations, was given extra water and was checked by a medic. "I found it quite telling," writes Fusco, "that it was the woman who acted like a weakling who performed the most convincing persona for these interrogators."[56]

We are left to wonder: was she merely acting or had she reached her limit for abuse? Fusco's objective was not to study the effects of stress and psychological violence on the "prisoners," however, but the psychology of the interrogators. But what do we learn that is new about the interrogators? Under the circumstances of a real interrogation, would they have gone easier on the woman who appeared weakest—or pressed harder on the weakest link? Isn't this interrogation course designed, ultimately, to serve the paying customers and protect themselves against lawsuits? Although their courage is admirable, the effect on the women seems potentially significant, for this is not "simulated" experience (except perhaps for Fusco), but real experience. Some of the women who revealed their mission information were subjected to a form of psychological torture known as "comrade pride," in which they believed that stand-ins were their comrades who were being beaten and could hear their screams as they were subjected to increasingly aggressive interrogation. Like Iraqi

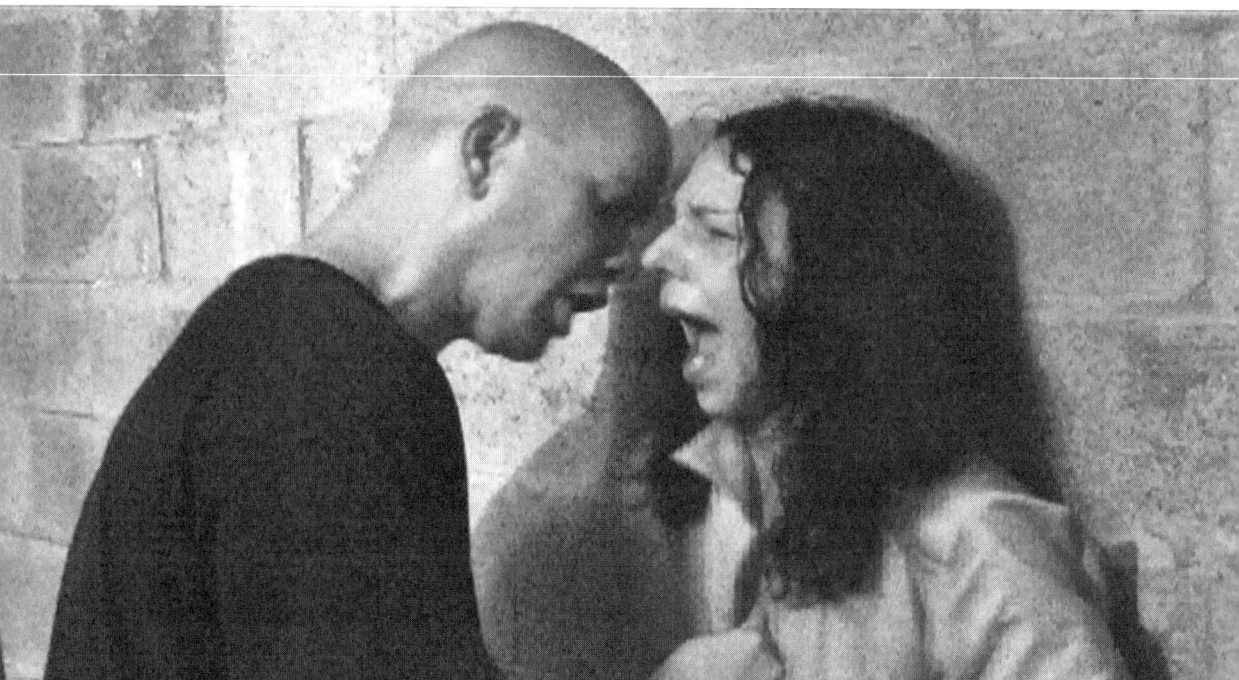

Figure 6. Coco Fusco, still from video *Operation Atropos*, interrogator and "detainee," 2006. (Courtesy of the artist.)

men whose wives and children were kidnapped and imprisoned in Abu Ghraib as a way of getting to the men, this is a form of psychological torture based on the imagination of violence. At the same time, the traumatic effects are physical and embodied.

Fusco concludes her *Field Guild* by summarizing the contradiction liberal feminists face: "First, American women continue to experience sexism, and second, thanks to their participation in the exercise of global power as Americans, women are called upon and agree to act in public capacities as aggressors, frequently by making strategic use of their femininity."[57] Indeed, it must be recognized that women often serve the interests of the state against the interests of women, minorities, the working class, and opponents of imperialist rule. In her work on female military interrogators and in *Operation Atropos*, Fusco presents some disturbing truths about the limits of "sisterhood" as well as the logic of military psychology.

Fusco's experiment is a brave one, yet its potential traumatic impact on some of the group members, who undertook the course with informed consent, nonetheless bears further consideration. A white paper published in June 2010 by Physicians for Human Rights on the unlawful collusion of physicians with torture and human experimentation under the Bush administration points out that soldiers involved in SERE survival training exercises, because of their exposure to "uncontrollable stress," experienced "marked stress responses as indicated by significant hormone spikes and troughs, and significant adverse psychological effects." Although they were exposed, with informed consent, to limited interrogation techniques over the course of only a few days, the report concludes that they were nonetheless harmed: "In fact, the SERE studies demonstrate that even mild applications of EITs [Enhanced Interrogation Techniques] were harmful, despite incomplete measures of their physical and psychological effects."[58] This occurred despite the fact that these soldiers were "stress hardy" and familiar with psychological testing. Although SERE soldiers experienced interrogation techniques such as waterboarding, which Fusco's group did not, her group might nonetheless be more vulnerable for being "stress naïve."[59] Only Fusco herself, well-seasoned in performance discipline, ended the training with no seemingly adverse effects.[60]

Bare Life Study #1 and *A Room of One's Own* shed light on the ruthlessness of military women, while *Operation Atropos* conveys the embodied experience that allows sympathetic identification with interrogation victims who are subjected to the ritualized humiliation, debasement, and psychological and physical violence that have become standard operating procedure in the American military. Atropos, one of the three goddesses of fate and destiny, was the one who administered the stroke of death, suggesting that this is what military women, like their male counterparts, are training for. However, *Operation Atropos* also raises challenging questions about works that explore the grueling experience of stress and trauma with human subjects. Like psychologist Philip Zimbardo's Stanford Prison Experiment in 1971 and Polish artist Artur Zmijewski's 2005 reenactment of that experiment, *Repetition*, this research into captor and captive psychology brings its own hazards as well as insights.

Repetition is a half-hour film documentary recording the reenactment of Zimbardo's study of human behavior in prison conditions in which Zimbardo isolated a group of student volunteers, some of whom played the role of "guards" and some "inmates." The experiment was meant to run for two weeks but was stopped after six days because of behavior deemed pathological, including sadism, violence, and humiliation. Zmijewski's reconstruction of the project in Warsaw utilized older unemployed Polish men and included psychologists acting as experts who could stop the experiment, a former prison inmate, and a sociologist involved in prison system reforms. This time it lasted for seven days, when participants collectively decided to leave the prison, after sadism, fear, frustration, anger, and humiliation again became manifest. Among reviews of Zmijewski's reenactment, Zimbardo's daughter, curator Tanya Zimbardo, raises some of the most probing questions about the project, noting that "we observe how an artist can enter the back door and avoid ethical considerations in order to open up for us the limits of what art can and cannot do."[61] Zimbardo notes that the impulse to re-create her father's infamous experiment predates *Repetition* in the form of television and cinematic renditions, and that it has been invoked countless times in relation to institutional abuses of power, especially in the wake of the Abu Ghraib torture scandal. "The visual parallels in the imagery of prisoner humiliation," writes Zimbardo, "are immediately striking," suggesting how easily similar results can be generated. The original experiment was "a powerful tool for understanding the dynamics of authority, the role of deindividuation, and the diffusion of responsibility," showing how the military prison environment consistently produces sadism and abuse, influencing human behavior as much as it is shaped by "individual disposition." As a result, notes Zimbardo, the works are "time capsules in the history of social psychology" and the Human Subjects Committee will no longer approve requests to reproduce either the Stanford Prison Experiment or its frequent comparison, the Milgram Experiment of 1963 (the Obedience to Authority Study).[62]

Zmijewski, however, at a panel at the California College of the Arts in 2006, insisted that his project challenged the original study's findings and claimed that the experiment had a positive result because the participants agreed to end it before it escalated further. Noting considerable differences between the original project and the reenactment, including the presence of the camera, Tanya Zimbardo objects: "The problem with collapsing the distinctions between art and social science is that the work's status as art is ultimately its legitimation. Using art to investigate these distinctions saves Zmijewski from being a pseudo-scientist." In such cases, the merging of social science with art raises challenging questions about "differences between art and life, the ethics involved in working with human subjects, and the extent to which artists will put others at risk in order to carry out an action."63

It is striking how the institutionally conditioned abuses of power, while quickly rejected in these limited and voluntary experiments, also were, at the same time, so rapidly internalized by the participants. Lynndie England, like most of the other actors at Abu Ghraib, never expressed remorse for the humiliation and torture in which she participated and was photographed, defensively asserting to Errol Morris in *Standard Operating Procedure*, "We didn't kill 'em. We didn't cut their heads off. We didn't

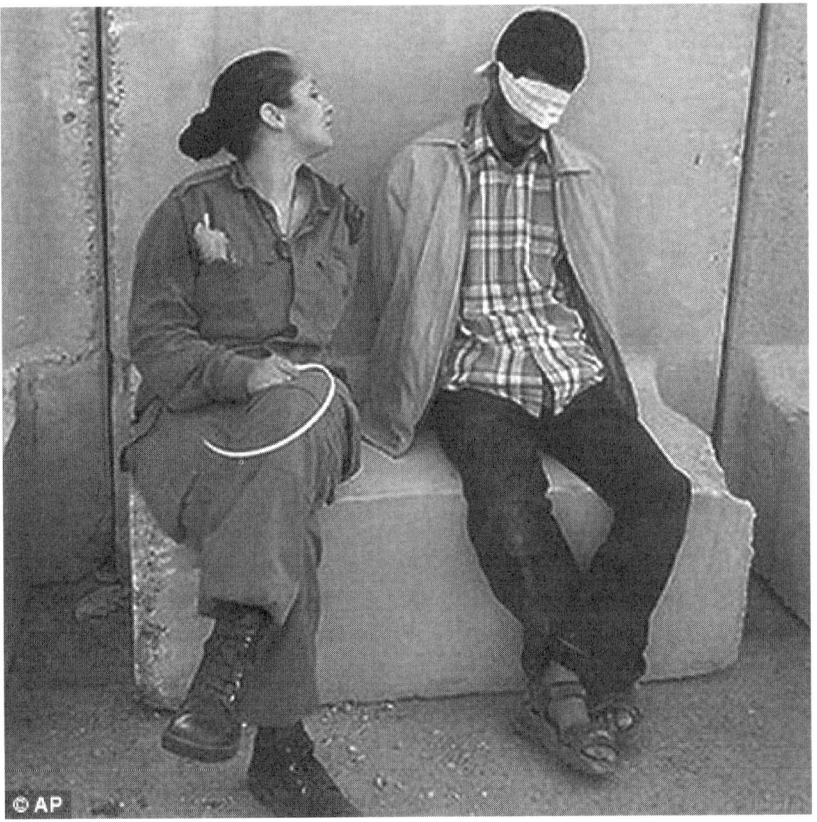

Figure 7. Photo posted on Facebook by former Israeli soldier Eden Abergil, posing with Palestinian detainee, 2010.

shoot 'em. We didn't cut 'em and let them bleed to death. We just did what we were told to soften 'em up for interrogation." In other words, it could have been worse and therefore, wasn't so bad. What she most regretted, as she made explicit in later interviews, was that pictures were taken. More recently, Israeli army soldier Eden Abergil rose to notoriety after she posted two trophy photos of herself with bound Palestinian prisoners on her Facebook page in an album titled "Army . . . the most beautiful time of my life." The photos found their way onto Israeli news sites and blogs and caused a scandal. In one photo Abergil squats before two handcuffed and blindfolded prisoners and smiles; in the other she sits beside a handcuffed and blindfolded prisoner and looks down her nose at him. The public outcry and comparisons to Lynndie England took her by surprise and she said she did not understand why the photos were viewed as offensive: "There was no statement in the photos about violence, about disrespect, about anything that would hurt that person. I just had my picture taken with someone in the background. When I understood that so many people were hurt by those pictures, I removed them. I did not humiliate those detainees. I didn't hit them, I didn't act toward them unpleasantly. It's completely different than the American soldier some are trying to compare me to."[64] This is telling for what it reveals about the normalization of the conditions of occupation in Israel/Palestine, the objectification of Palestinians ("I just had my picture taken with someone in the background"), and the sliding scale of acceptable behavior in the position of occupier. For England, anything short of murder was okay ("we didn't kill 'em"); for Abergil, the fact that they could not see her assuming a position of mocking dominance made that behavior and its posting on a public forum acceptable ("I didn't hit them"). The photos were taken in 2008 at Abergil's base in Ashdod where Palestinians trying to cross the Gaza border into Israel were sometimes bound with plastic handcuffs and blindfolded while awaiting questioning.[65]

Like England, Abergil internalized the prevailing ethos of the military and saw nothing objectionable in her behavior, clearly suggesting that it was a sanctioned norm. Similarly, both England and Abergil came to enjoy their position of mastery and commemorated it through photographic documentation. One of Abergil's Facebook friends commented that she looked "sexiest like that," and she responded, "Yes, I know. LOL . . . What a day it was, look how he completes my pictures. I wonder if he's got Facebook. I have to tag him the picture. LOL." The eroticism of the position of power and the license to mock and humiliate is explicitly part of the appeal.[66]

There is ample evidence that such behavior is widespread, as demonstrated by photos and videos of Israeli soldiers taunting, humiliating, or gratuitously assaulting Palestinians as any Internet search will turn up and observers have pointed out.[67] Director of the Public Committee against Torture in Israel, Yishai Menuhin, commented, "This reflects an attitude which has become the norm and consists in treating Palestinians like objects, not like human beings." Palestinian Authority spokesman Ghassan Khatib said, "This shows the mentality of the occupier—to be proud of humiliating Palestinians. The occupation is unjust, immoral and, as these pictures show, corrupting."[68] The Israeli military dutifully called the photos "disgraceful." While the state prosecutor decided in June 2011 not to open a criminal case against Abergil, who had been discharged from the army a year earlier, he announced at the same time that charges would be filed against a male IDF soldier who was videotaped belly dancing against a bound and blindfolded female Palestinian detainee. Yet the state and military institutions are primarily responsible for the framing of these photos and videos that reflect the discourses they themselves have naturalized: valorizing the dominance of the Israeli soldier and citizen while counting Palestinian lives as less valuable and worthy of respect, at best. Thus Abergil was indignant that the Israeli government did not defend her and that it was more concerned with international criticism, defiantly asserting that she "endangered her life for the country." After calling her actions "thoughtless and innocent" on Israeli radio, as she was perhaps counseled to say, Abergil nonetheless added: "I still don't understand what wasn't OK."[69] We believe her, since for her the photos merely frame her loyalty and service to the state and accurately represent the state's attitude that Palestinians have no rights that Israelis are bound to respect.

The Public Display of Torture Photos

Some observers have suggested that the low resolution quality of the Abu Ghraib photographs diminished their impact. In response, South African–born, San Francisco–based artist Clinton Fein hired models and reenacted some of the most notorious photos, including images of the human pyramids, men being forced to simulate fellatio, chained to bunks and bars with women's underwear on their head, in stress positions, and the Hooded Man, in order to produce large-format, high-resolution images. Beautifully lit, these high quality chromogenic prints mounted on panel have a strangely intimate, disturbing quality but convey a more staged and painterly sensibility than the original photographs (the originals and reenactments can be compared at clintonfein.com).

A First Amendment activist who has challenged notions of "decency" in representation and won a Supreme Court victory over United Sates Attorney General Janet Reno, Fein was disturbed by the blurring of genitals on the Abu Ghraib images disseminated on the Internet and in print sources. His website notes: "If one was to question which was obscene—the display of someone's ass cheeks or graphic displays of torture, I don't think there ought to be any confusion." Moreover, this "concession to good taste," as if these were ordinary porno pictures, as art critic Marcia Vetrocq asserts, obscures the sexual sadism and explicitly eroticized choreography staged for the camera in Abu Ghraib, which Fein seeks to restore in his reenactments pictures.[70] By emulating the actions of the torturers who staged the original scenarios, Fein ultimately set out to learn something about their sexual pathology and claims on his website that "there was something inexplicably erotic and sexually charged in choreographing the scenes."

While this is obviously true for Fein, and likely true for the soldiers as well, Fein's belief that with this insight he has gained full access to the experience of the Abu Ghraib torturers represents the fallacy of reenactment. What Fein did not and could not experience was the mental condition of the American soldiers after months of grueling war, fear, and boredom, their backgrounds as prison guards or youthful inexperience, or, most importantly, their sense of the political power they wielded over Iraqi prisoners whom they considered "other" in every way, all of which converged in those acts of abuse and degradation. Fein's photographs may usefully focus our attention on the staging and the torturers and the intoxicating eroticism of power over others, as opposed to just the victims, but their inflated hyperreal quality also creates a distinct sense of artificiality.

Indeed, the emphasis on slick high-resolution quality is misplaced. The very condition of low-resolution amateur photography is critical to the impact of the Abu Ghraib photos, giving them a familiar camera phone authenticity and authority. If the photos did not have as big an impact on American foreign policy as they might have, it is not because they were low-res vernacular images, but because of the way the Bush administration managed to politically distance itself from the outrage they generated and to contain the fallout; they nonetheless forced a reaction and became a global news media event, whereas print descriptions of the torture prior to the release of the photos did not. As media theorist Richard Grusin asserts, the affective intensity provoked by the Abu Ghraib photos depended on their "mediality," that is, the way in which the practices of taking digital photographs, uploading them on websites, and e-mailing them to friends and family echoed "our own everyday practices of photographing our pets, our vacations, or our loved ones, and then sharing these images with friends, family, or strangers via the same sociotechnical networks of file-sharing, email, and the web."[71] Grusin argues that the mediality of the photos in itself is what first activated the shock effect of the photos, the recognition that these were casual snapshots taken as souvenirs. Grusin's emphasis on the embodied affect of mediality helps explain the greater power of the original photos over the large high-resolution reenactments.

Not long after the scandal broke in 2004, seventeen of the Abu Ghraib images were on view in the exhibition *Inconvenient Evidence: Iraqi Prison Photographs* from Abu Ghraib, curated by Brian Wallis at the International Center of Photography in New York and at the Andy Warhol Museum in Pittsburgh. The exhibitions provoked questions about the wisdom or necessity of displaying these images. Likewise, when the exhibition of lynching photographs, *Without Sanctuary*, first shown in New York in 2000, was scheduled to open in Atlanta, a great deal of soul searching addressed the problem of whether such an exhibition would make the photographs available once again to a gaze of mastery, reinforcing their humiliating effect, or whether it was more important to expose this dark chapter of American history to critical public examination in a continuing dialog about race in America. Like images of rape and lynching, how and whether images of torture are shown are questions to be negotiated on the basis of how and whether such images make moral claims that must be heard. But unlike rape and lynching images, the photos of Abu Ghraib were already widely available on the Internet. What advantage, then, to public display? Is it true that overexposure to such pictures will produce a desensitized response, as some have argued?

Even Susan Sontag, who first posited the desensitization argument in her first book on photography, came to abandon it in her last one. Disturbing photographs do not fail to disturb us; on the contrary, we become desensitized to the events such pictures represent by *not* being able to see the visual evidence of their occurrence with our own eyes. Coco Fusco relates the story of a man who served as an archivist during the Vietnam War at the Department of Defense. Although he never engaged in combat, he nonetheless "suffered a mental breakdown from looking at scores of pictures of mutilated and defiled Vietnamese corpses, including some that featured heads with mouths stuffed with severed genitals." These images were circulated in secret by returning soldiers to his hometown. Fusco seems to assume a hardier or more sophisticated response to visual atrocity today and comments that "one would hardly worry about that sort of danger to our sensibilities now," though she asserts the importance of continuing to use images to affect political change.[72] While this archivist's response was perhaps extreme, people are potentially as deeply affected by images today as they have been in the past, and the global outrage generated by the Abu Ghraib images, despite their failure to bring down a presidency, is evidence of that; the continued efforts by the state to frame and circumscribe the public archive of images and to control the narratives that surround their public exposure are also evidence of that.

Certainly pictures of the tortured body are not new and have been represented in newspapers and other media for most of the twentieth century; yet photographs of American lynchings in the early decades of the 1900s, for example, as well as the tortures at Abu Ghraib fall outside the usual archives of images subject to marketing by commercial picture agencies, editors, and television networks through which the "right to look" is bought and sold.[73] Until a recent series of museum exhibitions, lynching photos were not considered part of the archive of "collective" public memory, but privately held and collected. Historically in lynching photos, "blackness" was made an exotic and eroticized spectacle for which only white supremacists retained the privilege of looking. Similarly, photos of the sadistic tortures at Abu Ghraib established the right of American soldiers and their friends, a right extended to U.S. officials and the U.S. Congress, to look at the nude and brutalized bodies of their Middle Eastern victims while denying that right to the public.

Presentations of torture photos in public institutions such as museums permit a common public viewing and acknowledgment of the crimes represented, shaming the communities that privately sanctioned them. They allow for a public grieving over the victims and provide a forum for collective discussion in which the moral claims and grievances of the photos and the atrocities they represent are acknowledged. Victims who were tortured or killed in the name of protecting "whiteness" in the case of lynchings, or "democracy" in the case of Abu Ghraib, are otherwise not recognized publicly as victims and such grieving is minimized or prevented, as a way of forestalling political opposition—and this makes the absence of photos of sexual assault on women all the more egregious. Taken by witnesses/participants and local professional photographers in the case of lynching photos, or by soldiers in the case of Abu Ghraib, these photos function differently on the larger national and international stage than in the smaller communities that perpetrated the crimes. On a local level, they were meant to reflect and consolidate the values of the community and to reaffirm a hierarchy of power; on the national stage, the same pictures reveal these acts as atrocities, invite moral positioning, and encourage political struggle. The museum presentations direct the viewer's attention to the political conditions of production, critically analyzing the initial framing of the photos and thereby reframing them.[74]

The first function of these exhibitions, then, is to formalize the right of all to "look" and by looking, to publicly avow the violence, the injuries, the losses, and their injustice, to take responsibility for the meaning now produced by these photographic statements. Viewing the images through the global media of newspapers, television, and the Internet may produce similar effects, but I am specifically concerned here with the implications of viewing such photos in public exhibitions that arguably have the unique effect of formally institutionalizing such photos while assuming greater latitude in framing their presentation and their meaning and producing prolonged observation. This creates new viewing conditions in which the spectator approaches the photograph not as a momentary distraction. The viewer becomes a civil spectator who considers the violence of the original frame, the conditions under which the photos were made, the address of the subjects within the image to the viewer, and takes responsibility toward the sense of the photographs by transforming them into emergency claims.[75]

The appeal and impact of such exhibitions has been enormous. The first exhibition of lynching photographs, *Without Sanctuary: Lynching Photography in America*, was shown at the Roth Horowitz art gallery in Manhattan in 2000, presenting lynching photos from the collection of James Allen and John Littlefield, the majority of which were taken in the first three decades of the twentieth century. The overwhelming public response to the exhibition caught the attention of the *New York Times* and other periodicals that noted the public's willingness to stand in the January cold for up to three hours in order to visit the tiny one-room gallery, which could only accommodate about fifteen people at a time. Some five thousand people saw the show before it closed.[76] The exhibition moved to the New-York Historical Society, which added material on the anti-lynching movement, and drew fifty thousand people in the first four months.[77] Exhibitions followed at the Andy Warhol Museum in Pittsburgh, where more than thirty thousand viewers attended, and, in its first southern venue, the Martin Luther King Jr. National Historic Site in Atlanta, 177, 000 visitors attended during the nine-month installation.[78] The exhibitions have been so popular, in part, because threats against black men are still common in the United States. In December 2003, for example, several black NFL football players were sent death threats by rope with the message to stop dating white women. Since the election of Barack Obama, death threats and attacks against black people have soared.[79]

While drawing record crowds of viewers, the exhibitions also elicited complaints. Some questioned the motives of white Atlanta antiques dealer James Allen, who collected the photos and profited from them, or questioned the virtue of publishing and displaying photos that evoke such a painful history. In an essay for the book *Without Sanctuary*, black author and *New Yorker* staff writer Hilton Als himself mused aloud that the "usefulness of this project . . . escapes me."[80] Als feared the reification of the black body as an object of fascination for whites. Although it may indeed be impossible to avoid the voyeurism that attends images of the tortured body, the risk of voyeurism must be weighed against the moral claims of the image and the useful effects of shame and opposition evoked by public acknowledgment of racial violence. In the discussions surrounding the Atlanta exhibition of lynching photos, Mark Bauerlein observed that the reasons for withholding such photographs from public view "are outweighed by the importance of showing how people who otherwise believed in basic democratic principles turned into self-exonerating murderers."[81] To withhold such photos is to repress an understanding of history that is uniquely conveyed through the power of images.

When *Inconvenient Evidence* opened at the International Center of Photography (ICP) in Manhattan and was presented concurrently at the Andy Warhol Museum in Pittsburgh, *New York Times* art critic Michael Kimmelman noted in an article titled "Photos Return, This Time As Art," that the Abu Ghraib photographs had "passed from the headlines to the art pages in half a year," and raised what he felt were key ethical questions: "Why Abu Ghraib but not images of beheadings, which are also on the Web, floating in the digital ether, fragments from the same new photographic universe? Would it be considered an invasion of the dead men's privacy? Too disgusting? Politically incorrect?"[82] The conservative right also has raised the issue of showing the beheadings or the crimes of Saddam Hussein's regime. These criticisms imply that U.S. atrocities are being unfairly targeted and that the presentations are politically one-sided.

These cynical calls for "parity" in presentation do not seek to establish an ideological "balance" for the crimes of Abu Ghraib; rather they seek to neutralize, excuse, or legitimate them. The crimes against Americans are regarded as "grievable" crimes, while those against Muslims and Arabs at Abu Ghraib are not. Because the bodies of Iraqi and Afghani others have been kept officially unnamed, uncounted, and unpictured since those wars began, they are kept from being "grievable bodies," in Butler's terms.[83] Despite the sneering title of his article, Kimmelman recognizes the vernacular rather than the "artful" quality of the photos, noting that they "imply no outrage about what's happening. In fact, the intent of the pictures is precisely to compound the humiliation." Though the ICP is an institution devoted to the history of photography, the photographs, as Kimmelman himself points out, are not "just one more artful provocation," but genuinely shocking, and this effect works against the intention of those in the sanctioning community.[84]

The charge of turning the images into "art" also was asserted in a critique of the installation at the Warhol Museum. Joseph Dugan, president of the Soldiers & Sailors National Military Museum & Memorial, said, "In reality, they're taking material off the Internet, that has been used in the tabloids, the newspapers, *Time*, *Newsweek*, and trying to present it as 'art,' which to me is totally ridiculous."[85] In fact, the ICP and the Warhol Museum presented the Abu Ghraib photos very differently. Avoiding the appearance of seeming to aestheticize the photos, the ICP mounted the computer printouts with pushpins in a room by themselves. The Warhol Museum presented *Inconvenient Evidence* with large photographic reproductions, interpretive text panels, newspaper headlines, and historical materials and placed them in one corner of the largest room on the second floor of the museum, in proximity to some of Warhol's paintings of camouflage, an electric chair print, and a print from his *Race Riot* series. This proximity positioned the Abu Ghraib photos in relation to an artistic practice that employed media photographs to produce a socially engaged art. The museum simultaneously presented the exhibition *Looking at Life*, including vernacular and media photos published in *Life* magazine, such as the My Lai massacre from Vietnam and stills from the Zapruder video of John F. Kennedy's assassination. This relationally positioned the Abu Ghraib photos within a history of photojournalistic documentary photography and the amateur or vernacular documentation of atrocities.

Dugan's suggestion that the Warhol Museum was trying to make the Abu Ghraib images into "art" is disingenuous and palpably false. He suspects a political agenda and means to suggest it is disrespectful to the soldiers—not their victims—to be placed on public exhibition, as he made clear when he argued that the photos unfairly condemned U.S. soldiers. Ben Butler, director of legislations for the national Association for Uniformed Services, put it more bluntly: "[Warhol] was an artist who tried to use art in a radical way, and to use these photos and this situation in that way seems inappropriate."[86] It is telling that conservative veterans' groups oppose the public exhibition of these photos, precisely because such exhibitions are successful in making visible what they would like to keep from view. The museum exhibitions invite the public to look at these photos differently from the way they are looked at when reproduced in the media, that is, to examine them more closely and at length, slowing down the consumption of atrocity, and to consider their implications under the greater impact of seeing them as a group and in relation to other atrocity photos. Is this what Ben Butler means when arguing that the photos should not be used "in a radical way"? For no one would mistake the photos of Abu Ghraib as "art" or admire them for their "aesthetic qualities."

The lynching and Abu Ghraib exhibitions were distinct from each other in that the lynching photos had not been seen publicly since the 1930s, while the Abu Ghraib images were easily available on the Internet. The revelatory purpose of the former exhibition did not exist in the same way for the latter, but both exhibitions were regarded as central to the mission of the Warhol Museum in creating a forum for public debate, supplemented with programming such as symposia. Distinct from other forms of media, both museum exhibitions, in a larger sense, constitute what is understood as the cultural heritage of our society. Both offered what Roger Simon calls "an affective force to thought," in which the embodied affect of seeing disturbing visual images produces an inherited form of difficult knowledge that becomes part of our culture, unsettling certainties, and provoking an ethical responsibility toward the suffering of others. The power of these exhibitions rests not only on their content but on their ability to "inhabit the present."[87]

The exhibitions bring to mind other recent exhibitions of atrocity photos, such as an exhibition that toured Germany in 1996–1997, *The War of Annihilation: Crimes of the Wehrmacht*, 1941 to 1944, with photos by soldiers from German archives showing atrocities committed not by the SS, but by the regular German army during World War II. Even fifty years after the end of World War II, they provoked a firestorm of controversy. The reality of atrocities committed by German soldiers in photos long buried in German archives was shocking to those who wanted to circumscribe such atrocities as the work of members of the SS only, not ordinary soldiers, although it should be no surprise that those who rule the state set the moral standards of behavior in warfare, which are conveyed through the chains of command. It was not only Germany under the Nazis that found itself subject to a culture of war in which torture, atrocity, and gratuitous killing was common practice, if publicly unacknowledged, although the massive industrialized death machine of genocide was unique and unprecedented.

Other atrocity exhibitions included photos taken at the Khmer Rouge death camp Tuol Sleng (known as S-21), *Photographs from S-21: 1975–1979*, mounted by the Museum of Modern Art in 1997, the video of the Rodney King police beating first shown at the Whitney Museum in 1993, and the Zapruder film of Kennedy's assassination shown at the Andy Warhol Museum. Thus it seems quite appropriate to view these images within the museum and to recognize the important relationship of the documentary photograph to artistic production, from Picasso's *Guernica*, which was first exhibited across from the German pavilion at the Paris World's Fair in 1939 as a political protest against the Luftwaffe's bombing raids that destroyed the ancient Spanish city of Guernica, to Richard Serra's 2004 lithographs of the Hooded Man, which depend upon the immediate recognizability of the original image. Serra's lithographic silhouette in *Stop Bush* and *Stop B S* serves as a kind of graphic logo of oppressive American occupation, a visual strategy that could not exist without the photograph that preceded it, yet which turns the image in the photograph into something else. Serra did not merely reproduce the effects of the photo, powerful as those effects are, but created new political meaning in the context of an American election, transforming a trophy war image into a searing antiwar image that branded the United States as a country that tortures despite its official denials.

What critics find objectionable about public display of the photos is the exposure of the careless enjoyment by the perpetrators over the gratuitous humiliations and tortures, revealing instead of concealing their culpability, and, by implication, the more important culpability of the military hierarchy. Images of the tortured body act against historical amnesia in ways that print does not, and exhibitions of such photographs help to keep alive a public sense of shame and moral outrage. More powerfully than words, the lynching and Abu Ghraib photos demonstrate the brutal excesses of white supremacy and American nationalism, which must not be ignored or forgotten. Thus the context in which these photos are represented makes all the difference in how they are understood and how they inhabit the present; by showing them as groups of images in public institutions, a new "global community" of viewers is produced, which not only alters the discourse surrounding the images but, potentially, the political conditions that lead to such atrocities. They make visible the brutalized bodies of "others," which historically have been considered unrepresentable except in highly coded ways. By picturing bodies that have previously been hidden from view, such exhibitions allow for a public grieving over those who have been injured and killed by the United States, or in the name of the greater national good of the United States, a grieving that is normally disallowed in the public sphere. Making such photographs publicly visible, then, formalizes the right of all to look, and by looking, to publicly avow the violence and the losses and to hold those responsible accountable. These exhibitions thus aid a political repositioning of such photos and the acts they represent, allowing the national public to recognize what has been hidden, to grieve, and to protest. And just as the initial production and limited circulation of these photos were political acts, so is their display in public venues, serving to expose American pretensions to racial, cultural, and political dominance and to reveal the imperialist brutality and sense of entitlement that is firmly rooted in U.S. nationalist ideology in the Middle East.

4

THE BODY AS POLITICAL CORPUS

In response to the revelations of torture and their justification in recently declassified CIA documents, Guatemalan artist Regina José Galindo enacts and externalizes bare life as constitutive of the new political body by submitting her own body to an act of torture. For *Confesión* (Confession), Galindo's 2007 performative reenactment of waterboarding, she traveled to Palma de Mallorca, the capital city on the island of Majorca off the coast of Spain, because it had been revealed that the CIA used it as a transit point for its "extraordinary rendition" flights of men they had kidnapped to countries where they could be tortured. Galindo hired a burly Spanish nightclub bouncer and instructed him to repeatedly force her head into a barrel of water, her own version of waterboarding, and staged this work on the "Night of Art" in Palma de Mallorca, an evening when the well-heeled take to the streets and make the art scene all over town.

A video of the performance shows a crowd of viewers gathered in the street outside the basement room where Galindo's performance took place; a few could look in through a cellar window while the rest watched on a large TV screen. The torturer pushes Galindo into the room and the waterboarding begins immediately. Galindo is seen as a diminutive woman while the bald-headed bouncer she hired is huge, muscular, and powerful, his physique that of a body builder. Although Galindo offers resistance, she is easily overwhelmed as he forces her head into the barrel of water, holding her down for an uncomfortably long time, then pulls her out, her hair spraying water around the room. The bouncer/torturer enacts his role with such enthusiasm that Galindo seems barely able to catch a breath before he plunges her back in, again and again. She gasps and whimpers as she struggles against his overpowering strength, gripping the edge of the barrel with both hands as he forces her head down. It is difficult to watch. The bouncer/torturer apparently enjoyed his role so much that he ignored a previously agreed upon stop signal and added his own flourish to the script by throwing Galindo onto the concrete basement floor, her body smacking the surface and crumpling into a heap.[1] Apparently, she had told him not to be gentle.[2]

There is nothing being asked or answered here; it is simply a reenactment of torture, though it can be no coincidence that the water is in a barrel that once held oil. Isn't this what all of those "unlawful combatants" have been tortured for? Isn't this what the invasion of Iraq was really about? Moreover, isn't this form of easy dominance and off-handedly cruel treatment the way the "superpowers" treat all less powerful countries that get in their way? How can we witness this without feeling complicit or troubled? "Their contest," writes Julian Stallabrass, who photographed the event while a videographer taped it, "could be read as an allegory of the absurdly skewed power struggles played out between nations: of the Iraq War, for example, in which the world's greatest military power, using the most advanced weaponry and with complete control of the air, destroyed an ill-equipped army of conscripts from a nation strangled by a decade of sanctions; but also of all those agreements on trade, privatization, 'regime change' and the law thrust on weak nations by the strong, and backed by the threat of poverty and devastation against those who say no."[3] The history of colonialism in Iraq goes back to the imposition of a system of direct military control by the British following World War I, which caused a nationwide revolt that resulted in thousands of Iraqi deaths and two thousand deaths among the massive number of British and Indian troops brought in to suppress it.[4] At the same time, the performance has a gendered dimension, in which the torturer enjoys his power and mastery over the body of a petite woman; like smaller, weaker countries, she is easy to dominate and brutalize.

The use of waterboarding, a near-drowning technique used as far back as the Spanish Inquisition and long regarded as a war crime, was a tactic defended by the Bush administration on the grounds that it was sanctioned by government lawyers and therefore not unlawful. Former vice-president Dick Cheney continued to defend torture even after it was outlawed by Congress. In February 2010, Cheney appeared on national

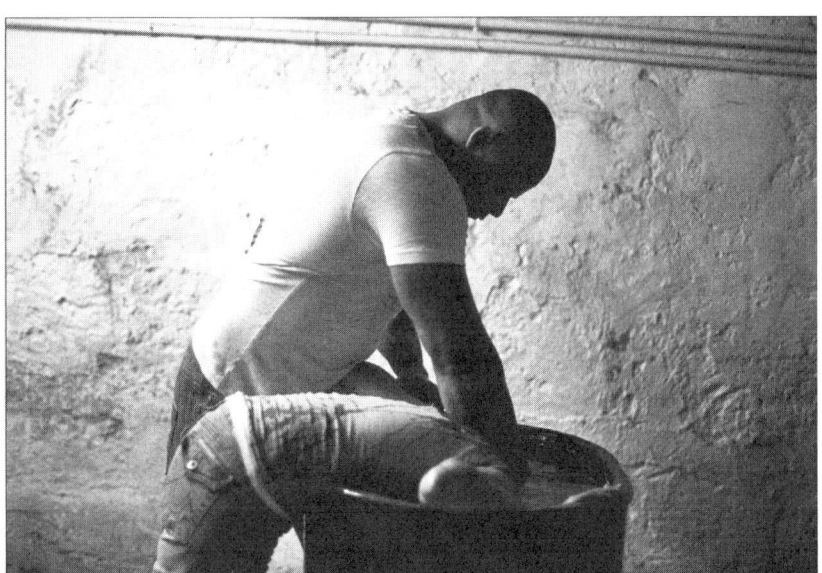

Figure 8. Regina José Galindo, *Confesión* (Confession), 2007, La Caja Blanca, Palma de Mallorca, Spain. Photo by Julian Stallabrass. (Courtesy Prometeogallery di Ida Pisani, Milan/Lucca.)

television in ABC's news program *This Week* and affirmed not only that he was still "a big supporter of waterboarding," but admitted that the Bush administration had not asked for legal opinions on the propriety of torture, as he and former president George Bush had long maintained, but instead openly acknowledged that the Bush administration had *instructed* the Justice Department to issue the legal opinions they needed to justify torture.[5]

As with other critically engaged reenactments (see chapter 2), Galindo's brave reenactment of torture creates a new social and political memory that not only makes torture visible to anyone, but indelible, unforgettable, deeply disturbing, and vicariously embodied by the viewer as they watch Galindo's voluntary near-drowning. The performance does not allow the status of waterboarding as torture to be questioned, as Cheney also once attempted to do, despite Galindo's change in format. But torture was not what the audience of La Caja Blanca, the commercial gallery that arranged the reenactment/performance, was expecting on the "Night of Art" in Palma de Mallorca. Some in the crowd objected, not to the brutality of the bouncer/torturer, or to state-sponsored torturers, but to Galindo herself, the tortured, for the violence of the action and the harrowing experience she created for her viewers.[6] We might see this as a failure, in the moment, to create a public sphere with a similar way of seeing, but there may be several reasons for this: first, this was a privileged audience of the class that identifies with the interests of capitalism; second, we have to wonder how well known it was among the elite that Palma de Mallorca was used as a transit point for extraordinary rendition by the United States? Would this have made Galindo's performance seem like an accusation or uncomfortable reminder of their acquiescence or complicity?

Stallabrass notes the privileged and uncomfortable position of those who record torture, where the image making itself becomes part of the torture. In *Confesión*, it is only the torturer who has real control, not Galindo herself, who structured the performance by effectively relinquishing control, and not Stallabrass, who witnesses the torture through the camera. At Guantánamo, too, photographs and videos were part of the torture. Prisoners were videoed as they were subjected to "Extreme Reaction Force" sessions in which they were severely beaten and abused. Printed photos were used for interrogation in the form of images of scantily clad women or the victims of bombings, which were shown to tortured prisoners and even stuck to their bodies.[7] Galindo's torture video echoes the grainy amateur quality of such videos, avoiding a slick finish and echoing the effects of digital media used to take amateur photos, such as those we are familiar with from Abu Ghraib.

So the audience was angry at Galindo for tricking them into witnessing violence, although the idea of violence against civilians obviously does not originate with Galindo. She was likely familiar with such torture, though, even before the CIA memo was unclassified. Following Naomi Klein's analysis in her book *The Shock Doctrine*, which demonstrates the long relationship between neoliberal economics and torture, Stallabrass explains: "A policy that impoverishes the large majority of citizens while enriching a small elite can only be imposed by force, and the favored method, certainly in large swathes of Latin America under the dictators who pioneered neoliberalism, was to murder and torture those that opposed them. Much in the treatment of detainees in the current wars would be familiar to those who have opposed the interests of the US worldwide—from Vietnam to Guatemala—for the techniques were researched and propagated by the CIA, and include hooding, stripping, beating and frequently electroshock."[8] Only electroshock was not openly embraced as a torture technique by the Bush administration, though we saw echoes of it in the wires attached to the Hooded Man of Abu Ghraib.

Galindo won the Golden Lion award for the best young artist at the 2005 Venice Biennale, for three videos and one live performance.[9] *Who Can Erase the Traces?* (2003) documents Galindo's breakout performance in the streets of Guatemala City, where she walked in a long black dress from the Constitutional Court Building to the old National Palace. As she walked she carried an enamel white basin with human blood, which she set down periodically in order to dip her feet, leaving a trail of bloody footprints from one building to the other. Her performance was a protest against the corrupt Constitutional Court, which had recently sanctioned the presidential run of the former military dictator, Gen. Ríos Montt, despite the fact that the constitution barred the ability of past presidents who gained power by military coup to run for office. Guatemalans in the street easily understood the ghostly footprints as representing the hundreds of thousands of civilians who had been murdered, primarily by the Guatemalan army, in the long years of civil war and after, which Ríos Montt helped orchestrate. For her live performance in Venice, *(279) Golpes* ([279] Blows), Galindo crawled inside a pale gray cube and whipped herself 279 times, one for each woman murdered in Guatemala so far that year. While not visible to the audience, the sound of each blow was amplified outside the box, the performance evoking the invisibility of the disappeared women whose deaths are never officially counted, grieved, or punished.

Formerly an advertising copy editor, Galindo has appropriated the methodology of boiling down the idea to a single powerful statement in her art.[10] What drives her to embody so much pain in her performances?

In an interview with Francisco Goldman, Galindo asserted, "My country has suffered an eternity of calamities of all shapes and sizes: a mortal conquest, the maltreatment of indigenous villages and the negation of their rights throughout our entire history, the Gringo intervention, an infernal 36-year war, evil governments, spine-chilling levels of corruption, a murderous army, histories of violence that are a daily nightmare of inequality, hunger, misery." The rage these injustices have generated finds its expression in her work: "I feel impotent, unable to change things, but this rage has sustained me, and I've watched it grow since I first became aware of what was happening. It's like an engine—a conflict inside me that never yields, never stops turning, ever."[11]

Also a published poet, Galindo's uncompromising performance works include, among others, having her body wrapped in plastic and thrown into a dumpster (*We Don't Lose Anything by Being Born*, 2000); being hosed down with cold water by a high-pressure water hose of the kind used against street protesters (*Social Cleansing*, 2006); being tied nude to a bed with umbilical cords in her eighth month of pregnancy and positioned with her legs splayed in the way the Guatemalan army prepares pregnant indigenous women for gang rape (*Why Are They Still Free?*, 2006); getting Tasered until she collapses (*150,000 Volts*, 2007); and living with her family in a cell of the type used to detain illegal immigrants in the United States (*America's Family Prison*, 2008). Galindo approaches her subjects with ferocious personal commitment and political conviction, establishing the body as a site of brutal conflict and political violence by offering her own vulnerable corporeal being as a representative specimen in order to call into place a public sphere with a shared way of seeing that will recognize the emergency claims of her work.

Decolonizing the Body

"We have all been standing atop a political, economic, cultural, and spiritual disaster site," writes Guillermo Gómez-Peña, in regard to *Corpo/Illicito*, the third installment of his ongoing *Mapa/Corpo* series of performance/installation projects performed with his group La Pocha Nostra and produced in response to the post 9/11 "body politic."[12] A warrior in the visual field of political performance art for more than thirty years, Gómez-Peña moved to the United States from Mexico in 1978 seeking greater artistic and intellectual freedom and has sought to explore and expose in his work, through "symbolic acts of transgression," the more subtle cultural and ideological sources of racism and nationalism. In *Two Undiscovered Amerindians Visit . . .* (1992–1993), Gómez-Peña and Coco Fusco exhibited themselves inside a gilded cage dressed as fictitious "Indians" to protest the quincentennial celebrations of the arrival of Columbus in the West. They allowed viewers to feed them bananas like animals in a zoo to illustrate the easy enabling and perpetuation of ethnic stereotypes.[13] In *The Cruci-fiction Project* (1994), Gómez-Peña and Roberto Sifuentes crucified themselves in "full mariachi regalia" to protest immigration policy. In *The Temple of Confessions* (1994), Gómez-Peña and Sifuentes posed as "end-of-the-century saints" inside Plexiglass boxes "to receive racist confessions from guilt-ridden audience members."[14]

Gómez-Peña employs performance art as the most ethical and effective format in which to convey the embodied claims and grievances of the marginalized and oppressed, in the hope that the audience member who allows herself to interact, respond, and become part of the performance will also embody, and therefore be transformed by, the intensity of the performed experience. It is not unusual for audience members to be deeply moved and even weep at such performances. The most eloquent exponent of his own work, its guiding ethos and ideological dilemmas, Gómez-Peña also has published several books and numerous essays.

Using the American art world as his base of operations became increasingly difficult during the eight-year-reign of the Bush administration, when cultural institutions became more and more nervous over offending patrons, being charged with cultural betrayal, and losing their funding; many lost funding in any case. The increased scrutiny in this atmosphere of paranoia and distrust led to offers of budgets reduced by half, scaled-down projects, and self-censorship among artists who did not want to be blacklisted and have their work suppressed altogether, dictating a constant delicate reckoning between reasonable compromise out of solidarity with the institutions on whom they depended and conceding too much, taking the edge off the work and hollowing out its meaning. In 2006, Gómez-Peña wrote: "Let's face it, overt censorship is happening throughout the United States, and not just in 'red America.' My performance art colleagues and fellow spoken-word poets are being monitored, interrogated, defunded, watered down, ignored, and un/dis-invited by our cultural institutions, many of which perceive themselves as 'liberal.' It's a major dilemma for critical culture in the United States, and at the same time it's an international embarrassment. Why? Because the whole world knows about it and because it's not happening anywhere else, not even in Catholic Latin America."[15]

There are many examples of exhibitions and other events that have suffered the chilling effects of political conservatism. *The Dialectics of Terror*, scheduled to open at the Chelsea Art Museum in New York at the end of September 2008, including works by well-known artists such as Josh Azzarella, Johan Grimonprez, Coco Fusco, Jake and Dinos Chapman, and Jenny Holzer, examined images of political violence and critiqued the war in Iraq and the Bush administration. Museum president Dorothea Keeser claimed that the exhibition "glorified terrorism and showed disrespect for its victims," causing museum chief curator Manon Slome to cancel the exhibition and immediately resign from her position. Slome claimed that Keeser had attempted to censor the exhibition catalog and asserted: "Nothing in the exhibition glorifies terrorism and there are no images that are in any way sensational."[16] In an example of bureaucratic restrictions, in April 2010 five Iraqi artists were denied entry to Britain for the opening of their own exhibition on the grounds that they could not provide bank statements, a nearly impossible demand for artists from an occupied country with a collapsed banking system. The exhibition *Contemporary Art Iraq*, which opened at Manchester's Cornerhouse Art Gallery, included the Iraqi ambassador and the British foreign secretary on the guest list.[17] Gómez-Peña notes that five visas were denied by the U.S. State Department for Mexican, Cuban, and Colombian artists that La Pocha Nostra attempted to bring to the United States to include in their performance work.

The performative/installation work *Mapa/Corpo*, created by Gómez-Peña and La Pocha Nostra, metaphorically colonizes the body on three separate stages. It originated with a performance that mapped war zones onto a living nude using large acupuncture pins tipped with national flags. Gómez-Peña describes it as a "poetic, interactive ritual that explore[s] neo-colonization/decolonization through political acupuncture and the reenactment of the post-9/11 'body politic.'" It was initially rejected by a dozen U.S. museums and universities when they learned that the central image was a nude body covered with forty acupuncture needles, each bearing the flag of one of the "coalition forces" that supported the invasion of Iraq, primarily those of the United States and Britain. Audience members would be invited to "decolonize the body" by extracting the needles tipped with flags, with the help of the acupuncturist. Finding so much rejection, Gómez-Peña and his performance group toured other countries and performed in the United Kingdom, Canada, Mexico, and Brazil, where they could perform their most sensitive material without curatorial pressure to tone down the work. But even international performance is not without its hazards. As Gómez-Peña explains, "Due to 'security restrictions,' our props, costumes, and art materials are carefully scrutinized at every airport we enter. U.S. Homeland Security officers are now even checking the titles of our books and opening our notebooks and phone agendas, both when we leave and when we return to the U.S. Frequently, our materials are confiscated. . . . Every performance artist dreads his/her next flight, especially if he/she is brown-skinned and/or 'alternative' looking or has a foreign name or accent."[18]

In September 2008, *Mapa/Corpo 3: Interactive Rituals for the New Millennium* was performed for two nights at the Detroit Institute of Arts (videos of other versions of *Mapa/Corpo* are available on YouTube). Every performance is different, but each includes Gómez-Peña, Violeta Luna, and Roberto Sifuentes, along with a local professional acupuncturist and sometimes a local performance artist. *Mapa/Corpo 3* in Detroit included the Chicano techno-artist and VJ (video jockey) René Garcia, the local performance artist Lisa Melinn, and the local acupuncturist Susan Jakary. Every performance is adapted to its unique space, its tableaux vivant mediated by the shamanic poetic voice of Gómez-Peña, the charged darkened atmosphere inducing a sense of sacred space. As one entered the space of Rivera Court through black curtains, there were four stages. A woman in a burqa at one stage, performed by Violeta Luna, began to transform herself many times, from a passive Muslim woman to one who brandished a gun, or lifted her veil to reveal a sexy persona beneath. She picked up bloodcurdling instruments, as if threatening to maim herself and painfully distorted her face with them. As an embodied Muslim woman, Luna placed a crown of thorns on her head and then pulled it apart into a long barbed wire in which she wrapped herself, grotesquely distorting her features, then offered the end of the barbed wire, like a leash, to audience members, one of whom briefly took hold of it in a momentary act of troubling complicity. When she removed her burqa,

Figure 9. Guillermo Gómez-Peña and La Pocha Nostra, performance still of *Mapa/Corpo 3* with Violeta Luna, Detroit Institute of Arts, 28 October 2008. Photo by Dora Apel.

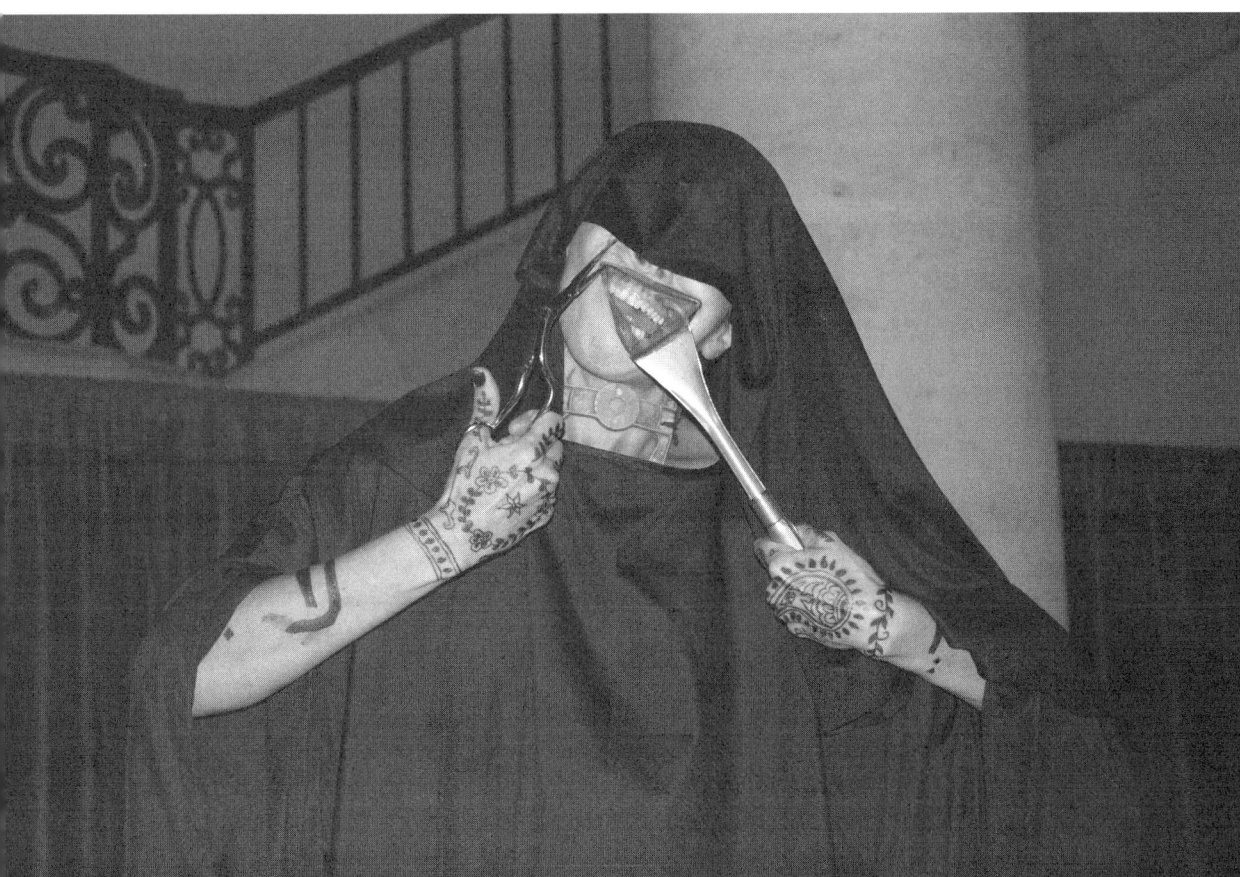

she was wearing a silver back brace studded with spikes. Luna's riveting transformations evoke a variety of associations as she creates her dioramas of personas alternating between perpetrator and victim, agency and passivity, stereotype and subversive counterstereotype. At different moments, her performance resonates with Shirin Neshat's black-and-white photograph of an Iranian woman who points a pistol at the viewer, disrupting stereotypes of the passive veiled woman; the bizarre gynecological instruments in David Cronenberg's *Dead Ringers*; the hooded prisoners of Abu Ghraib and the man on a leash; the mythologized persona of Frida Kahlo, with her many back surgeries and back brace, appropriated by feminists as a martyr and heroine.

At a second platform, the figure of Roberto Sifuentes lies on a gurney entirely wrapped in plastic, like the dead man packed in ice at Abu Ghraib, with an intravenous fluid stand. His figure embodies the universal immigrant or exile, the displaced and dispossessed, the political prisoner or asylum seeker, in short, *homo sacer*, the figure who cannot be sacrificed but can be killed with impunity, a man without statehood or citizenship. He is the New Barbarian, an immigrant from the South, a refugee without sovereignty and without human rights.[19] As the performance proceeds, a woman unwraps his corpse, then ritually shaves and washes his body as if preparing it for burial. Sifuentes eventually comes to life, and they enact alternating tableaux of tenderness and conflict, employing objects such as a rifle, a handgun, a pick axe, a whip. Every action by the performers seems to transform into an opposite reaction, creating a web of dichotomies and contradictions that evoke violence and death as well as compassion and connection. Eventually, with cheap red and black lipsticks, audience members are invited to write their messages on his body ("Leave Iraq," "Love and peace"), in effect redeeming and healing the body.

At a third stage, a nude woman lies on a surgical table covered by a United Nations flag. The acupuncturist, in a white lab coat, lays out her forty needles (the most a body can safely handle), slowly rolls up the U.N. flag, starting at the feet, and exposes the body section by section. The U.N. flag must be noted as a flag that symbolizes "human rights" yet represents no organized power, wields no authority, and evokes no allegiance. It alludes to that world body's inability to mitigate international conflicts even in a feeble way. Gómez-Peña writes, "If there is a central feature to globalization, it is violence, generalized violence, all-encompassing violence, in every corner of the 'global' village.... And now the world news: Since the end of the cold war, the 'center' of the ideological spectrum has moved 10 miles to the right. The U.S. and its cronies in the U.N. have established an international police force in charge of punishing rebel nations in the name of 'democracy.' Corporations displace indigenous communities, ravage their land and dump toxic waste wherever they please. Organized crime crosses all borders."[20] In his techno-shaman-in-drag persona (with studded glove and one high heel), Gómez-Peña struts around the tableaux and among the audience, erasing the boundaries between performer and audience, then steps up to a lectern and delivers a spoken-word multilingual poem on intolerance toward immigrants and minorities and the Iraq War, speaking in various languages and non-languages, evoking the preamble to the U.S. Constitution from the perspective of the Other ("We, the Other people/ We, the migrants, exiles, nomads & wetbacks"), while the acupuncturist methodically inserts the flag-tipped needles into the exposed body/map, "colonizing" the female body/world.

Finally, the U.N. flag has been rolled away and disappears altogether, unable to protect the bare life or modern political body; the body is completely exposed and covered with pins, with the tiny flag of Israel protruding prominently between the eyebrows, the apparent linchpin for all the British and U.S. flags in the body below. When audience members are invited to "de-colonize the Mapa/Corpo" by carefully removing the pins, they step up solemnly to perform this symbolic act of metaphoric healing. "It was in deep," said one participant. "Pulling it out was like removing a knife."[21] Many wish to pull the Israeli flag between the brows, which the acupuncturist saves for last. As the pins are removed, the acupuncturist places them into a cow's heart, brought in for that purpose, restoring the biological body to its human status, with the "right to have rights," in Hannah Arendt's terms.

The fourth station is that of the VJ, René Garcia, who controls two sets of images shown on four screens mounted high above the performers around the space in a montage of video footage, photo stills and sound. Flickering by are images of the Klan, the Confederate flag, medical images of the interior of the body, the Nazi army and Hitler, American bomber planes. They are taken from films such as *Gone with the Wind*, *Fahrenheit 9/11*, and *The Road to Guantánamo*, as well as Japanese sci-fi, NASA footage of the first *Apollo* mission, porn films, and footage from the making of the *Detroit Industry* murals by Diego Rivera in Rivera Court.

When the immigrant's body has been covered with writing, audience members help him sit up. On the second night of the Detroit performance, audience members spontaneously carried Sifuente's body entirely off the gurney and into the center of Rivera Court, where they tenderly placed him on the circular mosaic in the center of the court. Violeta Luna, "the decolonized body," joined him, and they lay head to toe like a human yin-yang while the audience silently gathered around them in a huge protective circle, as if this unscripted ritual of resistance and protection in sympathy with the figures represented by the performers was the most natural conclusion to the performance. In effect, the audience spontaneously constituted themselves as a radically activated public sphere with a sense of responsibility toward the "emergency claims" of bare life instantiated by the performers.

Heightening the intensity of the moment, in a remarkable fortuitous alignment, the visual narrative on the screens above the heads of the audience converged with the audience action as projected visitors to Rivera's murals in the early 1930s, standing on the mural scaffolding, also looked down upon the court. This unplanned visual and conceptual confluence joined the internationalist ethos of working-class solidarity in the Rivera murals at the height of the Depression, during ruling-class repression of workers' strikes, with the outpouring of solidarity on the floor of Rivera Court almost eighty years later in the context of the American wars in Iraq and Afghanistan and the ongoing conflict in Israel/Palestine. Different generations among the audience acted in concert to performatively decolonize the feminized world body of the Other and to create a new narrative on the body of the universal immigrant.

Mapa/Corpo uses ritual devices to create a sense of shared intimacy with both performers and fellow participants, thus creating a sense of collective agency. This shared sense of agency must be understood as a response to the grievances and claims of the tortured and oppressed as expressed through the bodies of the performers, underscoring the force of Gómez-Peña's claim that "our bodies are metaphors for the sociopolitical corpus."[22] Deploying our familiarity with documentary images to create palimpsests of those images that inform and haunt the arresting and constantly changing *tableaux vivants*, they leave the performative elements open ended and changeable. The emotional and embodied experience of ritualized participation creates a sense of living history whose outcome may yet be determined through the shared commitment and heightened political solidarity of communal experience.

The Grievable Body

When American editors were faced with the question of whether or not to publish the photographs of the gruesome killings of Blackwater mercenaries, known as "civilian contractors," in Fallujah in April 2004, they polled thousands of their readers about a particular photo taken by Khalid Mohammed for AP, which showed cheering Iraqis with two burned bodies hanging from a bridge. The response was mixed and represented opposing viewpoints:

"A lot of Americans do not understand why the military is in Iraq, and

I think this helps explain the necessity of a presence in Iraq," wrote Candice Tolman of Honolulu, Hawaii.

"The pictures should appear on the front page of every newspaper in the United States," said Charles Cavenaugh of Bend, Oregon. "A large number of people are supporting George Bush's war; let them see the results!"[23]

These two viewers read the picture of mutilated bodies and jubilant onlookers in diametrically opposed ways, according to larger political perspectives. For one, the picture appeared to confirm the Western orientalist stereotype of the East as barbaric, uncivilized, and in need of redemption by the West. It therefore seemed to "explain the necessity of a presence in Iraq." For the other, the picture appeared to demonstrate the justified rage and hatred felt by indigenous Iraqis whose country has been invaded and occupied by foreigners, putting Americans at dire and needless risk, with almost inevitable consequences, that nonetheless tend to be hidden from the American public, leading to the call to "let them see the results" of "Bush's war."

Charred and mutilated corpses hanging from a bridge over the Euphrates surrounded by jubilant Iraqis was a shocking picture for Americans, just as Canadian photographer Paul Watson's photos of dead American soldiers being dragged through the streets of Mogadishu, Somalia, in 1992, were shocking and led to the withdrawal of American troops. Americans were appalled at the horror of desecrated bodies from their "own" army because they are used to seeing themselves as victors, especially in third world and Middle Eastern countries, not as thoroughly vanquished and humiliated victims. But what do these pictures tell us about the political framing of the image? How does the horror of Fallujah offer simultaneous evidence of why the United States should and should not be in Iraq?

We might wonder how the people of Fallujah felt about the public mutilation of American bodies. There is plenty of evidence for popular outrage, however. An Iraqi journalist, Burhan Fasa'a, who worked for the Lebanese satellite TV station LBC and who was in Falluja for nine days during the most intense combat, told another reporter that Americans killed Iraqi civilians indiscriminately out of frustration when they could not speak English. "Americans did not have interpreters with them," Fasa'a said, "so they entered houses and killed people because they didn't speak English. They entered the house where I was with 26 people, and [they] shot people because [the people] didn't obey [the soldiers'] orders, even just because the people couldn't understand a word of English." He added, "Soldiers thought the people were rejecting their orders, so they shot them. But the people just couldn't understand them."[24] Unarmed civilians waving white flags were shot and tanks rolled over wounded civilians in the streets. Witnesses saw U.S. troops throw Iraqi bodies into the Euphrates River and helicopters fire on civilians trying to escape the carnage in the city by swimming across the river. Another witness noted, "They shot women and old men in the streets. Then they shot anyone who tried to get their bodies."[25]

In the photograph we see the jubilant faces of those near the burned and hanging torsos of the American mercenaries. They are mostly young men, some of whom raise their arms in victory gestures. One holds up a piece of paper with print we cannot make out and what seems to be a small image of a skull and crossbones. The photo might bring to mind the arrogant white faces in lynching photos or the grinning thumbs-up bravado in the Abu Ghraib photos. But Americans in Iraq do not occupy a position similar to that of blacks in the South, who never tortured southern whites, or destroyed their cities in the name of "liberation," nor are the Fallujans occupiers in another country. The Fallujah photo represents the culmination of a grossly mismanaged American occupation; the city became one of the main sites for the insurgency that spread to the rest of Iraq, and led to a failed American siege of the city in April 2004. This was followed by a week-long siege by Americans in November 2004 in which an unknown number of Iraqi insurgents and civilians died, the city was reduced to rubble, and 300,000 people became refugees in order to bring the destroyed city back under U.S. military control.

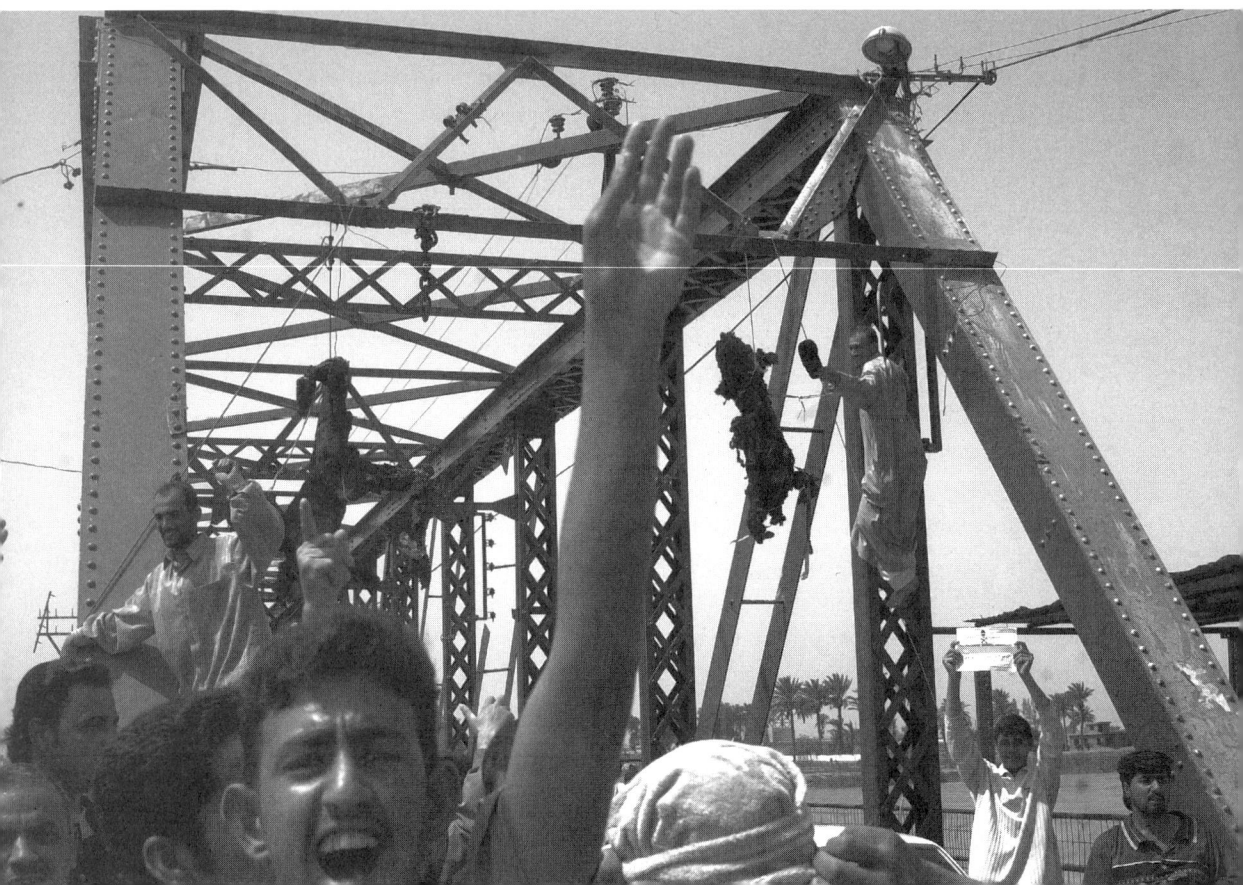

Figure 10. "Iraqis chant anti-American slogans as charred bodies hang from a bridge over the Euphrates River in Fallujah," 31 March 2004. (AP Photo/Khalid Mohammed.)

Fallujah had always been important as a crossroads city along the great desert highway that connected peoples in the Saudi, Jordanian, Syrian, and Iraqi deserts. It combined key religious, tribal, and nationalist aspects of Iraq's history. In addition, the killing of a British colonial officer by a local leader in 1920 sparked a great Iraqi revolt against the British, making Fallujah a symbol of resistance to foreign control up to the present day. The failure of the U.S. government to understand this history when it entered Fallujah led not only to control of the city at great political and human cost but helped produce the Iraqi quagmire that led to the assertion of American independence from international law on torture and open hostility to constraints on U.S. actions.[26] Fallujah was largely destroyed and its residents killed or driven out to become refugees. Like the bombing of Baghdad that began the war, the destruction of Fallujah was an anti-city strategy on a continuum with the tradition established during World War II of bombarding cities such as Guernica, Berlin, Hiroshima, and Nagasaki, and the more recent destruction of Gaza by Israel.[27] Yet many Americans, in a form of circular reasoning, pointed to the images of Fallujah and to the videotaped murders of Americans such as Daniel Pearl and Nick Berg, to suggest that such images and the events they represented constituted reasons for continued occupation and war, as if the United States were in Iraq on a "civilizing" mission, an unreconstructed colonialist perspective.

What American viewers rarely see in media outlets are the ongoing effects of the war and prolonged occupation. The American military does not count the number of Iraqi dead. These are not lives that are "grievable" in the American public sphere. Their lives do not count and therefore are not counted. This "prohibition on certain forms of public grieving itself constitutes the public sphere on the basis of such a prohibition," as Judith Butler asserts. "The public will be created on the condition that certain images do not appear in the media, certain names of the dead are not utterable, certain losses are not avowed as losses, and violence is derealized and diffused."[28] The Fallujah pictures are in part so shocking because the right to look at the tortured body under occupation, which has been denied to Americans by the state as a way of effacing the scale of the killing, has been captured and directed at the American body. That is, it is directed at the *coded* American body, which, regardless of the actual identity of those killed in Fallujah, is white, male, Christian, and grievable.

The Missing Body
British artist David Cotterrell spent a month in Helmand Province, Afghanistan, as a guest of the Joint Forces Medical Group for three weeks while he observed the work of military medical staff at Camp Bastion.

His official purpose was to produce photo documentation for the exhibition *War and Medicine* for the Wellcome Trust, a British charitable organization which presented the exhibition in London and Dresden. Cotterrell also kept a diary in which he tried to articulate the growing sense of shock and trauma that he experienced and the strain his absence created with his family. Writes Cotterrell about the latter: "I manage to ring home. Jordan seems tense and I struggle. I would love reassurance and warmth, but I sense her anxiety. She is worried about money. Struggling with the pressure of work and single parenting. I want her to feel supportive of me and to prop me up, indulging my angst with sympathy, but instead I realize how immersed I have become. Elijah is grumpy and angry that I am away. Kezia, as always, wants to tell me everything she can think of. I feel guilty. I am too far from home and too early in my trip to be able to offer reassurance, but I recognise my selfishness and it helps me to pull away from the self-righteous position that I have allowed myself to adopt."[29]

How many people in the military and their families are familiar with these feelings? Cotterrell and his family are contending with only a three-week absence while most confront an absence of a year or more, or they may never return except in a casket or with disabling wounds. In the United States, a novel form of imagery has been developed to staunch the longing for absent or dead family members who have gone to war. These are roughly life-size photographs known as Flat Daddies, represented from the waist up, or photos from shoulders up attached to sticks known as Heroes on a Stick. In a photo by Bridget Brown published in the *Bangor Daily News*, two boys, brothers, sit in the backseat of a car and have between them a smiling photographic cut-out of their father in army fatigues. He is a Flat Daddy, a U.S. soldier deployed in Iraq or Afghanistan. There are Flat Mommies too, available through a Flat Daddies website associated with a printing company in Ohio that provides them for $49.50. Children otherwise too young to remember what their fathers look like can recognize them when they come home on leave; Flat Daddy can always be there, even on a trip to the grocery store or at the breakfast table or in their room at night. Boys include Flat Daddy when they play with soldiers, indulging their idealizations of war and romantic fantasies about their mother's or father's role in it, or trying to psychologically defuse the apprehension they might feel. This portable simulacrum of the smiling soldier in uniform embodies not only the longed-for parent, but the romance of war. One boy in the Brown photo wears a camouflage pattern T-shirt while the other has an American flag on his T-shirt like the small flag on the sleeve of Flat Daddy. Each echoes the photo of their Flat Daddy, securely ensconced between them, signaling their identification

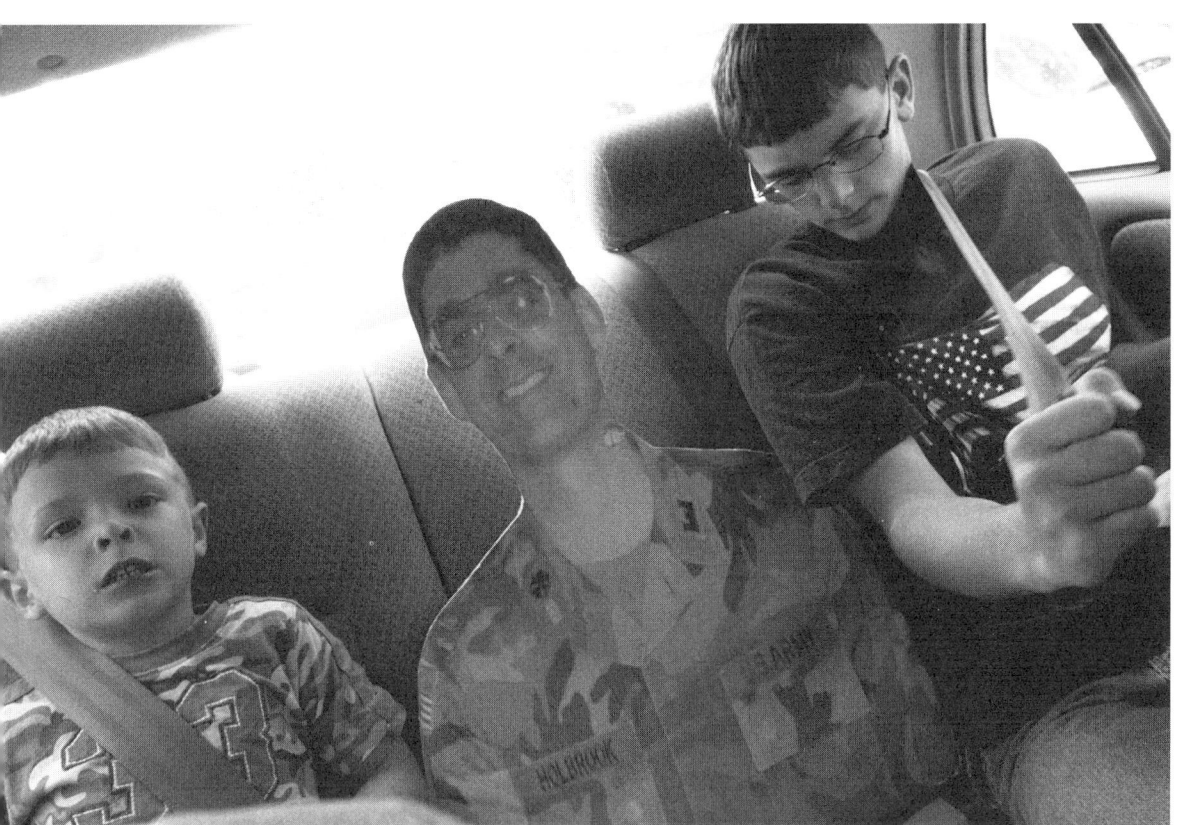

Figure 11. *Flat Daddy*, 2006. "Logan, 3, and Justin Holbrook, 14, rode to dinner with the life-size cutout of their father, Lieutenant Colonel Randall Holbrook, a Maine National Guardsman from Hermon, Maine." (*Bangor Daily News*/Bridget Brown.)

with and connection to their father as well as their emotional and psychological connection to his soldierly identity.[30] The identifying symbols help to prepare the next generation for the demands of current and future wars even as the military families recognize that their Flat Daddy only holds a place for the missing body.

Everyone associated with war is potentially traumatized, not only the families, but also the medical personnel who treat the wounded and the war photographers who document it. Dr. Mantador Taher was just finishing his medical training in Baghdad in 2003 when war broke out. In his essay for the *War and Medicine* catalog, he describes a bombing, the sounds of sirens getting louder and people screaming, "Open the hospital doors!"

> About two hundred wounded and dead people arrived at the hospital all at once. We had one emergency room, whose door fell off, and there were only about fifteen to twenty doctors in the hospital at that time. A horrible picture still sticks in my mind of people who were completely burned, people with no arms, people with their legs only attached to their body by a small piece of skin. I was shocked. The power went off, we were running out of medicine and fluids, the oxygen cylinders were empty, and it was extremely chaotic. By the end of that day it was quiet

again, but we had only been able to save a few people; most of them died because of the lack of fluids and resources to perform emergency operations.[31]

Doctors were threatened, kidnapped, or killed by militias and al-Qaeda or by desperate patients or their relatives in a fury over the inadequate care. Taher notes, "With a gun to my head, I gave 15 defibrillator shocks to a dead person because his son was convinced that this would bring him back to life. On another occasion, angry relatives tried to kill me with AK weapons because a member of their family, who had suffered a severe asthmatic attack, had died due to lack of oxygen and medication for his illness."[32] Many doctors fled the country, especially the more experienced ones, leaving junior doctors to cope with catastrophic conditions, a situation that only began to ease in late 2007 and 2008. This in part accounts for the many deaths among Iraqi civilians.

While the devastating power of weapons has increased, so has life-saving health care on the battlefield, which has driven medical advancements through many wars, including the Peloponnesian War that helped establish Hippocrates as the "father of medicine" because of his plague research conducted during that war.[33] The American Civil War led to the creation of the first ambulance corps, while the First World War introduced the Thomas splint, which reduced mortality due to compound fractures by 80 percent within two years; chemotherapy grew out of studies on the toxic effects of mustard gas. As a result of improved trauma care and body armor, nine out of ten soldiers survive in Iraq while 7.5 out of 10 soldiers survived in Vietnam. This advance, however, comes at a price. There are more seriously disabled veterans than ever before. Traumatic brain injuries, more than a thousand amputations (as of February 2008), and PTSD are higher than in any previous war, though this has fostered further research into prosthetics, rehabilitation, and greater recognition of mental-health issues.[34]

In Helmand Province, David Cotterrell records his guilt and anxiety and questions the usefulness of his role as artist-observer. As he is about to witness his first operation in the field hospital, he writes, "I have never been in the military and have never seen an operation. I am a trauma tourist desperately trying to justify my role—to others, but more difficultly—to myself." Following the operation and further traumatic injuries, he notes, "I feel dislocated and aimless. I am not certain if my anxiety comes from my ethical fears of delivering a facile response or from thwarting of adolescent fantasies. I am not certain of my own intentions." After a particularly horrific injury and surgery, he writes, "Fletcher is to remain sedated. I feel overwrought and tearful." Finally, he arrives at a rationale for his work: "I am constructing a logic for my presence, which involves attempting to document each state from arrival to repatriation. It is a tenuous logic but it helps me to justify my presence and provides a structure for my documentation."[35] The photos depict subdued doctors and nurses concentrating intensely on their work, helicopters arriving with the injured, and other scenes of the landscape and life at Camp Bastion. For the most part, Cotterrell abjures horrific shots of injuries during surgery, offering one or two that are riveting but quiet and contained, disappointing critics who expected the pictures to better reflect the diary extracts published in *The Guardian*.

Cotterrell later returned to Afghanistan as a civilian. Reflecting on his experience after his return to England, Cotterrell expressed disillusionment with what the camera could show and the views about war that he held before going to Afghanistan. If he thought, before going, that he would bring back dramatic views of the catastrophic impact of war on the human body, such imagery became incongruent with his own memories, which were framed by aesthetic and emotional distance. Failing to satisfy the desire for gory drama, Cotterrell wanted to convey another kind of truth: the silent and slow experience of isolation and disorientation that shapes the narrative of injury, and his own alienation from colleagues, friends, and family on his return to England.

Cotterrell ultimately traces his willingness to expose himself to the highly traumatic experience of a field hospital in Afghanistan—really, a tent in the desert—to his need to connect to the war experience of his grandfather, who was a Welsh working-class bomber in World War II, and a soldier deeply traumatized by the comrades he lost in burning planes. Eventually, Cotterrell's grandfather spoke about his experiences to his grandson, who understood himself to be both the repository for these memories and charged with the impossible burden of guilt and redemption for the past. Perhaps it was the guilt of survival on behalf of his grandfather, or guilt about a privileged life in which he was not commandeered into traumatic war experience. Keeping at bay his doubts and trepidation, Cotterrell volunteered not as a soldier but as a witness to the effects of soldiering. Selected by the Wellcome Trust from a short list of ten artists because of his previous bodies of work, which hint at war, aggression, absurdity, and remorse, Cotterrell was told that he was under no obligation to produce anything and was shown horrific photos of surgeries in advance of his deployment to acclimate him to the horrors. But nothing prepares one for the horrors. It is possible to detach from a photograph, to distance oneself, but you cannot anticipate, as Cotterrell points out, the buckling of your knees in the face of real torn flesh and splintered bone.[36]

How does one convey the interior trauma of disorientation and uncertainty? In *Serial Loop* (2007), Cotterrell creates a seamless and continuous loop of an arriving and departing Chinook helicopter along with images of a bleak desert landscape. His website (cotterrell.com) observes that "the banality of the film's fixed perspective masks the dramas that unfold within the ambulances as they travel to triage. A fire rages in the distance while antiquated ambulances lumber along to take wounded to treatment areas." The film is restrained, repetitive, seen from a distance, while masking the "dramas within." In *Theater* (2008), Cotterrell creates an immersive panoramic video projection on five screens that lasts for sixty minutes (ten minutes can be seen on his website) of an aeromed evacuation flight on a Hercules transport plane from the hospital at Camp Bastion to Kandahar. An injured body on a stretcher is surrounded by soldiers who sit and stand or walk about, performing various tasks or attending to the prone figure. Cotterrell creates from memory a simulation of a medical rescue, which serves to re-create the limbo of dread and anticipation central to the experience of witnessing combat trauma victims, who themselves remember little as they return to a civilian life of recovery and rehabilitation. The video across three walls in a darkened room, amid the constant noise, vibration, and motion, conveys a sense of suspension, indeterminacy, and liminal space. These are the kinds of experiences that constitute everyday life for the medical corps and for the wounded in the field, and that Cotterrell conveys in a decided rejection of anything that might romanticize war. Photographs of the operating theater take on the dramatic lighting, rich color, and heightened sense of reality of Rembrandt's *The Anatomy Lecture of Dr. Tulp* or Thomas Eakins's *The Gross Clinic*, or, in more contemporary terms, Gregory Crewdson's eerily staged photos. Yet in Cotterrell's work, the intensity and stillness suggest both a simultaneous inadequacy and excess of meaning.

Cotterrell describes his work as focusing on "the mundane, abstracted, and ambiguous experiences that remain un-newsworthy: the frozen, interminable, night-time evacuation flights, the uncertain waiting for casualties, the abstraction of trauma through codified military terminology, and the administrative burden of death and injury."[37] What Cotterrell experienced, along with many in the military, was "the collapse of the authority of the summary analysis," the profound gulf between how war is presented on the domestic front and how it is experienced in the field. In his analysis of his own responses, Cotterrell rejects the illusions of summary analysis offered through print and broadcast media as sensational images and conveys the altered consciousness that war trauma can produce: the need to subvert and complicate expectations already produced by the vast extant archive of war imagery. The strategies of distancing and restraint in his photos and videos attest to the effects of traumatic rupture.

The Wounded Body at Home

Nina Berman conveys the effects of war injury once veterans have been rehabilitated and return home, documenting the effects of war on the lives of maimed veterans whose dreams of a good life after military service have proven illusory. The photos of disabled veterans at home alone have been published as *Purple Hearts: Back from Iraq*, and are accompanied by statements from the veterans. Although there is no essay in *Purple Hearts*, the statement written by Berman to accompany the 2007 exhibition of the same title explains: "Since October 2003, I have been making portraits of American soldiers who were wounded in the

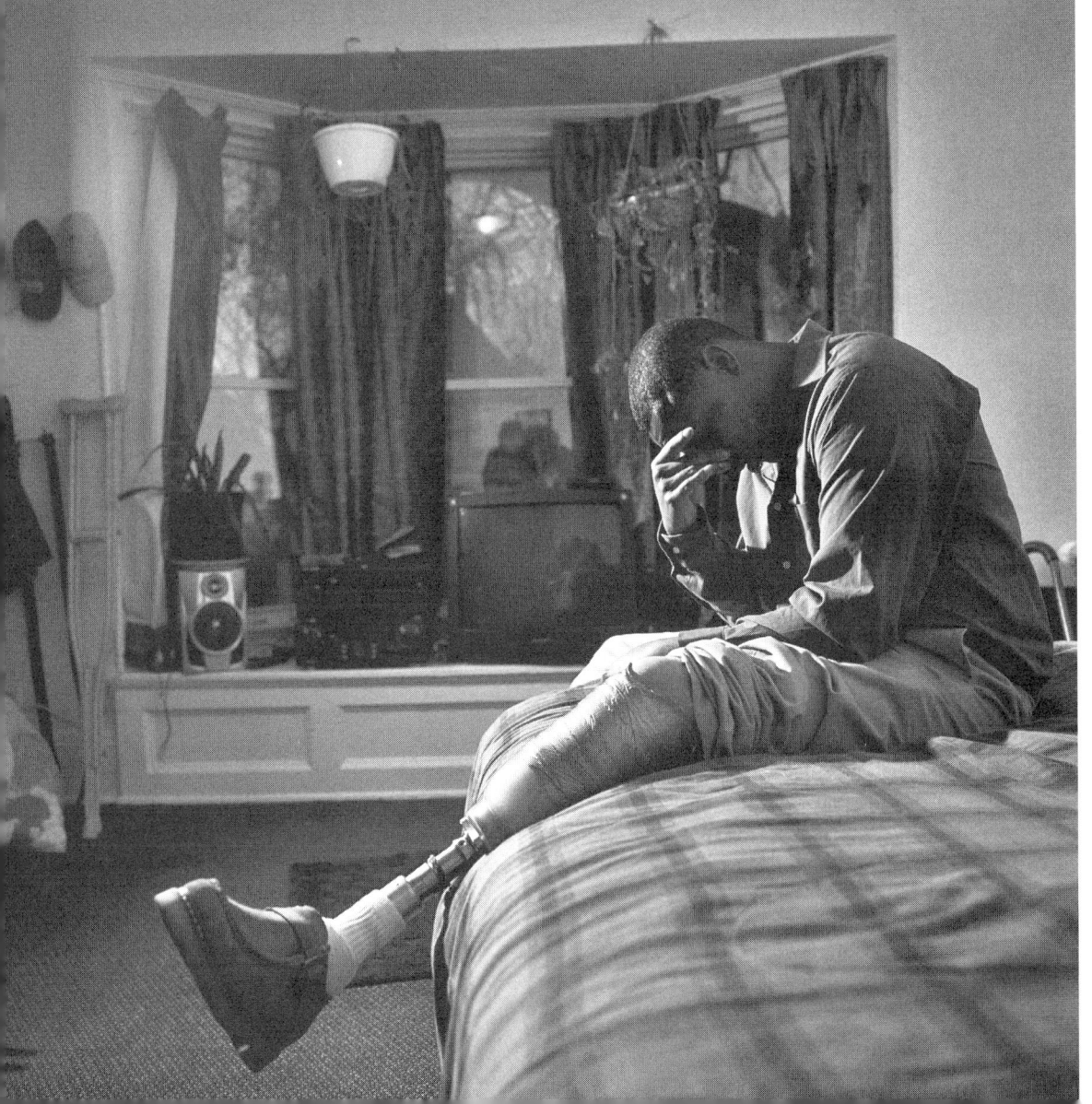

Figure 12. Nina Berman/NOOR, *Pfc. Alan Jermaine Lewis*, 2003, from series *Purple Hearts*. (Nina Berman/NOOR.)

Iraq War. I seek them out in their hometowns, after they have been discharged from military hospitals. I photograph them alone, mainly in their rooms, which to me feel like little cages. I strip them of patriotic colors and heroic postures. I see them alienated and dispossessed, left empty handed amid dreams of glory and escape."[38]

Berman's outraged agenda is clear: to "strip them" of pretensions to patriotic glory and heroism and reveal them as "alienated," "dispossessed," and "empty handed," left on their own in rooms that feel like "little cages." Berman echoes the idea of little cages by framing the photos in a square box format. The art critic Marcia Vetrocq is equally outraged, wondering whether Berman has posed her subjects according to her sense of their subjectivity rather than their own. Vetrocq asks, "Is there staging, not to mention exploitation, in 'stripping' the soldiers of signs of pride? Are the veterans really 'all alone,' or did Berman send the family from the room? Is there condescension in perceiving their homes (furnished with souvenirs, worn sofas, big-breasted pinups and hanging plants) as 'little cages'?"[39] For Vetrocq, it is important to foreground signs of pride, to consider the presence of other family members as evidence that the veterans are not really lonely or "alone," and to suppress signs of class condescension that might perceive working-class homes with "worn sofas" and "big-breasted pinups" as signifiers of being left "empty-handed." The photographer and the critic each prefer to see fixed a priori meanings produced by the photographs.

These fixed and conflicting meanings are what John Tagg might call the violence of meaning, produced by imposing a frame on which meaning must hang. The frame, in turn, is produced by the institutions and discourses that surround the image. We might see this as the discourse of the responsibility of the state, which is held accountable for the arrested development and truncated lives of the soldiers whom it uses up and spits out, versus the discourse of heroic individualism, which looks for signs of healing, hope, and hardiness as evidence that the free individual can transcend the most oppressive circumstances. This discourse of heroic individualism ultimately legitimizes a militarist ethos and is foundational to the liberal capitalist state.

Berman's images contrast markedly with portraits of disabled veterans taken by Timothy Greenfield-Sanders, in which Greenfield-Sanders more transparently poses and lights his subjects against monochrome white or black backgrounds in the same manner in which he takes glamorous celebrity portraits. These subjects are unambiguously hardy individualists. The photograph of Dawn Halfaker, for example, portrays an attractive and seemingly self-confident twenty-seven-year-old woman who squarely faces the camera in a sweater and jeans.

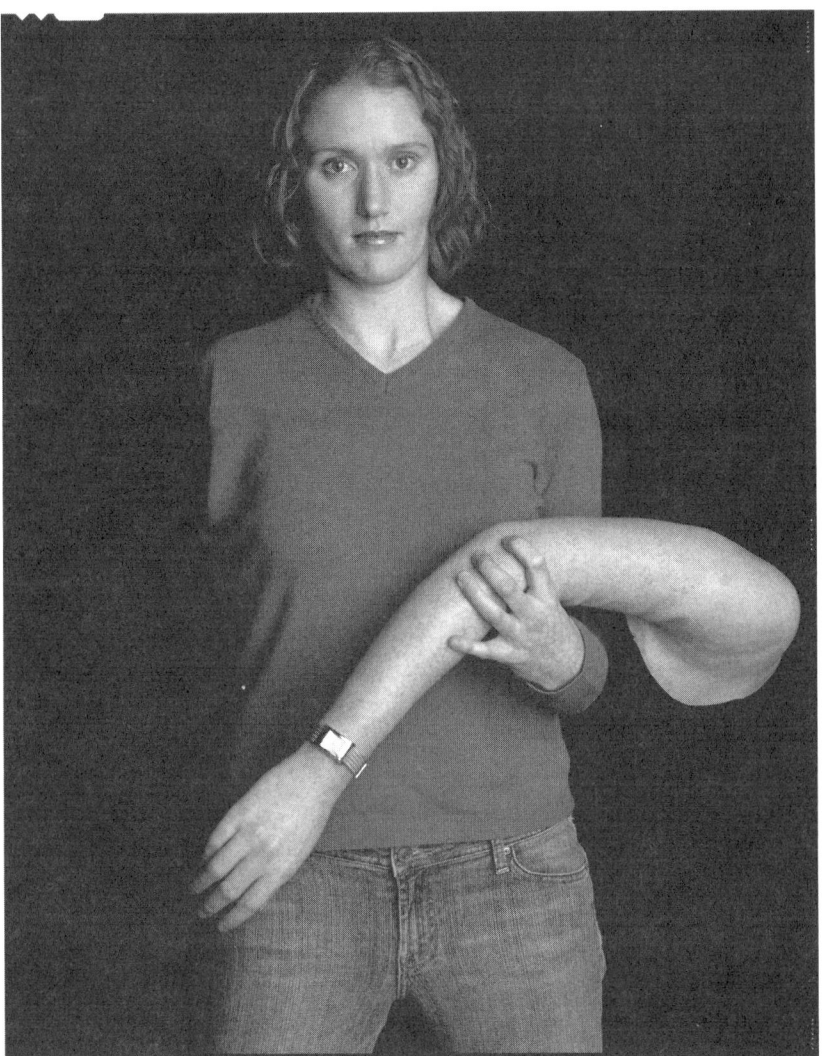

Figure 13. Timothy Greenfield-Sanders, *Dawn Halfaker, First Lt., U.S. Army*, 2006. (Courtesy of the artist.)

Unlike the veterans in Berman's portraits, she projects a strong sense of agency and self-possession. Halfaker lost her right arm in an explosion in Baqubah, Iraq, at the age of twenty-four. She holds a highly realistic looking prosthetic right arm across her torso with her left hand, almost defying the viewer to find her pitiable. A first lieutenant in the army, Halfaker was one of thirteen veterans interviewed by James Gandolfini for the HBO documentary "Alive Day Memories: Home from Iraq" aired in September 2007. An "alive day" is the day a soldier survives a traumatic injury. Greenfield-Sanders photographed each of the veterans, who first appeared in poster blow-ups on the street as part of an advertising campaign for the documentary. Proud and heroic, these are winning images, in the contest of images, which are regarded as most appropriate for dissemination on streets. Their real subject is the viewer who is recruited as a citizen and called to witness, in John Tagg's terms, at a time of crisis when national cohesion is needed.

The sense of heroic agency in Halfaker's visual portrait, however, is belied by the sense of loss, regret, and disillusionment with the romance of war that she registers in the brief telling of her story on the HBO website (hbo.com/aliveday). In the bio that records her place of birth, her injuries, her unit, and date of deployment, she says:

> I am in graduate school; I have a beautiful new condo in metro D.C. and I have a slew of friends who I trust and love and who make me laugh. However, through the windows of my "new" life, each day I find myself at one moment or another looking back at my service in the military and my injury, wondering how different, easy and wonderful my life would be like had I not become a product of the ravages of war. I could have gone to Yale. I could have branched—, rather than MP and sat behind a desk doing war-fighter's errands. My list of "I could be doing..." is quite long. And through my best efforts to skew my vision at something other than the past, I am reminded of it every day and every day it tears at my heart, mind and soul.

Even the photograph contains an excess that cannot be wholly contained. We see from the tension in the fingers of her left hand that her prosthetic arm is heavy and can guess that it is probably uncomfortable to wear, which she demonstrates for us by holding it instead of wearing it. This unwieldy false limb held between Halfaker and the viewer seems to embody the violent and traumatic experience that cannot be seen except as an absence where her real right arm used to be. Halfaker grasps her prosthetic limb like a burden she must carry, both as an emblem of her fortitude and a talisman against further incursions against her person. When later asked why she did not wear the prosthetic during the HBO interview, Halfaker replied: "I wanted to present myself to people as myself. I don't have an arm and to be quite honest I don't really wear my prosthetic that much: it's uncomfortable, it's cumbersome, it serves no function. When I talk about my experience I want it to be me. I want people to see me with one arm. Not wearing the prosthetic comes with the experience of moving on and being more comfortable with that. It's also being so busy and not having time for it."[40] The arm is not only awkward and heavy but "serves no function" and does not represent her. The relationship in the photograph between the tensed left-hand fingers and the permanently relaxed right hand sets up its own tension between the past, present, and future, marked by the ticking watch on the wrist. By placing the watch on the prosthetic arm instead of her "good" arm, the prosthetic becomes the carrier of time, a burdensome construct along with the burdensome arm. The removal of the arm suggests an open acknowledgment of the "ravages of war" and is a reminder of things "I could be doing," had she made different choices.

And yet, like most of the wounded veterans interviewed by Gandolfini for the HBO documentary, Halfaker asserted she would do it all again. Is she convinced, or is it part of the unscripted script for the heroic individual? When later asked why she had said she would do it again, Halfaker struggles to explain and instead talks about the support she received after the injury: "The big thing for me was getting a chance to see how many people care about you, are willing to support you and be your friend and be there for you, regardless of what you look like or what happens to you." She notes, "The tagline for the film is 'the fight has just begun.' And it really has in a lot of senses and it's not something we're ever going to really get used to." Thus the soldier must continue to "fight." This is not only the language of can-do American health jargon, but especially resonates for wounded combatants because to do anything other than "fight" would seem unpatriotic and un-American. "You can look back and say I learned so much, I grew so much," Halfaker continues. "Granted, on any day you could ask me would I trade all this to get my arm back and I would just say well you know I don't ever have to make that decision. That decision was made for me." The question, then, of choosing to do it again is finally rejected as a nonsensical question: there is no choice to be made after the fact. Halfaker admits that she never anticipated being wounded in combat and found it difficult to comprehend: "It didn't set in for me until I walked into a room [at Walter Reed] with 30 others amputees and thought, 'Oh my God, this is what's going on in this ward. This is the population of the world that I fall into.' This is a side they don't talk about, you don't know about even being in the military. I mean, anybody who thinks they know about combat before going into the military, they have no idea."[41] According to sources such as about.com and antiwar.com, the official count of wounded U.S. soldiers in Iraq as of December 2010 was almost thirty-three thousand, a number that excludes soldiers with psychological trauma.

Suzanne Opton's photographic project *Soldier* alludes exclusively to psychological trauma. Her subjects are all young, active-duty soldiers serving in Iraq and Afghanistan whose photos are taken close up, with their heads resting on tabletops. With only their heads and necks visible, they appear strangely vulnerable, their eyes dazed, ruminative, serene, shocked, or vacant, yet palpably close and intimate. The photos were presented as billboards (*Soldier Billboard Project*) with the word SOLDIER in the dark blue space above or to the right of the heads along with a web address for her blog on soldiers. Although shown in nine American cities from 2008 through 2010, the billboards at first provoked controversy when the company that owned the billboards in Minneapolis and St. Paul, where Opton planned to show five of the images during the Republican National Convention, abruptly canceled the contract, having decided that the images were an inappropriate representation of American soldiers. Many suspect this was a response to Republican pressure.[42] Opton notes, "I've been asked why anyone would want to be photographed in this position—as if they were dead. Although I don't know the answer to that, I surmise that these soldiers went along with my request because it resonated with them. They must think about dying all the time."[43] In these works, Opton deals only with the kinds of psychological affect and injury that are difficult to picture.

Nina Berman's most haunting work addresses the profound effects of physical injury and its cultural construction as heroic in the photograph of Sergeant Ty Siegel and Renee Kline taken on their wedding day, originally commissioned to accompany a story by *People* magazine, for which Berman won the 2007 *World Press Photo* competition. The photo is from the eighteen-part series *Marine Wedding* that was shown at the 2010 Whitney Biennial. Those photographs, produced in 2006 and 2008, tell a story about Marine Sgt. Ty Ziegel, who was severely injured in a 2004 suicide bomber's attack near his truck during a routine patrol. It was his second tour of duty in Iraq. The bomb's explosion trapped Ziegel in a ball of fire. "I was rolling around on the bed of a truck, yelling the whole time I was conscious," he relates. "The guy next to me kept putting me out—I guess I kept relighting."[44] He was in a coma for the next few months and was blinded in one eye, lost part of his left arm, fingers on his right hand, and most of his face, which melted in the extreme heat of the explosion along with most of the skin on his body. He underwent fifty reconstructive surgeries and his skull was so badly shattered that it was replaced with a plastic dome with holes where his nose and ears used to be. He was in Brooke Army Medical Center in Texas for nineteen months. His high school girlfriend Renee Kline, to whom he had gotten engaged before his second tour of duty, helped care for him, and when he returned home in 2006, Ty, then twenty-six years old, and Renee, almost twenty-one years old, got married.

Berman accompanied the couple to a commercial portrait studio for their formal wedding portrait in a small rural farm town in Illinois. Before the wedding photographer stepped up, Berman took her own photograph. In some respects it is a traditional wedding photograph, except for the fact that Ty Ziegel, decked out in his decorated Marine uniform, is in no respect an ordinary groom. He stands at an angle to the camera, gazing downward toward his bride's hands, which hold her bridal bouquet of scarlet roses. A single white flower sits at the center of the bouquet like a sprout of hope in

Figure 14. Nina Berman/NOOR, *Marine Wedding*, 2006, from series *Marine Wedding*. (Nina Berman/NOOR.)

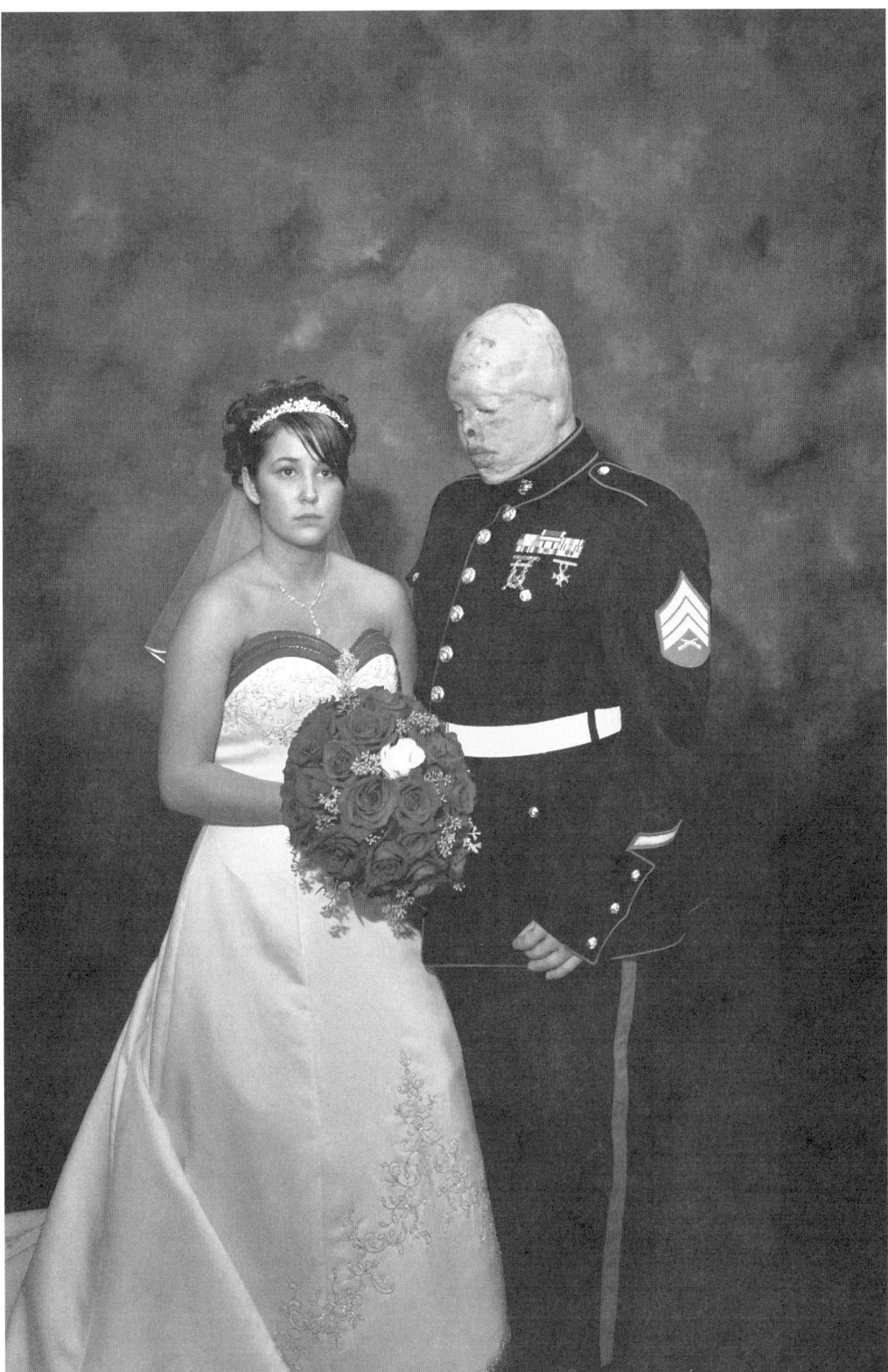

a circle of blood. The reconstructed mass of pinkish flesh that constitutes Ty Ziegel's head looks barely human, almost monstrous.

But this is not what is most shocking about the photo. Rather, it is Renee Kline, the small-town girl on her wedding day, who stands in her bridal finery, a white dress with scarlet trim to coordinate with her bouquet, her diamond tiara and matching necklace, her massed curls atop her head and small veil at the back, like a young bride who has pored over bridal magazines and imagined the perfect wedding. Renee Kline does not smile, or even look content, let alone happy. She stares off into some sobering vision of the future that brings no joy to her face, and it is clear that this is not the dream wedding for which she had planned. None of this is surprising. What is shocking about this photo is that she is there at all. Never has a groom and bride looked more alienated from each other. Renee looks numb or in shock, as if she was the one recovering from some recent traumatic experience. Her mind appears to be somewhere else. Ty's face is altogether unreadable, its normal elastic qualities destroyed.

Berman attempts to counter this reaction to the photograph, the apparent alienation they exhibit and the pity the portrait seems to evoke. She explains that the couple was hung over from heavy drinking the night before. Yet this bit of knowledge only adds to the pathos of the wedding portrait. Ty and Renee each seem not so much to be suffering the effects of a hangover as to be profoundly alone. Berman recognizes this. "I realized when I took this picture," she said, "that sometimes you can show being alone much better when there's another person in the frame."[45] Three months later, Ty Ziegel and Renee Kline divorced.

The photos leading up to the wedding include one of Ty seated outdoors while Renee stands behind him holding a bottle of water and gazing at his shattered hand; in a candy store, a little girl stares transfixed at Ty's face; Ty with his arms around Renee and seemingly smiling as she looks off into the distance. None of the photos show them looking at each other or in the direction of the camera. It is as if they do not wish to be seen being seen. The tension in the wedding photo is present in these photos too and only dissipates in the photos taken after the divorce, which show Ty alone at home or with his mother dispensing his medications in the kitchen, or Ty standing in his home holding a rifle aimed at the ceiling. This is the only photo in which his face appears almost human again. It seems to convey his continuing identification with and comfort in military culture, despite the devastating personal costs.

The traumatized disabled vets and their traumatized intimate partners are a permanent part of the postwar American landscape. Their visibility through Berman's documentary practice does not call a national patriotic audience into place; on the contrary, the benevolent, impartial, paternalistic state implicitly constructed by Greenfield-Sanders's "alive day" portraits is here implicitly represented as both utterly disruptive to "normal" civilian life and severely indifferent to that disruption. The wedding is transformed into a painful ritual of embarrassing formality while the scenes of the couple at home are a kind of mockery of the nostalgic idea of the American dream. Marriage and war are conjoined, not as the twin tropes of bourgeois democratic ideation, but as dual catastrophes.[46]

The Iconic Body

Public images, while historically specific to any given moment, often echo earlier representations and are constructed according to a long-standing range of conventions. Later images often achieve a certain cultural resonance by virtue of this echoing pattern, as W.J.T. Mitchell has shown in *Cloning Terror*, Stephen Eisenman in *The Abu Ghraib Effect*, and Robert Hariman and John Louis Lucaites in *No Caption Needed*, all in different ways. Write Hariman and Lucaites, "The circulation of images is indeed a fundamental characteristic of modern civilization, as is the remediation of the form and contents of earlier media in their successor technologies."[47] We can see this remediation, for example, between the outstretched arms of the Hooded Man of Abu Ghraib and the outstretched arms of the napalmed girl running down a road in Saigon, the iconic photo of the Vietnam War taken by Nick Ut. While the photographers of the Abu Ghraib photos (there was more than one) may not have consciously imitated the Nick Ut photo as the camera phone picture was snapped, this image was likely to be stored unconsciously in their mental archive; but even if it was not, the convention of the suffering figure with outstretched arms has a longer cultural history than this, one that gave the Nick Ut photo its resonance, too, which stretches back to the figure of the crucified Jesus and has been visually represented thousands of times.

Polish-born American artist Ewa Harabasz makes visible the effects of such remediation by combining photojournalistic images of contemporary war and suffering with painting techniques that emulate the aesthetic of medieval devotional icons, the International Gothic style of the late Middle Ages that introduced secular life into religious scenes, or the dramatic *tenebroso* lighting and radical naturalism of Caravaggio. Harabasz's paintings/photo collages draw on both contemporary photojournalism and artistic conventions more than five hundred years old to create images for contemplation in a secular world. As deliberately false religious images, they both display and subvert the conventions and sentiment that are the language of religiosity, demanding a more critical response to the visual protocols that turn hapless victims of violence and war into pietàs and Madonnas on the front pages of many newspapers.

Harabasz's works succeed because these conventions are familiar and comforting ways of picturing misery and suffering which are always already premediated for us by a long history of suffering figures. Plucked from the visual landscape of the mass media, the images in Harabasz's paintings become icons of "beautiful suffering" and suggest that some documentary practices are no more or less a "style" than the conventions of earlier forms of representation.

In her painting of a soldier and child, for example, Harabasz renders the image of rescue as a modern-day Madonna and child with a gender role reversal. The work is a contemporary icon, surrounded by gold, in which a soldier advances toward the viewer holding a small boy. Yet the halo that circles the soldier's head doubles as a rifle scope. The photo is from the Beslan school hostage crisis of 2004, when Chechen rebels seized a school in Russia's North Ossetia region that resulted in a shootout with Russian security forces and left 344 people dead, 186 of them children, and hundreds more wounded. Another nimbus surrounds the head of the child. The life-size scale of the work positions the viewer at the other end of the projected riflescope and we are suddenly in the midst of the uncertainty and danger that characterizes the modern condition, the precariousness of "sacred life." Harabasz renders the images of suffering as both more beautiful and more troubling.[48]

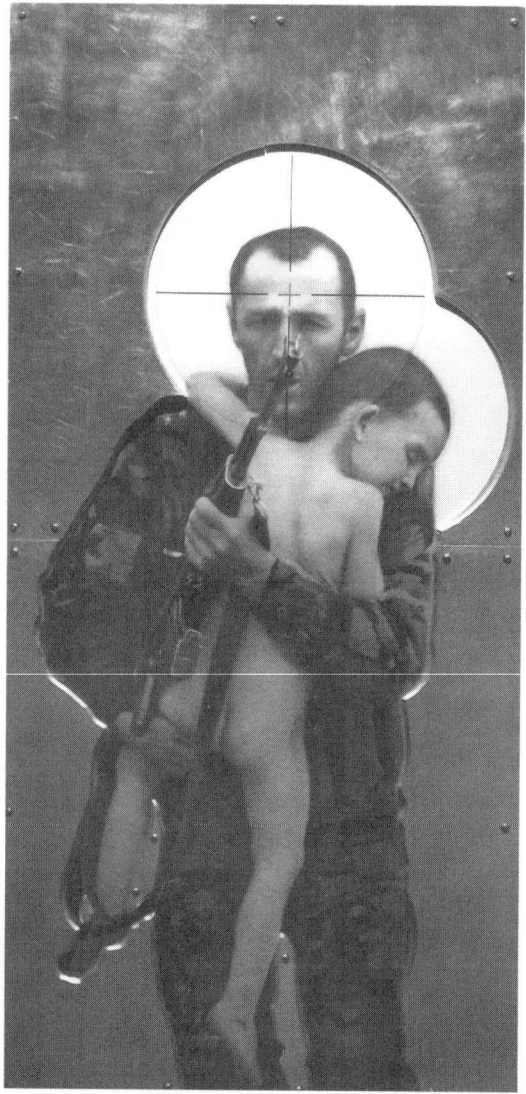

Figure 15. Ewa Harabasz, *Untitled*, 2005–2006, wooden panel, digital print, gold leaf, oil paint on canvas. (Signum Foundation Collection, Poznan, Poland.)

Political scientist Mark Reinhardt and art historians Holly Edwards and Erina Duganne, in their catalog for the exhibition *Beautiful Suffering*, address the long-standing censure of beauty in images of pain, despite the persistent presence of such images, which have been central to representation, in different forms, at least since the invention of Greek tragedy. "Without scenes of death, destruction, misery, and trauma," the editors suggest, "the contemporary image environment would be nearly un-

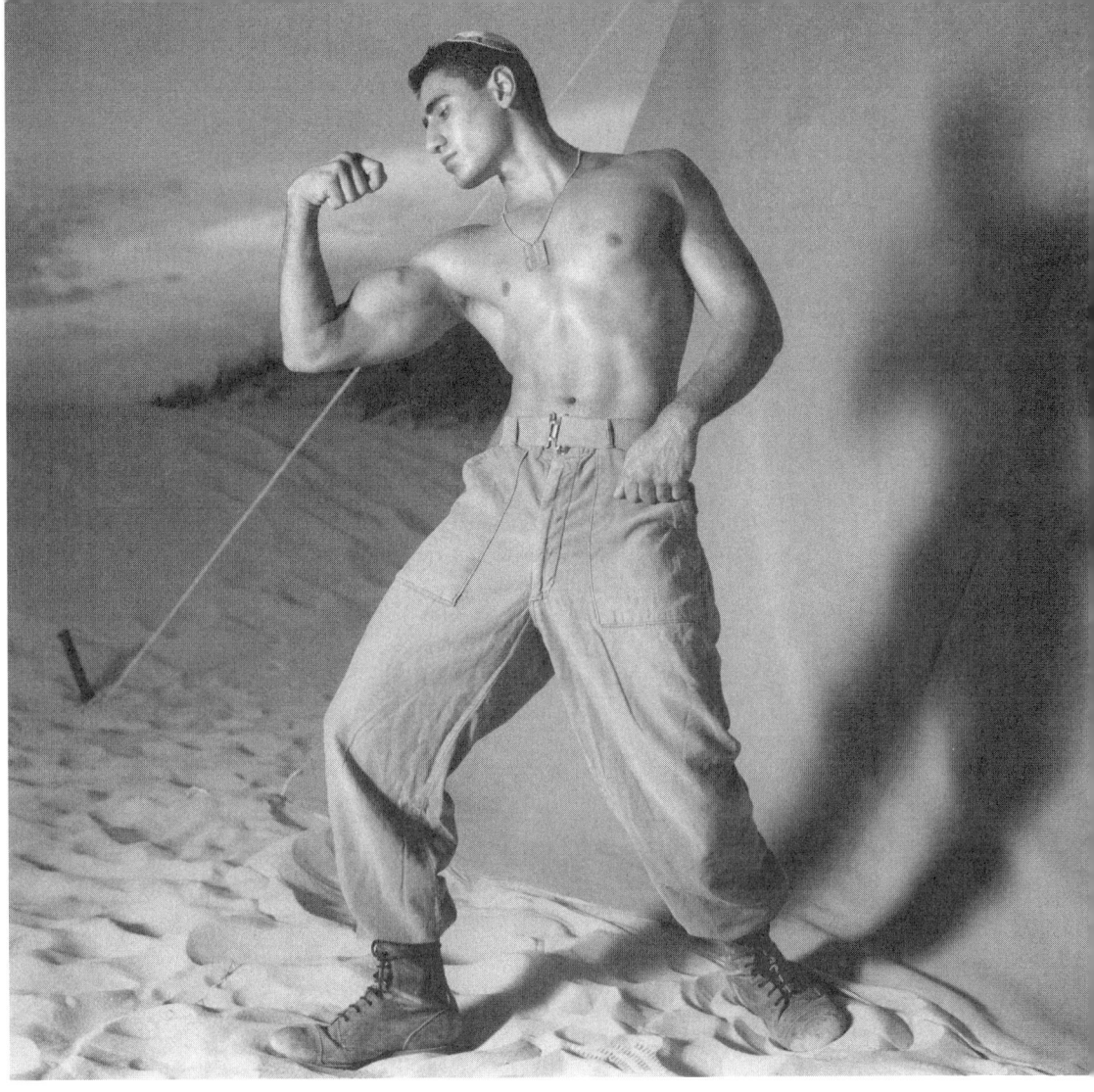

Figure 16. Adi Nes, *Untitled*, 1996. (Courtesy of Jack Shainman Gallery.)

recognizable."⁴⁹ In his introduction, Reinhardt argues against the anxiety of aestheticization that still makes documentary images of suffering suspect for some, which is different from the myth of "disinterestedness."⁵⁰ Reinhardt asserts that the aestheticization critique, which has become academically entrenched, is a "blunt instrument" and that the problems of representation should not lead us to a position that condemns any formal content in images of suffering. Without aesthetic choices to make the image bearable, the viewer would look away. In a review of *Beautiful Suffering*, David Levi Strauss observes, "This censure of beauty in the depiction of suffering is never applied to music, and seldom to literature or painting, but often to photography."⁵¹

Another artist who has relied on remediation of religious imagery to address contemporary life is Tel Aviv–based photographer Adi Nes, the son of Iranian and Kurdish parents who immigrated to Israel in the 1950s from Iran. Nes grew up in the immigrant community of Kiryat Gat, feeling further marginalized as an Eastern-derived (Mizrachi) gay man who did not fit the mythologized Israeli stereotype of the macho sabra, the Israeli-born New Jew constructed as a powerful warrior. The European-derived (Ashkenazi) sabra was meant to compensate for and expiate the memory of the "lamb-to-the-slaughter" stereotype of the weak diaspora Jew, who died by the millions in the Holocaust. At times composing his images with a dramatic contrast of light and shadow inspired by Caravaggio, or the forms of Michelangelo, Nes deflates the stereotyped opposition between the classically idealized heterosexual male body and the gay body by explaining that he was influenced by "gay artists or people considered to be gay—Leonardo, Caravaggio, Pasolini, Michelangelo."[52] In the 1980s, when Nes began making his images, homoerotic imagery was scarce in Israel, and homosexuality, seen as antithetical to the national myth of the sabra, was not openly discussed.

Nes's most well known photograph was made into an advertising poster that was placed in the New York subways for an exhibition at New York's Jewish Museum in 1998. Evoking both Greek sculpture and a strongman pose, the photograph pictures an olive-skinned, bare-chested, muscular soldier who stands in profile outside an army tent in a performative gesture of masculinity. Feet apart, he flexes his massive bicep. The nocturne is lit by a hidden spotlight that creates a soft, diffused light, focusing our attention on the hard male body atop the soft white sand, the tiny crocheted yarmulke (skull cap) on his head, the tent rope parallel to his body and seeming to bisect his bicep. The beauty of the male body emanates from the pose, yet the stereotype of the macho hero is undermined by the dark skin, cast shadow, and homoerotic overtones. Nes is primarily concerned with the treatment of Jewish ethnic minorities within Israel, the presence of Mizrachi men, and issues of masculinity. His focus on Israeli identity is centered on the crucible in which "Israeliness" is forged: the army, in which all Israeli citizens are required to serve and to meet the physically perfected warrior ideal of the sabra. The sabra in turn represents the Zionist reembodiment and transformation of the weak, effeminate diaspora Jew; he personifies "Judaism with muscles."[53] Nes playfully subverts that ideal with the image of dark-skinned homoerotic masculinity, drawing it from the repressed periphery to center stage. In her study of the Zionist body, Meira Weiss demonstrates that the ideal Israeli male is not only tall, white, with blue eyes and light-colored hair, but that this model is systematically cultivated through premarital and prenatal screening as well as liberal abortion practices in cases of fetal defects that are easily remedied, such as cleft lip. It amounts to a form of "eugenics turned into a selective prenatal policy backed by state-of-the-art genetic technology," and makes Israel "the world leader in the proportion of children who are rejected for physical flaws."⁵⁴

In Nes's version of a pietà, based on Giovanni Bellini's 1505 *Pietà*, a wounded IDF soldier lies in the lap of another soldier, a paramedic who tenderly cradles his wounded comrade's head and ministers to him, not by applying medical aid but by shaping the image and perception of masculinity. In one hand, the "paramedic" holds a makeup brush; an open makeup box, like a painter's palette, lies next to the "wounded" man's body, demonstrating the artifice and construction of all soldierly images, which are premediated in poses familiar from religious and classical imagery, here satirically revealed and focused on the construction of masculinity as a carefully designed product. The painted "wound" evokes the cut made by the sword of a Roman soldier in the chest of Jesus on the cross, mapping the sacrifice of the soldier onto that of the martyr and undermining it at the same time. One critic notes, "War is the new religion, and every soldier is a Christ."⁵⁵ In many of his images of soldiers, Nes conveys a sense of innocence and vulnerability as well as sensual youth and beauty, like an unwitting new breed of "lambs to the slaughter."

Nes produced a series of images commissioned by *Vogue Hommes* for their 2003–2004 winter edition dedicated to the Middle East. Ethnic and homoerotic tensions become subtexts for his photographic statements about fashion staged in another decidedly charged Israeli setting related to military life, that of the prison. Although editors asked that the works not be political, Nes posed and photographed his models, who were not professionals, in a fake prison setting, where they assumed the characters of prisoners and guards. In one photo a dark-skinned youth (a Palestinian boy from Jaffa) defiantly confronts a taller, more confident Israeli guard. The youth wears an expensive leather jacket, the guard designer shades, but in this context, their differing social and political status affects how we perceive what they are wearing. As one reviewer notes, the Valentino leather jacket looks like it might have been picked up at a flea market.⁵⁶ While serving on reserve duty in the Ketziot Prison in Ansar during the first Intifada (Palestinian uprising), Nes himself spent time as a guard of Palestinian prisoners. Nes became friendly with and was attracted to a Palestinian prisoner, producing a traumatic and conflicted experience that inspired this work. Nes says of his *Vogue Hommes* photographs, "I tried to express the idea that whenever you put a fence around the other, surround him with high walls, you put yourself in a prison as well." Nes speaks for many in expressing his conflicted views about the Israeli/Palestinian conflict, embodying both a democratic impulse and an Israeli nationalist perspective on Israel as a Jewish state: "I don't believe in occupation. But I can't run out from my duty because I am a good Israeli

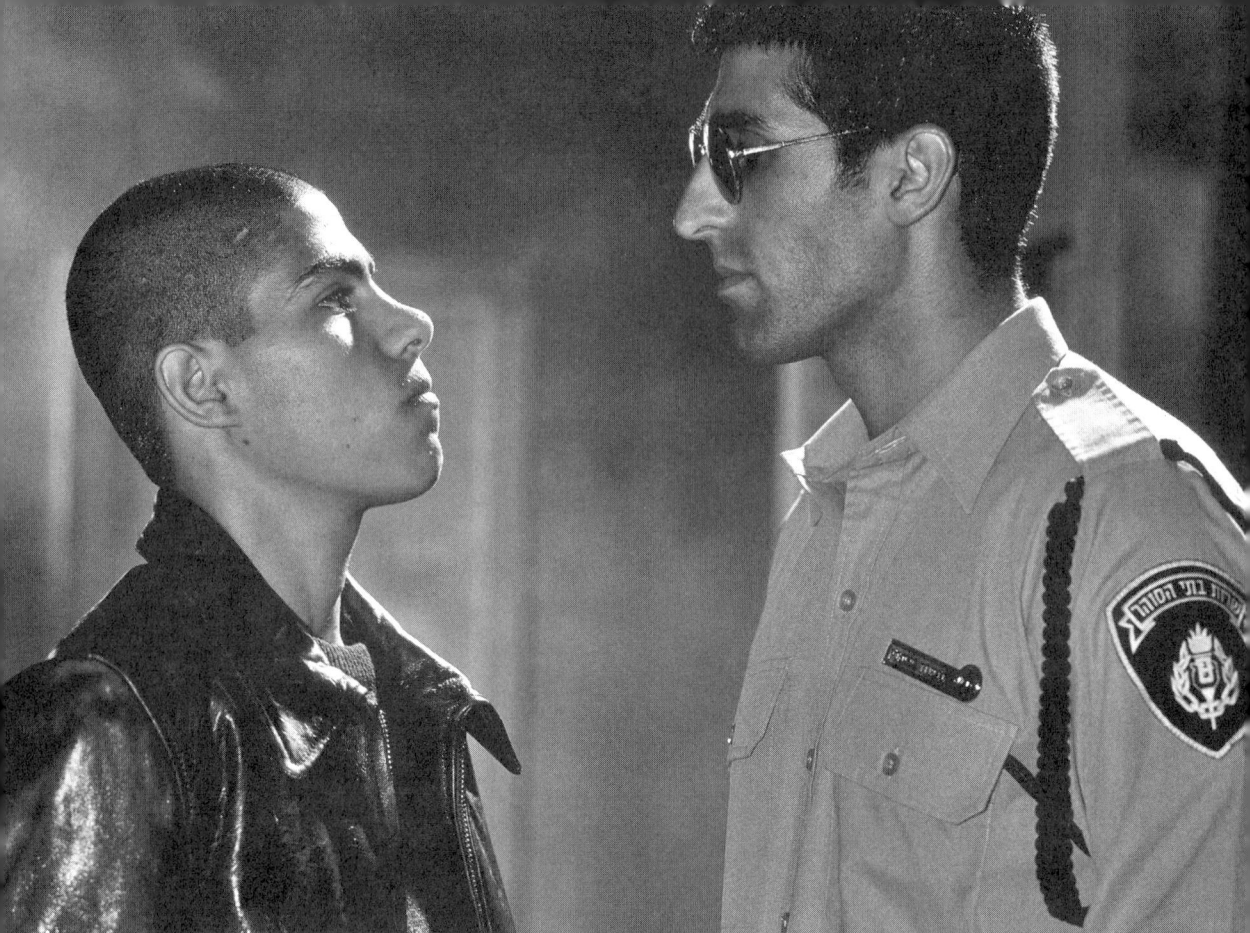

Figure 17. Adi Nes, *Untitled*, 2003, from series *Prisoners*. (Courtesy of Jack Shainman Gallery.)

citizen and know we are fighting for our lives. It's not by accident that these people are in prison. They want to kill us. . . . It's a very complex situation. You have to know how to live together with your neighbors. You have to be smart. You have to be sensitive to the other. And sometimes you have to give more than you think you have to, just to live in peace."[57]

In another photo by Nes, three Chinese workers dressed in matching red outfits by designer Paul Smith are lined up against a concrete wall with small windows at the top. Here the outfits seem to become prison uniforms and the photo comments on the prisonlike conditions in which such imported workers, many from mainland China, live in Israel and their treatment by immigration police. Nes also refers to the prisonlike factories in the Far East where workers labor under highly exploitative conditions. Regarding his compositional concerns, Nes observes, "I wanted to shoot red, and I had Barnett Newman's painting 'Who's Afraid of Red, Yellow and Blue?' in mind. Who's afraid of the yellow people? Why do you imprison them?"[58] Nes uses the prison as a metaphor for Israeli society, complicating the erotic, psychological, and political relationships among ethnic groups in Israel, including the dominant Ashkenazim, in an attempt to "voice the identity of the Sabra other."⁵⁹ His work reifies, complicates, and undermines the mythologized image of the heroic sabra, the masculine counterpart to the feminized diaspora Jew. Constructed as a fashion model, the sabra is both an object of desire and a subject of critique.

We conclude with the work of Martha Rosler, whose political work in the last forty years has been seminal in making visible the corporate drives of the capitalist state, and for whom the iconic American body is also the fashion model. Rosler presents the acute artifice of cultural fashions and their ideological underpinnings through elaborately staged scenes produced through the use of photomontage. The technique seamlessly combines found photographic images to create new meaning in the politically satirical tradition of German artist John Heartfield, who is best known for skewering the Nazis in his caustic montages. Rosler demonstrates the ways in which the "good life" in America depends upon the criminal activity of the U.S. government abroad. Like Heartfield, Rosler lampoons class privilege and its dependence on imperialist America's exploitation of resources abroad, leading to wars such as the one in Iraq. Her reimagined *Bringing the War Back Home* series, begun in 2004 in response to the U.S. invasions of Iraq and Afghanistan, continues her critique of capitalist war culture and globalization first produced in *Bringing the War Back Home: House Beautiful* (1967–1972) in response to the American war in Vietnam. In the new series she combines war imagery with glossy fashion imagery that implies an American war culture oblivious to the real costs of war. Unlike the Vietnam War series, which was originally produced in color but photocopied in black and white for distribution at demonstrations and in the underground press, these new photomontages take advantage of the publicity and distribution networks of the art world, forcing agitprop and fine art into "strategic alliance."⁶⁰ These works, color cut-and-paste images produced as larger digital prints, are shown in commercial galleries, print media reproduction, and small posters. Technology may be updated in war as in art, but Rosler's revived series recalls a history of U.S. military arrogance and aggression that has not changed at all in thirty years.

The 2004 series focuses on the militarization of everyday life, the violence and chaos of war, and the traumatic effects on soldiers, even as it shows how a streaming consumer culture obscures these conditions. Now, instead of Vietnamese refugees and maimed children haunting American domestic interiors, it is Iraqi orphans, the tortures of Abu Ghraib, and American GIs playing at being terrorist "gladiators" that haunt their well-appointed homes. *Saddam's Palace* (Febreze) combines an image of the bombed-out palace of Saddam Hussein with stills of a housewife who moves from spritzing her sofa to spraying the devastation of the palace with her bottle of fabric freshener, taken from a Febreze commercial. If only it were so easy to undo the destruction. In *Photo Op*, the duplicated image of a fashionable young woman enchanted with her cell phone camera is oblivious to the dead woman and child in her modernist living room, not to mention the war raging beyond her windows. Despite the digital era, we seem unable to communicate effectively across national and ethnic borders; the American user is blissfully unaware of what is going on beyond the boundaries of her privileged life, and the relation of domestic technology to war remains invisible to her, though we, as viewers, are invited to make that connection.

Invasion (2008) depicts the avatars of virtual capitalism and global exploitation. The photomontage represents several small tanks on burning streets with the entire area aflame in red and yellow explosions. A small sign in Arabic at the lower left (advertising a car repair workshop nearby) positions us in Iraq or Afghanistan. An army of young men identically uniformed in black suits march toward the viewer. Their hair is carefully parted and pomaded into pompadours, their mien is unswervingly intent, they wear skinny pencil ties and their shoes are shiny lizard or snakeskin, with three of them ending in sinister points like metal blades. The men are like replicants or apparatchiks but sleekly outfitted in Dolce & Gabbana couture.[61] The West prides itself on its fashion sense but the irony is that they all look the same, like an army of Harvard lawyers or investment bankers, upper-class playboys and privileged sons, the newly romanticized admen of the fifties, or new Young Republicans in sixties' Beatles suits. They are the next generation of the corporate elite, the drones of capitalism, the occupying army that stands behind the working-class grunts in fatigues, who exist as virtual capitalists with no sense of the real world. Performance artist Guillermo Gómez-Peña observes, "One of the scariest features of virtual capitalism is that it is run mostly by guys in their 20s and early 30s. These young millionaires are determining the new terms (or lack thereof) of our social contract, and the fundamental characteristics of our new culture.... Since the geography they inhabit is largely virtual, they have no sense of belonging to any community in reality other than their own corporation.... The great paradox is that virtual capitalists don't see themselves as conservative. On the contrary, they define themselves as carriers of the torch of 'a new revolution,' and holders of true 'alternative lifestyles.'"[62]

Rosler presents a surreal vision, a higher reality, in which corporate aspirations at home and the war abroad are creepily conjoined. Rather than picturing the domestic invaded by war, here Rosler brings the homefront

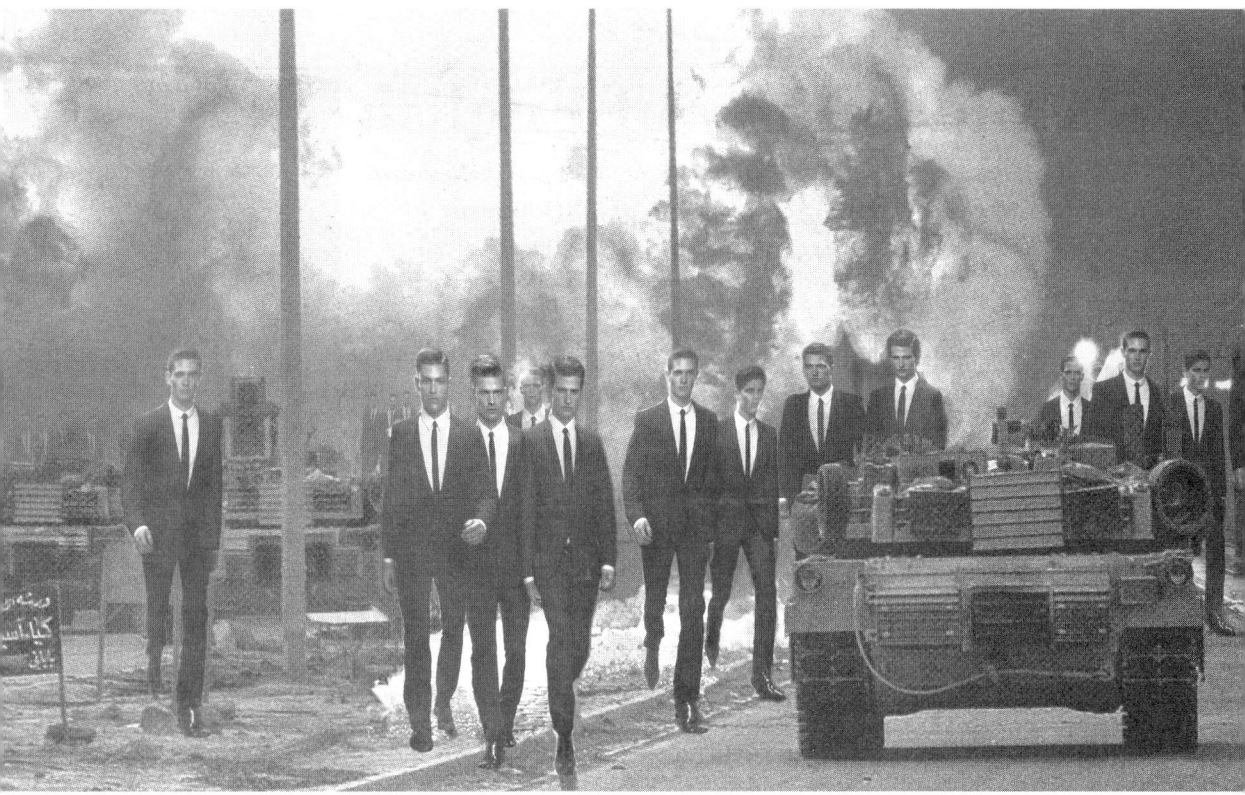

Figure 18. Martha Rosler, *Invasion*, 2008, photomontage. (Courtesy of the artist.)

to the battlefield. In the process she creates a seamless cinematic space that aligns fantasies of American military power and world dominance with popular military and sci-fi films that pit good against evil in ways that usually have satisfying endings. The portents of this scenario, however, are both faintly ridiculous and weirdly chilling as we gaze at these baby-faced masters of the universe, the Manchurian candidates whose personas seem to remain unchanged through decades of neocolonialist wars.

If military technology can be domesticated, like Humvees, which are a vehicle of choice for the domestic wealthy elite, the domestic can also be weaponized. These young unarmed corporate soldiers, embodying the political corpus of their class, are still shiny with certainty in their values and seem dangerously oblivious to the missiles exploding behind them, or worse, they emerge from that inferno eerily unscathed by the destruction they wreak as though blissfully protected by a greater controlling power they never imagine may one day crack. In a radical critique of capitalism and U.S. foreign policy, *Invasion* attends to the way the corporate elites profit from the suffering and destruction they produce, rising like the undead from the fiery inferno they have created.

PART III

THE **LANDSCAPE** OF **WAR**

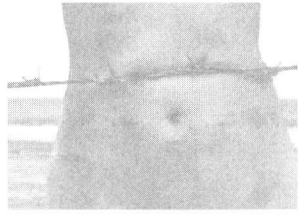

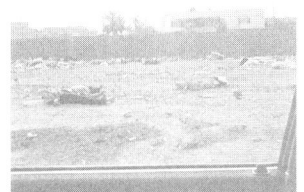  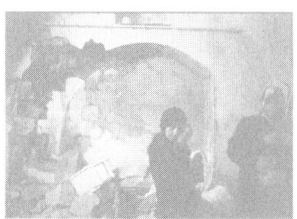

5

CONTROLLING THE FRAME: PHOTOJOURNALISM, DIGITAL TECHNOLOGY, AND "MODERN WARFARE"

I have been defining the public sphere as "the spaces, sites, and technologies available for public discourse that is critical of the state," in Peter van der Veer's terms, but with a focus on its constitution through documentary practices of visual representation that call into place a shared way of seeing, a "citizenship of photography" in Ariella Azoulay's terms, which excludes no one, even if they are not citizens of a sovereign power. For those who have no sovereign rights, this public sphere, which is constituted through photography, is the primary vehicle of visibility for their grievances and claims. It is also the primary source of war experience for the public sphere constituted by these images. Media theorist David Slocum asserts that there lingers in public discourse a sense of separation between war experience and media representation of that experience, and argues against this sense of separation. Such a distinction, asserts Slocum, fails to recognize that the public understanding of war through media images is not separate from or secondary to actual war experience but is *primary* war experience and therefore central to our social understanding.[1] Many photojournalists attempt to mitigate the depersonalized and distant relations produced by the official framing of war imagery through independent documentary practices that serve as tools of materialist analysis to produce new social knowledge and to promote democratic ideals and transformative politics. These photojournalists focus on the militarized, traumatized, and impoverished lives of the victims of capitalism and its relentless war machine and attempt to make both visible and palpable the violence that otherwise would remain silenced or repressed. While it remains true that in the courtroom of public opinion, the meaning of visual evidence is always "framed," it is also true that the photograph as visual evidence may serve to construct a shared way of seeing that rejects the viewpoints of ruling institutional regimes and exceeds their disciplinary frames.

To ensure a visual focus that calls the viewer into place as a national citizen who is part of a unified and patriotic national community, the U.S. government increasingly tightened restrictions on photojournalists until they arrived at a protocol that required any journalist first to be approved and then to be "embedded" with American troops before he or she would be permitted to travel to war zones. After the U.S. government censorship of photographs from World War II and Korea, pictures from the Vietnam War such as those by Nick Ut and Eddie Adams had a shocking effect on the American public, spurring renewed attempts at government control. The practice of restricting journalists began with Margaret Thatcher and the Falklands conflict in 1982 and was embraced by George Bush senior during the first Gulf War in 1991. The policy of "embedding" journalists, requiring them to sign a document agreeing to abide by military controls for "their own protection," was implemented by Bush junior in the Iraq war. "Hundreds of embedded photojournalists accepted this poisoned chalice," observes the English picture editor Colin Jacobson, "and virtually no images emerged from the professional phalanx that could be said to be revealing, challenging or even questioning of the nature of this conflict."[2]

By embedding photojournalists, the government hoped to control the narrative of war from without, to foster a natural identification between photographers and the troops with whom they lived and on whom they depended for their safety and security, to encourage an approach that supported nationalist aims and the larger militarist goals of the state, and to instill a sense of self-censorship. This official framing of war is not passive, but part of the war machinery, producing and enforcing a particular reality while actively excluding any alternative views, which cannot be perceived from the vantage point of the military's perspective. Until the rupture of Abu Ghraib, America became largely accustomed to photos made from inside the U.S. military cordon and removed from the day-to-day realities of war; reporters tended to identify with the troops, abandoning journalistic neutrality and referring to the movements of their units in the first person: "we" advanced, or "we" won that battle, and there was an impulse to focus on heroic tales of troops in danger.[3] As Martha Gellhorn wrote after the 1991 Gulf War, "In the Falklands, Grenada, Panama and the Gulf War, our governments have shown a fine skill in controlling and manipulating the press. The press is shown what the government thinks fit when the government ordains. The press is treated to military briefings instead of finding out for itself. An accompanying officer or minder is always at hand. The result of this press management... is that we have had no real press coverage. In the interests of national security or any phrase they wish to use, our governments have decided to neuter the press in war time."[4]

Certain themes of war remain constant in war photography, such as ruined architecture, war injuries, or the aftermath of battle, first registered by Roger Fenton with heavy, slow equipment during the Crimean War. In other ways, however, war photography has changed radically. The nature of war itself has changed greatly from men in brightly colored uniforms marching toward each other in formation to urban guerrilla warfare, and the greater accessibility to photographic technology has made possible the vast proliferation of representations of war, not only because photojournalists have much faster, lighter, more portable equipment and the greater capacities of digital cameras, but also because soldiers, civilians, insurgents, and refugees now have far greater ability to photograph their own circumstances outside the disciplinary frames of ruling institutions. These photographers and the imagery they produce exceed the instrumental photography of the state and legitimize alternative versions of reality. Despite the attempts of the U.S. government to control access to and monopolize the visual field and the nature of the image that emerges from the Iraq war, to crowd out "unauthorized" images, these attempts ultimately have failed, Jacobson's assertion notwithstanding, even if the unofficial, amateur, or renegade images do not always appear on primetime news or mainstream print venues—though sometimes they do. The effort has failed for several reasons, including the important fact that many photographers refused the "poison chalice" or found ways around it, so that even some of those who were initially embedded were able to pursue a more independent course and subsequently found alternative ways to present their images.

The effort to control the visual field also failed because technology has produced an uncontrollable excess of imagery. Soldiers, civilians, insurgents, and refugees have the capability of documenting war with photos and videos taken with their cell phones or other small digital cameras that can be immediately transmitted to social network or public media sites, allowing the images to travel around the globe within minutes. Even combat images of sniper attacks in which American soldiers are hit, or the effects of IEDs (improvised explosion devices) on armored Humvees or other military vehicles have been recorded and made available as videos, first in Baghdad shops and Jihadist websites, then on video-sharing sites such as YouTube and Google Video.[5] Many of these were taken down but quickly reappeared because the demand is great and the motivations many, ranging from the political to the voyeuristic. A nineteen-year-old YouTube user in Istanbul who posted more than forty videos of violence in Iraq told the *New York Times* via email that "antiwar feelings and Muslim beliefs (the religion of peace) motivates me." An American YouTube user and college freshman who sought out such videos, and who was related to American veterans, said, "I like watching stuff blow up."[6] American soldiers post hundreds if not thousands of videos as well.

The ability to post amateur photos and videos online or to independently publish professional photos takes political control of the war narrative out of the hands of official news media sources and makes visible realities of war that otherwise would be off limits to embedded photojournalists and inaccessible to most viewers. The unprecedented speed, accessibility, and ease of use of digital technologies has produced an explosion of imagery, whose digital nature, it may be argued, is no more or less subject to manipulation than other photographic technologies have ever been. In the contest of images, the prohibition and control of photographic technologies by the state has become nearly impossible to maintain in the digital era. This, in turn, gives the documentary image new impetus and potential for radical critique, and the ability to call forth a counterhegemonic public sphere.

Unsanctioned Images

The images most likely to be remembered from the Iraq war are not the staged images produced by the Bush administration's public relations apparatus, but the trophy photos of Abu Ghraib taken by soldiers on their cell phones, along with other images not officially sanctioned by the state, such as the leaked "Collateral Murder" video (discussed below), or the images that were made by independent photographers who took great personal risks to enter and move relatively freely in Iraq in order to avoid external and internal censorship. They spent months rather than weeks in the war zones, and photographed from the perspective of Iraqi populations, both civilians trying to live amid the ravages of war and Iraqi insurgent forces who fought against the occupation of their country by Americans. These photographers sometimes sent their images to editors at mainstream media print sources but more often, lacking venues for distribution, exhibited their images in photography exhibitions and books, blurring the line between photojournalism and fine art photography, or effectively dissolving it. This is not new. Many photojournalists have a relationship with fine art through exhibitions and book publications of their work, such as Robert Capa, Margaret Bourke-White, Lee Miller, W. Eugene Smith, James Nachtwey, Susan Meiselas, Larry Burrows, Alex Webb, Gilles Peress, Eugene Richards, and Sebastião Salgado. Such exhibitions and books avoid the ephemeral nature of press photos surrounded by other news or advertising, intensify the focus on their subject, and demonstrate how such photographs and videos not only reflect but also help to construct the meaning of war and social violence by what is made visible. By showing how the borders between the categories of media and artistic images are fluid, an examination of projects that cross the boundaries of these categories also demonstrates the integral relationship between them. Thus the once assumed differences between the "objectivity" of war photojournalism and the "subjectivity" of war photographs hung in museums has no purchase, as art historian Erina Duganne's analysis of the professed differences between Luc Delahaye's photojournalistic and artistic images of war also demonstrates.[7]

Marcia Vetrocq and others have also suggested that a succession of events, including the attacks on 9/11, Hurricane Katrina, the war in Iraq, the photos of Abu Ghraib, and the amateur and photojournalistic photos that proved indispensable to understanding those events and shaping public opinion, has catalyzed an upsurge of interest in "photo-based engagement with social and political reality." After thirty years of the "critique of truth" in photography, there is a renewed interest in evidentiary or documentary photos, all the more so because at moments the government has taken measures to restrict photographic access, not only through the embedding program, but also by attempting to ban specific kinds of images, such as the flag-draped military coffins arriving at Dover Air Force Base. When Kuwait-based cargo worker Tami Silicio took and provided such a photo for publication in the *Seattle Times* in 2004, she was fired from her job at the Maytag Aircraft Corporation for violating U.S. government and company regulations.[8] The Pentagon later released almost four hundred such photos, however, under pressure from open-government advocates who filed for their release under the Freedom of Information Act. The government's refusal to report on Iraqi civilian casualties or its censorship of photos of returning coffins with the American dead starkly contrasts the realities of war with officially approved and sanitized representations of the American presence in Iraq.

To counteract photojournalism's discredited objectivity, or the medium's susceptibility to aestheticization, contemporary photographers of reality-based work generally include an emphasis on research through captions, statements, interviews, or explanatory texts, so that the perspective of the photographer is always evident or implied, without pretense to "objectivity." Vetrocq writes, "It may be that the quality of photographic transparency, once presumed dead, has simply shifted from the picture to the picture maker. In such a practice, subjectivity and truthfulness are no longer at odds, and the acknowledgement of point of view is itself a precondition of photographic honesty."[9] Such captions and texts accompany all of the photographic projects by photojournalists discussed below, which activate the photographs and give them a voice.

Though on assignment for *Newsweek* magazine and embedded with American troops, Dutch photojournalist Geert van Kesteren found the story of the war in Iraq much bigger than anything *Newsweek* could accommodate. Embedded for only six weeks on assignment for *Newsweek*, van Kesteren stayed on in Iraq for seven months. With no magazine venue for in-depth coverage of the war, van Kesteren documented the traumatic and destructive effects of the U.S. occupation of Iraq and the growing refugee crisis with the 2005 exhibition and publication of *Why Mister, Why?* The book employs a deliberately low aesthetic of perforated edges and magazine stock, and is densely packed with images and texts, in both English and Arabic, and includes an introduction by Michael Hirsh, a senior editor at *Newsweek*. Hirsh was on assignment to interview L. Paul Bremer III, America's man in Iraq, but was persuaded by van Kesteren to spend two days in Samarra, from where van Kesteren had just returned. Together, they saw the counterinsurgency up close as they went from house to house with U.S. troops in the middle of the night looking for insurgent "cells" that failed to materialize while Iraqi civilians were repeatedly brutalized. "I realized the Bush administration truly had no clue what it was doing in Iraq," writes Hirsh in the introduction. "Like a hidden generator, the occupation itself, I realized, was sustaining the insurgency." Not without sympathy for American soldiers, Hirsh notes, "But they were now being pressed into a counterinsurgency role they'd never trained for. . . . 'Geneva Conventions' was not a term often heard at 3 a.m. in Samarra, not when you think everyone is against you." Hirsh identifies the moment when Bush lost the goodwill and support of the world, instead fanning the flames of anti-Americanism by revealing American power to be an unrestrained and arbitrary force: "It was when in the face of Saddam's cave-in—when the Iraqi dictator abruptly gave United Nations inspectors free rein and they found little WMD (and their assessments proved far more accurate than the CIA's)—Bush decided to invade anyway."[10]

The images include house raids, arrests, the grief of Iraqi men and women, Iraqi injured, cars exploding, Iraqi women being body searched by U.S. male soldiers, Abu Ghraib interrogations, soldiers with prisoners whose name and other key information is duct-taped to the sides of their heads on a white index card, the excavation of mass graves, and, overall, the growing tension between American troops and Iraqi civilians. In one photo, soldiers rummage through the belongings of an absent Iraqi family. The door to the bedroom has been kicked in and still shows the dried mud left by the boots of the American soldiers, one footprint higher than the door handle. Three soldiers are visible: one on the right edge of the page, with a rifle and night-vision device hanging from his neck; one in the background, looking through bedclothes; and most unsettling, one in the left foreground who crouches on the floor and casually rifles through a private family photo album.

He has turned to the last leaf with images, as if to rifle backward through the stiff pages. It has six pictures on it, four in color and two in black and white, neatly arranged in rows of matching sizes. Three have three figures in them, three have single figures, including a teenage girl and an even younger boy, who is dressed in a white shirt, jacket and tie, like a school photo. There is no sign of a neatly ordered life in the home that is pictured now, which shows crumbled plaster along the doorjamb

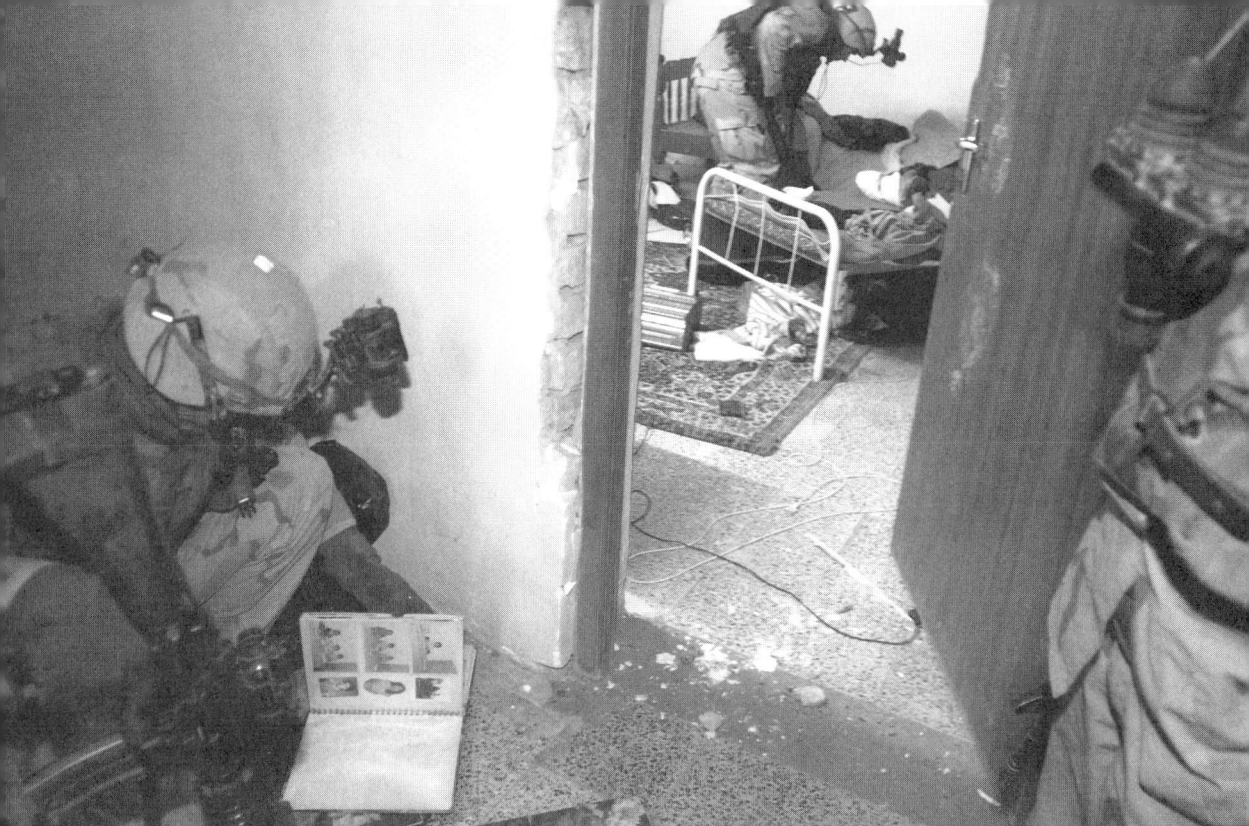

Figure 19. Geert van Kesteren, American soldiers raiding apartment in Baghdad, 2003–2004. [© Geert van Kesteren.]

that has been crushed underfoot on the floor, a space heater on a rug in the bedroom, and jumbled bedclothes. The moment of violent invasion over, the soldiers seem to take their time. The photo album is placed on the floor. There is a final page at the end of the album, which has been left blank, echoing the blankness of the white wall behind the curious soldier, and the blankness of his curiosity. He is not embarrassed to be photographed peering through this private family photo album any more than the soldiers are embarrassed to be photographed invading private homes and kicking in their bedroom doors. We do not see how the occupants were terrorized by such assaults or dragged from their beds and homes, although in other photos young men are forced to lie on the floors of their homes with their hands bound behind their back; in one a soldier's foot presses down on a boy's shirtless back as he grimaces with closed eyes. As was once said about American black slaves, they have no rights that the occupiers are bound to recognize. The private domain of the home is seamlessly militarized, its occupants made homeless and transformed into prisoners whose crime was to be in their home at the moment the Americans chose to invade it. There is no recourse to any force or power for redress, except through the public sphere constituted by photography that calls into place witnesses with a shared way of seeing.

Why Mister, Why? concludes with a series of horrifying car bombs, the streets soaked in blood and littered with glass, a close-up of the burned face of an Iraqi young man slathered with white salve, an old man beseeching the heavens, and freshly dug graves with an Iraqi flag-covered body ready for burial. Van Kesteren concludes his commentary by describing Jassin Jirza, who together with his son stood in a line to get work with the interim Iraqi government when a bomb exploded. "Jassin survived, but not his son. The man was drenched from head to toe in his son's blood. 'My life is over,' was all that he said."[11]

The exhibition accompanying *Why Mister, Why?* was organized by the production company Paradox at the Rotterdam Fotomuseum and presented the images as rolling projections on giant video screens underscored by a live news feed from Iraq. Van Kesteren's follow up 2008 publication, *Baghdad Calling*, for which he won the International Center of Photography's Infinity Award in Photojournalism for 2009, continues the story of the dispersal of Iraqi refugees. Images from *Baghdad Calling* also were part of the exhibition *On the Subject of War* at the Barbican Gallery in 2008–2009. *Baghdad Calling* is composed of more than one hundred images taken by Iraqis using cell phone cameras and posted on social networking websites, interspersed with only a few of van Kesteren's own photos taken of refugees in Jordan and Syria. Photos sent to van Kesteren include the wrecks of car bombs; a young man trying to look cool in sunglasses and hat against his souped-up red car; a large fam-

Figure 20. Dying Iraqi doctor in bed at hospital. Photo sent via cell phone for *Baghdad Calling*, 2005–2007. (Collection Geert van Kesteren/Baghdad Calling.)

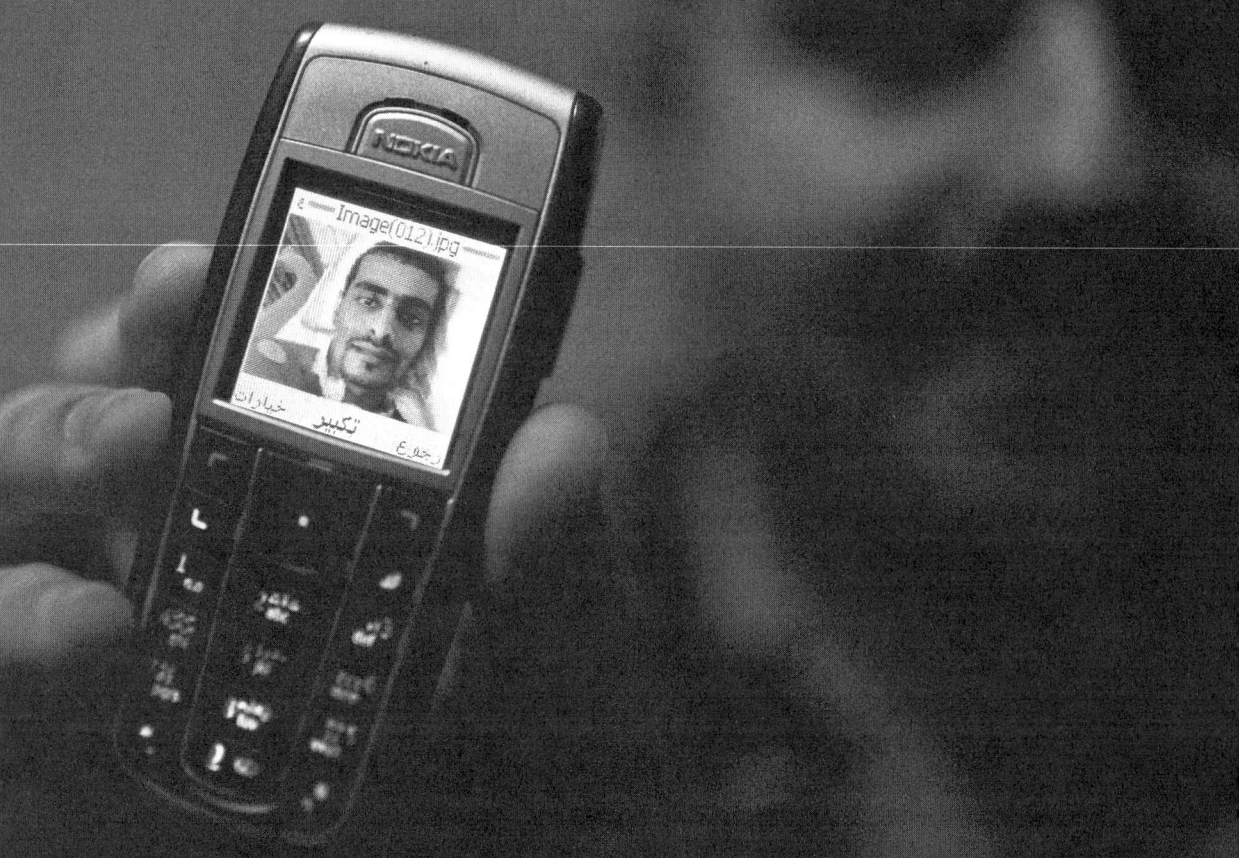

ily celebrating Christmas in red Santa hats; the skyline of a city with thick black smoke from an explosion on the horizon; a grinning young man at a bowling alley with colorful bowling balls; a handsome but desolate young man in a hospital, a bandage around his neck with a breathing tube, the light already fading from his eyes. This last photo, a cell phone image shown to van Kesteren by an Iraqi doctor who took this picture of his wounded and dying best friend, made van Kesteren realize that he could not capture the reality of Iraqis' lives in the way they themselves could, and inspired *Baghdad Calling*.[12]

In his introduction to the book, Jan Gruiters, director of IKV Pax Christi, notes the dire situation for Iraqi refugees in Syria and Jordan and writes, "These countries do not even acknowledge refugees as such and they restrict foreign humanitarian aid, allowing it to get through only intermittently. Most countries have now closed their borders to Iraqis or send refugees back into Iraq. Besides the two million refugees, at least as many people have been displaced within Iraq, where even less help is available. In the northern city of Kirkuk, for example, several thousand refugees have been sheltering in the local stadium for more than four years with no assistance from the Kurdish or central Iraqi governments, with all the attendant consequences: children do not go to school and people are denied any medical care."[13]

Van Kesteren received hundreds of pictures through his contacts, Facebook, and Iraqi chat groups by people eager to make their humanity visible, to appeal to the "citizens of the citizenry of photography" available only through the public sphere created through the documentary image. "The civil contract of photography enables citizens and noncitizens alike to produce grievances and claims that otherwise can't be seen and to impose them by means of, through, and on the citizenry of photography," writes Ariella Azoulay. We must look at the photos that assert these grievances and claims, and protest against power, even when looking is all we can do, because not to look is to collude with the state. "The civil contract of photography is frequently threatened by the ruling power. When the citizen's gaze is diverted from photographs, and directed toward the field of vision created by the ruling power, where, in fact, there are no images, individuals abandon their commitment to the contract and effectively collaborate with the ruling power even when they may be explicitly opposed to its actions."[14] The pictures by Iraqi citizens collected by van Kesteren make visible moments of horror in parts of the country where Western journalists could no longer travel, especially after 2005.[15]

An email message sent to van Kesteren by an Iraqi man from Baghdad captures something of the insanity of conditions in Iraq. "This summer," he wrote, "a workman wanted to quench his thirst by putting ice in his tea. A car pulled up, the driver stepped out and began to beat and kick the man, cursing him as an unbeliever. 'What do you think you're doing? Did the Prophet Mohamed put ice in his water?' The man being attacked was furious and asked his assailant: 'Do you think the Prophet Mohamed drove a car?'"[16]

In one photo that van Kesteren received, three murdered men, their hands still tied behind their backs, have been dumped in an empty lot, strewn with other trash. Houses are visible beyond the low concrete wall behind the lot. It is possible that one of the men has been decapitated. The image was taken by a citizen photographer as he or she drove by the lot and is framed by the car window. We do not know who the murdered men are or why they were murdered; nor do we know where this lot is located in the city, or how many cars drive past it every day. "This is not 'the war' but somebody's neighborhood," writes Robert Hariman, "a place where kids might be scrounging around looking for cool junk. Or worse, the car could be driving through the back lot because those inside are hoping they won't find the body of a loved

Figure 21. Three bodies dumped in a lot. Photo sent via cell phone for *Baghdad Calling*, 2005–2007. (Collection Geert van Kesteren/Baghdad Calling.)

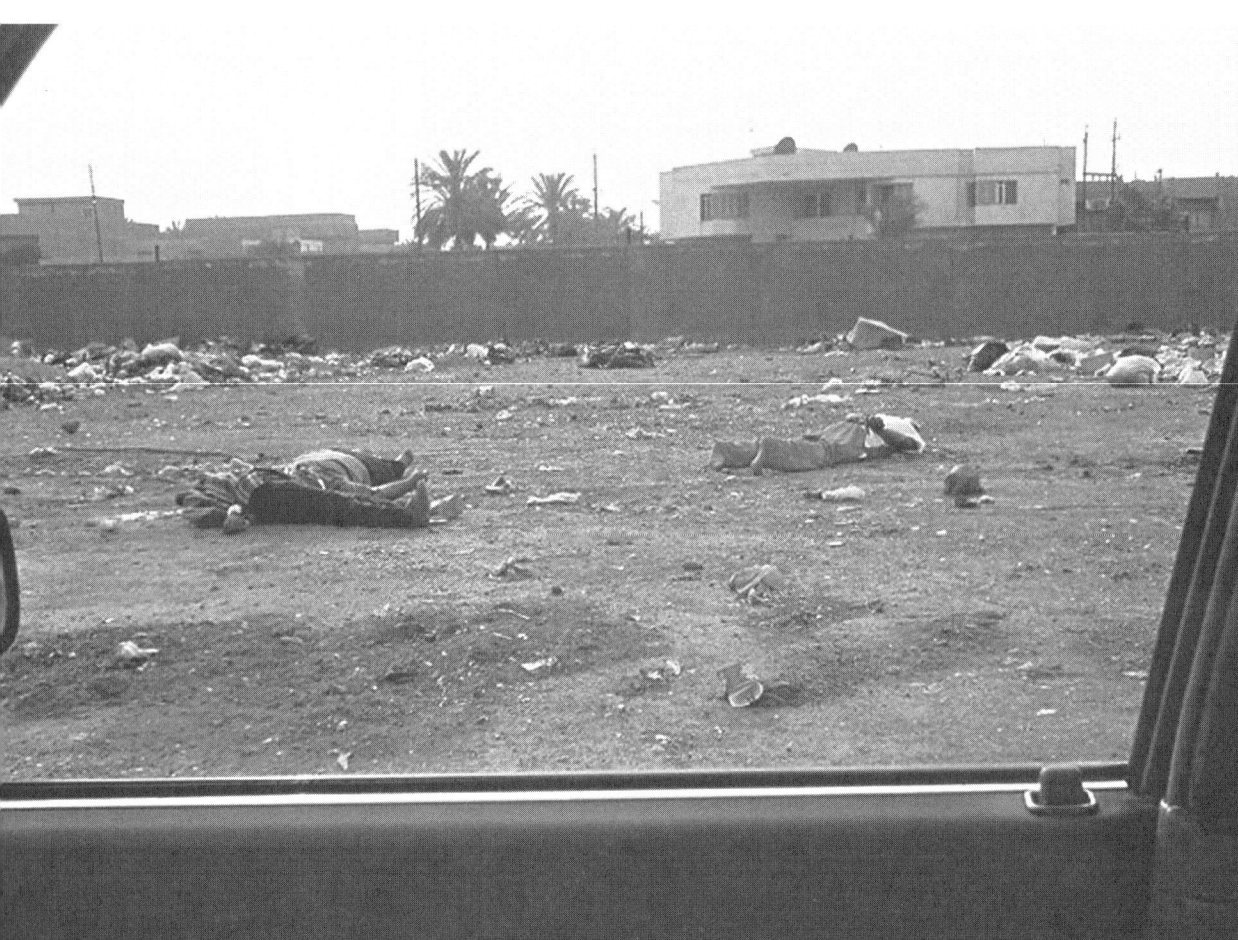

one."[17] In this case, it is the lack of a caption that says everything. These are unknown, uncounted, ungrievable lives, and this is the emergency claim of the photo.

It is no accident that most of these photos have been taken on cell phones, which are very cheap in Iraq, and Iraqis take cell phone pictures by the thousands, making everyone a producer as well as a consumer of photography. The low resolution of the images does not diminish their authority; on the contrary, as Roger Hargreaves notes, their amateurism heightens their sense of authority, avoiding "compositional slickness" and appearing "more real by being less hyper-real."[18] The mediality of the images, like the Abu Ghraib torture photos, adds to both the authenticity and the power of the images.

In a country where most utilities have become dysfunctional and landlines have broken down, cell phones also have become the best means of communication for kidnappers and coroners; the number of cell phones since the American invasion has jumped from 1.4 million to 7.1 million.[19] Van Kesteren relates an incident in which "the kidnappers called the family on the mobile phone because that's how it works. They kidnap you. They find the number of your father or mother and they're going to give a call. Those kidnappers first made the call and said 'can you recharge the credit on the uncle's phone?' It was because they didn't want to spend their own money on phoning the family to make their ransom demand. Two years ago, you paid ransom to get your son alive back. Today you pay ransom to be able to bury him."[20] Van Kesteren contends that the cell phone has become "an essential tool in modern warfare" that plays a crucial role in protecting human rights. He points to the importance of the cell phone image in the Abu Ghraib photos and the first images of the hanging of Saddam Hussein, not to mention the use of cell phones by civilians to avoid danger and by insurgents to detonate bombs. With control of the technology also comes control of the narrative and the possibility of presenting grievances and claims. *Baghdad Calling* gives Iraqi refugees both visibility and access to the visual field, called into place in part by their own documentary practices.

Four independent photojournalists who also went their own way in order to photograph what would otherwise remain underreported or invisible to audiences outside of Iraq were Americans Kael Alford and Thorne Anderson, Canadian Rita Leistner, and Iraqi Ghaith Abdul-Ahad. Like van Kesteren, they spent months reporting on Iraqi life without the protection of the military. Many of their photographs document the U.S.-led siege of Najaf in 2004, including such key perspectives as the insurgency seen from inside the separate resistance movements, civilians affected by the violent battles between the U.S. and insurgent forces, growing conservatism and fundamentalism and their effects on women, and the devastating effects of civilian casualties. Their work was presented jointly in a traveling exhibition and a book with explanatory captions and texts titled *Unembedded: Four Independent Photojournalists on the War in Iraq* in 2005.

In *Najaf, August 21, 2004*, a man in a white shirt with his back to the viewer holds a wailing child and raises his arm as he enters a devastated section of the city. Kael Alford writes, "A father shows his hand to snipers as he carries his terrified child across the front line between U.S. forces and the Mahdi Army at the wrecked outskirts of the old city." In *Baghdad, January 28, 2005*, the composition is filled with the thick, dark, billowing smoke of a car on fire, and a lone figure traverses the space in front of it. Ghaith Abdul-Ahad writes, "A car bomb burns next to a school in south Baghdad an hour after a suicide bomber targeted a police station in the same area. The city witnessed a surge of violence as the country prepared for elections." In *Abu Faloos, February 2, 2003*, a girl in white sits forlornly on the floor, her left hand in her lap, her chin lifted. Thorne Anderson writes, "Twelve-year-old Isra lost her right arm when her village, Abu Faloos, was hit with an American bomb during an attack in the 'no-fly zone' in southern Iraq in 1999. Five other children were injured and four were killed. The United States bombed Iraq regularly over a twelve-year period, in part to 'soften up' Iraqi air defenses in preparation for the 2003 invasion." In *Rashad Psychiatric Hospital, Baghdad, April 17, 2004*, Rita Leistner writes of a sobbing young woman in a hospital gown against a tiled wall, "A young patient, newly arrived from the southern Shiite town of Karbala, pleads to go home: 'I don't belong here. Please don't make me spend the rest of my life here.'" Accompanying texts suggest that women are often sent to psychiatric hospitals if they are ill because Iraqis fear that if one daughter has a mental disorder, it will affect the marriage chances of their other daughters; healthy women may seek refuge from beatings and honor killings; others are sent because their parents have died and their brothers want control over family property. "Most of the women have no choice but to live at the hospital for the remainder of their lives."[21]

Though conditions were dangerous, the four independent photographers were largely protected by their status as photojournalists under the aegis of the civil contract of photography. Although Iraqis conditioned by the fact that journalists in Saddam Hussein's Iraq worked for the state often feared that foreign journalists might be spies for their own governments, they also understood that photojournalists could present their grievances and claims. Rita Leistner, while in Najaf in 2004, recounts this incident:

"Follow me on foot to the shrine of Imam Ali," he said.

As we walked toward the city center, fighters standing in the doorways began chanting.

"This is a good song," an interpreter for *The Telegraph* said. "It's the song that signals to fighters up ahead not to shoot the journalists."

Leistner describes her harrowing entrance into Iraq on foot through the treacherous mountains of Syria and Iran, led by smugglers, and her ambush, with another colleague, in Latifiya by men who were "crazed with anger and adrenaline" and wanted to kill "the Americans." They were saved by their Canadian passports, by Iraqi women who sheltered them, and by their claims to be "good journalists." Their lives were spared in exchange for all their camera equipment and digital media, which were taken.[22]

Kael Alford first arrived in Iraq on a three-week visa but ended up spending more than eight months in Iraq on three separate trips. She photographed the casualties in the overrun medical centers and was on the spot when a marine radioed in a request to pull down the statue of Saddam Hussein with a tank, climbing on top of the tank to photograph the staged event. Alford describes the Iraqis who seemed to arrive with the Americans and the dispute over the flags—American or Iraqi—concluding that this ready-made "iconic" image was a "charade" that represented nothing she had experienced about the war.[23]

Baghdad-born Ghaith Abdul-Ahad studied architecture at Baghdad University and became a deserter from the Iraqi army during Saddam Hussein's rule. He lived underground for six years, changing residence every few months to avoid detection, and began writing for *The Guardian* and the *Washington Post* after the U.S. invasion in 2003. In his essay for Unembedded, he describes his detention by republican guards who believed he was a spy. His cameras also were confiscated in exchange for his life. Abdul-Ahad later photographed the strafing by U.S. helicopters of civilians on Haifa Street in Baghdad when a celebratory crowd gathered around a burning U.S. armored personnel carrier. The helicopters opened fire—very like the helicopter in the "Collateral Murder" video—killing twenty-two Iraqi civilians and injuring forty-eight.

In a sequence of two photos, we see death in motion. In *Baghdad, September 12, 2004*, two young men lie on the street, a burning tank behind them. A third young man sits up next to them. In the next photo, he has keeled over, and one of the other two, his head bleeding, is sitting up. Abdul-Ahad writes, "I watched as he lowered his head to the ground, rested his head on his arms, and stretched his hands toward something that he could see. It was the guy who had been beating his chest earlier, trying to help his brother. He was there dying in front of me. Time didn't exist. The streets were empty and silent and the men lay there dying together. He slid down to the ground, and after five minutes was flat on the street." Abdul-Ahad moved from his hiding place to photograph; then the helicopters returned and he ran back to his shelter "just as two more big explosions shattered the stillness. *They're firing at us*, I told myself." It is difficult for Abdul-Ahad to believe that the Americans are firing for no reason at civilians on the street and he must keep reminding himself. He concludes, "All the people I had shared my shelter with were dead. Every time I look at these pictures I tell myself I have killed those people. I should have helped them instead of taking pictures." But it seems there is only one way in which he can help them, and that is by taking pictures, as those who are disenfranchised but wish to present their grievances realize. Abdul-Ahad writes, "I ran into the entrance of a building and someone grabbed my arm and took me inside. 'There's an injured man. Take pictures. Show the world the American democracy,' he said."[24] As a 2001 study by the International Committee of the Red Cross makes clear, civilians have borne the brunt of modern war, "with 10 civilians dying for every soldier in wars since the mid-20th century, compared with 9 soldiers killed for every civilian in World War I."[25] Of course, that number may have climbed much higher since 2001.

Thorne Anderson describes the moment his primary contact, Haider, presented him with a gift of sweets and a photograph of himself and his wife on their wedding day. Anderson understood that Haider was preparing himself for martyrdom as his turn approached to enter the front lines of fighting. He also realized that a bond of friendship had grown between them, that Haider had protected him even as he deeply resented the domination of Iraq by a foreign force, the deaths of innocent Iraqi civilians in bombings and checkpoints, the fraud and corruption in the distribution of money for reconstruction, the breakdown of basic services such as water, electricity and security, the American insensitivity to local custom, and the installation of a new government that included many Iraqi exiles who had lived in Britain or the United States for the previous two decades. Anderson resisted the implications of an approaching martyrdom as Haider "pressed his gifts into my hands."[26]

The Perils of Embedding
Embedded photographers are in great danger as well, just as American troops are, their "protection" largely extending to not being shot at by the troops themselves who might mistake them for insurgents. Australian photojournalist Ashley Gilbertson was in Iraq from 2002 until 2008,

arriving, unaffiliated, on the eve of the U.S. invasion, to investigate the story of Kurdish refugees in Kurdistan in 2002–2003. Because he had heard so many horror stories of what Saddam Hussein's regime had done to the Kurds, he initially supported the American invasion. It was only after he drove with an Australian cameraman to Mosul, a city that survived the invasion but was destroyed by the looting, that he changed his mind. American soldiers and Special Forces drove by the chaos and did not respond even as the city burned; then-Secretary of State Donald Rumsfeld dismissed the looting with his infamous "Stuff happens." Gilbertson realized there was no plan for stopping the destruction.

He shifted course and began covering the looting and insurgency that followed Americans' claims of victory, the dramatic battle to overtake Fallujah, and the country's first national elections, returning and embedding with different military units for a total of eighteen months.[27] He earned the Robert Capa Gold Medal for his 2004 work in Fallujah and published a book of photos with essays about his experience titled *Whiskey Tango Foxtrot* (2007), with an introduction by *New York Times* foreign correspondent Dexter Filkins. "Whiskey tango foxtrot" is derived from the military radio phonetics for "what the fuck," and was a phrase Gilbertson heard over and over in the beginning without realizing what it meant, only later coming to appreciate the shock, frustration, and bewilderment it signified among American soldiers.

One of his most well-known photos shows an American soldier sliding down a banister in one of Saddam Hussein's palaces in Hussein's hometown of Tikrit, a city where the marines and the army had gathered shortly after the invasion. Gilbertson and the cameraman were told they could not talk to the troops unless they were embedded, but they found a few soldiers in the palace who were happy to have them along and Gilbertson photographed them playing around. He notes the very different responses to the photographs: among those who supported the war, it was an exuberant expression of Americans "winning the war," while those who opposed the war saw it as conveying a terrible American naiveté.[28]

How do we see it today, knowing what a catastrophe the war has been and that there was no "winning the war"? The long banister is a blur as Gilbertson focuses on the helmeted soldier who straddles the banister and leans back as he slides, holding his gun at one side while his other arm flies out freely, fingers extended. He is in the position of a boy on a bull at a rodeo, or a mechanical bucking bronco, his mouth wide open in a big smile. He is enjoying the moment and is entirely in the moment, giddy with pleasure. Careless of the domestic invasion his presence represents, the scene is a perfect emblem of American arrogance, ignorance,

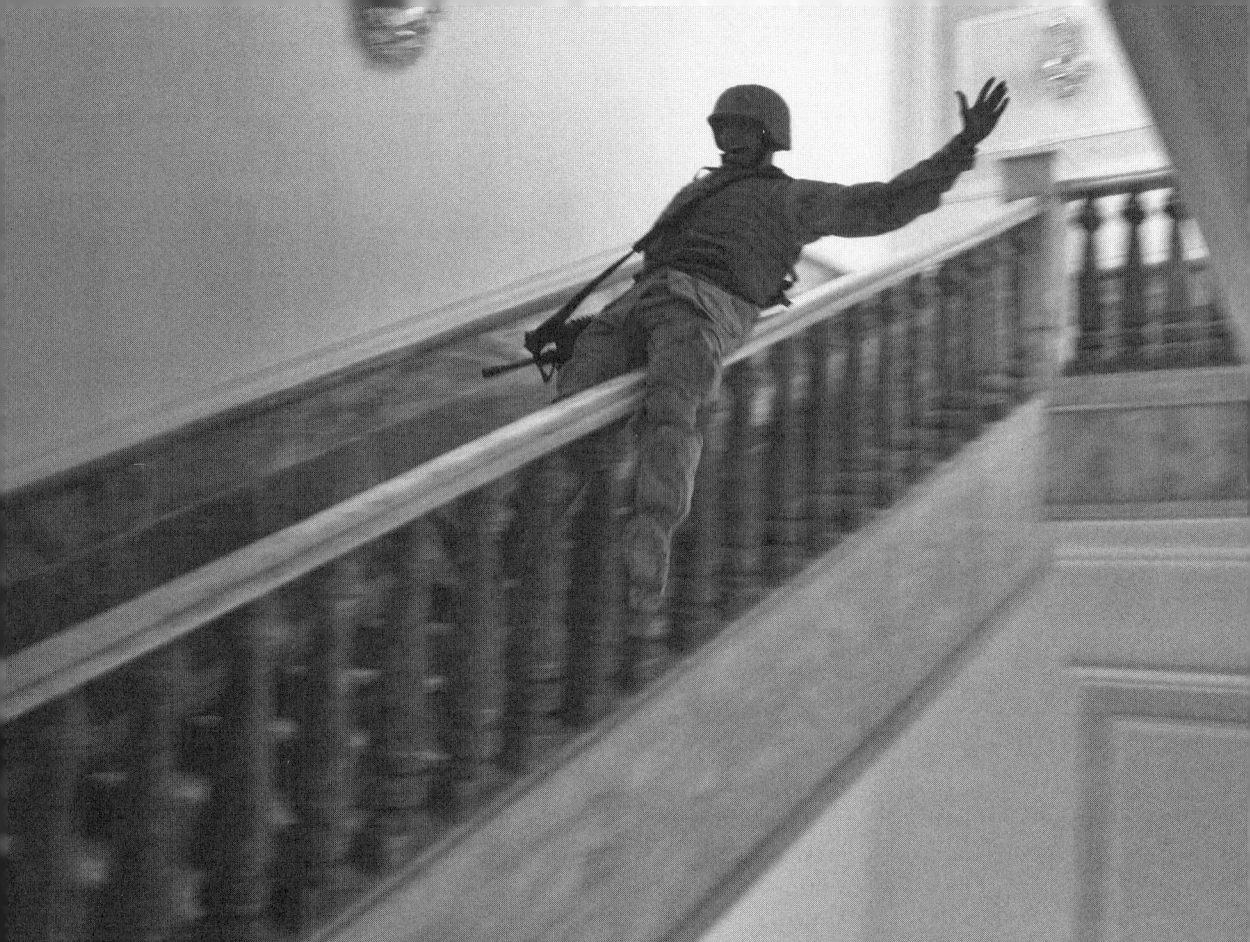

Figure 22. Ashley Gilbertson/VII Network, "A marine slides down the marble handrail in Saddam's palace in Tikrit," 2003. (Ashley Gilbertson/VII Network.)

and short-sightedness. The soldier is the serviceman counterpart to Bush Jr., the "cowboy" president, and to Donald Rumsfeld, who believed that the war would be won handily in a few weeks.

Many of the photographs portray American soldiers in ways that are designed to foster sympathy for their condition as they patrol, guard, shoot, carry their wounded, mourn their dead, rest and sleep, adopting the perspective of those on whom Gilbertson came to depend for his life while trying to maintain his critical independence. Gilbertson describes a moment when he realized he had "grown too close to the platoon and had unintentionally protected them" by failing to shoot an incriminating photograph.[29] He described it again when interviewed by fellow photographer Nina Berman, who inquired about the embed process.

BERMAN: Describe what if any compromises you had to make as an embed.
GILBERTSON: It only happened once, but it was bad, and it still drives me crazy today. I was out in Samarra on the big offensive up there, and I embedded with the New York National Guard. I was hanging out with one platoon a lot, and they'd stumbled across a suspect who had Osama Bin Laden book-

lets in his home. Their interpreter, Money Mike, an Iraqi national guardsman, beat the hell out of the man, trying to get intel, and I photographed the whole scene. The man wasn't talking, so Mike took out a bayonet and went to stab the guy, but he was stopped by the American Lieutenant, who said, "I hate to say this Mike, but put the knife away . . . I mean, I have to be frank: There's a reporter here."

I thought I had the picture and lied to the Lieutenant that I didn't take it. I found out just a few days ago, over beers with him back here in New York, he thought I was lying when I said it. I really thought he'd believed me. That night though, editing photos, I realized that I had unconsciously made the decision not to press the shutter, a way of protecting the platoon. It was the first and last time I let the embed process cloud my objectivity.[30]

Gilbertson may have understood that his bonds with the troops worked against his "objectivity" in this instance, but we must wonder about the more subtle effects of these bonds in terms of the shared suspicion of and alienation from Iraqi society. One of Gilbertson's most well known photos was produced in Fallujah of a hooded detainee seated on the ground and bent over, his wrists tied behind him with zip ties and a bandage covering a wound where he was shot in the back. Blood has run down his side and pooled on the ground. He sits in front of a wall under the looming shadow of his armed marine guard, whom we do not see directly and who occupies the position of the viewer, so that we too are placed in a position of dominance over the prisoner. In an interview with Alan Thomas, an editor at the University of Chicago Press, Gilbertson suggests that this image is emblematic of the war as a whole because both marine and Iraqi insurgent remain faceless, unknown and unknowable, and this is how each side regards the other. But there is no equivalence here: the wounded prisoner is bound, hooded and controlled by his guard; the American marine stands freely, armed. For Gilbertson the photograph signifies a "war fought by shadows and people that don't really exist" while capturing "the absolute distrust between the American military and the Iraqis."[31] But do the Iraqis really feel that the Americans are "shadows and people that don't really exist," or is this more particularly the American view of the insurgent forces, who know the cities, streets, and people far better than the Americans and are better able to blend into the scenery and disappear? Moreover, Gilbertson's label tells us that this is "one of four Iraqis who surrendered to the marines and said they were students trying to avoid the battle," which seems, in fact, to belie the assertion of "absolute distrust."

Gilbertson's book also includes a photograph of a severely wounded soldier on a stretcher being loaded onto a Blackhawk helicopter. The soldier

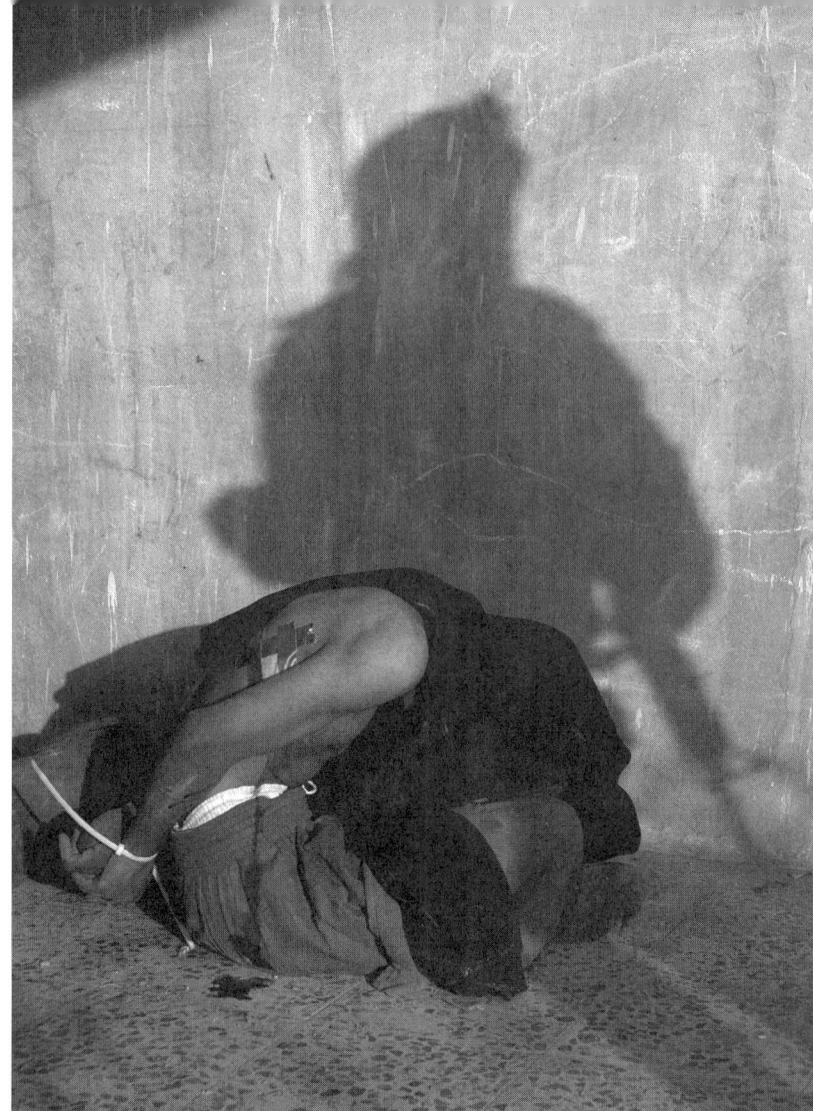

Figure 23. Ashley Gilbertson/VII Network, "One of four Iraqis who surrendered to the marines and said they were students trying to avoid battle," 2004. (Ashley Gilbertson/VII Network.)

died a few hours later. Such a photo could not be legally published today unless the photographer had gotten prior written approval from the soldier to photograph him while wounded, according to new military rules, which got war photographer Zoriah Miller "disembedded" in July 2008 after he posted images of the dead on his blog (following notification of the families). Zoriah (his professional name) asserts that various military officials tried to keep the photos from being published and actively prevented him from taking more photographs of the dead after an attack. He also refused to delete his memory cards or surrender his cameras as they demanded. "They embedded a war photographer," he said, "and when I took a photo of war, they disembedded me. It's as if it's okay to take pictures of them handing lollipops to kids on the street and providing medical care, but photographing the actual war is unacceptable."[32] Former photojournalist and communications professor Dennis Dunleavy suggests that "the media has acquiesced to the military's demands to keep offensive images off our breakfast tables" and asks, "Do embedded photojournalists actually work for the Pentagon?"[33]

Gilbertson calls the Pentagon policy "taking the death and destruction out of war" in his interview with Alan Thomas, and reiterates his position in his interview with Nina Berman:

> While I have some photographs of wounded and dying soldiers in the book, I am furious about Pentagon's directives that have since made it impossible to shoot those scenes. By not allowing the press to cover such awful events, it's created a sanitized and emotionless war. It not only gives the public an inadequate picture of what's really going on there, but it robs the men and women who are being wounded and killed of the recognition for the sacrifices they made. The numerous conversations I've had with parents of dead men I photographed, I know how painful it is for them to see the pictures of their children on stretchers, but I think in time, as a nation, we will look back at this war and ask why those pictures don't exist.[34]

As if to compensate for those missing pictures and the voids they leave in the landscape of the American political imaginary, Gilbertson's current project is *Bedrooms of the Fallen*, a collection of photographs depicting the intact bedrooms of service members who died in Iraq and Afghanistan. In 2009, a substantial part of the project was commissioned by the *New York Times Magazine* and published in March 2010, with a brief essay by Dexter Filkins. A sense of absence pervades every object and their configurations in each of the empty bedrooms, framing their meaning as haunting American loss. The elegiac quality of the work seems to grow out of Gilbertson's own posttraumatic stress disorder following nonstop combat in Fallujah when Americans tried to retake the city after the November 2004 U.S. elections and the death of a marine who was killed when Gilbertson wanted to photograph a foreign fighter inside a minaret. Gilbertson could not work after that and retreated from the war for twelve months, seeking therapy, before returning to see the effects of the Iraqi elections.

Other reporters have suffered PTSD as well as grievous physical injuries, such as Reuters' reporter Samia Nakhoul and her partner Faleh Kheiber. To showcase their work, Reuters collaborated with Idea Generation Gallery in London for the inaugural exhibition of *Bearing Witness: Photos of the Iraq War* in April–May 2008, which presented Kheiber and Nakhoul's interview with and photograph of twelve-year-old Ali Ismail

Abbas, whose entire family was killed when an American missile landed on his house, and whose arms were blown off in the blast. The day after Kheiber and Nakhoul filed their story, the Palestine Hotel where they and some two hundred international journalists were based was shelled by a U.S. tank in a controversial incident, killing two reporters and severely wounding three others, including Kheiber and Nakhoul. Samia Nakhoul required emergency brain surgery.[35]

Photographing the Homefront

Some photographers were denied permission to embed and decided to photograph the domestic effects of the war instead, such as Nina Berman. In her book *Homeland*, Berman makes visible the less obvious consequences of a permanent war culture on the American landscape, from large cities to small Midwestern towns. Fed by the Homeland Security industry and federal dollars distributed across the country following the attacks of 9/11 on the Twin Towers and Pentagon, Berman's photos, taken between 2001 and 2008, ruminate on the militarization of American culture. Berman portrays a country that "is having a love affair with war and violence." She observes, "We developed a sense of identity based on the fact that we were attacked."[36] Setting out to explore issues of security, or insecurity, and identity in America, Berman found a troubling sense of fantasy and theater that both elicited and responded to American fear, in the process making war "fun" and empowering. Berman describes her outrage:

> I saw Air Force bombers entertaining sunbathers on summer weekends; high schools taken over by the Department of Defense as a solution offered communities desperate for school funding; frequent simulation drills costing millions of dollars and involving thousands of participants where various war scenarios are imagined; recruitment scenarios where young children are transformed into smiling would-be killers.
>
> Some of these events have the look and feel of state sponsored performance art, where realism is replaced by theater giving participants a powerful sense of identity and value through a militarized experience. It is this identity, and the ambiguity between real and made up, so emblematic of post 9-11 political discourse, that interests me most.
>
> I came to this series after having spent the last few years photographing very graphic examples of the human cost of war. Many of the subjects I photographed said they grew up thinking war would be "fun." Many watched the first Gulf War on TV and thought it was "awesome." Several said that becoming a soldier meant they would finally do something good in life.

Rather than continuing to show evidence of war, it seems appropriate for me to show the fantasies of war, the selling of war, the institutions of war, the culture of war and with it the militarization of American life.[37]

Homeland includes pictures of soldiers marching on a red carpet in a New York City parade, military recruiting in the Bronx where children play with real weapons, massive Armageddon scenarios of nuclear war emergency exercises complete with elaborate sets and fake blood, Homeland Security signs with their confusing array of colors, and a stealth bomber flying over bathers on a beach who track its progress, making war practice seem like an engaging entertainment. Less successful is the fictional voice Berman assumes in short, written commentaries for the three sections into which the book is divided (Prepare; Believe; Defend), in which she presumes to speak in the voice of those who are pictured in the photos. In "Prepare," for example, Berman's fictional voice correlates with a photo of two older women in security uniforms, complete with berets and a security patrol car, who look rather puffed up and pleased with themselves. Berman writes: "I belong to the Homefront Security Patrol, a volunteer program that lets me wear a uniform and carry a radio and drive in a police car with a partner three mornings a week. We patrol our streets, public buildings and tennis courts, looking for anything or

Figure 24. Nina Berman/NOOR, *Human Target Practice*, All America Day, Ft. Bragg, North Carolina, 2006, from series *Homeland Insecurities*. (Nina Berman/NOOR.)

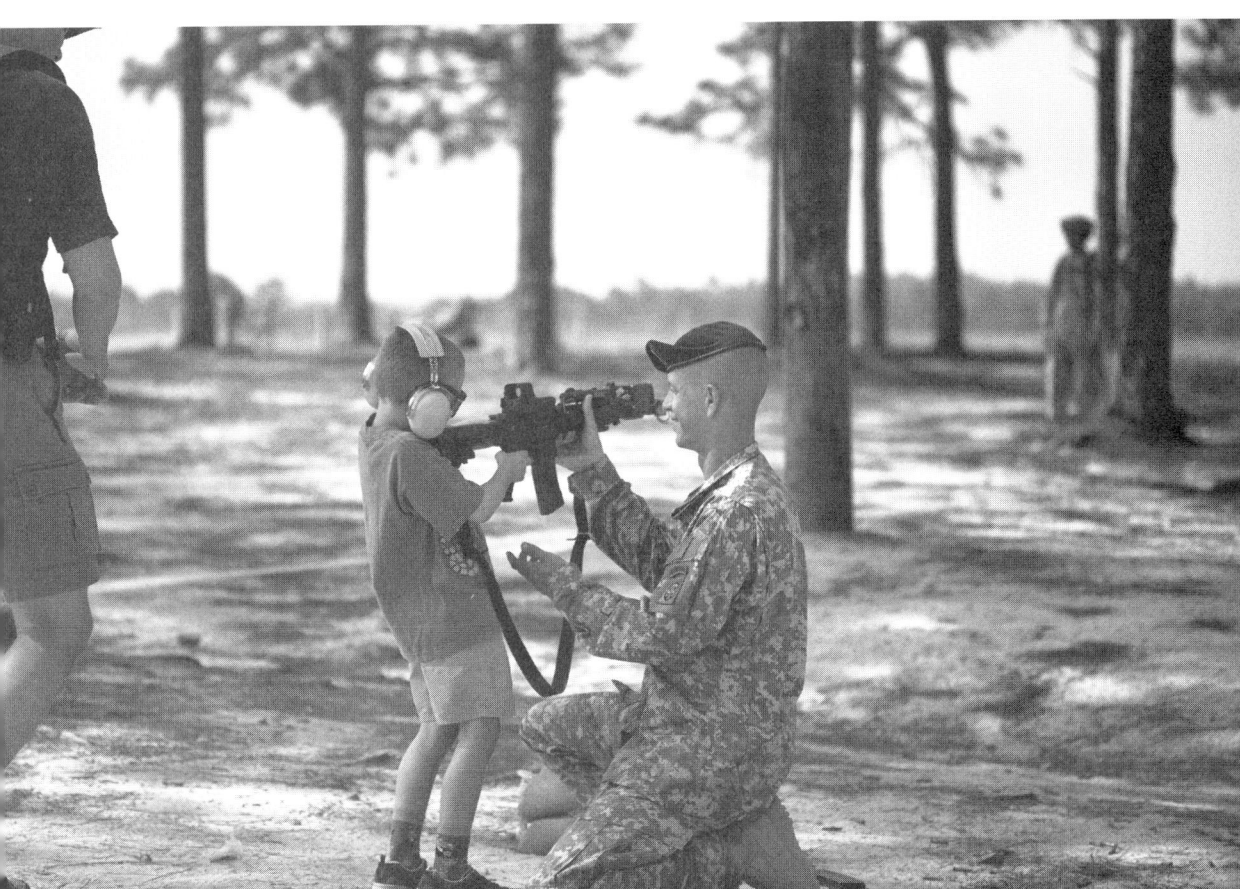

anyone suspicious—bombs, terrorists, and whatnot."[38] Berman's fictional voice perhaps says what the real women may be thinking, but we are left to wonder how revealing their own voices might have been. The larger point, however, is successfully conveyed: homeland "security" secures little and only adds to the deeper penetration of the state's surveillance technologies into domestic life.

In a chilling photo of "All America Day" in Fort Bragg, North Carolina, Berman photographs a soldier helping a boy fire a rifle equipped with a laser at a dark-skinned man in a turban who will drop to the ground and play dead when hit. This is a powerful recruitment tool in a country that fetishizes guns and serves as the primary source of weapons systems in the world, greatly expanding its arms sales during the Bush administration.[39] At the same time the lesson is clear: dark-skinned men in turbans are the paradigmatic enemy.

At a military training facility in Fort Polk, Louisiana, known as The Box, Berman photographed a simulated Iraq consisting of eighteen mock villages set on 100,000 acres. The Box is populated with Arabic-speaking employees and a thousand role-players who simulate Iraqi civilians and insurgents, many of whom are actual Iraqi immigrants who have taken on the performative role of "Iraqi" as a full-time job. Berman describes The Box as a place where soldiers go for a couple weeks before deploying to Iraq, where "you're supposed to learn about the culture." A cinderblock box carries a sign in English and Arabic that says "Freedom School." Berman asks, "Once you start building Freedom School, what are you really making? Whose imagination is this? Is this supposed to be someplace in Iraq? (Or) is this someone's fantasy of what Iraq is?"[40]

Americans have built numerous training camps to simulate Afghani and/or Iraqi villages in addition to Fort Polk. There are training camps in Playas, New Mexico; Camp Grayling, Michigan; Camp Atterbury, Indiana; and the Yuma ranges in California. A thirty-million-dollar complex opened at Camp Pendleton in southern California in 2011, and more are planned in Camp LeJeune, North Carolina (sixteen million dollars), and Hawaii (thirty-one million dollars).[41] These camps are unknown to most Americans except as they have been photographed by artists such as An-My Lê, Nina Berman, and Christopher Sims. On thousands of acres deep in the woods in Louisiana or North Carolina, or in a vast desert expanse near Death Valley in California, there are whole clusters of villages in pretend countries known as Talatha, Braggistan, or "Iraq." In addition to recent immigrants from Iraq and Afghanistan, who produce performative versions of how Americans expect "Iraqi" and "Afghani" villagers to behave, the "villagers" are also played by local residents, active-duty army spouses, and veterans of the wars in Korea and Vietnam, some of whom are amputees and play "the wounded."

Christopher Sims's photo series *Theater of War: The Pretend Villages of Iraq and Afghanistan* (2008), made over the course of recent years, includes lamps and knick-knacks painted onto the walls of rooms that hold only the barest, most makeshift furniture (*Jihad Lamp, Fort Polk, Louisiana*), a small plywood structure painted dark green and meant to be a "mosque" (*Mosque, Camp Mackall, Louisiana*), the head of a woman in a black veil painted onto the glass window of a door (*Village Residence, Fort Polk, Louisiana*), or a woman wearing round black glasses holding a basket that contains two dolls with clipped-on ID cards (*Mother with Babies, Fort Polk, Louisiana*). The cheap construction of the villages and dress of the "villagers" not only highlights their fakeness but makes them seem uncanny and surreal, their utterly artificial relation to the cultures they are meant to represent hopelessly inadequate.[42]

Sims, the 2010 recipient of the Baum Award for Emerging American Photographers, describes the way in which this low-budget simulation eerily fuses into normal life: "The villages are places of fantastic imagination. The actors continue playing their roles as police officers, gardeners, and café owners during the long stretches of day between training exercises. Some villagers plant crops that they harvest months later for food for their lunches and dinners. Others pass their leisure time painting murals on the interior walls to beautify their surroundings, or making arts and crafts to trade with other villagers." This wartime life, however, includes a high daily death count. Sims writes:

> Sometimes I visit the villages with access provided by the military's public affairs office; other times I am a role player myself, playing the character of a war photographer for the "International News Network." Here, backstage in the war on terrorism, I see insurgents planting a bomb in a Red Crescent ambulance; American soldiers negotiating with a reluctant mayor; a suicide bomber detonating herself outside of a mosque; and villagers erupting in an anti-American riot. The designers and inhabitants of these worlds take great pride in the scope and fidelity of their wars-in-miniature. By day's end, hundreds of soldiers and civilians lay dead—the electronic sensors on their special halters indicating whether friendly fire, an improvised explosive device, or a sniper's bullet has killed them.[43]

In *Guantánamo Bay* (2006), finding too many restrictions on photographing the people, Sims portrayed what he calls the "stage sets" of community and prison life on the forty-five acres of the American prison camp in Cuba, including a painted portrait of Martin Luther King in the naval station mess hall, a painted rifle on the wall of "Club Survivor, Camp America," a forgotten Christmas tree in the corner of an office at "Camp America," and a revealing photo of an administrative review board meeting room at Camp Delta. A small white plastic chair with a hook on the floor in front of it for affixing leg chains is dwarfed by two large black armchairs on its flanks. The edge of a desk in the foreground of the photo, though only a few feet from the chairs, holds a microphone on its edge. The surreal and the menacing commingle here as well.[44]

Homeland security has become a U.S. industry, a big business with billions of dollars in available funding so that various police and training groups perform and document their training in order to write grants for more funding in a self-perpetuating cycle of fantasy, fear, and employment. States vied for grant money from the U.S. Department of Homeland Security as a way of garnering contracts and attracting more businesses and jobs to their state. In 2010 the budget for homeland security was almost forty-three billion dollars.[45] The drive for funds also fuels research proposals for ever more invasive surveillance and sensors as "counterterrorism tools."[46] Lindsey Beyerman notes "a local police department beefing up its SWAT teams, or a Neighborhood Watch captain writing grants to hire his friends to patrol his small town for terrorists." Beyerman recounts a conversation with Berman about a gun dealer in Orlando, Florida, "who was trying to sell very long sniper rifles to a civilian police department in the name of counterterrorism. She asked why the police would need such a weapon. The gun dealer responded by presenting a highly complex scenario involving terrorists on a boat filled with explosives in the river preparing to ram into some seaside structure. In that case, he asked Berman, wouldn't she want the police officers to have extra-long sniper rifles?"[47]

Photographers of the homefront, such as Berman and Sims, like those in the war zone, establish considered political perspectives. Because we know that photographs are no less mediated than art and do not provide unfiltered access to the real, it is important to examine the ways in which war photographs taken by soldiers, civilians, and photojournalists, embedded or independent, *are* mediated and framed according to the beliefs, values, and circumstances of their producers and conditions of display, and to recognize, moreover, that there is, in fact, no unmediated access to war experience. What is different now than a decade or two ago, is the openly partisan perspectives of the photographers, who do not pretend to be omniscient or objective; they do not claim the position of the "eye of god"; on the contrary, through text and context, we know where they stand and, by analyzing the frame, we can determine how a photograph shapes political perspective and is shaped by it.[48] These documentary practices are therefore powerful weapons in the contest of images.

"Modern Warfare": First-Person Shooter Video Games

The effects of mediality, that is, the familiarity of most Americans with digital social media and the troubling way that familiarity bleeds into real war experience that is founded on the same kinds of digital technology, is all too chillingly demonstrated in the case of the leaked video footage of an American helicopter attack on twelve men in Baghdad in July 2007. The leaked footage was taken from a U.S. Apache helicopter gun camera and shows a group of twelve civilian men, most of them unarmed (one possibly armed), on a street in a section of eastern Baghdad, who are shot to death from above. The group included Namir Noor-Eldeen, a twenty-two-year-old photographer for Reuters news agency who lived in Baghdad, and Saeed Chmagh, his forty-year-old driver and assistant. The soldiers in the helicopter believed it was a group of insurgents, mistaking Noor-Eldeen's camera with a telephoto lens for a weapon. The thirty-eight-minute video, seen in infrared "negative," was decrypted and posted on the online whistleblower website Wikileaks in April 2010 and also shortened to a seventeen-minute version, titled "Collateral Murder." Both versions are also posted on YouTube.

The two Reuters employees, Noor-Eldeen and Chmagh, worked independently and were not embedded with the U.S. military, which meant that the military didn't know they were in Al-Amin, the section of eastern Baghdad where they were shot down that day. "Oh yeah," said one of the crew members in the Apache helicopter as he looked at the hanging camera, seeing what he expected to see, "That's a weapon." They tracked Noor-Eldeen in the cross-hairs of their gunsight. "Light 'em all up," was the command.

For many people, one of the disturbing aspects of the video is the callous chatter of the soldiers who joke and jeer as they gun people down. "Look at those dead bastards," says one. "Nice," responds another. More disturbing is what happens when a civilian van stops to pick up one of the unarmed wounded men crawling in his own blood. The soldiers open fire on the van, violating military Rules of Engagement, badly wounding two children who are inside the van and killing their father, the Good Samaritan who stopped to help. One of the soldiers remarks, "Well, it's their fault for bringing their kids into a battle."

Richard Grusin suggests that the powerful embodied affect of this video depends on its affinities with current practices of online video-game playing both on computers and video-game platforms like X-Box Live and PSN (Play Station Network), particularly a popular game called

"Modern Warfare," which has produced a series titled *Call of Duty*.[49] The *Call of Duty* series has sold more than fifty-five million copies, and the 2009 "Modern Warfare 2" became one of the best-selling games of all time. Serious shooter fans collectively spend millions of hours playing these games, and in 2010 another game, called "Battlefield: Bad Company," set out to rival "Modern Warfare." *New York Times* video-games reviewer Seth Schiesel notes that in "Modern Warfare" the combat arenas feel chaotic, whereas in "Bad Company" the teamwork and communications are more coordinated so that "the combat environments are more interesting and feel more akin to what I imagine a modern war zone to be." One wonders. The single-player first-person shooter stories (first-person shooters look at the world through their gunsight) in both games are six to eight hours long, but Schiesel favorably compares "Bad Company" to "Modern Warfare" primarily on the grounds that it is "more immersive" and "a boatload funnier," that the scripted narrative is more "profane, quirky and usually hilarious," and the characters "seem to be having a lot more fun."[50] Schiesel can only imagine what might constitute an authentic war zone and is more concerned, as a reviewer, with what provides the most fun, approaching the games from the perspective of their potential users. He notes that the *Call of Duty* games only took off in 2005 when Activision, the company that markets the franchise, moved *Call of Duty* games from World War II to the modern-day battlefield. With this gesture, the lag time that used to exist between war and reflection on its effects and meanings, at least ten years, has been shrunk to zero. War games, with modern-day Humvees, tanks, and helicopters, are set in the same time frame as the actual wars taking place in Iraq and Afghanistan, and reviewers of these games in major newspapers, like the players for whom they write, imagine what a modern war zone must be like based on the developing sophistication of the games themselves.

While recognizing that the embodied experiences of war games and shooting real humans from a helicopter in a real war are two different things, Grusin contends that the similar protocols and other parallels between games such as "Modern Warfare," "Bad Company" and the "Collateral Murder" video create an undeniable overlap of experience. In both games and gunship videos, players and real shooters must wait for permission to engage and are told what targets to avoid; targets are vehicles or people on foot; players interact with their targets through gun sights via video screens and black-and-white images, and even the dialogue programmed into the game after particular kills, like "nice shot" or "way to go," is echoed by the soldiers in the gunship video. The video screens and black-and-white images, in particular, serve to derealize the flesh and blood corporeality of the human "targets."

This is not to say that video games produce real-world violence any more than historical war reenactments do, but that each realm of experience is figured or "premediated" and then "remediated" in terms of the other, so that the game world may come to seem real and the real world may come to seem like a game in a liminal space of mediality. Grusin writes:

> Not only are video game designers basing the affective and social behavior of their algorithmically generated characters on the behavior of soldiers in the field, but it is undoubtedly the case that soldiers in the field are remediating affective behaviors that they have themselves experienced and participated in while playing video games at home. And when you remember that these games are not only being played by teenagers at home in the US and across the globalized West, but are being played by the soldiers themselves both before they deploy abroad and in between missions back at their base, then the force of Wikileaks' Collateral Murder video is to make the boundaries between these two experiences ever more difficult to secure. By premediating the sociality and affectivity of warfare for American youth, video games like Modern Warfare work not only to prepare a new generation of soldiers for combat but also (given the demographics of our current volunteer military) to modulate the collective affect of an even larger group of US and global citizens to accept modern war as an unexceptional feature of our everyday media landscape.[51]

Benedict Carey confirms this assessment in a *New York Times* article that cites veterans who explain the soldiers' actions in the "Collateral Murder" video by pointing out that fighters must create psychological distance from the enemy in order to do their job. "One reason that the soldiers seemed as if they were playing a video game," writes Carey, "is that, in a morbid but necessary sense, they were." Former Army psychologist Bret A. Moore reinforces the point: "Their job is to destroy the enemy, and one way they're able to do that is to see it as a game, so that the people don't seem real."[52] Thus the derealization of the enemy as fully human, akin to video games, becomes part of military strategy and training, and the spillover of this attitude to all Iraqis (or Afghanis or Palestinians), whether armed or unarmed, innocent or guilty, child or adult, becomes normalized and acceptable, perhaps even inevitable.

Indeed, the U.S. military has developed a video game called "America's Army" that millions of people play but which started as a military recruiting tool. The game merges real and virtual war and is one of the top ten games of all games downloaded from the Internet. According to Peter Singer, who wrote about "America's Army" for *Foreign Policy* magazine, "the game had more import on actual recruits than all other forms of Army advertising combined." Singer calls this "militainment" and points out that the military draws from the tools of entertainment in the development of its weapon and robotic systems. The Pacbot, for example, which is a tiny ground robot, is modeled after the Xbox and PlayStation controllers, because the military realized that video game companies had already spent millions of dollars designing these systems that "fit in your hand perfectly." Even more importantly, "the training costs had already been taken out because you hand these to an 18-year-old, and they automatically know how to use it."[53]

Advocates of "America's Army" as a recruiting and training tool suggest that more complexity can be built into it than a regular training program in the field, and that it can be repeated over and over. Singer argues that video games make no room for unforeseeable contingencies known as "the fog of war." He cites the example of a real-world battle during the invasion of Iraq, re-created in one package of the video game, in which a Green Beret team fights off an Iraqi battalion that had tanks. In the game, the player does what the Green Berets did. "What the game leaves out, though," notes Singer, "is that when the Green Berets called in an air strike, the air strike accidentally hit some of their own, and also killed some of our Kurdish allies. The unexpected is often hard for us to program in." War in a video game becomes much cleaner and death is abstract. Singer refers to what some have jokingly called "avatar fatigue" in which losing in the game means "you just reboot," because you've lost your avatar. "Whereas in reality, you actually have to call your buddy's wife and explain what happened." Singer also points to what the military calls "the O'Brien effect," referring to an incident in which the talk show host Conan O'Brien challenged Serena Williams, the tennis player, to a tennis match, and when she came out onto the set, he handed her a Nintendo Wii. O'Brien proceeded to beat Williams. "And the point here was that just because you excel in the video game of something, it doesn't mean that you excel in the real-world version of something."[54]

Under pressure from Reuters in the 2007 shooting, the U.S. government investigated the incident and came to the conclusion that every action taken by the soldiers in the helicopter was completely justified, including the firing on unarmed civilian rescuers, and declined to suggest any remedial action to prevent such events from occurring in the future. Thus the government confirmed that the soldiers did their jobs, received permission for every action they took, and demonstrated what all soldiers in Iraq know: that their actions constituted standard operating procedure in accordance with military policy. Like the Abu Ghraib photos, what is remarkable about this killing is not that it is common practice, but that it became visible to an outraged public because Wikileaks got hold of the videotape and because of the deaths of two Reuters employees. Unlike the tens of thousands of ordinary Iraqis and Afghanis who have been killed in this or similar ways, these two deaths raised demands for an investigation. But it is not the soldiers alone who should be indicted, as they were, conveniently, at Abu Ghraib, but the U.S. government and the war policies it pursues and defends. As Glenn Greenwald acidly observes, "There's a serious danger when incidents like this Iraq slaughter are exposed in a piecemeal and unusual fashion: namely, the tendency to talk about it as though it is an aberration. It isn't.... That's how we collectively dismissed the Abu Ghraib photos, and it's why the Obama administration took such extraordinary steps to suppress all the rest of the torture photos: because further disclosure would have revealed that behavior to be standard and common, not at all unusual or extraordinary."[55]

The "extraordinary steps" of the Obama administration to which Greenwald refers is the active support for a bill jointly sponsored by Senators Lindsey Graham and Joe Lieberman called "The Detainee Photographic Records Protection Act of 2009." Greenwald explains that this bill "literally has no purpose other than to allow the government to suppress any 'photograph taken between September 11, 2001 and January 22, 2009 relating to the treatment of individuals engaged, captured, or detained after September 11, 2001, by the Armed Forces of the United States in operations outside of the United States.' As long as the Defense Secretary certifies—with no review possible—that disclosure would 'endanger' American citizens or our troops, then the photographs can be suppressed *even if FOIA* [Freedom of Information Act] *requires disclosure*. The certification lasts 3 years and can be renewed indefinitely."[56] This law has no other purpose than to empower the president to suppress photographic evidence of war crimes and retroactively changes a transparency law despite Obama's repeated vow to make his administration "the most open and transparent in history." These extraordinary lengths testify to the degree to which the Abu Ghraib photographs and videos and the helicopter gunship video have become the inverse of the 1991 Gulf War abstracted high tech images, which erased the human effects of war from the visual field and made death invisible. These controversial videos from the Iraq war turn those derealized prisoners and victims back into palpable flesh and blood. At the same time, these videos from gunships in the battlefield are structured as war images imagined by video-game makers, deliberately employed by the military to overdetermine how warfare itself is understood by those in front of the lethal gunship screen.

Although "Collateral Murder" may be the first Apache video to cause a national scandal, it is not the first such video to appear on the Internet. Thousands of similar Apache videos have been made available on

Liveleaks.com, an Internet video sharing site founded in 2006 by Hayden Hewitt, where the videos look very similar and usually end with "a group of people on a FLIR camera being killed," according to Hewitt, referring to the infrared equipment made by FLIR systems.[57] There are also other sites where soldiers upload their own filmed footage of their war experience, easily making the wars in Iraq and Afghanistan the most filmed wars in history. In a study for the online multimedia journal *Vectors*, Jennifer Terry lists fifteen video-sharing Internet sites for military videos from Iraq and Afghanistan.[58] As Terry points out, most of these videos are "radically decontextualized" so that "we learn very little about where they occurred, when they occurred, who is taking the footage, who is fighting, and why they are fighting. Some videos offer information that is either not very specific or inaccurate." This decontextualization leads to a larger political obfuscation in which the politics and circumstances are reduced to a visual and auditory spectacle while the "differing rationalities of the warring groups are submerged into obscurity." This phenomenon parallels that of war reenactment in which context is lost and political motivations are mystified and obscured. Crucially, as Terry notes, "if a video clip offers no information about the historical or political context in which its action takes place, the likelihood of simplistic racist and xenophobic logics organizing the viewing practice increases."[59]

The U.S. Army has produced its own videos, in the form of games, for a traveling road show and recruiting event called "Virtual Army Experience" that travels cross-country to NASCAR races and air shows. In his photography series *Hearts and Minds* (2007), Christopher Sims produced a series of portraits of adolescent boys playing the army video games. The boys wait in line at these events to enter a large tent where they not only can play the video games but meet decorated veterans who have served in Iraq and Afghanistan. Sims writes, "The army reveals itself to be a keen reader of American adolescent emotions and passions, and employs this understanding through a brilliantly designed and bloodless simulation of the thrill of the fight."[60] In Sims's photos, one boy wears a Boy Scout uniform, another a "Civil Air Patrol" camouflage shirt, a third wears a T-shirt that says "Chevy Trucks." The intensity of their involvement and absorption is written on their faces.

The point, however, is not that video war games produce a militaristic mentality. This would be too reductive, suggesting that the elimination of video war games might eliminate the appeal of war. Both war and war games, in predigital form, have been around for a long time, and it is just as likely that war games are produced by actual wars as the other way around. The question, then, is how to understand the implications of such digital technology in the context of similar technology that is currently employed in actual war. To put it another way, recruits who are already familiar with this technology, as we saw above, are seen by the military as having an advantage; yet we also have seen how it puts them at a disadvantage by distorting and undermining a larger understanding of war because the very idea of war has been premediated through a technology that has been learned and internalized as a game. This disadvantage is seen as an advantage by the military precisely because it makes it easier to train recruits to kill, both because the technology is familiar and because it provides a strategy for having "fun" and overcoming the prohibition against killing. The "hearts and minds" of the boys in Sims's photos already have been won by gaming technology, making the military's job much easier with those who also sign up.

Young men are also watching the thousands of videos of firefights and aerial bombings posted by soldiers in Iraq and Afghanistan, which Jennifer Terry suggests are made almost exclusively by male soldiers and watched by male viewers.[61] A large percentage of these videos come in highly edited form and are set to music, as if they were music videos, including a video parody of Lady Gaga's "Telephone" made by male soldiers in Afghanistan and viewed more than five million times on YouTube. "Certain songs have become established scene-setters," notes the *New York Times*, "particularly the heavy-metal song 'Bodies' by Drowning Pool, with its mantra: 'Let the bodies hit the floor, let the bodies hit the floor.'"[62] Like video games, the footage of war experience edited and set to music appeals to the young and creates a decontextualized and depoliticized effect that heightens visceral sensation while derealizing the less entertaining effects of war.

One of the most chilling examples is that of military predator drone operators who sit in comfortable offices in the United States and remotely pilot overseas drones with cameras, reporting the results to American ground commanders in the Middle East who make life and death decisions based on these reports, which are often highly inaccurate. In just one example, a predator drone in Pakistan, carrying a powerful camera that beamed real-time images to its operators in Nevada, tracked a convoy of three vehicles, a pickup truck and two sports utility vehicles for three and a half hours but failed to notice that the vehicles contained women and children, even after intelligence analysts who were monitoring the drone's video feed sent two computer messages warning the drone operators and the ground commanders that children were visible. The drone operators insisted that all the occupants were military-age men and the ground command called in an airstrike, killing twenty-three innocent civilians.[63] According to a U.N. report, airstrikes accounted for about 60 percent of the nearly six hundred civilians killed by NATO and allied Afghan forces in 2009.[64] According to various news sources, hundreds of innocent civilians have been killed in drone attacks in Pakistan. The exact number is difficult to determine because the U.S. government keeps out news organizations and blocks aid groups, including Doctors without Borders.[65] Videos of drone attacks from drone cameras have been posted on the Internet, where they are known as "drone porn" and have attracted tens of thousands of viewers. The videos are posted by the Defense Department itself in a show of prowess and technology advertisement, while serving as entertainment for those who like to watch people and things blow up without seeing the blood and gore.[66]

In September 2010, a new game called "Medal of Honor" aroused controversy when it allowed players to assume the role of the Taliban and shoot at American soldiers. Soldiers' families and politicians complained, and Seth Schiesel speculated that the protests arose because it allowed the enemy to seem too human, a soldier rather than a "terrorist."[67] The name "Taliban" was changed in the multiplayer mode to "Opposing Force" or "OpFor." But there are larger questions raised by such video war games. As Greg Goodrich, "Medal of Honor" executive producer, explained to the *New York Times*, he used consultants to help make the game "authentic and plausible" rather than "accurate and realistic," which was confirmed by one of these consultants who said, "There's nothing so close where it's a re-enactment. In my eyes, that would be wrong." Andrew Exum, an army platoon leader in 2002 and now a fellow at the Center for a New American Security observed that nearly eighty thousand Americans are deployed in Afghanistan while 2.2 million people played "Modern Warfare 2" on Xbox Live during a single day in fall 2009. "There's something annoying," he said, "that most of America experiences the wars in Iraq and Afghanistan, which are actually taking place, through a video game." What makes this "annoying" is that no matter how interactively engaged participants are or how persuasively they feel they are virtually reenacting authentic war experience, the war game is necessarily fiction that does not reflect the experience of real soldiers in Iraq and Afghanistan on either side. As *New York Times* writer Chris Suellentrop notes, "Military shooters turn the classic description of war on its head, converting the experience into long periods of sheer terror punctuated by moments of boredom." One veteran told Suellentrop, "No one would dramatize the real experience" of a platoon in Afghanistan "because it's too boring. How do you make a game out of drinking chai with an elder?"[68] The relentless thrills and excitement of video war games that last six or seven hours not only mislead the millions of players who think they understand the nature of these wars, but cause those who are recruited through the games' seductive appeal to arrive on the real battlefield ill-prepared for modern warfare; instead, they are ready to play "Modern Warfare."

6

ISRAEL / PALESTINE AND THE POLITICAL IMAGINARY

As a Jew, I was taught it was ethically imperative to speak up.
—Judith Butler, *Ha'aretz*, 24 February 2010

The technologies of video and surveillance fundamental to "homeland security" and the "war on terror," the pursuit of perpetual war on the domestic front, and the ensuing collapse of public and private space are all nowhere more deeply entrenched than Israel/Palestine. At the same time, the production of documentary photography and artistic interventions deployed against the logic of the Occupation of Palestine and the militarized homefront has produced among the most compelling uses of documentary practices. An example of the contest of images may be seen in the dueling videos that were aired on television and the Internet following the Israeli strike on the aid ship *Mavi Marmara* on 31 May 2010. The *Mavi Marmara* was the lead ship in the first flotilla attempting to break the Israeli blockade of Gaza, which had begun in 2007. When the ship refused to divert its course to an Israeli port, Israeli naval commandos attacked it during the middle of the night while it was still in international waters. Israeli Defense Forces (IDF) commandos threw stun grenades and fired a hail of rubber bullets from above before boarding the ship from helicopters and speedboats that surrounded the ship. Expecting the rubber bullets to disperse the crowd and to encounter only passive resistance from the 546 aid activists on board, the naval commandos instead were set upon as they invaded. One was stabbed and a total of seven Israeli commandos were injured. The soldiers who rappelled down the ropes after them fired live ammunition. Israeli commandos killed a total of nine aid activists and injured more than thirty. News of the killings evoked intense international condemnation. Like the Occupation of Palestine itself, this attack was seen as open defiance of international law, causing wanton death and injury, which is exactly the accusation Israel made against the activists.

The Israeli government held the ship's passengers in prison for several days and confiscated all film and video from passengers and some sixty reporters aboard the *Mavi Marmara* in order to control the visual narrative of what had occurred. Both sides nonetheless released videos in an effort to prove that the other side was the aggressor. Many observers asked how an unarmed group defending itself against armed invaders could be said to initiate violence under any circumstances. The Israeli video includes arrows, yellow circles, and captions describing the action and shows naval commandos sliding down ropes and apparently being beaten by activists. According to reports, however, the footage of passengers hitting IDF commandos "bore signs of heavy editing, including the obscuring or removal of time stamps." It was also noted, "Much of the footage released by Israel (after heavy editing) was taken from journalists aboard the ship after their equipment had been confiscated. The move was strongly denounced by Israel's Foreign Press Association (FPA), which stated on 4 June: 'the use of this material without permission from the relevant media organizations is a clear violation of journalistic ethics and unacceptable.'"[1] Although no commandos were shot and activists who took guns off them emptied them of bullets, or, in one case, were videotaped throwing a rifle overboard, Israeli news tried to claim this was evidence that the activists were armed. Some of those onboard, such as Cultures of Resistance filmmaker Iara Lee, successfully hid and retained some of their recordings despite Israeli efforts to confiscate all footage, and the flotilla's organizers, from the Turkish group Insani Yardim Vakfi, the Free Gaza Movement, and other groups, webcasted live from the open seas as the confrontation started, using the services of Livestream, a New York–based company that hosts free webcasts. Iara Lee's video shows hovering helicopters, speedboats, and gunships, activists using slingshots against IDF navy commandos rappelling from the helicopters, as well as efforts to treat both wounded and bleeding activists and two injured Israeli soldiers. At the end of a fifteen-minute video, a woman is heard shouting, "We have no guns here, we are civilians taking care of injured people. Don't use violence, we need help."[2]

What is clear is that in Israel's determination to stop the ship in this manner, and by killing nine unarmed Turkish civilians (one of whom was also an American citizen), Israel created for itself a huge public relations fiasco. The peace activists, who never expected a bloodbath, nonetheless succeeded in bringing the world's attention to the Israeli blockade of Gaza, which is regarded internationally as both illegal and responsible for the inhumane suffering of the population of Gaza by preventing all but the most basic humanitarian aid and food from entering. Israel cites the kidnapping of IDF soldier Gilad Shalit and rocket fire into Israel following the parliamentary election of Hamas in 2006 as the cause of the blockade, but many observers note that the gradual closure of Gaza began in 1991, when Israel canceled the general exit permit that allowed most Palestinians to move freely through Israel and the Occupied Territories.[3]

This international focus on the Gaza blockade occurred not only because of the violence against the activists but, more importantly, because the events were instantly available for global viewing. The debate over what actually occurred in the contest of images roused passions around the world in a way that many other acts of violence have been unable to do without such immediate global visibility, if they have been noticed at all. The nine killings on the *Mavi Marmara* and repeated playing of the footage galvanized demonstrations in the Middle East, Europe, North America, and South Asia, with thousands of demonstrators gathering in Istanbul, Cairo, Athens, Baghdad, Stockholm, Oslo, Rome, New York, and many other cities in the United States and Canada. The U.N. Security Council condemned the deaths and called on Israel to release all the prisoners from the ships, which Israel finally did by 6 June, but the incident severely strained relations with Turkey. Under intense pressure, Israel subsequently eased the blockade to allow in more basic goods, although this action does not resolve the suffering of the population in Gaza, a strip of land only twenty-six miles long and seven miles wide along the Mediterranean Sea with its borders controlled by Israel and Egypt. With a population of 1.5 million, it is one of the world's most densely populated areas; most residents are Palestinian refugees from families that fled there when Israel was established in 1948. Despite Gaza's high literacy rate, unemployment runs as high as 40 percent and at least 70 percent of Gazans live below the poverty line. The three-week military assault and massive bombardment that Israel launched against Gaza in December 2008 destroyed much of Gaza's infrastructure, leveling factories, government buildings, hospitals, schools, and entire neighborhoods. In addition to much gratuitous and wanton destruction, over thirteen hundred Gazans died and tens of thousands were left homeless.[4] In response to attempts to defend the Israeli attack on Gaza, Professor of Humanistic Studies at Hebrew University David Shulman refers to "the current wave of nationalist hysteria, racist legislation, self-righteous posturing, and self-destructive policies that has engulfed the State of Israel and now informs much of its public discourse."[5]

Although Israel justifies all of its actions on the basis of "security," the two sides are vastly unequal: Israel maintains total institutional domination, immensely superior military strength, and controls the country's borders and resources, while Palestinians are subject to occupation, containment, and control under Israeli rule but with no democratic rights that Israel is bound to respect, and any formal appeals for rights must be made to Israeli authorities. Israel's security framing and denial of Palestinian national rights is premised on its exclusive claim to the entire country and its insistence on Israel as an ethnocracy or "Jewish state." With room for only one people, "Arabs" are demonized, making clear that there has never been any serious intention to create a "two-state" solution; on the contrary, Israel has acted in a systematic way to make this impossible. In any case, there is no fair and humane way to occupy and rule people against their will; thus an unending landscape of war endures in Israel/Palestine.

The land is often figured as a metaphor for the social, political, and physical body of the people, making the landscape neither simple nor transparent. Both the object of war as battlefield, and the subject of war as confirmation of national or ethnic identity, the landscape of war is not just a ruined environment, but a symbolic entity and product of a national political imaginary that defines and grounds identity through place.[6] The landscape of war is discursive and physical, ideological and topological, as is vividly apparent in the Israeli-Palestinian conflict. This chapter will examine the relationship between the traumatic effects of war on the landscape—what has been called "war's silent casualty"[7]—and the responses of Israeli, Palestinian, and international artists to the landscape as defined and redefined in relation to collective identity and the goals of war. The very fact that the landscape may be redefined suggests that such definitions, to a great extent, are arbitrary.[8] But the destruction of the landscape becomes the destruction of the natural basis of cultural identity—thus, on the one hand, the landscape is a sign of the peaceful home of those who by birth and generations of habitation have a right to live there, and, at the same time, it is a sign of the foreignness of others who have no claim to the land. A foreign claim on the landscape thus legitimizes war, making the landscape always a sign of both war and peace.[9] Yet an essentialized relation between landscape and war may also be seen as false or misleading because, as the "war on terror" demonstrates, we are in an era of war that requires no landscape. In an undefined war against terror, there is no defining territory, so that the war zone is everywhere and nowhere at once; it may shift without warning from a hotel lobby to an internet site to an airplane.[10] It may be an aid ship in international waters or even devolve to the body of the Palestinian, which in itself is seen as a threatening object of war. As Judith Butler asserted in an interview with the Israeli newspaper *Ha'aretz*: "So any and all Palestinian lives that are killed or injured are understood no longer to be lives, no longer understood to be living, no longer understood even to be human in a recognizable sense, but they are artillery. . . . Because everyone who is a living Palestinian is, in their being, a declaration of war, or a threat to the existence of Israel, or pure military artillery, materiel. They have been transformed, in the Israeli war imaginary, into pure war instruments."[11]

On the Israeli side, the landscape of war as a symbolic entity and product of a national political imaginary is firmly anchored in the fictive rhetoric of reclaiming and "redeeming" the ancient biblical land of Judea and Samaria, of "making the desert bloom" and of "a land without people for a people without a land," culminating in the war of 1948, which Israelis call the War of Independence and Palestinians call the *Nakba*, or catastrophe. The ensuing conflict for the last sixty years has never been one of more or less equal forces; rather, the Israelis have been enormously more powerful, despite claiming a defensive stance, and have perpetrated more wars to extend the boundaries of Israel's national borders and scarred the land with military structures, roads, detritus, and, most recently, a permanent barrier wall. Paradoxically, then, in order to claim the land, the military often must destroy it; confirming identity through the land by means of perpetual war becomes self-defeating.[12]

Among Israeli artists who are sympathetic to the plight of Palestinians, their artistic practice is part of a political trend that addresses the problems and contradictions of the Jewish state as an occupying power and questions the official fixed meanings and mythologies of *Eretz Israel*, the land of Israel. In examining the traumatic effects of war on the landscape and the responses of Israeli artists to that contested national political imaginary, we may begin with the notion of Israeli "double vision," which describes the contradictory relationship between seeing and imagining the land of Israel. Israeli architect and theorist Eyal Weizman analyzes the effects of architecture and urban planning on the landscape and posits the paradox of "double vision" among Israelis who look at the landscape but do not see the Palestinians. Weizman notes that the Jewish settlers in the hilltop settlements of the West Bank, who effectively act as security agents for the Israeli state, are not in fact induced to move there on this political basis. In addition to the high level of services and the cheapness of state-subsidized housing, the settlements are conceptually constructed as reestablishing the relation between the terrain and the sacred text of the Bible, so that prospective settlers see themselves first and foremost as returning exiles to the land. The hilltops of the West Bank therefore are not only a physical entity but also "an imagined, mythical geography" that provides a biblical panorama with spiritual power and significance. Israeli settlers are able to reenact religious-national myths in a way that maps the modern onto the ancient, the present onto the past. What the settlers *think* they see is a pastoral biblical landscape and its ancient figures. What they *actually* see are the stone houses and olive terraces of the Palestinian villages as well as the diminished lives and impoverishment of Palestinians under occupation. "Within this panorama lies a cruel paradox," writes Weizman, "the very thing that renders the landscape 'biblical' and 'pastoral'—its traditional habitation and cultivation in terraces, olive orchards, stone buildings and the presence of livestock—is produced by the Palestinians, the very people whom the settlers would like to displace." The Palestinian vernacular architecture is seen as both an authentic "biblical" style and as the style that Israeli culture must define itself against. The Palestinian people are seen as both "latecomers to the land" and "custodians of ancient Hebrew culture."[13] Thus the

Palestinians exist in a landscape of biblical authenticity that legitimizes contemporary Israeli identity *and* in a state of political invisibility that delegitimizes their own identity in relation to the land. It is the embodiment of the trope "a land without people for a people without a land."

Even the Palestinian right to "look" at the settlements is a contested right. The mountaintop settlements necessitate building on steep slopes and result in the arrangements of homes in rings around summits. This fosters visibility both outward and down toward surrounding landscapes, and upward and inward, toward common public spaces and other homes, promoting both "unconscious policing" of public behavior and the consolidation of communal identity. The outward visual gaze, however, serves the state's security aims by transforming civilian settlers into observers who "investigate and report" on Palestinian movements in the West Bank; they help transform the occupied territory into an "optical matrix radiating out from a proliferation of lookout points/settlements scattered across the landscape." For safety, the settlements are intensely illuminated, further underscoring this vision matrix; however, while the circular layout of the settlements promotes both inward and outward gazing, the right to look belongs exclusively to the Israelis in "a hierarchy of vision." Weizman observes, "According to rules of engagement issued by the occupying forces at the end of 2003, soldiers may shoot to kill any Palestinian caught observing settlements with binoculars or in any other 'suspicious manner.' Palestinians should presumably avoid looking at settlements at all."[14]

B'Tselem, an Israeli organization that champions human rights in the Occupied Territories (West Bank, East Jerusalem, and Gaza), provides Israelis with a way of looking and seeing abuses that might otherwise be invisible to them. They do this through their camera distribution project, begun in January 2007, which provides Palestinians living in high-conflict areas with video cameras. Videos of Palestinian life become globally available on B'Tselem's website so that we might see, for example, the youth who spend their days working in the tunnels of Gaza or the improvised club for Internet games created for children in a Gazan refugee camp where they play "Counterstrike," a war game.[15] The website includes testimonial, video and photographic documentation of house demolitions, attacks on agriculture, beatings, interrogations, the water crisis, and other violence against Palestinians, including the willful destruction of Palestinian land for ostensible security reasons. The separation zone for the building of the Barrier Wall between Israel and the West Bank alone has consumed 3,700 acres of Palestinian land, destroying more than 100,000 trees and isolating more than 24,700 acres of cultivated land, including centuries-old olive trees, which are the most valuable. While Palestinians estimate tens of thousands of trees uprooted, the exact number is unknown; however, as René Backmann notes, "The Israeli daily *Yedioth Ahronoth* confirmed that in July 2003 one of the companies in charge of building the barrier put 'an unlimited quantity' of olive trees up for sale in Israel at the price of 1,000 shekels ($265) each."[16] There is a deeper violence in the destruction of trees that also destroys ancient family legacies and prepares for the destruction of Palestinian architecture, culture, and history, just as the imposition of the Wall on the topography of the Occupied Territories proceeds with little regard for the way it cuts through Palestinian land and towns, separating farmers from their fields and children from their schools. The primary concern in determining the sinuous route of the Wall, as aerial photos show, is to annex the nearly seventy West Bank Jewish settlements to Israeli territory, along with extra land necessary for their expansion.

The separation of farmers from their land and the proliferation of checkpoints, barriers, and Jewish-only access roads, along with the permit system imposed on the Palestinians, have devastated the West Bank economy, sending employment up and GDP down so that by 2008, close to 800,000 West Bank residents needed U.N. food assistance.[17] Palestinians are not allowed to open their own banks; tariffs and import controls prevent serious competition with Israeli products; economic ties with other Arab countries have been curtailed; the expropriation of farmland and the checkpoints closure policy prevent Palestinian produce from reaching Israeli markets and even internal markets, all creating a steadily tightening economic noose, so that 70 percent of Palestinian firms have either closed or severely curtailed production while access to the Israeli labor market is almost completely denied to Palestinian workers.[18] Israeli anthropologist and activist Jeff Halper, who founded and heads the Israeli Committee Against House Demolitions (ICAHD), describes Israeli policy as one of convincing Israelis that no political solution is possible. Halper argues that as long as the goal of the Israeli government is to maintain a Jewish ethnocracy, the counterpart is necessarily *nishul*, forced migration or "silent transfer," meaning the mass dispossession and displacement of Israel's Palestinian inhabitants, a crime according to international laws. This "de-Arabization" is the flip side of "Judaization," which also may be understood as ethnic cleansing.[19] The process takes many forms, including restrictions on citizenship, whereby, for example, Israel prohibits spouses of Arab citizens of Israel who come from the West Bank, Gaza, or any Arab country from entering Israel or receiving residency rights or citizenship, including the children of such marriages. Palestinian citizens of Israel, who constitute 20 percent of the population, are confined by law to only 3.5 percent of the country. Denied housing permits, Palestinians who live in "unrecognized villages" are denied sewage, electricity, roads, or schools, and the state may destroy their homes. In 2006, 868 Palestinian homes were demolished inside Israel, and in 2007, four Bedouin villages were destroyed. To further the goal of induced emigration, a similar system exists in the West Bank, where land is zoned as "agricultural" so that Palestinians are forbidden to build on their own land and their "illegally" built houses are subject to demolition.[20]

Journalist Naomi Klein astutely analyzes Israel as an "apartheid state" that has "crafted an economy that expands markedly in direct response to escalating violence." It has done so by pioneering the homeland security industry years before the United States and European companies grasped its potential. As a result, Israel leads the post-9/11 world market, even as it continues hostilities against its neighbors and the Occupied Territories; indeed, Israel's booming prosperity is precisely built on "an economy based on the premise of continual war and deepening disasters."[21] Motivation for a successful "peace process," if it ever existed, has been nullified. While some observers thought the 1993 Oslo Accords might lead to stability, foreign minister Shimon Peres made it clear that the Israeli government was seeking "a peace of markets," rather than "a peace of flags," meaning that Israel wanted only to open its borders and join the globalization trend and saw the effects of the bloody conflict with the Palestinians as blocking that path. If Israel ended the Occupation, Arab states would end their boycott of Israel, leaving it perfectly positioned to become the Middle East's free-trade hub. A variety of factors contributed to the failure of this plan. Israelis blamed suicide bombings and the assassination of Prime Minister Yitzhak Rabin (by a right-wing Israeli), while Palestinians pointed to the escalation of illegal settlement building in the Occupied Territories, which even Israel's foreign minister Shlomo Ben-Ami called "neocolonialist" activity designed so that "when there will finally be peace between us and the Palestinians, there will be a situation of dependence, of a structured lack of equality between the two entities."[22] Many question whether peace was ever the real goal of the Oslo process, which did not begin to resolve any of the most contentious issues, such as the fate of Jerusalem, Palestinian refugees and the right of return, Jewish settlements, or even the right to Palestinian self-determination. However, Klein points to two factors that did not figure in the debates about what happened but which played an important role in Israel's retreat into unilateralism. These factors relate to Klein's thesis that the Chicago School free-market crusade led by Milton Friedman since the 1970s, which treats disasters as exciting market opportunities and has led to economic "shock therapy" and disaster capitalism around the world, also played out in Israel.

One factor was the influx of Soviet Jews into Israel (a result of Russia's own shock therapy experiment), and the other was "the flipping of Israel's export economy from one based on traditional goods and high technology to one disproportionately dependent on selling expertise and devices relating to counterterrorism." With the arrival of roughly one million Soviet refugees, a huge influx, Israel was no longer reliant on cheap Palestinian labor, and the mutual economic dependence between Israel and Palestine was suddenly over. Israel already had taken aggressive measures to prevent Palestinians from developing an independent trade relationship with Arab states, thus leaving the Occupied Territories economically isolated. Zionist goals also were furthered by the massive infusion of Soviet Jews because they not only provided cheap labor but increased the ratio of Jews to Arabs and were often the people who populated the settlements, often without quite knowing where they were going. From 1993 to 2000, the number of Israeli settlers in the Occupied Territories doubled, the settlements became lush and fortified suburbs, and key water reserves in the West Bank were appropriated to feed the settlements and diverted back to Israel. Israel also began its policy of "closure," sealing off the border between Israel and the Occupied Territories, at first temporarily, but quickly establishing it as the norm along with increased policing and a more elaborate system of checkpoints. All of this had a catastrophic effect on Palestinian economic life and created the conditions for the Palestinian rebellion of the second Intifada in September 2000.[23]

The second factor was success in security and surveillance systems, data mining, and terrorist profiling, which allowed for Israeli dominance in the global security boom. Such success did not require peace with the Palestinians; on the contrary, it depended and continues to depend on continual deployment of Israeli antiterrorism technologies. The loss in tourism because of security fears is offset by Israeli hosting, since 2002, of homeland security conferences, which are effectively trade shows, for lawmakers, police chiefs, the FBI, and CEOs from around the world. Counterterrorism technology, in 2007, made up about 60 percent of all exports.[24] Inequality between Israel's wealthy few and the poor has also grown exponentially while wars have become transformed, in part, into branding opportunities and promotional campaigns, causing Israel's economy to grow even as it wages war. With the building of the Barrier Wall to make "closure" permanent, the entire country is transformed into a "gated community" while Gaza and the West Bank have become militarized ghettos with severely contracted economies, which many have compared to South African Bantustans.

192 THE LANDSCAPE OF WAR

As Klein notes, however, Bantustans were also work camps, designed to regulate and control cheap labor for African mines, while Israel has constructed a system designed to keep workers from working and has created instead "a network of open holding pens for millions of people who have been categorized as surplus humanity."[25]

The Tree Is the Enemy Soldier

The struggle for cultural identity rooted in the landscape has led to appropriation of its symbols by both Israelis and Palestinians. Yet these symbols themselves have become objects of violence in a proxy war by Jews against Palestinians. In 2006, Israeli artist, designer, and activist David Tartakover produced a New Year's postcard with the cheerful words "Season Greetings from the Middle East" printed across a vista of blue sky above a grove of olive trees that have been beheaded. A quotation across the bottom from Deuteronomy refers to what is known as the Seven Species, which are regarded as symbols of the earth's fertility

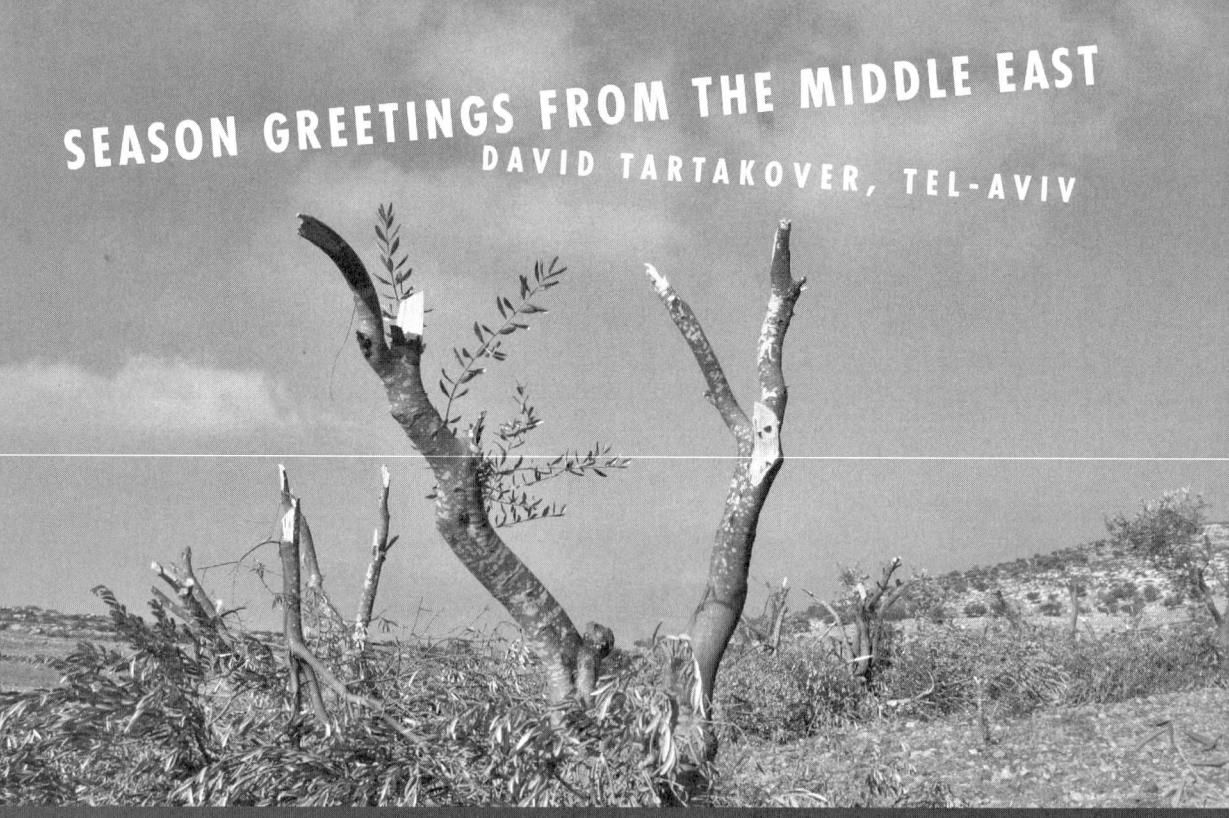

Figure 25. David Tartakover, *Greeting Card*, 2006. Photo by Alex Levac. (Courtesy of the artist.)

and thought to represent Israel's biblical relationship to the land: "A land of wheat, and barley, and vines, and fig trees, and pomegranates, a land of olive oil, and honey." The hacked-off and naked branches of the olive trees do not contradict this description of the bounty to be treasured but suggest something more sinister: its human contravention in a paradise turned dystopic. For his postcard, Tartakover appropriated a photo taken by *Ha'aretz* photographer Alex Levac of a Palestinian olive tree grove near the Jewish settlement of Itamar, which is close to the Palestinian village of Aqraba.[26] Although the IDF is required to protect Palestinian farmers during the olive harvest, residents of Itamar and its outposts have been reported "harassing local Palestinians, damaging their property and obstructing their access to land, particularly during the olive harvest. They have reportedly stolen olives, prevented Palestinian farmers from reaching their land, even when accompanied by international activists, shot at farmers picking their olives, or grazing their animals. It is alleged that they have set fire to hundreds of olive trees and thousands of dunam of cultivated land belonging to local Palestinians."[27] Many of the Jewish settlers are religious extremists who vandalize Palestinian property whenever the government sends in police or soldiers to dismantle outposts, an effective tactic known as the "price tag" and of which the breaking of these trees is thought to be an example.[28] By representing the brutal treatment of trees, the implied and latent violence insinuates a parallel to violence against the Palestinian body. Indeed, the olive tree is strongly associated with Palestinian identity and serves as a surrogate and metaphor for the Palestinian. Yet the olive tree has been claimed as a symbol of peace by the Israeli state, which incorporates two olive branches into the Israeli flag. Lashing out at the olive tree, then, is also an act of self-laceration, another example of destroying the land in order to "save" it.

In true proxy fashion, the Palestinian-Israeli conflict has been fought out on one level as a war between olive trees and pine trees, the former representing Palestinians and the latter representing Jews. Pine trees have been planted in Israel since 1901, when the Jewish National Fund was established by the Fifth Zionist Congress to purchase land in biblical Israel. The JNF has planted more than 240 million trees, mostly pines.[29] Pines were chosen because of their fast growth and were planted in areas declared "state land," mainly around Jerusalem in what is called "the green belt." Such plantings have been undertaken to prevent Palestinian planting and to maintain land reserves for future settlements or for the expansion of existing ones, while also making the land unusable as pasture for Palestinian shepherds. Pines have become the primary symbol of the Zionist project of turning the Holy Land into a European-looking landscape, while the olive tree has become the principal emblem of Palestinian resistance, each kind of tree assuming a totemic quality for the people it represents.³⁰ Subject to Article 78 of the Ottoman Land Code, which grants a longtime cultivator the right to land possession on the West Bank, the visibility of trees has led to tree wars in a fight for legally recognized control over territory. Originally meant to encourage cultivation of the land, the Israeli state has used Article 78 to declare all uncultivated land Israeli state land, working around international law, which prohibits an occupier from making irreversible changes to existing property rights, which also makes the settlements illegal. Between 1979 and 1993, Israel used Article 78 to declare more than 40 percent of the land in the West Bank, approximately 400,000 acres, state land.³¹ To do this, the state refused to consider cultivation or development more broadly as land used for industry, grazing, recreational purposes, or housing, let alone for common space, effectively restricting development of the land to narrow agrarian purposes. This may be seen as a primitive use that stereotypes the Palestinians as culturally undeveloped peasants. This construction of Palestinian identity as agrarian is juxtaposed to Jewish identity as modern and highly technological, reflecting a central feature of colonialist ideology that maintains the division between the urban, modern power and the rural, traditional people over whom it rules.³²

The figure of the peasant or *fellahin*, who is "close to the soil," also has been significant for Palestinian nationalism and has been used to naturalize the Palestinian relation to the land, especially since that relationship has been under siege. Following the 1948 war, the figure of the Palestinian peasant took on mythical qualities as a unifying historical agent and in the early 1970s became celebrated by Palestinian poets, artists, and theater groups, while previous to the war the peasant had connoted someone "lower-class, backward, and uneducated."³³ The Palestinian worker, on the other hand, is seen as a product of Israeli colonial dependency and as disconnected from the land. Thus only the peasant can serve as a national signifier despite the fact that by 1990, only 30 percent of Palestinians subsisted from agriculture. The loss of an agricultural way of life was symbolically elevated in significance as its economic impact declined.³⁴

The use of Article 78 to constrict Palestinian land use also explains why Palestinians have been reduced to the monocultural cultivation of olive trees, which can live for a thousand years and are easy to care for. Nonetheless, the Israeli state has uprooted a million trees, sometimes replacing them with pines, for a variety of reasons: to obliterate former Palestinian villages following the 1948 war, to establish an "Israeli" presence in the West Bank, and for "security reasons," including the building of the Barrier Wall. Israeli film director Eran Riklis explored the issue in his powerful film *Lemon Tree*, based on real events, in which a Palestinian widow (played by Hiam Abbass) fights to keep the state from razing her lemon tree field when a new Israeli defense minister moves next door to her, and security agents deem the lemon trees a potential hide-out for terrorists. In addition, Jewish settlers have uprooted, burned, or stolen many olive trees. Yet the uprooting of fruit trees is biblically prohibited, even when they are enemy trees in times of war. Chief Inspector Kishik, an Orthodox Jew and a settler, explains how contemporary uprooting fits with this biblical prohibition: "[T]he tree is the *source* of the problem. It's not just an incidental thing like [it is] in the Bible. Here, the tree is not only a symbol of the Arab's occupation of the land, but it is also the central means through which they carry out this occupation.... It's not like the tree is the enemy's property, in which case the Bible tells you not to uproot it because it has nothing to do with the fight. Here it has everything to do with it. The tree is the enemy soldier."[35] In a breathtaking double displacement, the illegal occupation of the land is here ascribed not to the Jewish settlers or the Israeli state that has seized the land from the Palestinians who have been living on it for generations, but to the Palestinians themselves, who not only "carry out this occupation" through their trees but who also are embodied by the trees, which are not property, but which themselves become "the enemy soldier." Thus when not outright uprooted, their "beheading" becomes a form of military execution. This narrative of Palestinian occupation is based on the Zionist assertion that Palestine was "a land without people for a people without a land," construing the Palestinians as foreign intruders, just as the American West was regarded as unpopulated according to the ideology of Manifest Destiny in nineteenth-century America. Even the Israeli insistence on use of the term "Arab" and taboo on the use of "Palestinian" becomes a way of "decoupling" Palestinians from the land of Palestine.[36]

Cactus is also associated with Palestinian identity and has become a symbol of the *Nakba*, the Arabic word for "catastrophe," which is used to describe the expulsion of the Palestinians in the 1948 war. The hardy cactus was traditionally planted as a protective fence by Palestinian farmers. When Israelis in 1948 demolished and bulldozed Palestinian villages, the cactus grew again, graphically outlining the boundaries of former family homes and plots of land and turning sites of erasure into memory traces. In many cases, cactus is the only remaining trace of the 418 Palestinian communities that vanished during the 1948 mass expulsion of Palestinians from Israel, functioning as a *memento mori* for the hundreds of years of habitation and occupation by the Palestinians.[37] Villagers claim that the cactus springs back even after Israeli settlers burn it to the ground, asserting a vicarious refusal to be eradicated and signifying survival of the nation.[38] Palestinian artists such as Rana Bishara and Mohammed al-Hawajri often employ cactus in their work, which is symbolic in part because it has tenacious roots and seemingly grows wherever it is thrown.[39] In Arabic, cactus is *sabr*, which is also the word for patience, making the cactus a symbol of resistance and endurance. Even a small cut piece can take root, transforming it from a fragile, rootless object to one that bears hope. Bishara, originally from the northern mountains town of Tarsheeha, near the Lebanese border, has sewn the withered leaves of dried cacti together (*Home*, 1995) or cut and stuffed living cacti into a jar in *Homage to Palestine*.[40] For Gazan artist al-Hawajri, prickly cactus sandals serve as painful surrogates for a difficult return but also suggest their ancient ineradicability in *Cactus Borders*, a work produced after the December 2008 Israeli assault on Gaza. In different ways, both Bishara and al-Hawajri address the frustration of feeling cut off from the land and the desire for return; they point to the pressures and restrictions that have ensued for the Palestinians, the tightly sealed and guarded borders, and the denial of citizenship rights. These works speak of exile, longing, humiliation, displacement, and the contraction of livable space. At the same time, they suggest tenacity and the ability to survive against all odds. Israelis, however, also appropriate the cactus as a symbol of their connection to the land and the word *sabra*, meaning a Jewish person born in Israeli territory, comes from the Arabic *sabr*. This makes the burning of cactus yet another contradictory act of mutilating the self to destroy the other.

Photographer Shai Kremer, a former member of the IDF (three years of service is compulsory for Israeli boys at the age of eighteen; two years for girls), documents the effects of an occupying army on the land in his series *Infected Landscape: Israel, Broken Promised Land* (1999–2007), showing how the military contaminates, controls, and reshapes topography according to the logic of "security needs" and the larger need to assert mastery of the land through roads, concrete barriers, settlements, fences, camps, training facilities, and other forms of building and technology.[41] These are forms of land transformation that Israelis also tend not to "see." In *Separation Wall, Jerusalem* (2004), Kremer represents the ruined Israeli landscape in front of a section of the Barrier Wall in the distance, vividly portraying the landscape as "infected" by the dominance of a repressive architecture that nonetheless depends on the rhetoric of the sanctity of the land while wreaking destruction on the actual topography.

Infected Landscape also includes several photographs of the Israeli military training camp, Tze'elim, built in the middle of the Negev Desert to simulate an Arab town (*Path, Urban Warfare Training Center, Tze'elim*, 2007; *Panorama, Urban Warfare Training Center, Tze'elim*, 2007).[42] The fake Arab town, nicknamed Chicago to invoke the bullet-ridden myth

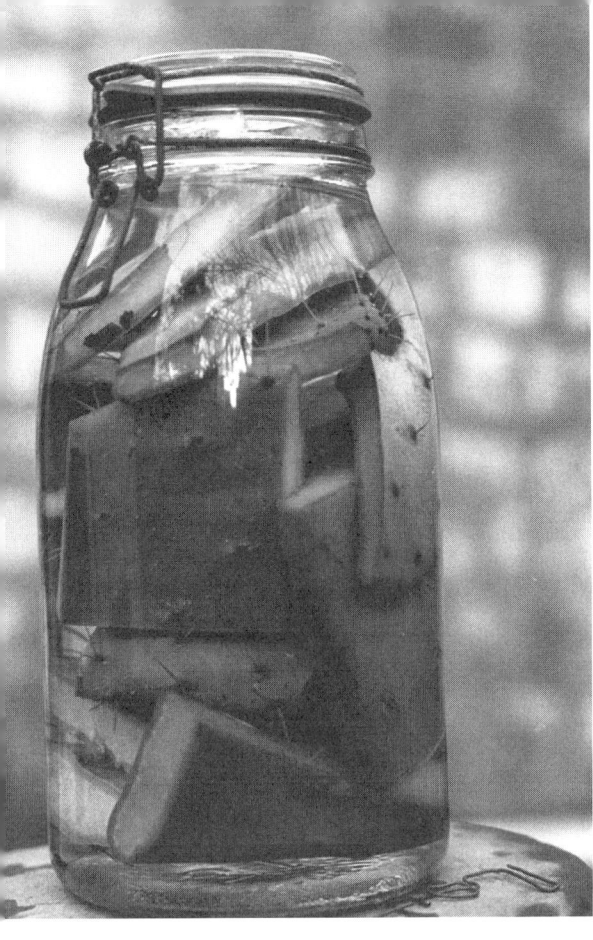

Figure 26 (left). Rana Bishara, *Homage to Palestine*, 1999. (Courtesy of the artist.)

Figure 27 (below). Mohammed al-Hawajri, *Cactus Borders*, 2010. (Courtesy of the artist.)

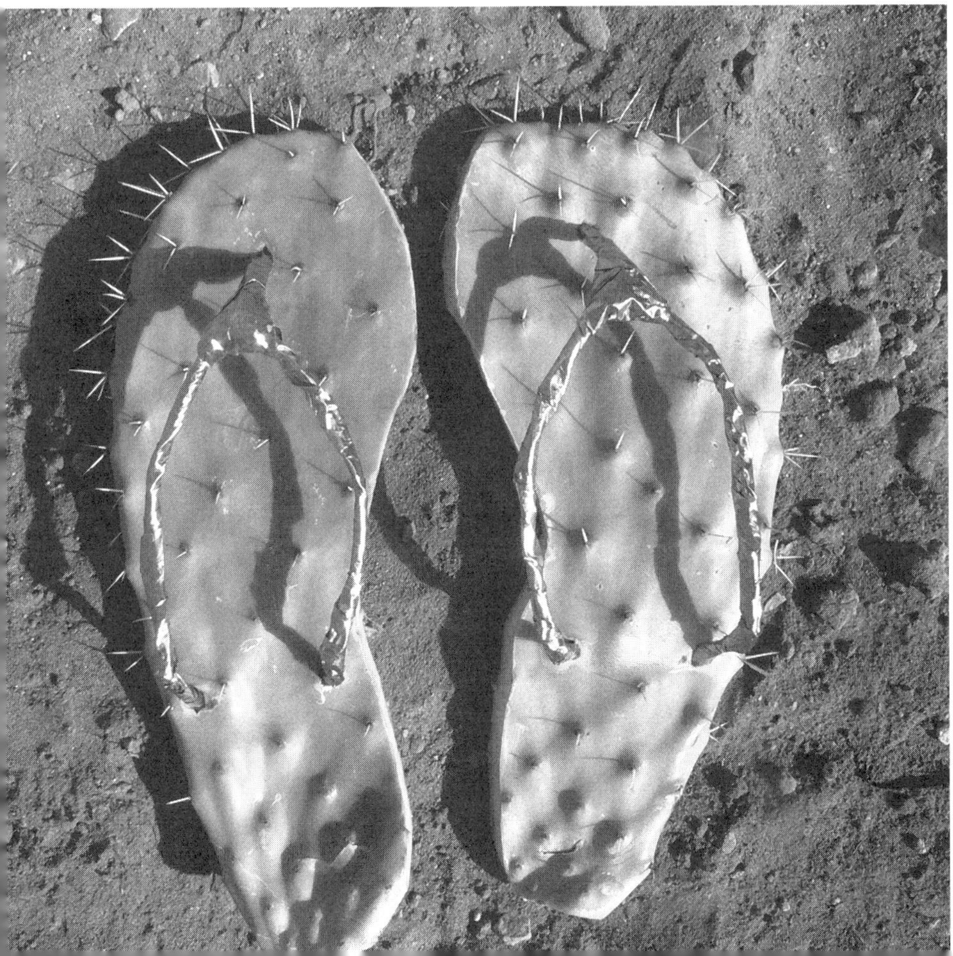

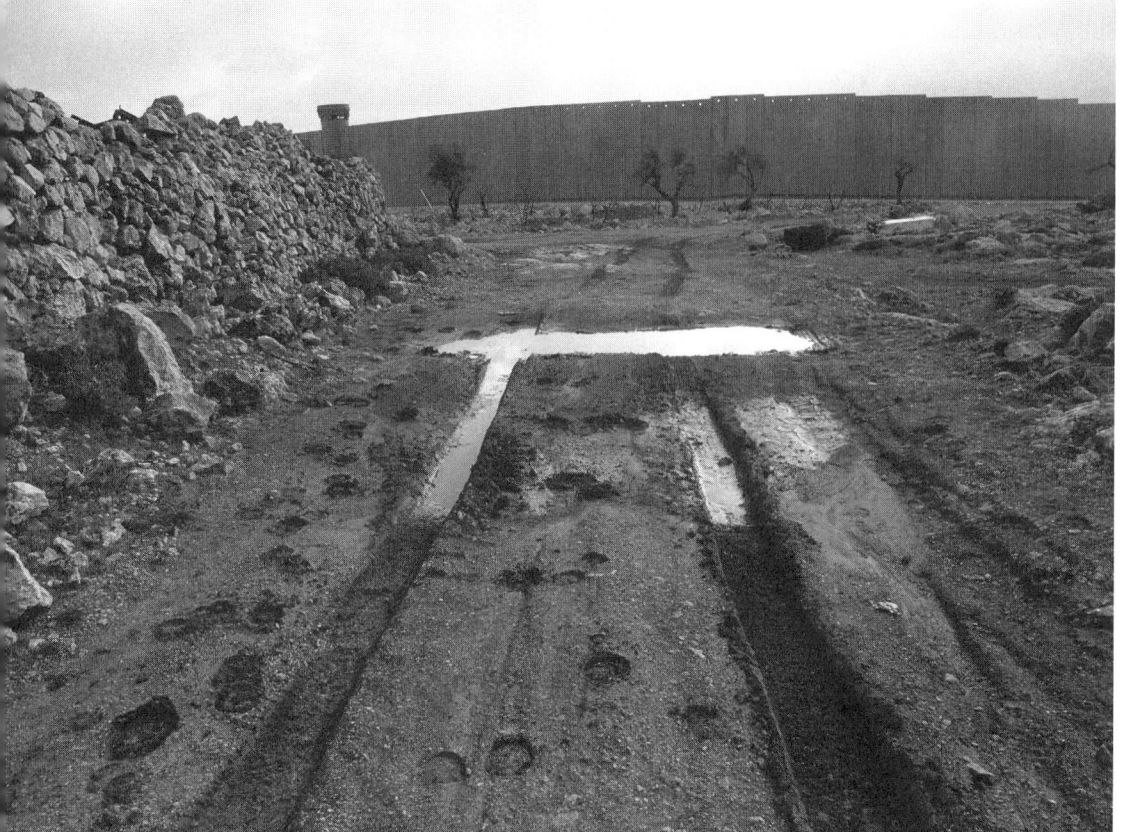

Figure 28. Shai Kremer, *The Separation Wall, Jerusalem*, 2005, from series *Infected Landscape*. (Courtesy of the artist.)

of that city, is where the takeover and destruction of Palestinian cities, villages, and refugee camps is practiced. The simulated site has gone through several incarnations since the 1980s and now includes a Kasbah quarter, a street market area with narrow alleys, a section simulating a refugee camp, a downtown area with broader streets, and a neighborhood resembling a rural village. This landscape is not usually perceived as part of the national political imaginary because violence is usually framed as defensive, but for the military that trains here, the simulated architectural ruin of a generic Arab town commemorates the effectiveness of destroying real Palestinian towns and villages populated with real people. Evoking feelings of loss and abandonment, the photos convey a sense of nostalgia—for a future that already lies in ruins along with the past. Yet as fabricated and generic ruins without real cultural and historical specificity, they cannot be romanticized; they are ruins, like all such simulated village training camps, that have been designed to conceal rather than reveal real human loss and suffering. They are meant to premediate destruction, to make it imaginable, to rehearse the Occupation over and over. As Eyal Weizman observes, "Images of war and conflict could be seen as *performative* in the sense that they are able to create the conditions that replicate the events they have themselves portrayed. Wars are both conflicts and conceptual imaginary systems, whose categories are reproducible. The ghost town of Chicago represents Middle Eastern cities but trains soldiers to make ghost towns out of living cities."[43]

In *Interior, Urban Warfare Training Center, Tze'elim*, Kremer represents a fabricated house with a precut hole in the wall for soldiers to practice going through. The practice of creating wall holes was developed as part of a siege warfare strategy that involved literally walking through walls as well as using hand-held imaging devices that allowed IDF soldiers to detect bodies through walls and to shoot and kill through solid walls. "Walking through walls" evokes what Gordon Matta-Clark called "unwalling the wall," whereby he dismantled abandoned buildings through cuts and slices. In Matta-Clark's case, this could be understood as subverting the repressive order of domestic space. Remarkably, the building cuts of Matta-Clark were featured in the presentation material of a think tank established by the IDF known as the Operational Theory Research Institute (OTRI). OTRI also includes on its reading list the writings of Deleuze and Guattari, Guy Debord, and Georges Bataille. Debord conceived of adapting buildings to new purposes, Bataille spoke of a desire to attack architecture, and Deleuze and Guattari's idea of rhizomes and war machines composed of a multiplicity of small groups that can split up or merge with one another depending on contingency all resonated with IDF military ideals, along with the theories of Matta-Clark, in a chilling instrumentalization of poststructuralist ideas.[44] There is something deceptively romantic about Kremer's photo in which the

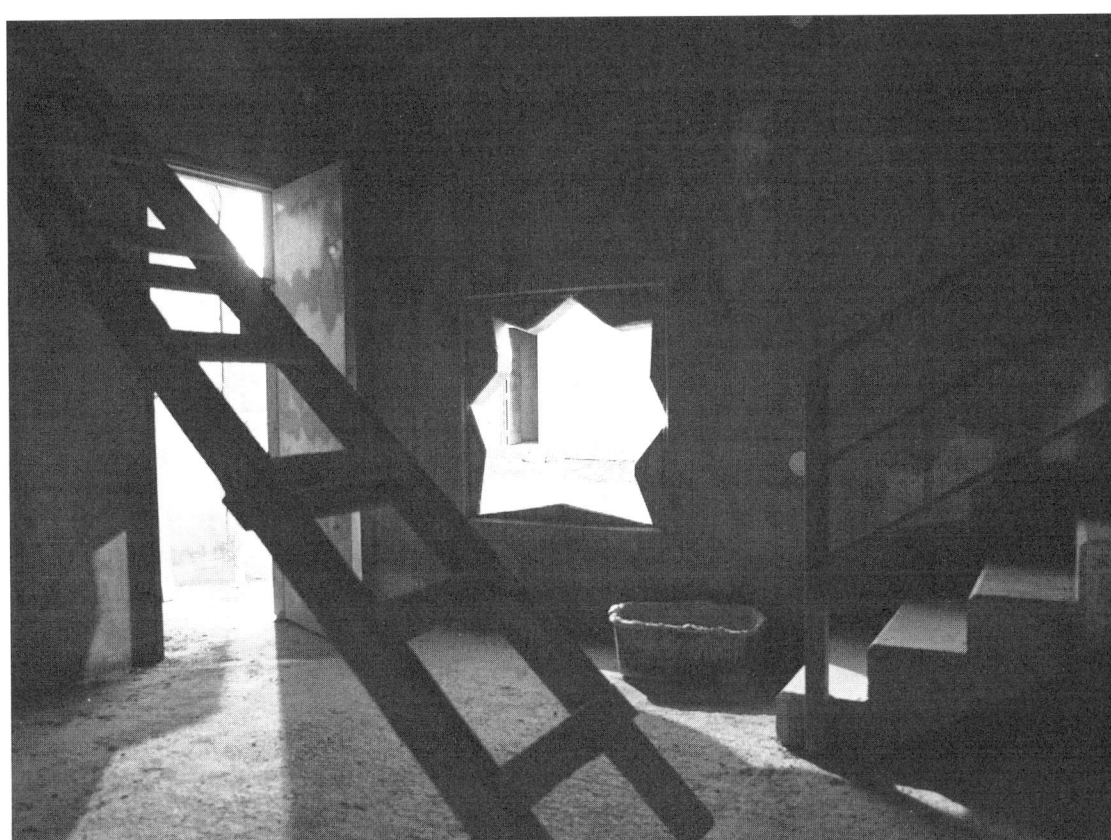

Figure 29. Shai Kremer, *Interior, Urban Warfare Training Center, Tze'elim*, 2007, from series *Infected Landscape*. (Courtesy of the artist.)

precut hole vaguely echoes the six-pointed Star of David, as if walking through walls were a transcendent spiritual act, leaving no messy aftermath. The sanitized simulated structure gives no hint that the invasion of people's homes is a deeply traumatic event, as attested to in an interview in the *Palestine Monitor* with Aisha, a Palestinian woman who described an attack on her home in November 2002:

> Imagine it—you're sitting in your living room, which you know so well; this is the room where the family watches television together after the evening meal ... and suddenly, the wall disappears with a deafening roar, the room fills with dust and debris, and through the wall pours one soldier after the other, screaming orders. You have no idea if they're after you, if they've come to take over your home, or if your house just lies on their route to somewhere else. The children are screaming, panicking.... Is it possible to even begin to imagine the horror experienced by a five-year-old child as four, six, eight, twelve soldiers, their faces painted black, submachine guns pointed everywhere, antennas protruding from their backpacks, making them look like giant alien bugs, blast their way through that wall?[45]

Aisha pointed to another wall now covered by a bookcase that the soldiers blew up in order to continue to her neighbor's house. The strategy of "walking through walls" blithely obliterates all distinction between public and private, transforming all Palestinian space into a liminal war zone that exists in a perpetual state of exception, where anything can happen, and the inhabitants have no rights or recourse—the conditions of bare life. This is what Susan Buck-Morss would call "the wild zone of power," which exists at the core of every state, even the most liberal.[46] This arbitrary and violent power is made manifest not only through the founding act of the state, which is always violent, but also when a state of exception is declared, when there is an ongoing interethnic civil war, or when there is a military occupation that produces a geographical "wild zone" where the state acts in unlawful ways that otherwise would not be sanctioned.

Miki Kratsman's photograph, *Nablus*, documents the actual result of "walking through walls," sans the clean starlike opening. The hole pictured in this photograph was made during the attack that began on this West Bank city in April 2002. Both Aisha's description and the Nablus photo demonstrate the strategy of "swarming." As Weizman explains, this is "a non-linear principle of problem-solving based on the interaction and communication of unsophisticated agents like ants, birds, bees, and soldiers" with little centralized control. "A swarm 'learns' through the interaction of its constitutive elements, through their adaptation to emergent situations, and in reaction to changing environments."⁴⁷ The process of walking through walls involves explosives or a large hammer to break a hole large enough for assembled soldiers to pass through, sometimes preceded by stun grenades or random shots into what is usually a private living room. Unsuspecting inhabitants are usually searched as "suspects" and locked inside one of their own rooms where they may remain for up to several days without food, water, medicine, or sanitation until the military has concluded its operation. According to Human Rights Watch and B'Tselem, dozens of Palestinians have died during such attacks. Demonstrating that the wall of the Palestinian home is no longer solid also demonstrates that, for Palestinians, the boundary between city and home may be dissolved without notice, and the domestic is always already exposed to the dominance of the colonial state. More than half of the buildings in the Nablus Kasbah had routes forced through them, and the attack was so "successful" that Israeli brigadier general Aviv Kochavi, commander of the operation, "ignored Palestinian requests to surrender and continued fighting, trying to kill more people," until the deputy prime minister ordered the attack over.⁴⁸

From the microcosm of safe domestic space that has been reduced to nothing, we may zoom out again to the macrocosm of the crowded refugee camp. The claustrophobic contraction of livable space ceded to Palestinians driven from their homes in the 1948 war is chillingly conveyed

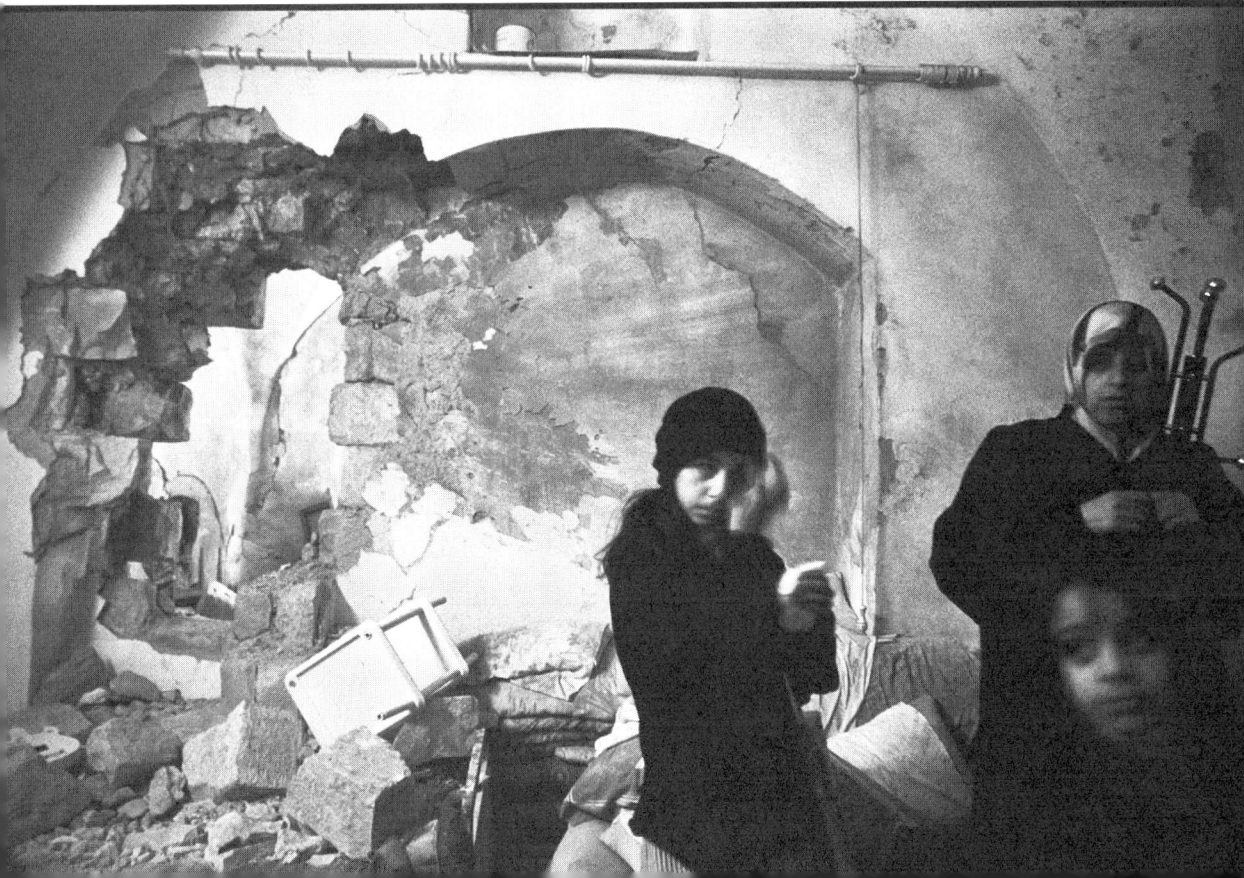

Figure 30. Miki Kratsman, *Nablus #2*, 2003, from series *West Bank and Gaza Strip* (1986–2008). (Courtesy of the artist and Chelouche Gallery, Tel Aviv.)

in Nir Kafri's photo *Balata Refugee Camp*, the largest refugee camp in the West Bank. Near the city of Nablus, Balata contains about thirty thousand people and was originally set up in 1950 for Palestinian refugees from Jaffa. The buildings are densely situated because they were built on the plots originally given to families to set up tents, and they were not allowed to expand, creating very narrow alleyways between the houses. When the IDF planned an attack on Balata because many activists in the Intifada came from there, navigating its dense architectural structure became one of the key reasons the army developed its method of breaking through the walls of houses from the perimeter into the center. Buoyed by the success of this strategy, General Kochavi's forces attacked Nablus and the Balata camp eight more times, helping to provoke international calls for Kochavi to face a war-crimes tribunal.[49] In addition, a strategy of cultural and economic destruction was carried out by bombing, from the air, historic buildings in the old city center of Nablus. Attacks on architecture, as Robert Bevan argues, is as much about killing cultures and destroying identities and memories as it is about killing people and occupying territory.[50] Moreover, the violent destruction of buildings and cultural property has been explicitly prohibited by the 1954 Hague Convention for the Protection of Cultural Property in the Event of Armed Conflict, which says in its preamble: "Cultural property has suffered

Figure 31. Nir Kafri, *Balata Refugee Camp*, 2002. (Courtesy of the artist.)

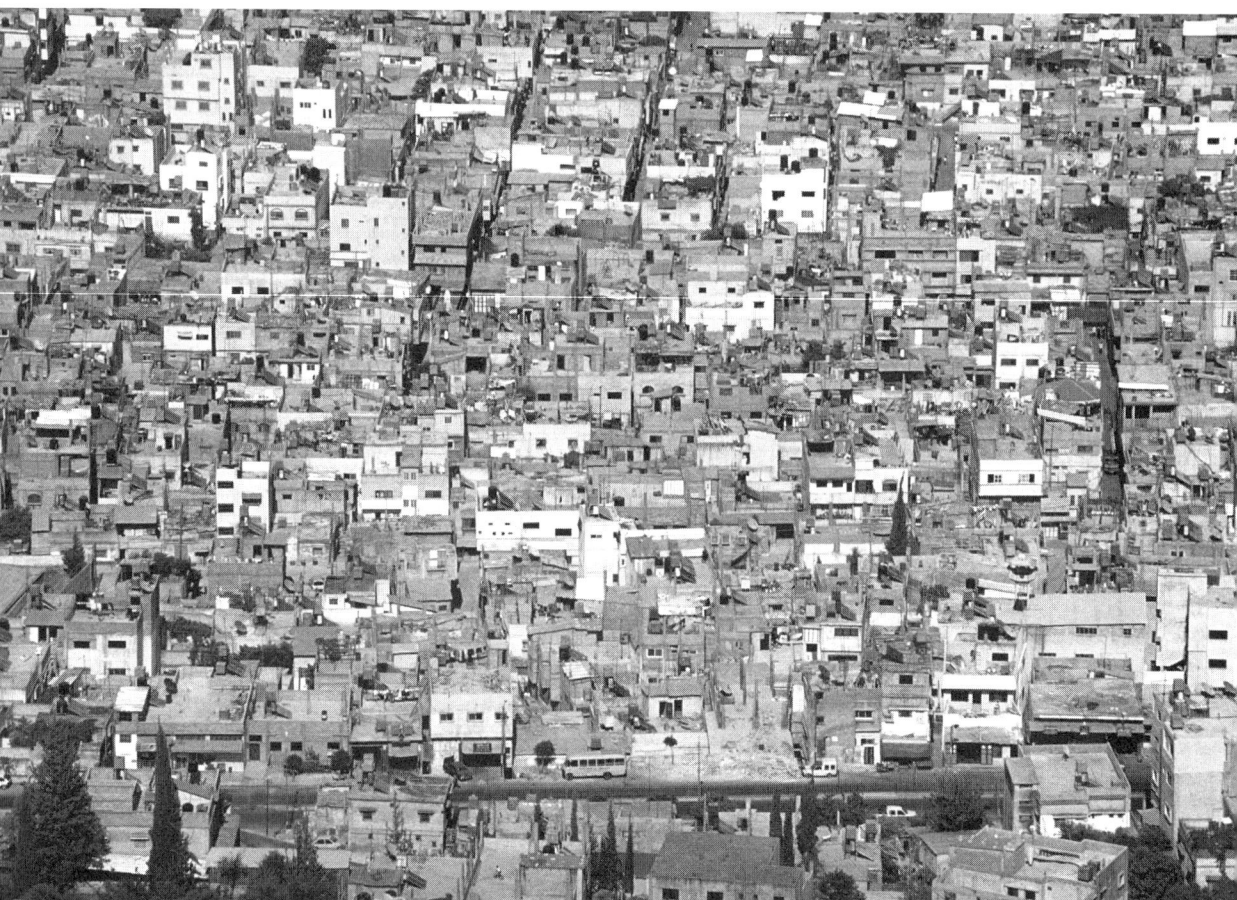

grave damage during recent armed conflicts, and that, by reason of the developments in the technique of war, it is in increasing danger of destruction ... damage to cultural property belonging to any people whatsoever means damage to the cultural heritage of all mankind, since each people makes its contribution to the culture of the world."[51]

Bevan notes that the injunction against the damage to cultural property may be disregarded "only in cases where military necessity imperatively requires such a waiver," a "generous loophole" that was modified but still exists in the 1977 Hague Convention provisions incorporated into the humanitarian laws of the Geneva Convention. The destruction of buildings following the 1948 war, however, was a deliberate policy designed to wipe out cultural memory and to make the transformation of British Mandate Palestine into the State of Israel "permanent and irreversible."[52] In addition, civilian Jews, as part of their army duty, were required to settle in the depopulated Palestinian villages already occupied by the Jewish army so as to prevent the return of Palestinians.[53]

In Nablus, many buildings were completely destroyed, including historic buildings such as the eighteenth-century Ottoman Caravanserai of al-Wakalh al-Farroukkyyeh, and the Nablusi and the Cana'an soap factories, while other buildings, such as the Abdelhade Palace, the Orthodox Church, and the al-Naser Mosque were badly damaged. In Balata, more than four hundred buildings were destroyed. Weizman argues that the destruction of these buildings must be understood, at least in part, as a deliberate reconstruction of the camp layout that widened existing narrow alleyways and cut new ones through existing buildings in order to create new and widened roads that allowed Israeli military tanks and armored bulldozers to easily reenter the camp and penetrate to a newly cleared open space at the core of the camp in order to support the ability of the state to regulate and control a rightless population under its command.[54]

Kremer's photo of the interior hole in the wall of the training camp and Kratsman's photo of the enactment of that strategy perform their own contest of images, though both reveal the ideology of the state. One is a fantasy stage set produced by the army's sophisticated theoretical discourse, its romanticized ideological sanctification emphasized in the photo through the dramatic contrast of brilliant sunlight and cool shade in a space that resembles no one's living room. The other represents the devastating results of that discourse on the violated private space and terrorized lives of those on the receiving end of the state's violence.

From 1996 to 2000, Israeli photographers Gilad Ophir and Roi Kuper produced a project that documented the effects of army training on the desert, including deserted army camps, abandoned fortifications, and firing ranges. Entitled *Necropolis*—the city of the dead—they documented the dead entities left behind to scar and disfigure the desert, making visible, for example, the rusted and disintegrating hulk of a captured military vehicle that litters the landscape like the decaying skeleton of a dead animal. This bullet-riddled iconography contains a latent violence that signals the applied violence of war, but this sort of ruination is hidden from view for most of the Israeli public by the national political imaginary of the biblical pastoral. Such photographs therefore present an alternative landscape that suggests a different political imaginary, a dangerous rather than a protective power, revealing the paradox of defending the national imaginary landscape while destroying the topography. Such photos represent a landscape that is inconsistent with the idealized terms of the national topos, signaling instead sovereign violence and the detritus of lives and structures left in its wake.[55] As Shai Kremer observes of his *Infected Landscape* series, "The aesthetic, orderly compositions parallel the defense mechanism of Israeli citizens striving for normalcy, while the scars concealed in the landscape correspond to the wounds in the collective

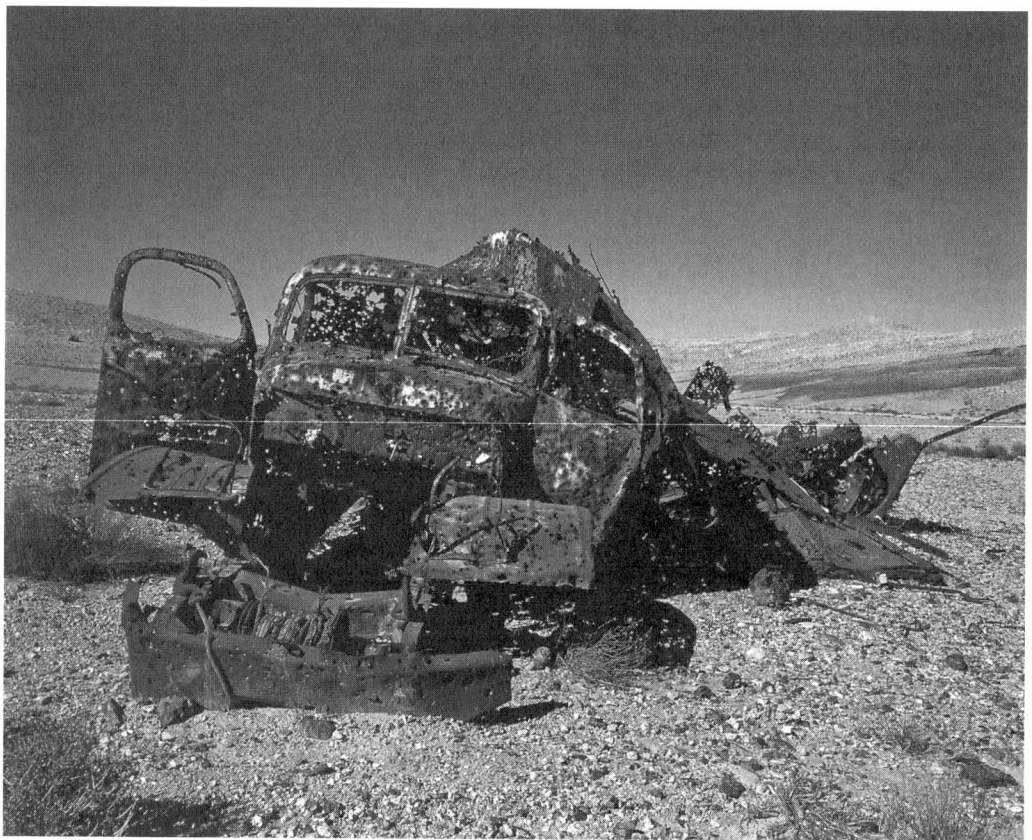

Figure 32. Gilad Ophir, *Untitled*, 1997. (Courtesy of the artist.)

unconscious of the country.... If the accumulation of ruins and military remnants turns out to be a defining trait of the Israeli landscape, what to think of the society that grows out of it?"[56]

The Wall

One of the most oppressive blights on the landscape and destructive forces on Palestinian daily life is the separation barrier built to enclose the West Bank. Most of the Wall consists of a multi-layered fence system with the ideal being three fences, allowing IDF soldiers to see and shoot through them, but in the more densely populated areas there are concrete slabs as high as twenty-six feet. Begun in July 2003, it is 425 miles long (twice the length of the 1967 Green Line). This makes it four times as long and, in places, twice as high as the Berlin Wall. Built not along the Green Line but well into West Bank territory and curving circuitously around the Israeli settlements, it is clear that annexation of the settlements as part of Israel is the determining factor in the route of the Wall. The term "settlement" itself is a misleading term because it makes one think of a small outpost. The rapidly growing settlements, by July 2007, contained nearly 450,000 settlers, including 190,000 Israelis living in the ten "urban" settlements of East Jerusalem, which Israel considers "Holy City" neighborhoods, but which are east of the Green Line. This means that one out of every six residents in the West Bank is a settler.[57] The largest city settlement of Ma'ale Edomim has thirty-two thousand inhabitants and displaced the Bedouin tribe that previously inhabited the hills. It also has succeeded in severing the north of the West Bank from the south by having the Barrier Wall routed around it and has isolated Jerusalem from the rest of the West Bank.

Israeli Committee Against House Demolitions (ICAHD) founder Jeff Halper describes the Wall as helping to fulfill the Israeli policy of dispossession and transfer. "The Palestinians," writes Halper, "now imprisoned within hundreds of miles of concrete walls that carve their lands, cities and villages into tiny, disconnected enclaves, now have no hope of a viable state of their own."[58] He further notes, "The severe restriction on their movement *within the West Bank*, the demolition of eighteen thousand homes, the uprooting of a *million* olive and fruit trees, the devastation of Palestinian agriculture, industry and infrastructure, the crazy route of the Separation Barrier intruding far into Palestinian areas—*none* of these measures could be explained by security."[59] Unless, of course, one defines security differently, as Weizman asserts the state does: "In Israel, 'security' has always been associated with the ability of the state to remain sovereign and Jewish. This is the very reason why the demographic growth of one category of its citizens—Arab Palestinians—can always be presented as a 'security problem.'"⁶⁰ It is indeed difficult to see how Israel's restrictive and oppressive occupation policies serve any purpose other than that of making Palestinian life so difficult as to force emigration in support of Israel's exclusive claim to the land.

Miki Kratsman has documented Palestinian life under Israeli occupation for over two decades, and his photographs attest to his constant effort not to simply reproduce the privileged position of the occupier. "Hence," writes Ariella Azoulay, "the series of decisions rising out of the photographs: to place the Israeli soldier next to the weeping Palestinian kid, as directly responsible for his suffering, while at the same time cutting off his head and leaving it out of the frame since his individual identity isn't relevant; to show the soldier's shoulder obstructing the view to acknowledge [to] the spectator that the photographer's viewpoint is dependent and limited by circumstance; to keep a relative of the wounded woman next to her as a sign for the fact that it cannot be taken for granted that anyone in any situation can look at the other's injured body, and that not all spectators enjoy the same status."⁶¹ Kratsman photographed the Israeli evacuation of Bedouins from their houses and the demolition of an entire village, and produced a series of Bedouin portraits taken at three Bedouin villages in the south of Israel (*Displaced*, 2010–2011).⁶² In another project, he addresses the rhetoric of the IDF used for targeted assassinations known as "focused foiling," a term employed against those whom the state considers to have violent intentions. Using a special lens employed by IDF unmanned aerial vehicles from the vantage point of Mount Scopus, Kratsman photographs innocent Palestinians in the villages below as they go about their daily lives, demonstrating how easily their quotidian activities can be made to seem "suspicious" once these moments are framed as the instant before a "targeted killing" (*Targeted Killing*, 2010–).⁶³

His series *Panoramas of Occupation* (1999–2009) conveys many of the architectural effects of the Occupation on the landscape. One photo represents a road that runs on the eastern side of the Wall in the West Bank but is for Israeli use only, with all Palestinian entrances to it barricaded by huge concrete blocks with steel reinforcements that are produced in Israel expressly for the purpose of blocking roads and reinforcing checkpoints (*Road 443 #12*). In *Road 443 #9*, we see how the road itself has become a massive barrier to Palestinian movement because of the high barrier walls built alongside it. The Israeli side has a mural painting representing a kind of stylized aqueduct, which transforms the wall into the sign of a peaceful, imaginary landscape while obscuring the actual landscape of Palestinian towns and villages behind it. Around the Palestinian cities of Tulkarem and Qalqilia, the Wall has become largely invisible

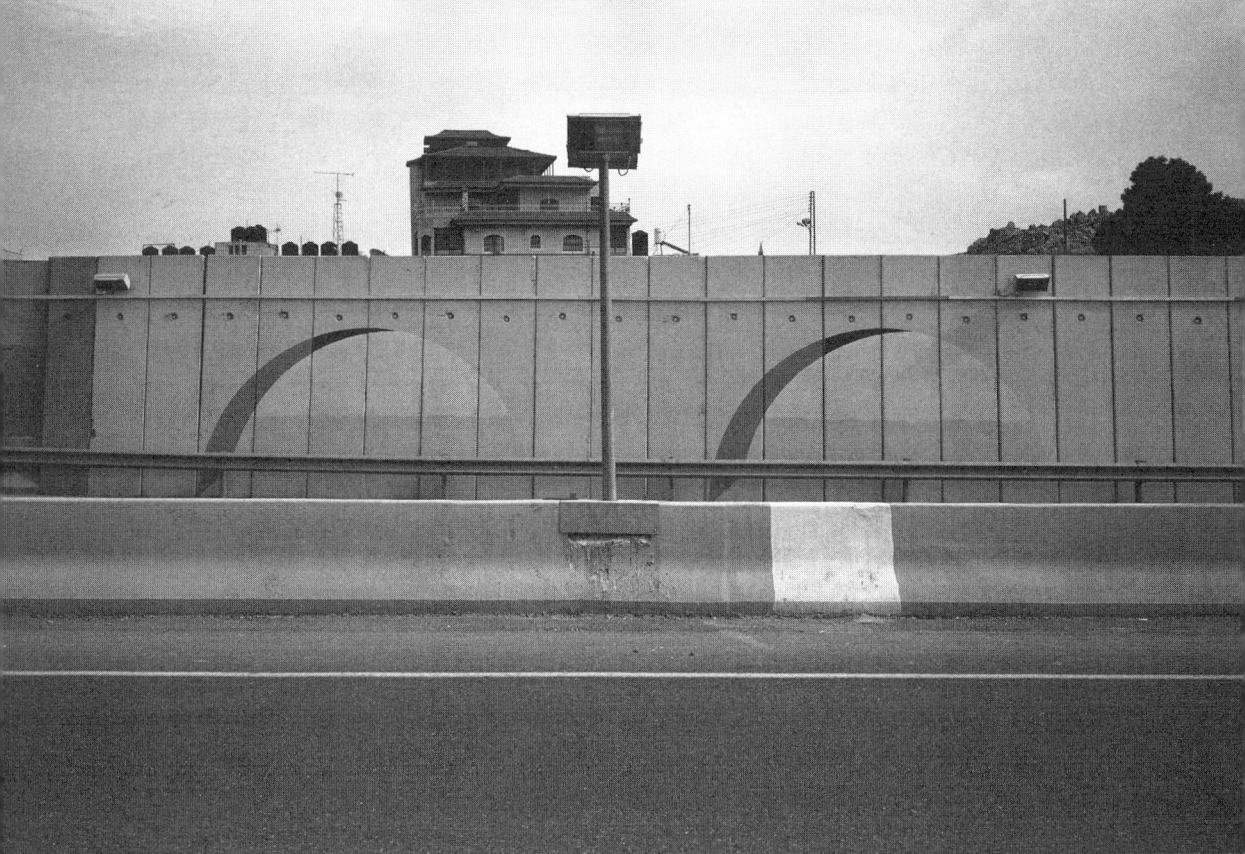

Figure 33. Miki Kratsman, *Road 443 #9*, 2001, from series *Panoramas of Occupation* (1999–2009). (Courtesy of the artist and Chelouche Gallery, Tel Aviv.)

to Israelis driving along the adjacent Highway 6 because it is covered by trees, plants, heaps of soil, and bushes. The Israelis seek to naturalize the Wall; the Palestinians refuse to beautify it, which would imply its acceptance. For the Israelis, it is another form of "double vision" in which they see only the Israeli national political imaginary in which no Palestinians are present. For Palestinians, the Wall is covered with messages and calls to solidarity. The most commonly painted slogan is "To Exist Is to Resist."

Other photos from *Panoramas of Occupation*, such as *Gilo 1*, represent the wall around Gilo, an Israeli neighborhood on the outskirts of Jerusalem that originated as a settlement built after the 1967 war. It was built on approximately seven thousand acres of annexed Palestinian land on the Palestinian side of the Green Line, the border that has separated Israel from the West Bank since 1949.[64] A wall was built at the start of the Al Aqsa Intifada in 2000 (the immediate trigger was Ariel Sharon's controversial visit to the Temple Mount—Al-Haram al-Sharif to Muslims) to shield the Israeli settlement from snipers, but because it obscured the beautiful view of Bethlehem, Israeli residents brought in Russian immigrants to paint the obscured landscape onto it. Kratsman notes, "If you look closely, you notice that the houses in the wall painting are more European than what is really there. A lot of them don't

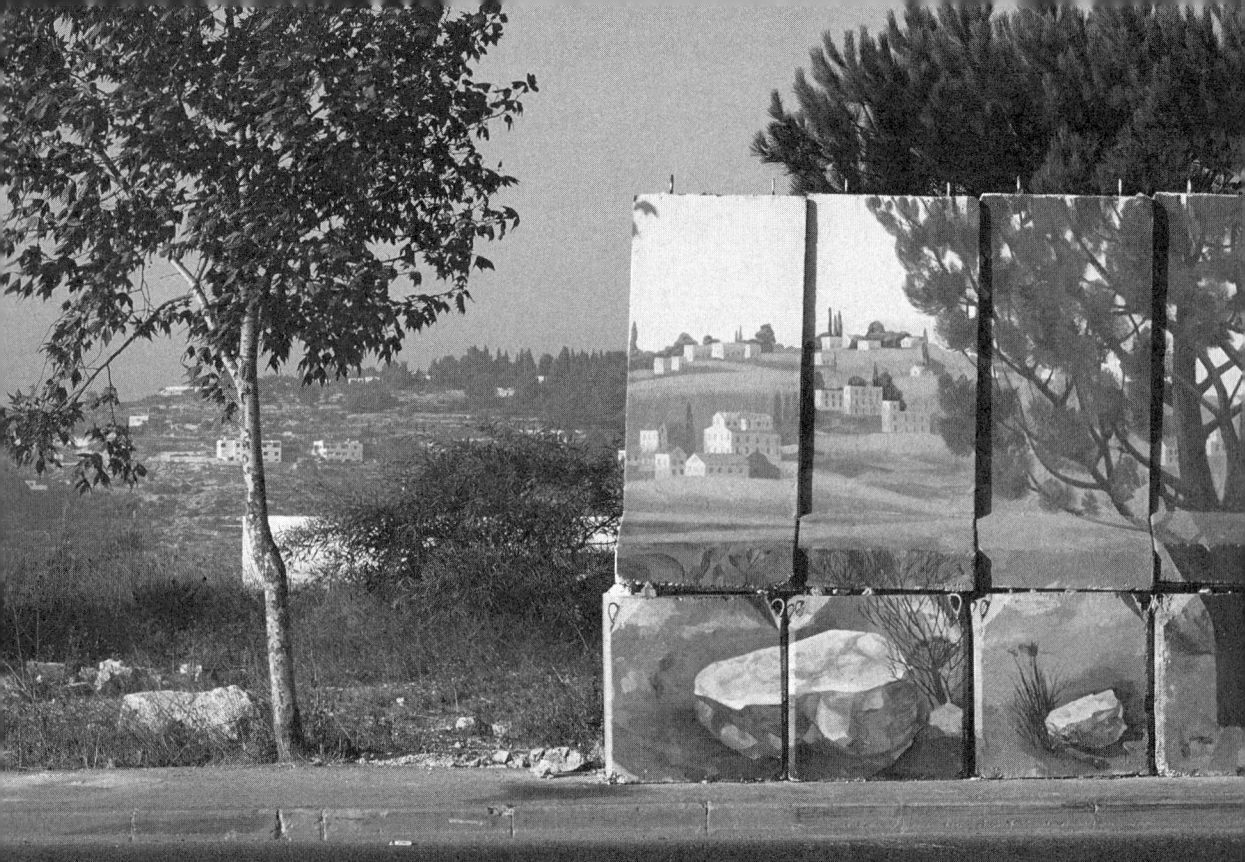

Figure 34. Miki Kratsman, *Gilo 1*, 2001, from series *Panoramas of Occupation* (1999–2009). (Courtesy of the artist and Chelouche Gallery, Tel Aviv.)

even exist anymore because we bombed them. It's an illusion that has nothing to do with the real situation."⁶⁵ The illusionary and unpeopled landscape that renders invisible what is really behind the wall may be seen as yet another example of Israeli double vision. Similarly, in *Gilo 2*, the mural landscape has been painted as empty and pastoral. The Palestinian town of Beit Jalla, where artist Rana Bishara lives, which is close to Bethlehem and actually exists behind the wall, is erased altogether; for ten years, only the Israeli landscape and city were visible and therefore real, while the Palestinian landscape was displaced from time and space, and therefore from history.⁶⁶

What is not evident is the way in which Gilo demonstrates the transformation of Israeli architecture in an effort that is meant to reproduce the Old City. This is done in order to naturalize the urban Jewish settlements as part of a greater Jerusalem. As Eyal Weizman explains, the "Housing Cluster" designed by architect Salo Hershman in Gilo in the early 1970s, which is laid out in several "walled-city-like ensembles" entered through large gates and clad in "Jerusalem Stone" (itself an Israeli invention meant to look "old"), is part of a strategy to consolidate "a new national identity and the domestication of the expanded city" in an "eternally unified capital of the Jewish people" and thus not negotiable in any diplomatic discussions with Palestinians. "The modernist, standard, cheap, prefabricated apartment block," notes Weizman, "formerly the basic unit of state-sponsored housing, was replaced ... by 'pseudo historical creations of oriental and Mediterranean mimicry ... embodying an association with antiquity and national roots.'"[67] Demographic policies in Jerusalem are designed to promote the construction of Jewish housing and limit Palestinian expansion, causing massive overcrowding in Palestinian neighborhoods and a rapid increase in real estate values that have forced many families out of Jerusalem and into the West Bank, where housing is much cheaper. By leaving Jerusalem, however, Palestinians lose their "Israeli residency" status, which allows them access to state services and health care as well as the right to enter and work in Israel. Since 1967, more than fifty thousand Palestinians have lost their residency status in this way, and tens of thousands more have moved out of the city but maintain a residency address in order to retain their right to work in Israel. As Weizman points out, "One of the factors in the routing of the Separation Wall around Jerusalem was to cut these Palestinians out of the city, and close this loophole. The Palestinian residents of Jerusalem now face having to choose which side of the Wall to live on—a

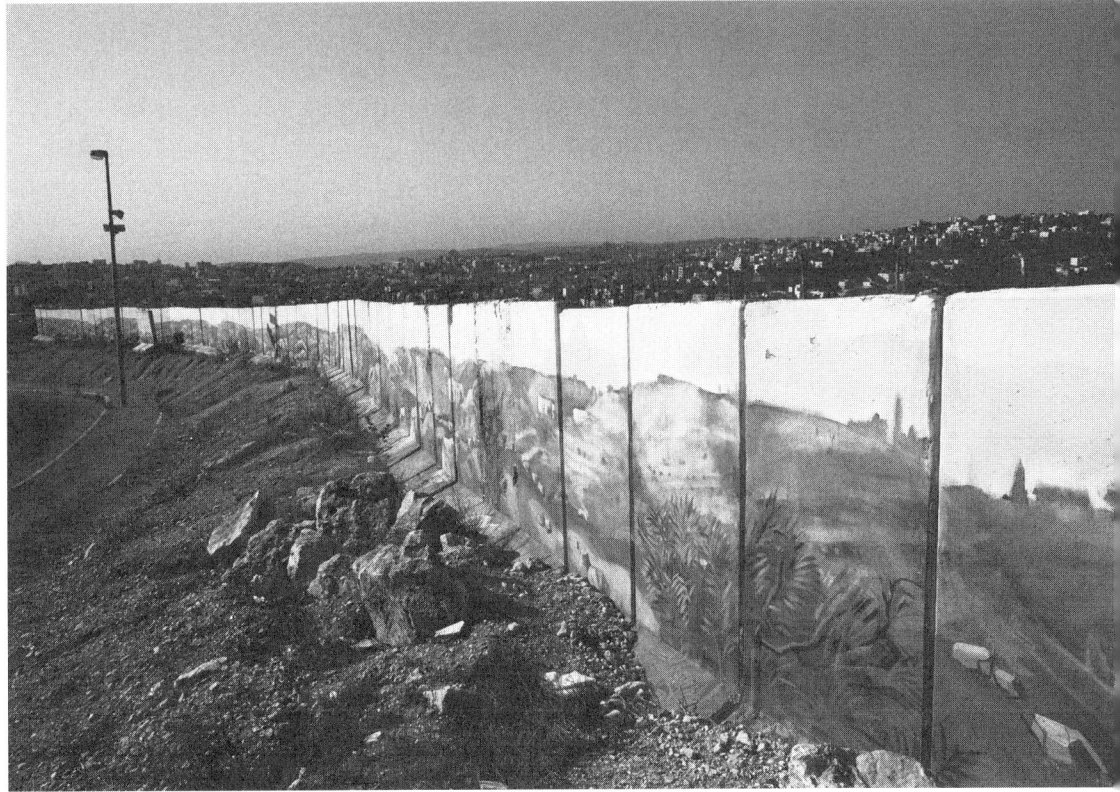

Figure 35. Miki Kratsman, *Gilo 2*, 2001, from series *Panoramas of Occupation* (1999–2009). (Courtesy of the artist and Chelouche Gallery, Tel Aviv.)

crowded and expensive Jerusalem, where they cannot build, or give up the rights they previously had and live in the surrounding towns and villages of the West Bank."[68]

Artists from other countries have traveled to the West Bank to photograph or produce art on the Wall. The most famous may be Banksy, a semimysterious British graffiti artist whose real name is thought to be Robert Banks. Although he started out with freehand graffiti, Banksy devised a series of intricate stencils to minimize time and avoid either being caught or unable to finish the art in one sitting. The stencils have come to characterize his style. In 2005 Banksy traveled to the West Bank with the artists' collective Santa's Ghetto and together they produced nine murals on the West Bank side of the Wall. In 2008 he went back and produced six more. Noting that the Wall "essentially turns Palestine into the world's largest open prison," Banksy's works address the desire for escape in a fashion both whimsical and political. The Wall has been declared illegal by the U.N., which has ordered it dismantled. Israel says the Wall protects it against suicide bombers; the Palestinians say it protects the Israeli settlements and gives them room to grow while making life miserable for the Palestinians. Apparently the army found Banksy's stenciled works threatening, and his spokesman, Jo Brooks, asserted, "The Israeli security forces did shoot in the air threateningly and there were quite a few guns pointed at him."[69] Palestinians were not always receptive, either. Banksy noted that an old Palestinian man said his painting made the Wall look beautiful. Banksy thanked him, only to be told: "We don't want it to be beautiful, we hate this wall. Go home."[70]

Indeed, Palestinians who live in the shadow of the Wall disagree on whether to beautify it with art or whether the art draws the world's attention to the disgrace of the Wall, but most welcome the solidarity it represents, while taxi drivers and business owners welcome the tourist trade it attracts.[71] In 2004, two visiting muralists from San Francisco's Break the Silence Mural Project, Susan Greene and Eric Drooker, along with members of the International Women's Peace Service, Anarchists Against the Wall, and friends from the Palestinian village of Biddia joined with twenty children and five adults in Mas'ha, in the West Bank's Salfit District, to paint a mural on the Wall over the course of six hours that represented a green valley with flowers and a soaring yellow bird. The mural faces the home of the family of Hani Aamer, which is surrounded on all four sides by the Wall. Aamer told the artists, "When you come here to paint with the children like this, you make them feel that they can live."[72]

Banksy's images show a boy with a sand bucket atop a rock with open sky behind him; an imprisoned horse's head; the silhouette of a young girl floating over the Wall by holding on to a bunch of balloons; a big square

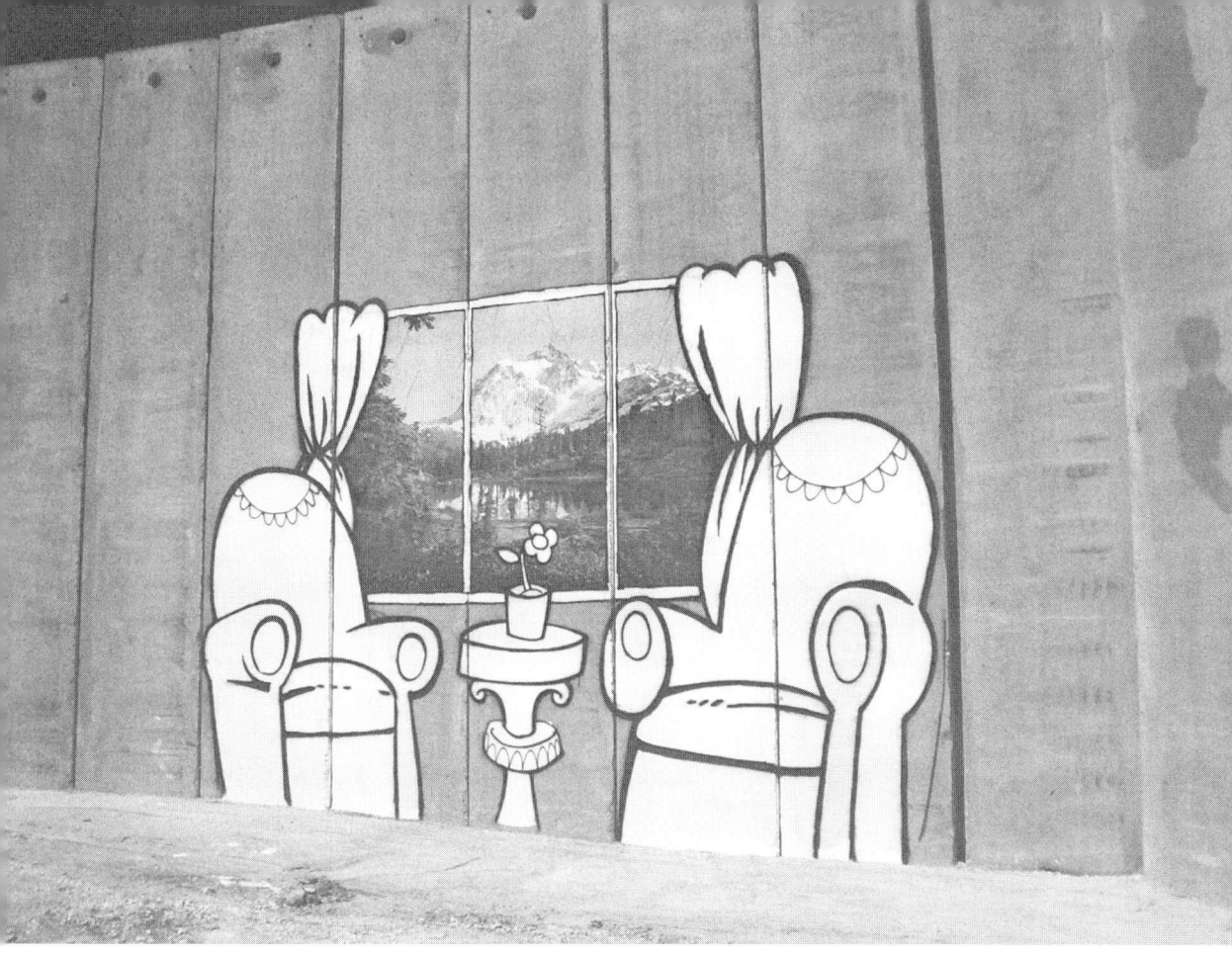

Figure 36. Banksy, Palestine, 2005. Stenciled image of living room on the barrier wall around West Bank. (Banksy image courtesy of Pest Control Office.)

cutout created with a dotted line and a pictured pair of scissors; a painted white ladder that reaches to the top of the Wall; children playing below a stenciled hole in the Wall that reveals a tropical paradise; a "living room" with two overstuffed chairs and a framed picture of a lake and mountains. Banksy was not always attuned to clashes in cultural perceptions, however. Journalist and photographer William Parry shows how the "living room" underwent stages of "debeautifying," first with parts of the idyllic framed scene scraped off, then painted over as a brick wall. The tropical paradise above two playing boys was scraped off and painted over as well, with the added text beside it, "Missing the point" and a drawing of a gate with the word "Auschwitz" over it. The blue sky behind the boy with a bucket was painted white and the slogan "Free Palestine" added. Many of these works are near Qalandia checkpoint and Bethlehem, the main point of access into Jerusalem from the north West Bank. Another graffiti work by an anonymous artist on the Wall near Qalandia checkpoint represents a boy with a long paintbrush who has written in large white letters, "NOTHING TO SEE HERE!" as if in defiance of Banksy's attempts to "beautify" the Wall.[73]

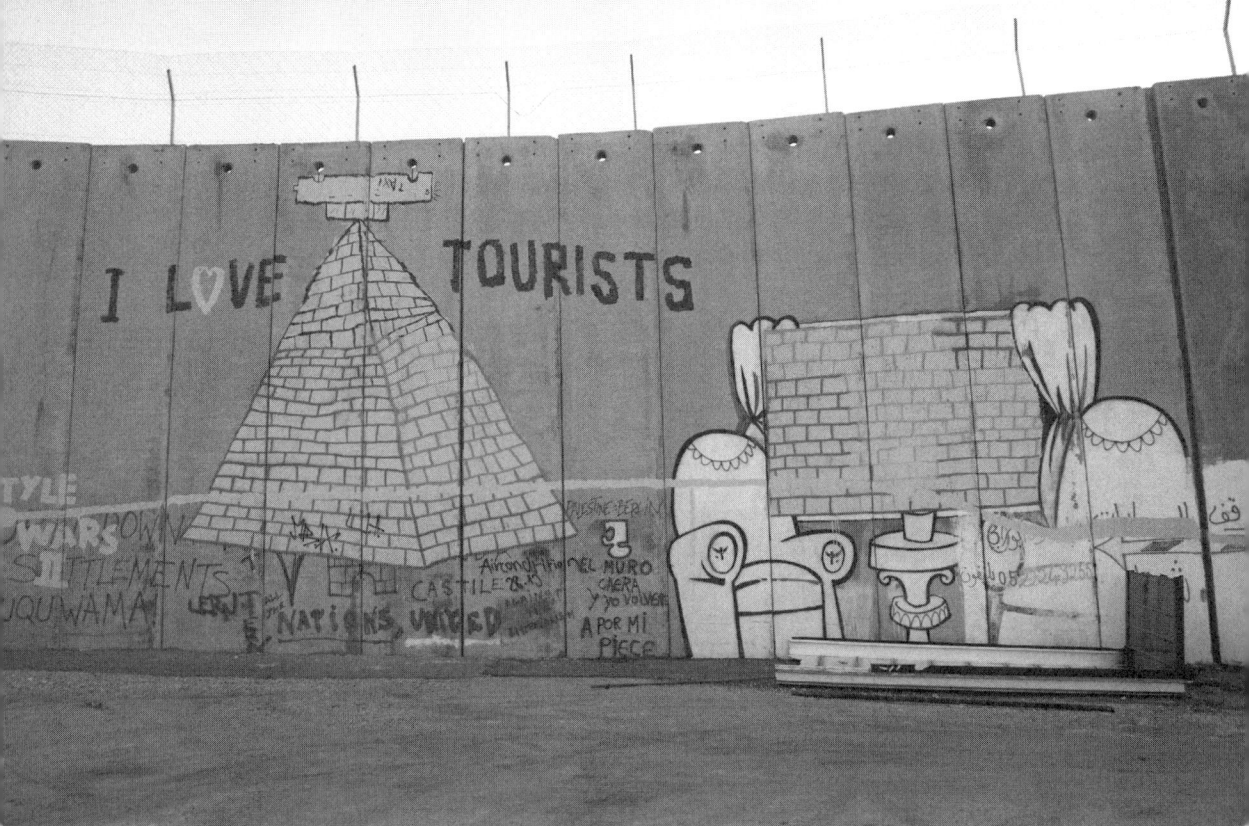

Figure 37. Banksy, stenciled image of living room with view painted over. Photo by William Parry.

Even more problematic, but with a profitable outcome, was Banksy's stenciled silhouette of an Israeli soldier checking the identity card of a donkey. While Banksy meant to satirize the absurdity of the "security" checks and reports that Israeli soldiers were not allowing donkeys through agricultural gates without security permits, locals were insulted and thought the image seemed to equate them with donkeys. Parry reports that the work disappeared but was not destroyed: "Rather, the owners of the building where it was painted, a canny family with a prominent local business selling a range of items to tourists, realized they had landed a valuable and original art work." They removed the section of the Wall, replaced the missing part and put the carefully preserved original up for auction, selling it for $200,000 to someone from the West in December 2009.[74] Two other 2007 Banksy works that backfired were stencils of rats armed with slingshots. Locals were offended by the comparison and destroyed the images.[75] Artists who worked with Banksy as part of Santa's Ghetto included Palestinian artist Suleiman Mansour as well as Swoon, Blu, Paul Insect, Faile, Sam3, Erica il Cane, and Ron English. Other notable graffiti works include a sculptural leg breaking through the Wall by Palestinian artist Wissam Salsaa (the leg has since disappeared leaving only the painted cracks), and the words in blue paint CNTL+ALT+DELETE by Filippo Minelli (2007), which seems a succinct statement of both official policy toward the Palestinians and the Palestinian attitude toward the Wall.⁷⁶

Video artists also address the Wall in innovative ways. The group "Artists without Walls," composed of Israeli and Palestinian artists, produced the video project *Eastern Side/Abu Dis* (2004), consisting of real-time video projections from one side of the Wall onto the other side, in effect temporarily dematerializing the Wall by creating a virtual window through the concrete. "The effect is startling," noted a reporter for *Die Tageszeitung*. "For a moment, both worlds seem transparent.... Palestinian youths wave at Israeli children sitting on their parents' shoulders. The later it gets, the greater the crowd and the waving."⁷⁷ The work was produced in DVD form and shown in the exhibition *Three Cities against the Wall* in Tel Aviv, Ramallah, and New York, which included sixty-six Palestinian, Israeli, and American artists. Oren Sagiv, a founder of Artists without Walls, explained to the *Tageszeitung* reporter that the idea for the live-transmission projection grew out of frustration with the usual protest demonstrations: "At one point, I was fed up with it: You demonstrate at the wall, the police come, and then they break everything up. That was the repeating structure." Artists without Walls has members in both Tel Aviv and Ramallah, but meets only in Ramallah, since the Palestinian members cannot cross the border.⁷⁸

Artists without Walls also supported a film by Eytan Heller (*Love Sum Game*, 2006), showing a tennis game taking place on both sides of the

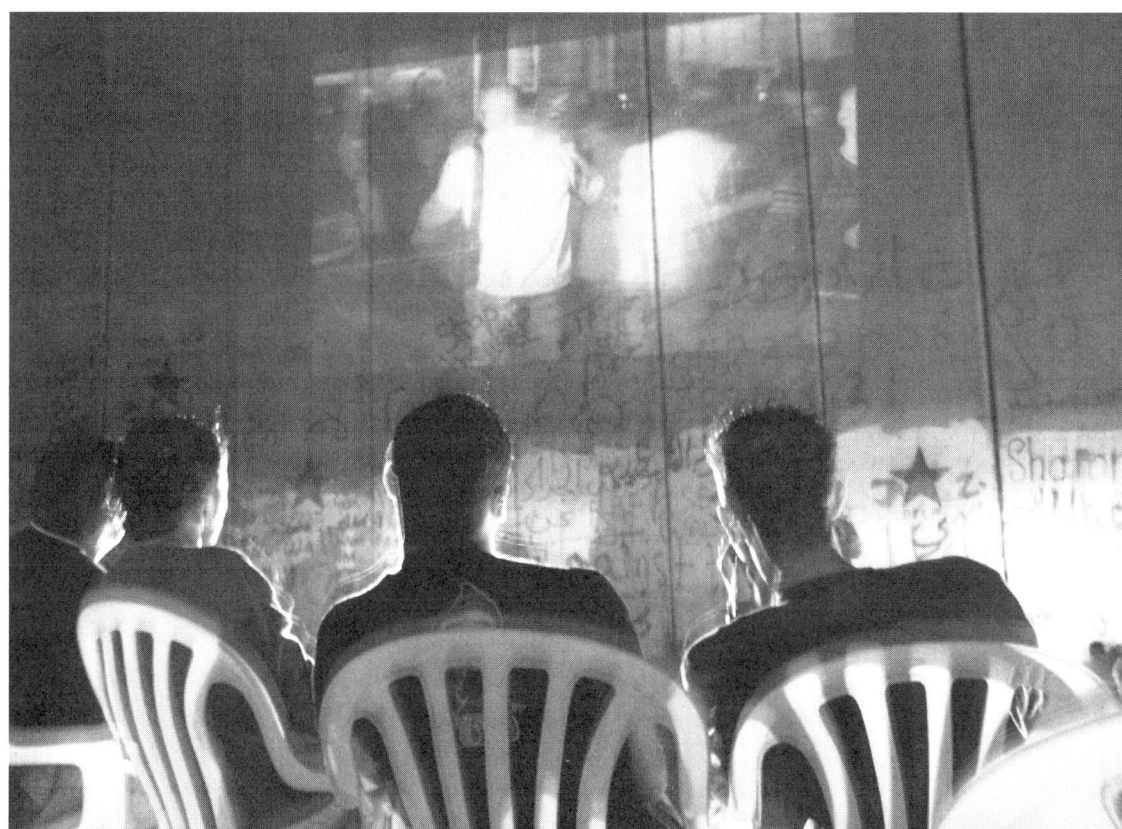

Figure 38. Artists without Walls, *Eastern Side/Abu Dis*, 2004, installation shot of video projection on barrier wall around West Bank. Photo by Oren Sagiv, Artists without Walls.

Wall, which is made absurd by the inability to see. Rona Yefman produced a video (*Pippi at Abu-Dis*, 2008), featuring Danish performance artist Tanja Schlander in striped knee-socks and flying red pigtails representing Pippi Longstocking. As Pippi, the rebellious fictive character with socially subversive ideas who self-identified as "the strongest girl in the world," she tries but fails to move a giant concrete block in the Wall at Abu Dis.[79] Yefman's video suggests the need for individual effort to effect political change even as it registers the frustration and failure of one person's singular efforts, even when they are "the strongest girl in the world," making the video both comical and poignant.

Miki Kratsman and others also have photographed the Wall and various checkpoints, but Kratsman, as a photojournalist with press privileges that allow him to travel unrestricted into the West Bank and Gaza, has exemplified the self-aware documentarian who claims the frame and has produced some of the most iconic and condemnatory images of the Wall. His photo *Abu Dis* (2006), for example, renders the Palestinian side of the Wall at this village due east of Jerusalem from an angle that maximizes its towering dominance and the sense of being imprisoned by it. Emphasizing the dehumanizing scale of the Wall, which nearly fills the entire picture, the photo foregrounds its height in relation to that of the woman who walks alongside it. This perspective signals the way that the Wall arbitrarily cuts off and separates rural populations, destroys

Figure 39. Miki Kratsman, *Abu Dis*, 2003, from series *Panoramas of Occupation* (1999–2009). (Courtesy of the artist and Chelouche Gallery, Tel Aviv.)

the natural landscape, artificially amputates space, and isolates people. While many families are forced to face thirty feet of concrete outside the windows of their homes, some seventy-five thousand residents are now also cut off from emergency medical assistance. Before the Wall, an ambulance would take people to one of two Palestinian hospitals in East Jerusalem within fifteen minutes; now these hospitals are inaccessible on the other side of the Wall.[80] Kratsman's photo includes a glimpse of red graffiti that says "Ghetto Abu Dis," ironically figuring the Wall in terms of yet another wall, one that once imprisoned the Jews, that of the Warsaw Ghetto. The Wall thus maps the containment and persecution of the European Jews onto the containment and persecution of the Palestinians, and the oppressive iconography of the Holocaust returns as the repressive iconography of the Occupation, as if to suggest that the Palestinians are the new Jews.

Photos such as those by Kratsman, Kremer, Ophir, and others make it impossible to edit out the topographical features of the land that do not fit with an Israeli political imaginary or do not represent the landscape in heroic or defensive terms. These images of latent violence render before our eyes what has long been hidden from view by the imagined political landscape, and they must be understood as creating a shared way of seeing that makes visible their implicit claims for justice. These photographers are part of the generation that has experienced the Israeli occupation of Palestinian territories and the Palestinian intifadas, an experience that has undermined the justifiability of the Jewish state as an ethnocracy and thrown into question the official dogma that the state is both Jewish and democratic. These artists address the fact that Zionism has not resulted in the utopian enlightened state. Instead, the dogma of Jewish victimization that is institutionalized in schools and through public rituals has produced a reaction among Israeli intellectuals and artists who may be seen as constituting a "post-Zionist" generation. As theorist Gene Ray notes, they view official memory with "skepticism and irony" and are "willing to ask critical questions about the ethical and political costs of Jewish power and nationhood,"[81] pushing the boundaries of political discourse and imagery of the land into new and disturbing areas. Israeli historian Moshe Zuckermann observes that Israel/Palestine is "a landscape praised by its occupiers for the sanctity of its lands—and saturated by its occupiers with the pollution of oppression, with endless human suffering, as well as with the death of hopes of a home and of homeliness, safety, tranquility and peace."[82]

Israeli political scientist Ilan Pappé regards mainstream Zionism as an ideological current challenged by two opposing streams: post-Zionism and neo-Zionism. Since the 1980s, post-Zionism has been a challenge from the left that criticizes Zionist policy and conduct during the 1948 war, accepts many of the Palestinian claims concerning the war, and envisions a non-Jewish state in Israel as the best solution for the conflict. An alliance with the Palestinian national minority is needed for this view to represent a meaningful political alternative; however, the post-Zionist perspective, largely an academic, media, and cultural phenomenon, has succeeded in legitimizing formerly taboo topics such as the nature of Zionism, Israel's conduct in 1948, the refugee problem, and policies toward Sephardic Jews (Mizrahim). Neo-Zionism, the challenge from the right that interprets Zionism in a violent and extreme way, emerged after the 1967 war and in the 1980s formed alliances with the settlers in the Occupied Territories and with other marginalized sectors of society.[83] Neo-Zionists do not recognize the existence of Palestinian refugees and would like to see a future Israel without secular Jews and without Palestinians, which would mean "transferring" all Palestinians out of Israel and the Occupied Territories in some form of ethnic cleansing. Pappé points out that the term "post-Zionism" should be used advisedly because there is no clarity on what kind of entity would replace the Jewish state in order to safeguard both Israeli and Palestinian human rights. For many post-Zionists, their goal is a return to the 1967 borders demarcated by the Green Line. Thus the term has become controversial in Israel, where rightists use it as an accusation of disloyalty to the state.

Haunted by the Holocaust

The Holocaust and antisemitism have been deployed repeatedly to justify Israeli policies and attacks against the Palestinians. While I do not in any way justify Palestinian attacks on innocent Israeli civilians, it must be emphasized that there is a vastly asymmetrical power between the state and a stateless people. It is a tragic irony that Israeli identity is built upon overcoming victimization and the cult of the fallen even as it instrumentalizes that identity in order to perpetrate its own atrocities on a victimized people. The cult of the fallen is associated with the Holocaust, with the fallen soldiers of Israel, and with the legend of Tel-Hai, where six Jewish settlers died in 1920 while defending a small northern settlement against Arab forces; it is also identified with biblical myths, in particular the story of Masada and of David and Goliath, which are seen as stories that transform victimization into heroism and survival. Museums of the Holocaust outside of Israel are thus seen as focusing too intently on Jewish victimization, while Yad Vashem, the Museum of the Holocaust and Heroism in Jerusalem, by its very title, celebrates survival and resistance. By situating Yad Vashem in Israel, rather than in Europe, where the slaughter happened, the museum has come to symbolize Jewish renewal and rebirth of the nation while sacralizing Holocaust memorialization.[84] Israeli anthropologist Meira Weiss shows that bereavement and commemoration take on special significance in Israeli society where "themes of idealized sacrifice and heroism of 'the fallen' are ... deemed essential to the persistence of the 'Jewish state' in the 'promised land,'" where the fallen have become a national symbol of immortality.[85]

A number of Israeli artists gesture toward the ways in which Israeli and Palestinian identity are structured in terms of each other in relation to the Holocaust. Kratsman's *Territory* series (2005), taken at Gush Katif, for example, a few months before the Israelis evacuated this bloc of seventeen Israeli settlements in southern Gaza and demolished the Israeli settlers' homes, constitutes one such example. *Territory* of course refers to the Occupied Territories, which in the late 1970s translated a military occupation into a civilian occupation and paved the way for colonization by settlements, forcing the Palestinians into the territorial patchwork of land fragments. As Eyal Weizman demonstrates, Israel controls not only all the areas around these fragments but also the vast water aquifer beneath the land and the sky above in a "vertical occupation." At Gush Katif in Gaza, strategically positioned near Palestinian cities and refugee camps, eight-to-twelve-meter-high concrete walls (twenty-six to thirty-nine feet) were constructed at the start of the second Intifada in 2000, using the same modular components as the Wall in the West Bank. Weizman notes, "Hundreds of Palestinian homes and hundreds of acres of Palestinian orchards surrounding the settlement walls were destroyed in what the IDF called 'landscape exposure operations,' aiming to remove cover for putative Palestinian attacks."[86] Kratsman's photographs of abandoned structures and objects, fences, walls, and watchtowers evoke nothing so much as the specter of the Holocaust. The use of black and white photography and the all too familiar nature of watchtowers, walls, and fences not only suggest surveillance and separation, but seem deeply dependent on the knowledge of the Holocaust that haunts Israeli life and disturbingly resonates with Nazi concentration camp photos of watchtowers and concrete barriers. Although the Jews are occupiers controlling the landscape, in such documentary images we see the return of the Holocaust imaginary, revitalizing and redeploying iconic images once abandoned by postmodern artists as clichés of the Holocaust even as they picture the Jewish settlements as their own prisons.

A color photo from the series *Settlement* (2006) by Israeli photographer Gaston Zvi Ickowicz, who documented Israeli settlements in both the West Bank and Gaza, represents a demolished Israeli settler's home in Gaza after the evacuation. When Israel decided to pull Israeli

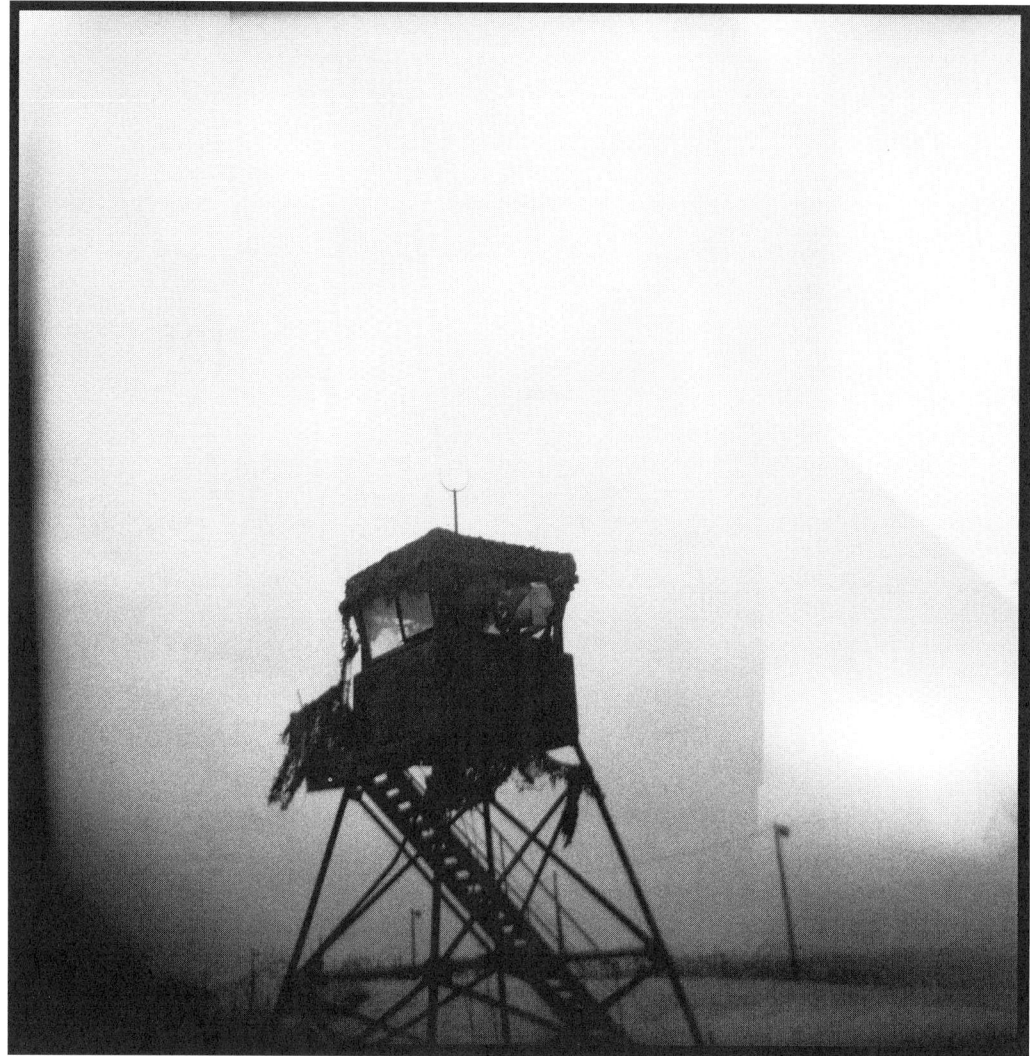

Figure 40. Miki Kratsman, *Territory 0201-2*, 2005, from series *Territory*. (Courtesy of the artist and Chelouche Gallery, Tel Aviv.)

settlers out of the Gaza Strip in 2005, the use of the evacuated buildings became the subject of intense discussion between Palestinians and a variety of organizations, including different U.N. agencies, the World Bank, foreign governments, and international investors, who outlined proposed uses for the evacuated settlements. Israel, however, focused on the symbolic effect of Israeli architecture under Palestinian control and demanded that all settlement homes and synagogues be destroyed. Israel demolished three thousand settler homes so that Palestinians could not move into them, and openly stated that Palestinians moving into former Israeli homes would create an undesirable political image. This can only mean that it would reverse the image of occupation and colonization of Palestine by Israel and suggest not only the collapse and takeover of the "first world" by the "third world" but the reversibility of the Zionist project itself.[87] In the contest of images, Palestinians moving into former Israeli homes would be an image defeat, conceptually reversing the image of the appropriation of Palestinian homes that was central to the founding of Israel. The photo by Ickowicz, however, reveals what may nonetheless be another undesirable image—a landscape of wreckage in which the flimsy character and insubstantial construction of the settlement buildings seems to portend their fate as a future of ruins. The pile of debris does not resemble the ruins of a destroyed home so much as a mound of trash. The Israeli flag seems to have been planted atop it in an attempt, as Simon Faulkner notes, "to assert Israeli sovereignty over land ceded to the Palestinians, yet it also sets up a pictorial dialogue between the rubble pile and the flag. Instead of topping a public building, army base, or a site of triumphal victory, the flag tops a scene of devastation."[88] This suggests that the Israeli landscape is one of "destruction and ruination" and more broadly that the Jewish connection to the land is tenuous and dangerous.

Video works by Israeli artist Yael Bartana also comment on the way the Holocaust infuses the contemporary political life of Israel. In her work

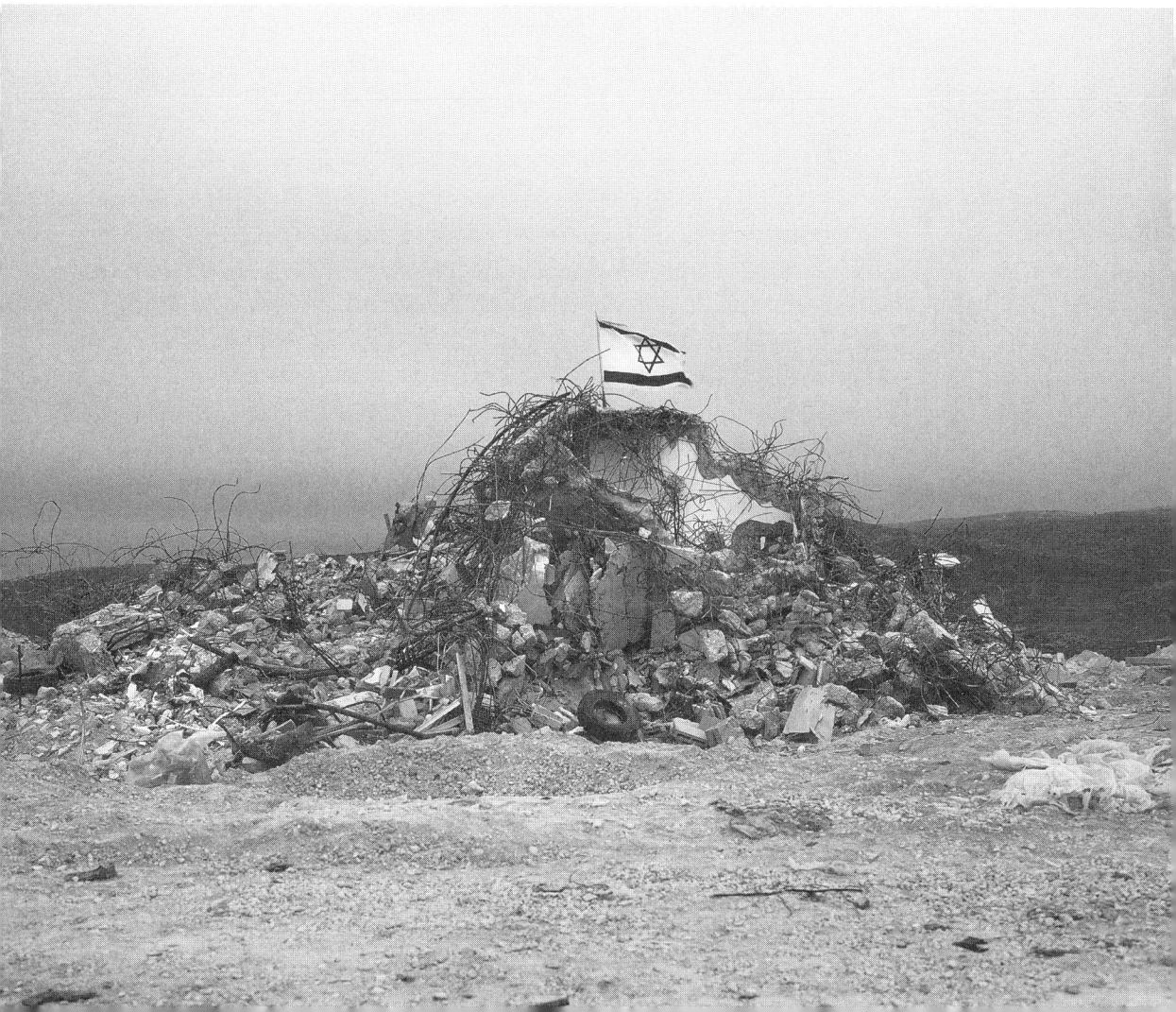

Figure 41. Gaston Zvi Ickowicz, *Untitled*, from series *Settlement*, 2006. (Courtesy of the artist.)

Mary Koszmary (Nightmares, 2007), the first in a trilogy, Bartana directs left-wing Polish founder and chief editor of *Krytyka Polityczna* magazine Slawomir Sierakowski, who gives a rousing speech in the abandoned National Stadium in Warsaw, both evoking Nazi architecture and its ruin. To the sounds of the Polish national anthem, Sierakowski asks three million (implicitly Israeli) Jews to return to the homeland to help the Poles deal with their nightmares. He acknowledges Poland's tradition of virulent bigotry and argues that Jews and Poles together can overcome the trauma of their history to create a more dynamic and diverse nation. Bartana turns Leni Riefenstahl on her head while using her cinematic techniques, substituting this young politico for Hitler, but instead of expelling the Jews he's calling on them to return. Instead of propagandizing for a so-called pure nation, he is mourning the lack of diversity. Many Poles at the screening in Warsaw were confused and didn't know whether to take it seriously or not, prompting Bartana to found a quasi-fictive movement for the return of the Jews.[89] By implication, the question of Israel without the Palestinians and the Palestinian right of return lurks in the shadow of this work about Poland without the Jews. Bartana sees both Poland and Israel as two nations still coming to terms with the Holocaust, still struggling with the search for their identity, and still grappling with ethnic difference and the ability to coexist. *Nightmares* addresses the contradictions of continuing antisemitism in Poland and the longing for a Jewish past among liberal Polish intellectuals, while evoking a lost Palestinian culture in Israel's future.

The second work in the trilogy, *Mur i wieża* (Wall and Tower, 2009), stages the return of the Jews, which Bartana conceived in the form of a kibbutz in front of the Monument to the Ghetto Heroes in the heart of Warsaw, on the site of the future Museum of the History of Polish Jews. This area, known as the Muranów district, had been the Jewish residential area before the war and subsequently became part of the Warsaw Ghetto. Employing a group of young male and female "pioneers," Bartana constructed a kibbutz according to the actual scale and "wall and tower" method used to build illegal kibbutzim overnight in Palestine in the 1930s. Complete with a watchtower and surrounded by barbed-wire fencing, Bartana evokes the early Zionist era and constructs "the first kibbutz in Europe," while also referencing Israel's continuing obsession with security. She notes, "I quote the past, the time of Socialist utopia, youthfulness and optimism—when there was a project of constructing a modernist idea of a new world."[90] *Wall and Tower* symbolically revives Jewish life in Poland while simultaneously evoking the failure of the utopian project in Israel; as barbed wire surrounds the completed kibbutz, it suggests both the concentration camp and the guarded settlements in the West Bank.[91]

Bartana's quasi-fictitious "Jewish Renaissance Movement in Poland" (JRMiP) is premised on the call for return and has its own flag, which combines the Polish eagle and the Star of David in a mingling of national symbols with fascist overtones. The reversal of immigration from Israel to Poland, however, would not simply reverse an earlier historical moment. Although the symbolic return of the Jews from Israel in Bartana's work underscores the real absence of the Jews in Poland, Bartana notes, "Jews coming to Poland today would not constitute a Diaspora anymore, but would be closely linked to a specific nation-state, to the militaristic rhetoric and politics of Israel."[92] Her project uses the method of the early Zionists, and the aesthetics of early Zionist and Nazi propaganda films, to effect another kind of reversal, which recognizes that if the early Zionist dream of a utopian state is no longer possible, a return of Israeli Jews to Poland would signal a kind of Israeli colonization of Europe. While playing on issues of homeland and return, Bartana raises the question of the problematic nature of nationalism itself.

The final film, *Zamach* (Assassination), premiered at the Venice Biennale in 2011 in conjunction with the first two parts in an exhibition entitled "... and Europe will be stunned." *Zamach* is set in the near future and documents the funeral of the assassinated movement leader, Slawomir Sierakowski. It takes place in Warsaw's monumental Palace of Culture

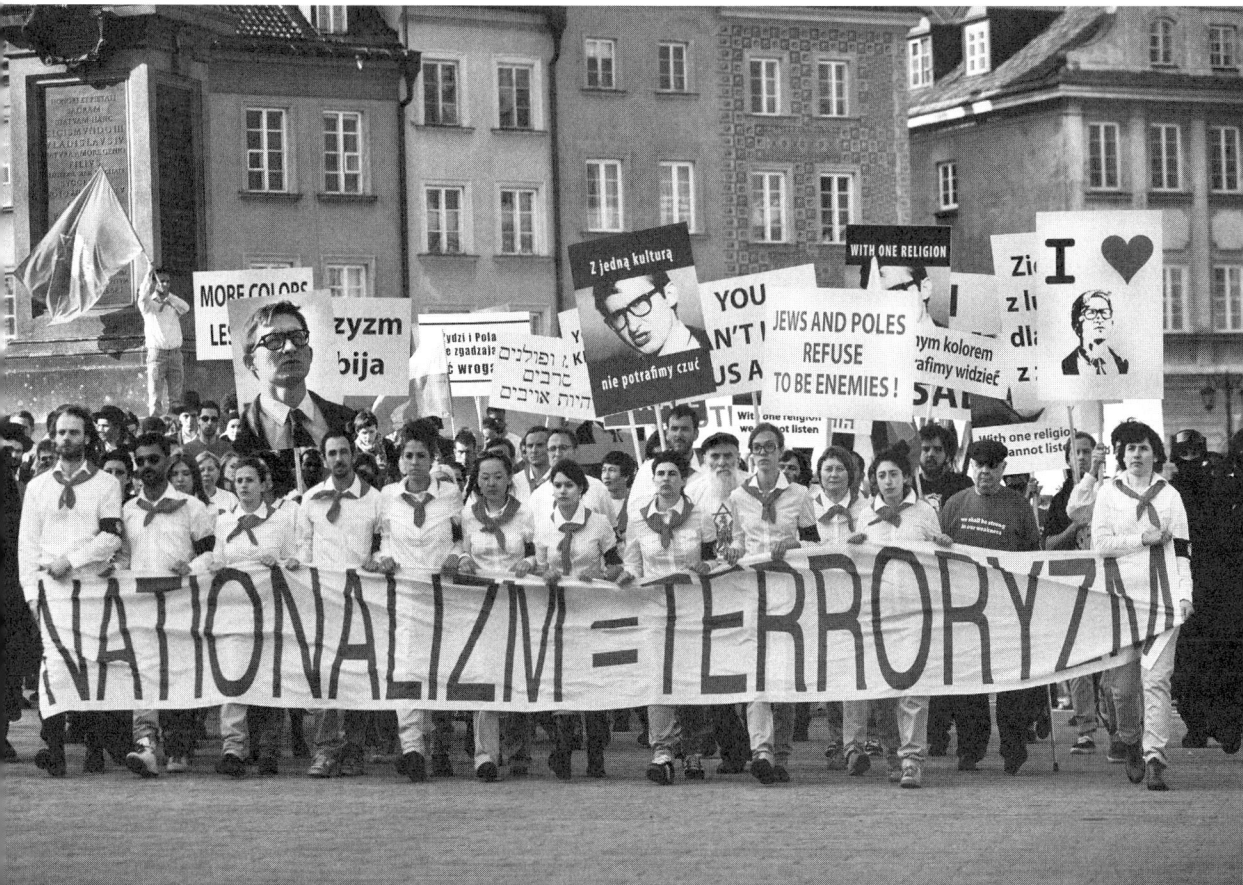

Figure 42. Yael Bartana, still from *Zamach* (Assassination), 2011. Production photo by Marcin Kalinski.

and Science in Pilsudski Square and is attended by Polish, English, and Hebrew-speaking mourners who dream of building a multiethnic community even as they dress in identical uniforms, engaging the trappings of political conformity. The accompanying publication for the Venice project, *A Cookbook for Political Imagination*, is a manual of political instructions, manifestos, stories, artistic contributions, and recipes, written by more than forty international authors. In their introduction, the editors and Bartana write, "The Polish trilogy can be read in a broader context, apart from the complex Polish-Jewish relationship, as an experimental form of collective psychotherapy, through which national demons are stirred, and dragged into daylight."[93] The first non-Polish artist to represent Poland, Bartana's deeply ironic project not only confronts the difficult issues of nationalism, ethnic oppression, and the right of return, but implicitly troubles the nature of the national pavilions at the Venice Biennale itself.

In an earlier video, men with four-wheel-drive trucks conduct war on the outskirts of Tel Aviv, not with weapons but only with the trucks themselves, reenacting in microcosm the larger war over the land (*Kings of the Hill*, 2003). Like enormous dumb creatures fighting for dominance on a dunghill, they are macho, ludicrous, and relentless, while providing entertainment for the spectators who watch the show. Another video features teenage boys and girls playing a real game called "Evacuation of Gilad Farm," based on the evacuation of Israeli settlers from the Gilad Farm settlement in the West Bank—surely, a uniquely Israeli game (*Wild Seeds*, 2005). One group tries to hold a patch of ground while the other group tries to forcibly remove them, instantly creating a sense of community among members of the opposing sides while providing a pretext for close bodily interaction and a sanctioned form of violence.[94]

We can see two general trends in Israeli art that evoke the Holocaust: one is specifically political and addresses the contradiction of the Jewish state as a democracy and as an occupying power; the other is psychoanalytic and more directly concerned with locating the self in relation to history. The first trend is exemplified by artists such as Kratsman, Ickowicz, and Bartana, whose works make visible what has long been hidden from view in Israel, and also in the United States, by the heroic and redemptive political imaginary. They often draw on the visual and verbal rhetoric of Holocaust victimization to reframe an understanding of the Israeli/Palestinian conflict by figuring the two kinds of victimization in terms of each other. Israeli-born artist Alan Schechner offers another example of this trend in his video work *The Legacy of Abused Children: From Poland to Palestine* (2003), in which he creates a continuous loop of two photographs of figures that slowly zoom inward: one is the little boy with his hands up as Jews are arrested by Nazis in a famous photograph of the Warsaw Ghetto; the other is a Palestinian girl being arrested by Israeli soldiers. Schechner has digitally altered the two photos so that each child holds a photograph of the other, thereby figuring one child's experience in terms of the other in a seemingly endless cycle of terror and oppression. Schechner also has critiqued Israeli commercialization and political manipulation of the Holocaust in other works, such as the controversial photograph in which he digitally inserted himself into a well-known photo in a concentration camp barracks, holding a can of Diet Coke (*Self-Portrait at Buchenwald: It's the Real Thing*, 1991–1993), and a video in which the striped pajamas of camp inmates morph into a commercial bar code (*Bar Code to Concentration Camp Morph*, 1991–1993). Both were shown in the 2002 exhibition *Mirroring Evil* at the Jewish Museum in New York City.[95]

The psychoanalytic trend in Israeli art concerned with locating the self in relation to history is particularly engaged by the enormous latent power that the figure of Adolf Hitler has come to assume in the Israeli political imagination. Both trends ultimately overlap in questioning the official meanings and mythology of the Holocaust that are a key part of the ideological agenda central to the founding of Israel, which has resisted visual interrogation by artists for decades. As part of the post-Zionist trend, a number of artists have set out to destabilize the solemn reverence in which Hitler is perversely held and to satirize the stubborn enthrallment the idea of Hitler produces in the Israeli psychological landscape. In Tamy Ben-Tor's performance video, *Women Talk about Adolf Hitler*, for example, Ben-Tor assumes the personas of six different women who "talk about Hitler." Among them is the "gender studies" writer who babbles on about how Hitler "didn't like dentists" and was "ashamed of his knees"; the Southern author of *Healing Hitler*, who talks about "coming to terms with evil"; the distraught Eastern European who says "Hitler makes me so ill I refuse to even talk about him"; the giggly Mitzi, who says that she "[likes] his little mustache"; and the girl who laments "my parents never told me about Hitler." Finally, there is the prim girl who dons a Hitler mustache and caresses a portrait of the Führer. Ben-Tor's fiercely funny work simultaneously makes visible and subverts the mass fascination and fetishization of Hitler.

Similarly, Roee Rosen's installation *Live and Die as Eva Braun* commands the viewer to assume the subject position of Adolf Hitler's mistress. The work consists of a set of numbered narrative texts written by the artist and printed on narrow fabric banners. The banners are accompanied by a heterogeneous group of drawings in the tradition of children's book illustrations that incorporate Nazi references. Rosen's texts are addressed to the

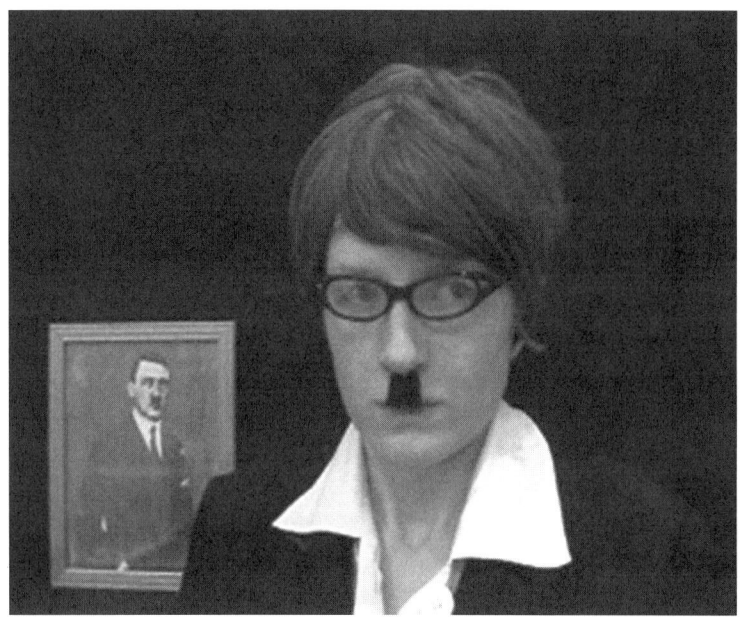

Figure 43. Tamy Ben-Tor, *Women Talk about Adolf Hitler*, 2004, digital video, 7:40, edition of 5. (Courtesy of Zach Feuer Gallery, New York.)

viewer, who is invited to assume the role of Hitler's lover as she shares a last tryst in the bunker, enjoying a lover's embrace, before their joint suicide. When first shown at an exhibition at Jerusalem's Israel Museum in 1997, the work became the center of a ferocious controversy. Both detractors and enthusiasts, however, pointed to the exhibition as a turning point in Israeli art, in which the image of Hitler and even the Holocaust more generally had been suppressed, seeing Rosen's work as deviant, unusual, and disturbing. Israeli curator Ariella Azoulay suggests that the sense of sacrilege lay in the fact that the work "doesn't concern Holocaust remembrance at all but ... concerns a set of fantasies and desires.... The fabrication of images and memories is not part of the familiar and reassuring game of Holocaust remembrance ... which is a framework that provides each person with a predefined role."[96] Thus Rosen's work makes visible the limits of Holocaust discourse and the predetermined expectations of the museum spectator. Like Tamy Ben-Tor, Roee Rosen attempts to come to terms with a fetishized and imaginary Hitler, both of them departing from official history and official forms of remembrance.

Rosen's work helped pave the way for Boaz Arad's videos, which also focus on the figure of Hitler, a figure that is traditionally visible in Israel only on Holocaust Remembrance Day, when film clips are shown on television. Arad has made seven short videos about Hitler using altered archival footage. He presents Hitler standing before a microphone with his hand in his pocket, masturbating (*100 Beats*, 1999), or, in another video, Arad himself wears a Hitler mask and discusses a clip from a film by Leni Riefenstahl that shows Hitler greeting admirers, then holds a photo of the latrines at Birkenau and discusses its aesthetic proportions (*Immense Inner Peace*, 2001). In *Safam* (Mustache, 1999), Arad focuses on the key visual signifier for the cinematic image of Hitler by depriving Hitler—in a clip from one of his speeches—of the one thing the viewer depends on, the signature mustache, which cannot be erased without destroying or trivializing the image of Hitler.⁹⁷ At the same time, Arad makes this manipulation apparent so that we are aware, via the dancing blank space above Hitler's lip, of the fetishistic significance of the mustache's absence.

In his video *Hebrew Lesson* (2000), Arad used footage of Hitler speaking and painstakingly spliced together German syllables to make Hitler say *Shalom Jerushalayim, ani mitnatzel* ("Hello Jerusalem, I apologize"). This mesmerizing video is only thirteen seconds long and ends with Hitler smoothing back his hair with both hands in a self-congratulatory moment of narcissistic self-regard. There is something both laughable and poignant in this difficult Hebrew lesson, a kind of yearning on the part of the audience that can never be fulfilled, an allusion to our collective frustration with Hitler's suicide and inability to hold him accountable, which might have allowed some small comfort in a sign of his remorse.⁹⁸ For Arad, the issue in these works is the complexity and difficulty of locating the self in relation to history, a constant negotiation between the subjectivity of the self and the other. In a sense, Arad humanizes Hitler in order to understand the self. He is careful to always make the manipulation visible, to show the artifice and ridiculousness of the attempt, yet in the process Arad questions the permanently fixed positions of victim and perpetrator in contemporary Israel.⁹⁹

A companion video to *Safam*, *Marcel Marcel* (2000), only twenty-seven seconds long, also addresses Hitler's mustache (the sound is audible but clearly subordinate to the image). The title evokes the work of Marcel Duchamp, who famously vandalized the *Mona Lisa* by adding a mustache and goatee to an image of the iconic painting. In *Marcel Marcel*, the mustache takes on a life of its own, waving like wings and taking on new shapes, becoming a fly buzzing around Hitler's head and zooming into his mouth, acting like windshield wipers on his eyes, or growing into a lush beard. This evokes other famous figures with mustaches and beards, such as Karl Marx or Che Guevara, as well as the full beards of Orthodox Jews and most specifically Theodor Herzl, the founder of Zionism. For Arad, Hitler has a Lacanian context, what Lacan calls the "Name-of-the-Father," who is twofold.

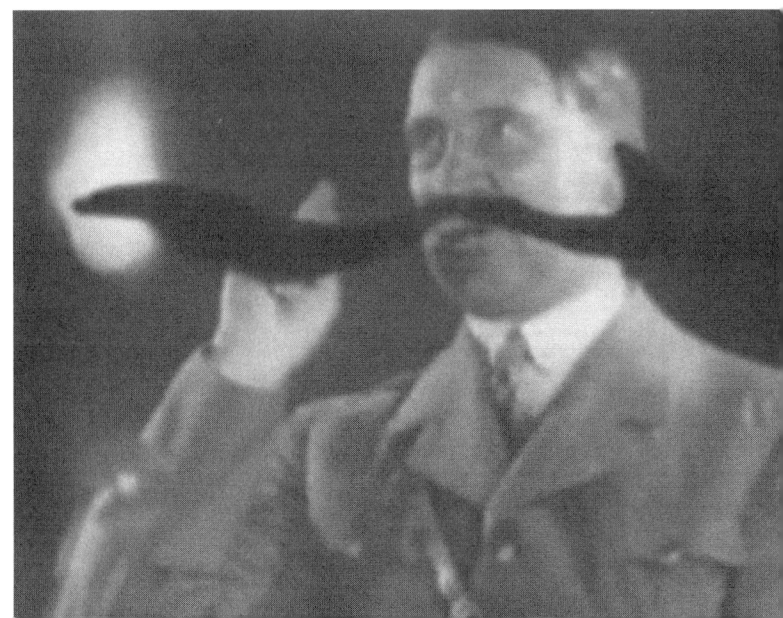

Figure 44. Boaz Arad, *Marcel, Marcel*, still from video, 2000. (Courtesy of the artist.)

Thus if Herzl is the father, Hitler is also the father. Herzl represents the good father, while Hitler is the monster father. In this sense, Arad sees Hitler as a father figure in Israel, but Arad notes, ironically, "He is also a consolation, because we think that we could never become such a monster, we could never reach such a level."[100] Arad's work was produced at a time when memory of the Holocaust was being instrumentalized as "moral cover" for the occupation of Gaza and the West Bank led by Ariel Sharon and alludes to the ways in which the Holocaust not only has scarred Israel, but also how it has been misused by Israel.

Referring to such use of the Holocaust as ideological justification for Israel's policies, Slavoj Žižek wrote: "Many political theorists, from Blaise Pascal to Immanuel Kant to Joseph de Maistre, have elaborated on the ways in which nation-states have manufactured heroic national mythologies to replace and ultimately erase their 'foundational crimes,' i.e., the illegitimate political violence necessary for their creation. With regard to this notion, it is true what has often been said: The misfortune of Israel is that it was established as a nation-state a century too late, in conditions when such 'founding crimes' are no longer acceptable (and—ultimate irony—it was the intellectual influence of Jews that contributed to the rise of this unacceptability!)." Žižek further notes, "The very need to evoke the Holocaust in defense of Israel's actions implies that its crimes are so horrible that only the absolute trump-card of the Holocaust can redeem them."[101] Indeed, the Holocaust is built into the training of Israeli soldiers, who are taken as high school students to Yad Vashem and encouraged to see the Palestinians as Nazi-like.[102] The work of artists such as Tamy Ben-Tor, Roee Rosen, Alan Schechner, and Boaz Arad seeks to counter this fetishized indoctrination, just as Yael Bartana's work evokes the early idealism of Zionist rhetoric to demonstrate the destructive results of the discourses that now flow from it. Ben-Tor, Rosen, Arad, and Bartana were among twenty-three post-Zionist Israeli artists in the 2003 exhibition *Wonderyears: New Reflections on the Shoah and Nazism in Israel*, organized in Berlin by the Neuen Gesellschaft fuer Bildende Kunst (a large artist-run collective), which refused to accept the victim/perpetrator opposition as an immutable form of collective identity.[103] Implicitly or explicitly, post-Zionist artists raise the question of the ironic relationship of the Jews as persecuted victims and exiles to the Palestinians as persecuted victims and exiles. Similarly, Miki Kratsman and others document the military training, occupation, and containment of the Palestinians directly, while their images of barbed wire, watchtowers, and concrete pillars recall the terrors of the concentration camps and construct present-day oppression in terms of what we know about previous forms of historical oppression.

Post-Zionist artists are part of a new generation that regards the Israeli occupation as a betrayal of the early ideals of the state. As Michael Sfard, an Israeli lawyer who refused to do his required reserve service, explained,

> I belong to a generation that has known only one side of Israel: that of the occupier. I grew up in a country where a small group of Jewish fundamentalist settlers benefitted from a level of political power out of all proportion with their modest number, where both the Right and the Left supported settling in the Palestinian territories—and, for this occupation, for this colonization, Israel pays a very high moral price. Our code of ethics is degraded. Even our culture has been affected. The place was founded on values of humanism, pluralism and democracy; the idea of the State of Israel to which I am attached no longer exists.... In 2002, four hundred and fifty Reservists, most of them between twenty-five and thirty-five years old, signed a petition that was published by the Israeli press, declaring that they refused to participate in the Israeli occupation or to serve on the other side of the Green Line. I was one of the signees, and I served as legal aide for several of the others.[104]

Like these reservists, a number of contemporary artists are reconsidering the ethical costs of Jewish nationhood, official mythology, and the contradictions between ethnocracy and democracy and drawing on documentary practices, past and present. Their works serve as weapons of social critique and help to create a more radically democratic public sphere as part of a political struggle for an egalitarian future.

Threatening Art

Palestinian artists have had a great deal of difficulty in achieving greater visibility because their movement and opportunities to exhibit have been greatly restricted by Israel. Palestinian artists in the West Bank are subject to having their exhibitions ransacked and their art galleries destroyed. Like all Palestinians, Palestinian artists cannot move freely because of the complex web of Israeli checkpoints, settlements, and the Barrier Wall, and there are no exemptions made for artists. On the contrary, the arts are subject to scrutiny for their political content and potential. During the first Intifada (1987–1989), when there were many Palestinian art exhibitions, the Israelis went so far as to ban the use of the colors of the Palestinian flag, severely hampering artistic freedom. Painter Vera Tamari notes, "It was very exciting, but the Israelis soon became aware of the importance of these exhibitions and started hitting the League of Palestinian Artists.

They made us get permits to show our work, censoring art and invading artists' studios. Several of us were imprisoned, usually on charges that they were painting in the colors of the Palestinian flag. They would say, 'You can paint, but don't use red, white or black,' and they would imprison you if you used those colors. You couldn't paint a poppy, for example, or a watermelon: they were the wrong colors. Often it was up to the artistic judgment of the particular officer in charge."[105]

Palestinian art is also controversial in the United States. At Chicago's Spertus Museum in May 2008, the exhibition *Imaginary Coordinates*, featuring the work of eight internationally known Palestinian- and Israeli-born women including Ayreen Anasta, Yael Bartana, Emily Jacir, Mona Hatoum, Sigalit Landau, Enas Muthafar, Michal Rovner, and Shirley Shor was closed more than two months early.[106] The exhibition presented work challenging notions of space, geography, and boundaries. Spertus director and the show's curator, Rhoda Rosen, explained the exhibition's premise as presenting divergent notions of national identity and place while pointing to the "critical disparity between maps and lived experience."[107] After opening a new fifty-five-million-dollar building in downtown Chicago, Rosen asserted that Spertus was adopting "a new mission, aiming to speak to people of all backgrounds," and while "the new Spertus' starting point continues to be Jewish experience, the institution does not operate from a partisan point of view."[108] But the trustees exerted heavy pressure when some viewers objected. The *Chicago Reader* noted, "Word on the street was that the exhibit had proved too controversial for some key members of the Spertus audience. The Jewish United Fund, a major Spertus supporter, had taken a look and promptly canceled a May 13 fund-raising dinner booked for the tenth floor boardroom. Michael Kotzen, executive vice president of the Jewish Federation of Metropolitan Chicago, says he moved the event after hearing from "'a number of people who thought the exhibit wasn't appropriate' in 'content and point of view.'"[109]

An attempt by the museum to modify walls, texts, and institute hourly tours in order to more fully explain the works did not mollify critics, and the show was closed. Philip Gordon, a Spertus trustee, insisted in a conference call with members of the press, "This has nothing to do with censorship," but he added, "This exhibition caused pain for members of our audience."[110] Arts writer Susan Snodgrass noted, "For some observers, the decision appears antithetical to the museum's revamped mission to present challenging exhibitions that educate diverse audiences and foster dialogue about the Jewish experience."[111] Barbara Kirshenblatt-Gimblett, who leads the core exhibition development team at Warsaw's Museum of the History of Polish Jews, asserted, "I don't think museums should be about consensus. They should be a catalyst, and then they should be prepared to deal with the repercussions."[112]

What works were found to be so painful? Though never specified, one of the works in the exhibition was a video by Palestinian artist Enas Muthaffar, who was born in Jerusalem. She addresses the issue of mapping in *A World Apart within 15 Minutes*, in which she drives around the ultra-Orthodox neighborhoods in West Jerusalem asking for directions to Ramallah (available on YouTube). There are subtle shifts in attitude as Israelis reject the question or have no idea, or send her in arbitrary directions and suggest that Ramallah is more than an hour away, though it is only fifteen minutes by car from Jerusalem. Nothing could make clearer the gulf between two peoples who live so close yet are separated by a vast social and political abyss.

Palestinian artist Emily Jacir, who won the Hugo Boss prize in 2008, showed *Crossing Surda (A Record of Going to and from Work)*. Jacir made the video documenting the difficulty of simply going to work after being humiliated at an Israeli checkpoint, already active for eight months, where soldiers held her at gunpoint in the winter rain after they saw her

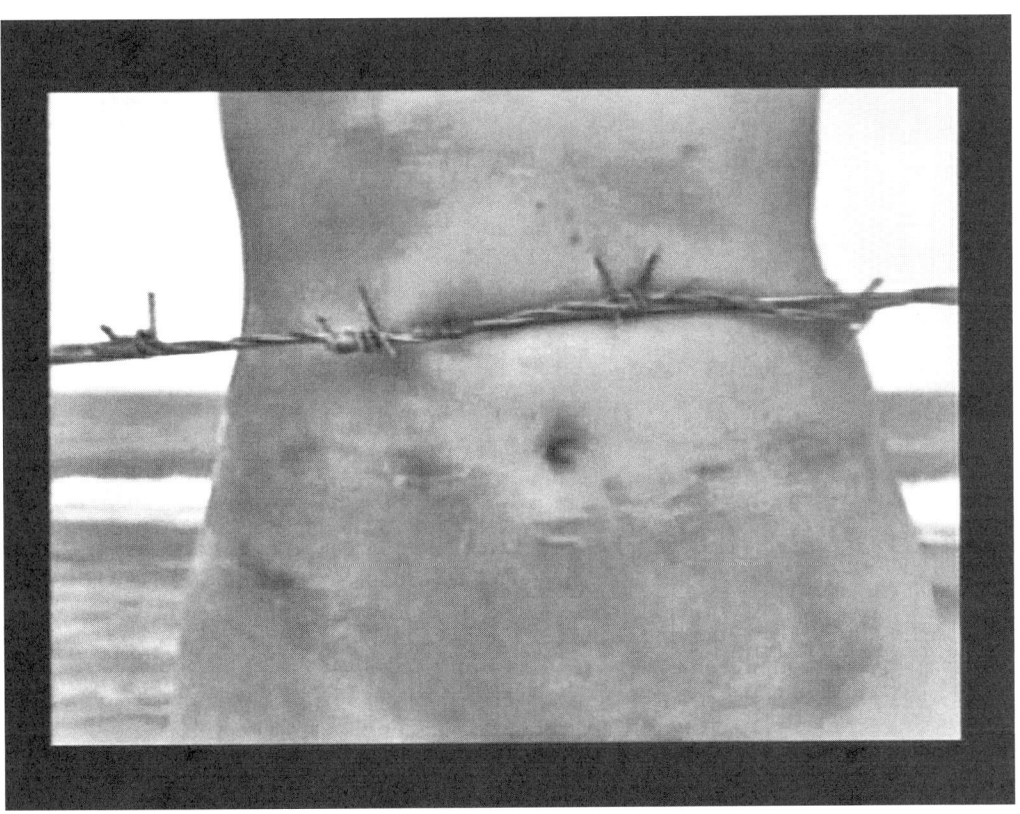

Figure 45. Sigalit Landau, *Barbed Hula*, still from video, 2000. (© Sigalit Landau. Courtesy of the artist and kamel mennour, Paris.)

filming her feet as she walked. They detained her for three hours, threw her American passport in the mud, told her she was in "Israel," and confiscated her videotape. In response, she cut a hole in her bag and for eight days surreptitiously recorded her daily walk to work from Ramallah to Birzeit University, including the Israeli checkpoint.[113]

Perhaps most controversial was Israeli artist Sigalit Landau's video *Barbed Hula*, which shows the artist swirling a hula-hoop made of barbed wire around her waist while nude on a beach in Tel Aviv. This painful yet gripping twenty-three-second video (part of a trilogy that includes *DeadSee*, 2005, and *Day Done*, 2007) becomes a visual metaphor of the Occupation (available at videoartworld.com). *Barbed Hula* evokes a deliberate kind of self-defeating game, the torment of prisons and concentration camps, and the closed and militarized borders in Israel. The work resonates with ritual and sacrifice, religious fanaticism, exclusionary and self-mortifying torture. The "imaginary coordinates" marked by the wire barbs signal an agonizing place to be, physically and psychologically, the body a surrogate for the political imaginary about the land and the results it has produced. It is difficult to watch the self-inflicted wounding, yet the action seems to echo the momentum of violence, even as every motion appears to be a willed effort, reiterating a history of violence, produced in view of the Mediterranean, "the only calm and natural border Israel has," as Landau observes.[114]

At the heart of the Israeli/Palestinian conflict is the impossibility of achieving national justice for geographically interpenetrated peoples within a capitalist framework bent on amassing profit through the booming industry of perpetual war. Both peoples who claim the land have a right to live there, yet the "two-state solution" is no solution at all since Israel has destroyed the possibility of a viable Palestinian state and claims all the land in any case in the name of a Jewish ethnocracy; two states could exist in name only, as Israel would maintain effective control of Palestinian borders and resources. Moreover, two states could only be created through the forcible separation of peoples, exacerbating the forced population transfers that have been central to Israeli strategy all along and would uproot thousands more Palestinians. The democratic right of self-determination cannot be effectively exercised by the Palestinians in the current conditions of Israel/Palestine, leaving the only possibility for a democratic solution in a social transformation that would transcend the national question on both sides. As long as the struggle remains entrenched in nationalist terms, the heavily armed and far more powerful Israeli state will prevail, and the oppression of the Palestinians will only deepen. The overthrow of the political system in Israel and the surrounding Arab states, however, could produce a new social order that would represent the national emancipation of the Palestinians along with the overthrow of oppressive Zionist and Arab regimes. Naturally this would represent a great political change in consciousness, in which Arab working masses would break from Islamic fundamentalism and bourgeois nationalism and Israeli workers would break from Zionist ideology. The alternative to this difficult task, however, is the continual threat of military conflict and oppression. As always, the weaker of the two national groups, along with other minorities and the poor, suffer the most. Those whose visual practices represent that experience, however, keep alive what the state would like to make invisible: the right of the rightless to have rights. Artists such as Muthaffar, Jacir, Landau, and many others challenge the shibboleths of Zionism in which the state's oppressive policies are rooted or make visible those who are deprived of rights, and help pave the way for emancipatory social struggle by calling into place a counterhegemonic public sphere through their quiet, beautiful, outraged, ironic, and passionate documentary practices.

CONCLUSION

ON HUMAN RIGHTS

While images are easily framed to serve the interests of the state, contemporary documentary images are also used to construct counterhegemonic narratives and to call into place public spheres, based on shared ways of seeing, that are critical of and outside the control of the state. In addition, critical documentary practices have merged with artistic genres such as video, reenactment, performance, and conceptual art in powerful and dynamic ways. Such practices make visible the state violence that often remains invisible, either because it is normalized by the institutions and discourses of the state, or because it has been left outside the official frames of vision. These documentary practices support democratic ideals and transformative social struggle by calling attention to those who might otherwise remain invisible were it not for the public sphere that is called into place and constituted by these documentary practices. These are the rightless, the people who have lost the right to have rights.

Let us then return to the question of "human rights." The liberal defense of "the human" through a universalist defense of human rights shifts emphasis away from the role of the liberal state to that of democratic reform, despite the fact that the inherent violence of the paternalistic state is the underlying cause of human rights abuses. The problem with humanitarian organizations is that they unwittingly support "a secret solidarity with the very powers they ought to fight," as Agamben argues. Put differently, the urgent concern for the immediate amelioration of suffering displaces the long-term concern with the political structures that produce that suffering.[1] As a result, human rights organizations rely on bare life as the object of their aid and protection by separating human rights from politics. "A humanitarianism separated from politics," writes Agamben, "cannot fail to reproduce the isolation of sacred life as the basis of sovereignty, and the camp—which is to say, the space of exception—is the biopolitical paradigm that it cannot master."[2] Human rights and the state are intrinsically related such that a state that cannot support human rights is a state that cannot be politically supported. Yet the capitalist state, premised on the concentration of wealth in the hands of a tiny minority which depends on the exploitation and impoverishment of the many to maintain an expanding rate of profit, is supported by nationalist ideologies that are racist, sexist, and xenophobic and inevitably produces the conditions of bare life and the corresponding indifference to "human rights," whether foreign or domestic. As Slavoj Žižek puts it, those who combat subjective violence are effectively hypocrites who support or even produce, in the case of philanthropists such as Bill Gates and George Soros, the systemic violence that generates "the very phenomena they abhor."[3]

Law scholar John Parry also argues that the difficulty with the idea of "the universal rights of humanity in general" is that "these claims lead directly to violence, both discursive and physical."[4] Parry points out that only the state can create the conditions, that is, citizenship, in which rights can be successfully claimed and that these rights are as much about restricting the individual as liberating him or her; at the same time, they create an "abstract autonomous individual or citizen" who is defined as equal in formal terms, but this condition of abstract equality depends on participation in a particular set of social structures and conventions. Those who do not share these structures and conventions are excluded from the group of equal-rights holders. The state, in an effort to provide equal rights, may perforce create "sustained domination or violence for the purpose of turning those people into the abstract individuals who will eventually have rights that are recognizable within a liberal order."[5] Such logic underwrote colonial rule and continues to support the open-ended domination of peoples by state powers, as we have seen. Thus liberal theory assumes a paternalistic stance toward those it deems incapable of having or insufficiently prepared to have equal rights; indeed, Parry argues that the very idea of rights developed in conjunction with colonialism, imperialism, and modern systems of production and trade, depends on them, and serves the interests of the modern state.[6] Those who have fewer rights are defined either as not ready for rights, that is, implicitly or explicitly less than human, or as having rights when in practice they do not. What is terrifying is the ease with which governments can shift categories of people from those who have rights to those who do not, as demonstrated by the Bush and Obama administrations' use of the term "terrorist" or "illegal combatant" to characterize people whom they deem nonparticipants in the social structures and conventions that confer rights, including American citizens. Such people are thereby counted out as human and redefined as "fanatics," "brutal," "barbaric," evildoers," "uncivilized," and "animals" who have lost the right to have rights, or simply are not ready to have rights.

The Missing Picture of the Dead Bin Laden
The denial of rights has become more open and unapologetic, as demonstrated by the Obama administration's summary execution of Osama bin Laden. But why withhold publication of the photograph verifying bin Laden's death? In the contest of images, we must go back to the destruction of the Twin Towers, which began the "war on terror" by constituting a catastrophic "image-defeat" for which the Bush administration tried,

but failed, to find a suitable and equally powerful counterimage.[7] The later capture and execution of Saddam Hussein did not suffice to counter this image of a mighty blow against U.S. capitalism, especially since Hussein had nothing to do with the attacks of 9/11 and was executed by his own people. But what about the image of a dead bin Laden, the architect and mastermind of the attack, for whom the U.S. government had hunted for almost ten years? Following the U.S. Navy SEALs team assassination of bin Laden on 1 May 2011, President Obama rejected the idea of making the image public by voicing concerns that it would be seen as a trophy photo and incite more violence.[8] Obama understood that publicizing the photo of the al-Qaeda chief, shot in the head and chest by an American death squad, would be seen as a form of imperial triumphalism and gloating. Yet this refusal to publish the photo also must be understood as an attempt to downplay the fact that bin Laden was summarily executed and dumped in the ocean, despite being unarmed, despite the fact that the seventy-nine commandos faced little resistance and quickly put it down, despite the multiple violations of international law that this represented, and despite initial assertions by a government spokesman that the government's intention was to take bin Laden alive if possible. It has since been shown that the government's intention was instead to avoid taking bin Laden alive, which would have made him a prisoner to be tried in a court of law and would have presented a plethora of legal and political headaches for the U.S. government while riveting the world on his trial.[9]

Observers such as Glenn Greenwald, Noam Chomsky, and Yochi Dreazen, senior correspondent on military affairs and national security for the *National Journal*, among others, have all questioned the ethical implications of the planned assassination and violation of elementary norms of international law. Dreazen, for example, writes: "The administration had made clear to the military's clandestine Joint Special Operations Command that it wanted bin Laden dead, according to a senior U.S. official with knowledge of the discussions. A high-ranking military officer briefed on the assault said the SEALs knew their mission was not to take him alive."[10] Dreazen notes that former West German chancellor Helmut Schmidt "told German TV that the U.S. raid was 'quite clearly a violation of international law' and that bin Laden should have been detained and put on trial," while U.S. Attorney General Eric Holder defended the decision to kill bin Laden, even though he posed no immediate threat to the Navy SEALs, telling a House panel that the murder was "lawful, legitimate and appropriate in every way."[11] This followed the retraction of the government's initial report that bin Laden was armed and using one of his wives as a human shield; White House spokesman Jay Carney quickly admitted that bin Laden was neither armed nor using his wife as a shield.

Bin Laden was not accorded the rights given even to Nazi war criminals, whose crimes were far greater. As British barrister Geoffrey Robertson notes, "When the time came to consider the fate of men much more steeped in wickedness than Osama bin Laden—namely the Nazi leadership—the British government wanted them hanged within six hours of capture. President Truman demurred, citing the conclusion of Justice Robert Jackson that summary execution 'would not sit easily on the American conscience or be remembered by our children with pride . . . the only course is to determine the innocence or guilt of the accused after a hearing as dispassionate as the times will permit and upon a record that will leave our reasons and motives clear.'"[12] Dreazen observes that the killing was in part motivated by revenge: "For many at the Pentagon and the Central Intelligence Agency who had spent nearly a decade hunting bin Laden, killing the militant was a necessary and justified act of vengeance."[13]

Not only was the prospect of a bin Laden trial apparently terrifying to the state, but so was the gruesome image of the bloody head of the al-Qaeda leader.[14] One can understand the administrations' concerns: What more potent symbol of the sovereign's power to declare a state of exception, suspend the law, and strip a man of all rights? What greater evidence of the sovereign's supremely arrogant defiance of international law? Such a photograph signifies the systemic violence inherent in the liberal capitalist state itself, which may suspend the rights of anyone, anywhere—the refugee, the impoverished, the dissenter, the rogue individual—openly and before the world, without the usual demurral or excuses, in this case transforming the ruthless and deservedly reviled bin Laden (whom the same state nevertheless once armed when he was fighting the Soviet Union in Afghanistan) into the most famous example of *homo sacer*, a man who, whatever his alleged crimes, was placed outside the law, answerable only to the sovereign, who could—and did—murder him with impunity. This unseen photo becomes a shadow version of the most infamous image of these wars: the Hooded Man. Unhooded in the mind's eye and with a Middle Eastern face, the morally questionable rationale that produced this image and that its visibility would highlight confirms that it is an image defeat in absentia, another failed response to the image of the Twin Towers crumbling. This defeat is precisely constituted by the government's inability to show the photograph as an image victory, one that would be instantly flashed around the world as part of the contest of images over the rule of capitalist "democracy."

The Politics of Radical Critique

The left has largely retreated from trenchant anticapitalist critique, and no one in academia has been more penetratingly critical of this than cultural and political theorist Slavoj Žižek. In his self-proclaimed magnum opus, *The Parallax View*, Žižek attempts to rehabilitate a dialectical materialist analysis of world capitalism, founded on the understanding that social oppression is rooted in social and economic structures marked by class contradictions, a view that has been in retreat now for at least a generation.[15] Žižek recuperates the merits of even a Stalinized communism as against Nazi fascism, with which it is often falsely twinned, though without accepting the important Trotskyist critique of Stalinism. Žižek maintains that the Stalinist deformation of the Communist project was a "historical necessity." Writes Žižek, "The proper task is thus to think the *tragedy* of the October Revolution: to perceive its greatness, its unique emancipatory potential, and, simultaneously, the historical necessity of its Stalinist outcome. We should oppose both temptations: the Trotskyite notion that Stalinism was ultimately a contingent deviation, as well as the notion that the Communist project is, at its very core, totalitarian."[16] The Russian Revolution of 1917, still the foundational event for an understanding of emancipatory politics today, was thus neither fish nor fowl in Žižek's view: communism was neither totalitarian at its core, nor was Stalinism a contingent outcome. Yet these two possibilities are mutually exclusive, and one or the other must be true. Žižek himself offers a persuasive historical explanation for the Stalinization of the October Revolution on the basis of material scarcity, suggesting that since communism did not expand to more advanced countries in Europe, the Stalinist degeneration became inevitable. Lenin and Trotsky themselves pointed out this danger, and it is *only* at this point that degeneration became inevitable. It cannot be argued that the failure to spread to an advanced capitalist country, such as Germany, where the revolutionary movement was strong, was itself inevitable, and to do so strips away historical agency from the people and parties who made decisions that led to that outcome. Had the Soviet party supported the Communists in Germany in the revolutionary upheavals following World War I and formed a united front with the German Social Democrats, as the Trotskyist Left Opposition urged, to prevent the victory of the Nazis in 1933, history surely would have unfolded very differently in both Europe and the Soviet Union.[17]

It is telling that after decades of decline, interest in revolutionary theory and history is reviving in response to the "Arab Spring" and has made its way into such publications as *Bookforum*, published by *Artforum*, in the article "Reading Trotsky in Tahrir: What the Russian Revolutionary Can Teach Us about the Arab Spring," in which Graeme Wood describes Trotsky's *The History of the Russian Revolution* as "among the most thrilling works of history ever written." He notes, rightly, that it is not only "riveting and intelligent" but its depiction of the February

Revolution that preceded the October Revolution is "capable of nourishing any reader who wants to know what the Arab Spring feels like from inside."[18]

Despite his critique, Žižek has little sympathy for the academics and liberals he characterizes as "the usual gang of democracy-to-come-deconstructionist-postsecular-Levinasian-respect-for-Otherness-suspects"[19] and expresses impatience with liberal longings for multicultural harmony as "the self-defeating vicious cycle of self-postponing, of a permanent 'to-come.'"[20] As theorist Terry Eagleton notes, Žižek finds U.S. fundamentalism more bracing than *"bien-pensant* liberalism" because, among other reasons, "adherents to the former believe in struggle while proponents of the latter believe only in difference." Though Eagleton mocks a renewed materialist analysis of the world crisis, he acknowledges Žižek's credibility: "As a child of Yugoslav neo-Stalinism and its bloody collapse, he has at least had a taste of real political conflict, however unpleasant, in contrast to the kind of gentrified leftism that is embarrassed by talk of class struggle."[21] Indeed, class struggle, in the past period of increasing conservatism, has become the idea that "cannot be spoken." Žižek also analyzes the flaw in the liberal critique of subjective violence—evil men doing evil things—as seen against a background of zero-level nonviolence, which makes the violence inherent in the normal state of things invisible. Žižek calls this normal state of things "objective violence": "Objective violence is invisible since it sustains the very zero-level standard against which we perceive something as subjectively violent."[22] This is the normal state of liberal capitalism.

Gene Ray also refers to the collapse "in confusion and despair" of the radical systemic critique of capitalism following the fall of the Berlin Wall in 1991 and the rise of neoliberal hegemony, which has produced "capitalism plus liberal democracy triumphalism" and legitimized the unbridled operations of finance capital while trampling the rights of labor and environmental protections.[23] As Naomi Klein demonstrates, the disastrous consequences of such neoliberalism, also called "free trade," "globalization," and "neoconservatism," can be seen as focused on advancing corporate goals by using "moments of collective trauma to engage in radical social and economic engineering" through privatization, government deregulation, and deep cuts to social spending, which effectively transfers public wealth into private hands.[24] Examples in the last three decades demonstrate that infamous human rights violations were committed with the deliberate intention of terrorizing populations in order to accomplish radical free market "reforms," including the Argentine junta's "disappearance" of thirty thousand people, mostly leftist activists, before imposing such Chicago School policies; China's 1989 Tiananmen

Square massacre and subsequent arrest of tens of thousands before converting the country into an export zone; and the Russian state's 1993 decision to send in tanks to set fire to the parliament building and arrest opposition leaders, paving the way for Russian privatization and the rise of the notorious oligarchs.[25] The accumulation of human, economic, and environmental disasters, including the 2008 global financial collapse and the increasing assaults on privacy, democratic rights, unions and labor rights following the attacks of September 11, the continual war on terror, the faulty safeguards on nuclear power leading to the Fukushima Daiichi partial meltdowns, and the ongoing rebellions against entrenched repressive regimes across North Africa, have put global anticapitalism and systemic critique back on the table and opened a larger space for critical and oppositional artistic and political practices. Because the vast majority of people do not benefit from the corporatist transfers of wealth from public to private hands, however, the spreading discontent, opposition, and protest also have produced an increased need for "aggressive surveillance" and "bottomless spending on security" as well as "mass incarceration, shrinking civil liberties," and a liberal use of torture, veiled in secrecy and resistance to accountability.[26] In the face of deepening crises produced by corporate capitalism for most of the world's population, the mastery of images by oppositional forces has become as important as the mastery of facts on the ground.

As many have noted, demoralization and despair followed the failed uprisings which took place over the course of the twentieth century, especially, for recent generations, the uprisings of 1968. This has resulted in the fears that seizing state power only leads to new forms of bureaucratic exploitation and control—something we see playing out in countries such as Egypt, where control has fallen to the military. Yet we must understand the specific historical conditions that lead to these failures and recognize that people all over the world are fighting to throw off oppressive regimes and have begun once more to revolt as the capitalist ethos of deregulation, privatization, and the free reign of corporate power only accelerates the degradation and destruction of the lives of the world's peoples and the environment we all share. The problem is that these revolts often lack clear leadership and anticapitalist programs. Against the system of advanced capitalism, which is incapable of supporting the world's population, eliminating poverty, or husbanding the earth's resources, there is no alternative to an organized political party that would fight for an anticapitalist egalitarian system. And in a global culture where everyone can produce as well as consume public imagery in a contest of images, the mastery of images and their polemical power is crucial to any emancipatory and transformative program of social and political struggle.

NOTES

Introduction

1. Judith Butler, *Frames of War: When Is Life Grievable?* (New York: Verso, 2010).
2. Ibid., xiii, xviii.
3. Peter Maass, "The Toppling: How the Media Inflated a Minor Moment in a Long War," *The New Yorker* [online], 10 January 2011.
4. Dora Apel, "Cultural Battlegrounds: Weimar Photographic Narratives of War," *New German Critique* 76, Special Issue on Weimar Visual Culture (Winter 1999): 49–84.
5. Guy Lane, "Jorge Ribalta on Documentary and Democracy," *Foto8 Magazine* [online], 2 July 2009.
6. Ibid.
7. John Tagg, *The Disciplinary Frame: Photographic Truths and the Capture of Meaning* (Minneapolis: University of Minnesota Press, 2009), 86–87.
8. Ibid., 80.
9. Jorge Ribalta, critical review of *The Disciplinary Frame* in caareviews.org, 28 April 2010.
10. Jorge Ribalta, "Introduction," in *Public Photographic Spaces: Exhibitions of Propaganda, from Pressa to The Family of Man, 1928–55*, ed. Jorge Ribalta (Barcelona: Museu d'Art Contemporani de Barcelona, 2008), 17.
11. Lane, "Jorge Ribalta."
12. Ariella Azoulay, *The Civil Contract of Photography* (New York: Zone Books, 2008), 126–127.
13. Anthony Downey, "Thresholds of a Coming Community: Photography and Human Rights," *Aperture Magazine* (Spring 2009), available at aperture.org. Also see John T. Parry, "Finding a Right to Be Tortured," *Law & Literature* 19, no. 2 (2007): 207–227, and Serena Parekh, "Resisting 'Dull and Torpid' Assent: Returning to the Debate over the Foundations of Human Rights," *Human Rights Quarterly* 29, no. 3 (2007): 754–778.
14. Giorgio Agamben, *Homo Sacer: Sovereign Power and Bare Life* (Stanford, Calif.: Stanford University Press, 1998); Anthony Downey, "Zones of Indistinction: Giorgio Agamben's 'Bare Life' and the Politics of Aesthetics," *Third Text* 23, no. 2 (March 2009): 111.
15. Downey, "Thresholds."
16. Charles Savage, "Secret U.S. Memo Made Legal Case to Kill a Citizen," *New York Times*, 8 October 2011. The quote is from "Al-Awlaki Assassination: U.S. State Terror," *Workers Vanguard*, no. 988 (14 October 2011).
17. Jacques Rancière, *Dissensus: On Politics and Aesthetics*, ed. and trans. Steven Corcoran (New York: Continuum International Publishing Group, 2010), 64–67, 4.
18. Ibid., 106–107, 68–69.
19. Azoulay, *Civil Contract*, 130.
20. Judith Butler, *Precarious Life: The Powers of Mourning and Violence* (New York: Verso, 2004), 128ff.
21. Azoulay, *Civil Contract*, 134, 132.
22. Ibid., 119.
23. Robert Hariman and John Louis Lucaites also suggest that photojournalism helps to construct public life and constitutes a shared way of public and collective seeing that potentially reconnects the personal and private concerns of the individual with that of the larger social collective and allows people to unite in defense of basic democratic rights. See Robert Hariman and John Louis Lucaites, *No Caption Needed: Iconic Photographs, Public Culture, and Liberal Democracy* (Chicago: University of Chicago Press, 2007), 18–19.
24. Parry, "Finding a Right," 212.
25. For a history of photography as an art-historical discipline, see Douglas R. Nickel, "History of Photography: The State of Research," *Art Bulletin* 83, no. 3 (2001): 548–558.
26. Lane, "Jorge Ribalta."
27. Erina Duganne, "Photography after the Fact," in *Beautiful Suffering: Photography and the Traffic in Pain*, ed. Mark Reinhardt, Holly Edwards, and Erina Duganne (Chicago: Williams College Museum of Art and University of Chicago Press, 2007), 60–61.
28. Ibid., 65–74. Duganne refers to Sally Mann's series *What Remains*, Serrano's staged photographs of torture published in the *New York Times Magazine*, 12 June 2005, and Jaar's *The Eyes of Gutete Emerita*, among other works.
29. Mark Reinhardt, "Introduction," in *Beautiful Suffering: Photography and the Traffic in Pain*, ed. Mark Reinhardt, Holly Edwards, and Erina Duganne (Chicago: Williams College Museum of Art and University of Chicago Press, 2007); Susan Sontag, *Regarding the Pain of Others* (New York: Farrar, Straus and Giroux, 2003), 39, 114–115.
30. John Taylor, *Body Horror: Photojournalism, Catastrophe and War* (New York: New York University Press, 1998), 4. Documentary practices predominated at Documenta 11 in Kassel, Germany, in 2002, a five-year biennial for which Okwei Enwezor served as the first non-European artistic director. In an essay published six years later, Enwezor defended the prominence of documentary practices (which he calls "vérité") as responding to the "unhomeliness" of the

contemporary world, that is, the widespread permanent migration produced by the catastrophic effects of global capitalism as well as our subjective alienation from consumerism and capitalist social relations. Enwezor asserted that a return to formalism would be "a great emptying out and banishment of the content of the political in artistic matters, as if this would provide a cure for the anxiety of modernity." See "Documentary/Vérité: Bio-Politics, Human Rights, and the Figure of 'Truth' in Contemporary Art," in *The Green Room: Reconsidering the Documentary and Contemporary Art #1*, ed. Maria Lind and Hito Steyerl (Berlin: Sternberg Press and the Center for Curatorial Studies, Bard College, 2008), 65–66.

31. Examples are exhibitions (with accompanying catalogs and/or symposia) such as *Memory of Fire: The War of Images and Images of War* at the Brighton Photo Biennial in 2008; *Zones of Conflict* at the Pratt Manhattan Gallery in 2008–2009; *The Greenroom: Reconsidering the Documentary and Contemporary Art* at CCS Bard in 2008; *Image War: Contesting Images of Political Conflict* at the Whitney Museum of American Art in 2006; *Thy Brothers' Keeper*, organized by The Alternative Museum in New York for the Flint Institute of Arts in Michigan in 2006; *Nature/Nation* (2009) and *Bare Life* (2007) at the Museum on the Seam in Jerusalem; and *Beautiful Suffering: Photography and the Traffic in Pain* at the Williams College Museum of Art in 2006.

Technologies of War, Media, and Dissent in the Post-9/11 Work of Krzysztof Wodiczko

1. Dale F. Eickelman, "The Middle East's Democracy Deficit and the Expanding Public Sphere," in *Media, War, and Terrorism: Responses from the Middle East and Asia*, ed. Peter van der Veer and Shoma Munshi (New York: Routledge, 2004), 66. The video can be found online in English at ciaonet.org.
2. Declan McCullagh, "Post 9/11 Antiterror Technology: A Report Card," CNet News.com, 7 September 2006.
3. Tim Weiner, "The Long War: How Little Has Changed," *New York Times*, 22 July 2007, Week in Review, 12.
4. Beatriz Colomina, *Domesticity at War* (Cambridge, Mass.: MIT Press, 2007).
5. John G. Hanhardt, "Dé-collage/Collage: Notes Toward a Reexamination of the Origins of Video Art," in *Illuminating Video: An Essential Guide to Video Art*, ed. Doug Hall and Sally Jo Fifer (New York: Aperture Foundation Inc., 1990), 71–72.
6. Martha Rosler, "Video: Shedding the Utopian Moment," in *Illuminating Video*, 31.
7. Peter van der Veer, "War Propaganda and the Liberal Public Sphere," in *Media, War, and Terrorism*, 13.
8. Andrew J. Bacevich, *The New American Militarism: How Americans Are Seduced by War* (New York: Oxford University Press, 2005), 5.
9. George Will, "On the Health of the State," *Newsweek*, 1 October 2001, 70, quoted in James Der Derian, "9/11: Before, After, and In Between," in *Terrorism, Media, Liberation*, ed. J. David Slocum (New Brunswick, N.J.: Rutgers University Press, 2005), 322.
10. Robert Ricigliano and Mike Allen, "Cold War Redux," in *Rethinking Global Security: Media, Popular Culture, and the "War on Terror,"* ed. Andrew Martin and Patrice Petro (New Brunswick, N.J.: Rutgers University Press, 2006), 85–103.
11. The installation was shown at Galerie Lelong in New York from 10 September to 22 October 2005, and at the Museu d'Art Contemporani in Barcelona from 22 September to 27 November 2006.
12. Raphael Cuir, "Krzysztof Wodiczko," *Artpress*, December 2005, 78.
13. John Haber, "Political Art and Architecture, Fall 2005: Luc Tuymans, Krzysztof Wodiczko, and Sam Durant," *Haber's Art Reviews* [online]. For other reviews, see Nancy Princenthal, *Art in America* 93, no. 10 (November 2005): 170, and Roberta Smith, *New York Times*, Arts & Leisure, 14 October 2005; Dore Ashton, "If You See Something," reprinted by Galerie Lelong from *The Brooklyn Rail*.
14. See Krzysztof Wodiczko, *Critical Vehicles: Writings, Projects, Interviews* (Cambridge, Mass.: MIT Press, 1999); on the Bunker Hill Project, see Lisa Saltzman, "When Memory Speaks: A Monument Bears Witness," in *Trauma and Visuality in Modernity*, ed. Lisa Saltzman and Eric Rosenberg (Hanover, N.H.: University Press of New England, 2006).
15. For an interview between Patricia Phillips and Krzysztof Wodiczko on the central premises of his work, see "Creating Democracy: A Dialogue with Krzysztof Wodiczko," *Art Journal* 62, no. 4 (Winter 2003): 32–47; also see Patricia Phillips, "(Inter)Disciplinary Actions," *Public Art Review* 15, no. 1 (Fall/Winter 2003): 11–15, and Elizabeth Ellsworth, *Places of Learning: Media, Architecture, Pedagogy* (New York: Routledge, 2004). For the most comprehensive volume on his work, see *Krzysztof Wodiczko*, ed. Duncan McCorquodale (London: Black Dog Publishing, 2011).
16. Colomina, *Domesticity at War*, 264–269. The multiscreen installation was first employed by Ray and Charles Eames at the Moscow World's Fair in 1959, and again at the 1964 World's Fair in New York.
17. Wodiczko, *Critical Vehicles*, 120.
18. See Lauren Berlant, *The Queen of America Goes to Washington City: Essays on Sex and Citizenship* (Durham, N.C.: Duke University Press, 1997), 62.
19. Quoted in Holland Cotter, "Remembrance of Downtown Past," *New York Times*, Weekend Arts, 1 September 2006, B24.
20. According to the MTA website, dozens of municipalities in the United States and

around the world have requested permission to use the campaign slogan. In early 2008, the MTA began a new campaign that added to the original slogan ads with pictures of police dogs and the slogan "You use your eyes. He'll use his nose." See "MTA Rolls Out 'The Eyes of New York' Ad Campaign," mta.info.

21. The U.N. first called for the closure of Guantánamo in 2006, denouncing the torture and abuses there as well as the arbitrary detention. See "UN Calls for Guantánamo Closure," *BBC News* [online], 16 February 2006. Two years later, the former Chief Prosecutor at Guantánamo, Colonel Morris D. Davis, resigned his position, testified on behalf of Salim Ahmed Hamdan, an alleged driver for Osama bin Ladin, and became one of the most outspoken critics of the military commissions process he had formerly supported. See Josh White, "From Chief Prosecutor to Critic at Guantanamo," *Washington Post* [online], 29 April 2008. The case of Mahar Arar, a Syrian-born Canadian who was arrested by the U.S. government during a stopover at JFK airport, falsely labeled an Islamic extremist, and sent to Syria where he was tortured for almost a year, aroused outrage regarding the practice of extreme rendition. See Daina Lawrence, "Wrongly Deported Canadian Is Offered Dollars 8.9m, Terrorism Ordeal," *Financial Times* (London) [online], 27 January 2007. Signed into law by Obama as this book goes to press is the National Defense Authorization Act of 2012, which authorizes indefinite detention without trial.

22. Geoffrey Stone, "Classified Information and the Press," University of Chicago Law School Faculty Blog, 26 May 2006, available at uchicagolaw.typepad.com.

23. See fulana.org, under "projects." The "see something, say something" campaign also has inspired three theater works: *The Fear Project* at the Barrow Group Theatre, with works by seven playwrights; *(I Am) Nobody's Lunch* by Steven Cosson; and *Major Bang, or How I Learned to Stop Worrying and Love the Dirty Bomb* by Kirk Lynn; the film *If You See Something, Say Something* (2005) by Josh Safdie was shown at the Underground Film Festival in New York in 2006.

24. See "Random Observations on Life, the Universe and Television," triborough.org, 17 December 2005.

25. "Know Your Rights!" aclu.org.

26. Excerpt from installation transcripts, courtesy Galerie Lelong.

27. "Guatemalan Refugees Return to a Hard Life," *Refugees International* [online], 1 May 2002.

28. Carolyn Lochhead, "Give and Take Across the Border: 1 in 7 Mexican Workers Migrates—Most Send Money Home," *San Francisco Chronicle* [online], 21 May 2006; also see "Labor and the Fight for Immigrant Rights," *Workers Vanguard*, 26 May 2006.

29. Roger Lowenstein, "The Immigration Equation," *New York Times Magazine*, 9 July 2006.

30. Paul Harris, "Illegal Immigrants Caught in a Fight for the Headlines," *The Observer*, 3 February 2008, available at guardian.co.uk.

31. Patrice Petro and Andrew Martin, "Introduction," in *Rethinking Global Security*, ed. Patrice Petro and Andrew Martin (New Brunswick, N.J.: Rutgers University Press, 2006), 5.

32. Cuir, "Krzysztof Wodiczko," 78.

33. Bill Christensen, "Covert Iris Scanner Close to Minority Report Future," Telenovelegy.com, 19 July 2007.

34. Wodiczko chose window washers for his project who specialized in cleaning the windows of art galleries, and even joined, as a Polish-speaking immigrant himself, such window-washing crews as a "trainee" on several occasions. Telephone conversation with Krzysztof Wodiczko, 18 August 2006.

35. Slavoj Žižek, *The Parallax View* (Cambridge, Mass.: MIT Press, 2006), 301.

36. Haber, "Political Art and Architecture."

37. A complete list of groups and organizations can be obtained from Galerie Lelong. Most of the participants in this project, whose gradual involvement and trust were accomplished over time, did not meet each other until the opening of the exhibition. Telephone conversation with Krzysztof Wodiczko, 5 June 2006. For theorizing on questions of audience and community, see Miwon Kwon, *One Place after Another: Site-Specific Art and Locational Identity* (Cambridge, Mass.: MIT Press, 2002); Grant Kester, *Conversation Pieces: Community and Communication in Modern Art* (Berkeley: University of California Press, 2004); Doug Ashford, Wendy Ewald, Nina Felshin, and Patricia C. Phillips, "A Conversation on Social Collaboration," *Art Journal* 65, no. 2 (Summer 2006): 58–82.

38. The installation was first shown at Galerie Lelong in conjunction with *If You See Something* . . . in 2005 and at the Galerie Gabrielle Maubrie in Paris from 18 March to 15 May 2006. I thank Buzz Spector for sharing his experience of the "speaking flames," in a telephone conversation on 6 June 2006, on which this description draws.

39. Installation transcripts, courtesy Krzysztof Wodiczko, Galerie Lelong, New York.

40. Deborah White, "Iraq War Facts, Results & Statistics at November 30, 2010," About.com, 3 December 2010.

41. For documents on Haditha, see PBS *Frontline* [online]; on Korea, see Charles J. Hanley and Martha Mendoza, "AP Updates Its 'No Gun Ri' Pulitzer Winner: New Document Reveals Order to Shoot Refugees," *Editor and Publisher* [online], 29 May 2006; on Vietnam, see Patricia Sullivan, "Samuel Koster, 86, General Charged in My Lai Killings," *Washington Post* [online], 10 February 2006.

42. Manuel Delgado, "Symbolic Wars: Struggle, Play, Festival," in *At War*, ed. Antonio Monegal

and Francesc Torres (Barcelona: Centre de Cultura Contemporania de Barcelona, Institut d'Edicions de la Diputacio de Barcelona, Forum Barcelona and Actar, 2004), 52, 48.
43. Mieke Bal, "The Pain of Images," in *Beautiful Suffering: Photography and the Traffic in Pain*, ed. Mark Reinhardt, Holly Edwards, and Erina Duganne (Chicago: University of Chicago Press, 2007), 110–111.
44. Robert Hariman and John Louis Lucaites, *No Caption Needed: Iconic Photographs, Public Culture, and Liberal Democracy* (Chicago: University of Chicago Press, 2007), 188.
45. MegofMegs, *Get Yer Art Here! (Denver Connects)*, dencx.com, 25 August 2008.
46. Telephone conversation with Krzysztof Wodiczko, 30 August 2008. The seven-and-a-half-minute video is available at kwodiczko.com/WarVeteranVehicle/.
47. Judith Herman, *Trauma and Recovery: The Aftermath of Violence—From Domestic Abuse to Political Terror*, 2nd ed. (New York: Basic Books, 1997).
48. Telephone conversation with Wodiczko, 2008.
49. Terri L. Tanelian, *Invisible Wounds of War: Psychological and Cognitive Injuries, Their Consequences, and Services to Assist Recovery* (Santa Monica, Calif.: Rand Corporation, 2008), 144 [online].
50. Tanja Frančišković et al., "Secondary Traumatization of Wives of War Veterans with Posttraumatic Stress Disorder," *Croatian Medical Journal* 48, no. 2 (April 2007): 177–184 [online].
51. Stacy Bannerman, "Veteran Domestic Violence Remains Camouflaged," *WeNews* [online], 13 April 2009.
52. Ibid.
53. Description of this project relies on the unpublished preliminary text for "The War Veteran Vehicle Project," emailed to me by Krzysztof Wodiczko, 27 September 2007.
54. Ibid.
55. Ibid.
56. Susan Buck-Morss, *Thinking Past Terror: Islamicism and Critical Theory on the Left* (New York: W. W. Norton, 2003), 71.
57. Colomina, *Domesticity at War*, 301.
58. See Wodiczko, *Critical Vehicles*. For discussion of another project on the homeless, see Rosalyn Deutsche, "Krzysztof Wodiczko's Homeless Projection and the Site of Urban 'Revitalization,'" in her *Evictions: Art and Spatial Politics* (Cambridge, Mass.: MIT Press, 1998).
59. The phrase is Wodiczko's.
60. Andrea Shea, "The Horrors of War within Museum Walls," WBUR.org, 10 November 2009.
61. Interview with Krzysztof Wodiczko, Michael Anthony, and Tala Khudairi on *The Callie Crossley Show*, WGBH [online], 10 February 2010.
62. Greg Cook, "Narrative Truth: Krzysztof Wodiczko's War Story at the ICA," *Boston Phoenix*, 19 November 2009.
63. "Casualties of the Iraq War," *Wikipedia* [online].
64. Dr. Michael Merzenich, "Do Iraqis Suffer from PTSD? The 'Tour of Duty' for the Average Iraqi Citizen Is Now Over 5 Years," democraticunderground.com, 20 July 2007.
65. "Iraqi Children Suffer from PTSD," findingDulcinea.com, 26 August 2008; César Chelala, "Iraqi Children: Bearing the Scars of War," theglobalist.com, 21 March 2009.
66. Email from Krzysztof Wodiczko to author, 14 June 2010.
67. Krzysztof Wodiczko, as told to Brigid Sweeney, "My Agenda," *Boston Magazine*, 1 November 2009, 1.
68. Sebastian Smee, "Theater of War," *Boston Globe* [online], 1 November 2009; Cook, "Narrative Truth."
69. John T. Parry, "Finding a Right to Be Tortured," *Law & Literature* 19 no. 2 (2007), 209–210.

Historical Reenactment

1. See chapter 3 for a discussion of Artur Zmijewski's 2005 reenactment of Philip Zimbardo's Stanford Prison Experiment in 1971, and chapter 4 for Regina Galindo's reenactment of water torture.
2. Jenny Thompson, *War Games: Inside the World of 20th-Century War Reenactment* (Washington, D.C.: Smithsonian Books, 2004), 79, 82.
3. *Wapedia*, "Wiki: Historic Reenactment" [online].
4. James O. Farmer, "Playing Rebels: Reenactment as Nostalgia and Defense of the Confederacy in the Battle of Aiken," *Southern Cultures* 11, no. 1 (Spring 2005): 65–67.
5. Thompson, *War Games*, 71–72, 200–202.
6. Rory Turner, "Bloodless Battles: The Civil War Reenacted," *Drama Review* 34, no. 4 (Winter 1990): 124.
7. Farmer, "Playing Rebels," 71.
8. Robert Blackson, "Once More . . . with Feeling: Reenactment in Contemporary Art and Culture," *Art Journal*, Spring 2007, 30.
9. The phrase belongs to World War I German militarist and author Ernst Jünger, who wrote books glorifying war, such as his memoir *Storm of Steel* (1920) and *Fire and Blood* (1925). Thompson recounts a belief that the first World War I reenactment group was formed after its members read *Storm of Steel*.
10. Thompson, *War Games*, 134.
11. Kevin Walsh, *The Representation of the Past: Museums and Heritage in the Post-Modern World* (London: Routledge, 1992), 1, 102–103.
12. George L. Mosse, *Fallen Soldiers: Reshaping the Memory of the World Wars* (Oxford: Oxford University Press, 1990), quoted in Jenny Thompson, "Playing Wars Whose Wounds Are Fresh," *New York Times* [online], 5 June 2004.
13. Thompson, *War Games*, 85.

14. Ibid., 156.
15. Ibid., 234.
16. Peggy Phelan, "Hinckley and Ronald Reagan: Reenactment and the Ethics of the Real," in *Life, Once More: Forms of Reenactment in Contemporary Art,* ed. Sven Lütticken (Rotterdam: Witte de With, Center for Contemporary Art, 2005), 157.
17. Ron Suskind, "Without a Doubt," *New York Times Magazine,* quoted in Phelan, "Hinckley and Ronald Reagan," 167.
18. Thompson, *War Games,* 161–162, 281.
19. Brett Sokol, "Weekend at War," *New York Times,* 27 February 2009, Escapes, D1.
20. Thompson, *War Games,* 135.
21. Sokol, "Weekend at War."
22. Thompson, *War Games,* 84–85.
23. Earnhardt also performs in another National Guard recruiting video with Kid Rock, who wrote the song "Warrior" for the National Guard.
24. Although often critical of the way military history details are portrayed in films, reenactors have participated in films on the Revolutionary War and such films as *The Patriot* (2000) and *Saving Private Ryan* (1998). In October 2008, a seventy-three-year-old retired police officer and reenactor portraying a Union soldier for a documentary film was shot in the shoulder by a Confederate reenactor, upsetting the reenacting community, which is sensitive to public opinion. Reenactors ban loaded weapons, but walk-on reenactors unaffiliated with units are often employed at film shoots. See "Civil War-style CSI: Who Shot the Reenactor?" AP, 25 October 2008, available online at msnbc.msn.com.
25. "National Guard Drained by Iraq," *International Herald Tribune,* military.com, 1 March 2006.
26. Quoted in Matthew Eddy, "*Nations Have the Right to Kill: Hitler, the Holocaust, and War* by Richard A. Koenigsberg," *Journal for the Scientific Study of Religion* 48, no. 4 (December 2009): 840. Although Koenigsberg writes from an anthropological perspective and refers to the ritual of human sacrifice, his formulation nonetheless serves as an apt political metaphor.
27. Tony Horwitz, *Confederates in the Attic: Dispatches from the Unfinished Civil War* (New York: Pantheon, 1998).
28. Shawn Martin, "NAACP Chapter Opposes Civil War Reenactment," freerepublic.com, 16 February 2003.
29. Farmer, "Playing Rebels," 48.
30. Martin, "NAACP Chapter."
31. Turner, "Bloodless Battles," 133.
32. John W. Howard III and Laura C. Prividera, "The Fallen Woman Archetype: Media Representations of Lynndie England, Gender, and the (Ab)uses of U.S. Female Soldiers," *Women's Studies in Communication* 31, no. 3 (Fall 2008): 293.
33. Thompson, *War Games,* 226.
34. Turner, "Bloodless Battle," 129.
35. Thompson, *War Games,* 226; Vanessa Agnew, "Introduction: What Is Reenactment?" *Criticism* 46, no. 3 (Summer 2004): 327–339.
36. Quoted in Richard Handler, "Overpowered by Realism: Living History and the Simulation of the Past," *Journal of American Folklore* 100, no. 397 (July–September 1987): 340.
37. Alexander Cook, "The Use and Abuse of Reenactment: Thoughts on Recent Trends in Public History," *Criticism* 46, no. 3 (Summer 2004): 490.
38. Ibid., 489–493.
39. Rayna Green, "The Tribe Called Wannabee: Playing Indian in America and Europe," *Folklore* 99 (1988): 30–55.
40. Sven Lütticken, "An Arena in Which to Reenact," in *Life, Once More: Forms of Reenactment in Contemporary Art,* ed. Sven Lütticken (Rotterdam: Witte de With, Center for Contemporary Art, 2005), 60; Blackson, "Once More . . . with Feeling," 30.
41. Handler, "Overpowered by Realism," 337.
42. See Alice Correia, "Interpreting Jeremy Deller's *The Battle of Orgreave,*" *Visual Culture in Britain* 7, no. 2 (2006): 95.
43. Quoted in Katie Kitamura, "Recreating Chaos: Jeremy Deller's *The Battle of Orgreave,*" in *Historical Reenactment: From Realism to the Affective Turn,* ed. Iain McCalman and Paul A. Pickering (Houndmills, U.K.: Palgrave Macmillan, 2010), 39.
44. Quoted in Christina Schaffer, "It Is What It Is: Conversations about Iraq," *Philadelphia Citypaper* [online], 24 March 2009.
45. Vesna Krstich, "On the Road Again with Jeremy Deller: Conversations about Iraq," *Art Papers* 33, no. 4 (July/August 2009), 19.
46. Quoted in Sarah Hromack, "What It Is: A Conversation with Jeremy Deller," *Art in America* [online], 4 March 2009.
47. My work on reenactment began with postwar artists who reenacted events related to the Holocaust, often retracing the steps of their parents or grandparents, or an event in which their parents' generation participated. This includes the work of Mikael Levin, who retraced the steps of his American journalist father, Meyer Levin, who, with photographer Eric Schwab, documented the liberation of the concentrations camps and simultaneously searched for his wife and Mikael's previously deported mother; and the work of Susan Silas, who reenacted a forced death march from Helmbrechts, Germany, to Prachatice in the former Czechoslovakia. See my *Memory Effects: The Holocaust and the Art of Secondary Witnessing* (New Brunswick, N.J.: Rutgers University Press, 2002).
48. Lütticken, "An Arena in Which to Reenact," 55.
49. Thompson, *War Games,* 48.
50. "Interview: Hilton Als," in *Small Wars: An-My Lê* (New York: Aperture, 2008), 121.

51. Conversation with author, New York City, 17 May 2005.
52. "Interview: Hilton Als," in *Small Wars*, 119.
53. Karen Irvine, Curator's Statement, "An-My Lê: *Small Wars*," Museum of Contemporary Photography [online], Columbia College, Chicago.
54. "Interview: Hilton Als," 119.
55. Irvine, Curator's Statement.
56. "Interview: Hilton Als," 122.
57. Lê has also produced a two-part film called *29 Palms* that shows close-ups of young soldiers being briefed on the left screen, and an immense landscape on the right where battalions practice maneuvers, overall suggesting "a Hollywood extravaganza." See "An-My Lê," in the exhibition *Ecotopia: The Second ICP Triennial of Photography and Video* at the International Center for Photography [online], 9 September 2006 to 7 January 2007.
58. "Interview: Hilton Als," 123.
59. David Montgomery, "Far from Iraq, A Demonstration of a War Zone," *Washington Post*, 20 March 2007, washingtonpost.com.
60. The video is available online at washingtonpost.com.
61. Quoted in Amy Goodman, "'Operation First Casualty': Outside Democratic Convention, Iraq Veterans against the War Re-Enact Raids on Iraqi Civilians," *Democracy Now: The War and Peace Report* [online], 27 August 2008.
62. B. Colby Hamilton, "Bringing the War Home," *Brooklyn Rail* [online], June 2007.
63. Martha Rosler and Iwona Blazwick, "Taking Responsibility: Martha Rosler Interviewed by Iwona Blazwick," *Art Monthly* 3 (2008): 1–7.
64. The IVAW also engages in a range of other activities. On 19 March 2008, for example, IVAW members seized the National Archives Building in Washington, D.C., in front of hundreds of surprised museum visitors, holding it for ninety minutes while reading the terms of the Citizens Arrest Warrant in a call to arrest Bush and Cheney for war crimes. They then proceeded to the Justice Department and the White House, where they repeated the call for the arrest of Bush and Cheney. Members of IVAW also testified at the National Labor College in Silver Springs, Maryland, about their experiences in the Iraq and Afghanistan wars. Those testimonies are available online at youtube.com/ivaw.
65. See "Lynching Reenactment in Georgia Dramatizes Call for Indictments in 59-year-old Case," *Democracy Now* [online], 28 July 2005; AP report "Georgia Lynchings Reenacted," msnbc.msn.com, 25 July 2005. For a detailed history of the lynching, see Laura Wexler, *Fire in a Canebrake: The Last Mass Lynching in America* (New York: Scribner, 2003). Videos of the later reenactments are available on YouTube.
66. AP, "Georgia Lynchings Reenacted."
67. See Wexler, *Fire in a Canebrake*; also my *Imagery of Lynching: Black Men, White Women, and the Mob* (New Brunswick, N.J.: Rutgers University Press, 2004), 166–171.
68. Shaila Dewan, "Group Lynching Is Recreated in a 'Call for Justice,'" *New York Times*, 26 July 2005.
69. Eric Lott, *Love and Theft: Blackface Minstrelsy and the American Working Class* (New York: Oxford University Press, 1995).
70. In 1991, Clinton Adams, who claimed to be a witness to the original events, told reporters that Loy Harrison had been one of the gunmen.
71. Mark Auslander, "'Holding on to Those Who Can't Be Held': Reenacting a Lynching at Moore's Ford, Georgia." *Southern Spaces* [online], 8 November 2010.
72. Ibid.
73. Ibid.
74. Ibid.
75. Giorgio Agamben, *Homo Sacer: Sovereign Power and Bare Life* (Stanford, Calif.: Stanford University Press, 1998).

Abu Ghraib, Gender, and the Military

1. For a discussion of World War II imagery and censorship, see George H. Roeder Jr., *The Censored War: American Visual Experience during World War Two* (New Haven: Yale University Press, 1993).
2. See translation of statement provided by Abdou Hussain Saad Faleh, 16 January 2004, in Mark Danner, *Torture and Truth: America, Abu Ghraib, and the War on Terror* (New York: New York Review of Books, 2004), 230.
3. Philip Gourevitch and Errol Morris, *The Ballad of Abu Ghraib* (New York: Penguin, 2009), 183.
4. W.J.T. Mitchell, *Cloning Terror: The War of Images, 9/11 to the Present* (Chicago: University of Chicago Press, 2010), 159.
5. Dora Apel, "Torture Culture: Lynching Photographs and the Images of Abu Ghraib," *Art Journal* 64, no. 2 (Summer 2005): 88–100; also see my *Imagery of Lynching: Black Men, White Women, and the Mob* (New Brunswick, N.J.: Rutgers University Press, 2004, and, with Shawn Michelle Smith, *Lynching Photographs* (San Francisco: University of California Press, 2004).
6. Also see Stephen Eisenman, *The Abu Ghraib Effect* (London: Reaktion Books Ltd, 2007). Eisenman argues that the Abu Ghraib photos unconsciously mimic the classical pathos formula, in which the suffering of anonymous supplicants at the hands of torturers is eroticized or aestheticized so as to reiterate the conqueror's superiority; he analyzes Western visual art, starting with Ancient Greek and Roman sculpture and painting, to illustrate how the Abu Ghraib photos resonate with the symbolism of empire and racism.
7. Walter Benjamin, "Theses on the Philosophy of History," *Illuminations*, trans. Harry Zohn (New York: Schocken Books, 1968), 255.

8. Colin Dayan, keynote address delivered at the conference "Violence and Visibility," Berlin, 24 June 2010.
9. Judith Butler, *Precarious Life: The Powers of Mourning and Violence* (London and New York: Verso, 2004), 98.
10. A fuller account of Jamadi's death and Harmon's role appears in Gourevitch and Morris, *The Ballad of Abu Ghraib*, and in Errol Morris's film *Standard Operating Procedure* (2008).
11. On the role of the father of Ivan Frederick, one of the accused soldiers, in getting the pictures to *Sixty Minutes II*, which broadcast them on 28 April 2004, see "Here's How the Abu Ghraib Photos Got Out," available online at talkleft.com. Specialist Joseph M. Darby also turned over CDs with photographs of the torture. See "In a Soldier's Words, An Account of Concerns," *New York Times* [online], 22 May 2004.
12. The memo was sent by Col. Thomas Pappas, who was in charge of military intelligence personnel at Abu Ghraib prison. Gourevitch and Morris, *The Ballad of Abu Ghraib*, 247–248.
13. In February and March of 2006, *Salon* published a more extensive archive of photographs and videos of the abuse online, most of which had already been seen, but they do not include rape images. See Jane Walsh, "Introduction: The Abu Ghraib Files," salon.com, 14 March 2006.
14. Coco Fusco, *A Field Guide for Female Interrogators* (New York: Seven Stories Press, 2008), 12–13.
15. Ibid., 26.
16. Ibid., 35, 39.
17. *Dateline NBC*, 2 October 2005, quoted in John W. Howard III and Laura C. Prividera, "The Fallen Woman Archetype: Media Representations of Lynndie England, Gender, and the (Ab)uses of U.S. Female Soldiers," *Women's Studies in Communication* 31, no. 3 (Fall 2008): 298.
18. Gourevitch and Morris, *Ballad of Abu Ghraib*, 137.
19. *Dateline NBC*, 2 October 2005, quoted in Howard and Prividera, "The Fallen Woman Archetype," 299.
20. Gourevitch and Morris, *Ballad of Abu Ghraib*, 234.
21. Ibid., 139.
22. Howard and Prividera, "Fallen Woman," 287.
23. Carol Mason, "The Hillbilly Defense: Culturally Mediating U.S. Terror at Home and Abroad," *NWSA Journal* 17, no. 3 (Fall 2005): 1.
24. Ibid.
25. Americans, however, were not the only ones to practice such forms of violence and abuse. Revelations about Camp Bread Basket, near Basra, under British control, followed by a trial in Germany and the court martial of five British soldiers in 2005, made clear that the British also perpetrated abuses on their Iraqi prisoners similar to those at Abu Ghraib, including sexual violence, and that they also photographed their abuses.
26. Letter dated 20 October 2003. Gourevitch and Morris, *Ballad of Abu Ghraib*, 111.
27. Written in November 2003. Ibid., 200–201.
28. Shawn Michelle Smith, "Afterimages: White Womanhood, Lynching, and the War in Iraq," *Nka: Journal of Contemporary African Art*, Special Issue: Strange Fruit: Lynching, Visuality, and Empire 20 (Fall 2006): 72–87; also see Thomas Conroy, "The Packaging of Jessica Lynch," in *Constructing America's War Culture: Iraq, Media, and Images at Home*, ed. Thomas Conroy and Jarice Hanson (Lanham, Md.: Lexington Books, 2008), 61–84.
29. Senior U.S. military officials admitted to journalists whom they escorted around Abu Ghraib in 2004 that rape had taken place. At the same time, they forbid journalists from talking to five women in the prison, who were accused of no crimes but were kept in solitary confinement for twenty-three hours a day, with only a Koran. See Luke Harding, *The Guardian* [online], 11 May 2004.
30. For translated statements, see Danner, *Torture and Truth*, 248; also see Apel, "Torture Culture."
31. Jasbir K. Puar, "Abu Ghraib: Arguing against Exceptionalism," *Feminist Studies* 30, no. 2, The Prison Issue (Summer 2004): 533. Puar thoughtfully addresses interpretations that focus on homophobia in the narration of the sexual abuse of Iraqi men and its intersection with U.S. imperialist violence. Also see her *Terrorist Assemblages: Homonationalism in Queer Times* (Durham, N.C.: Duke University Press, 2007), which includes a chapter on Abu Ghraib.
32. Ariella Azoulay, *The Civil Contract of Photography* (New York: Zone Books, 2008), 270–272.
33. Susan Sontag, *Regarding the Pain of Others* (New York: Farrar, Straus and Giroux, 2003), 68.
34. See Leonard Downie Jr., "Iraq: New Abuse Details," *Washington Post* [online], 21 May 2004; John Byrne and David Edwards, "Seymour Hersh Reveals Shocking New Details of Abu Ghraib; 'Father and Son Forced to Do Acts Together,'" rawstory.com, 17 June 2007.
35. See Duncan Gardham and Paul Cruikshank, "Report: Unreleased Abu Ghraib Abuse Photos 'Show Rape,'" alternet.com, 28 May 2009; Greg Mitchell, "Judge Orders Release of Abu Ghraib Photos," editorandpublisher.com, 29 September 2005.
36. See "Secret Iraqi Prisoner 'Rape' Photos Obama Wants Blocked," dailymail.co.uk, 29 May 2009. In 2007 Major General Antonio Taguba revealed to Seymour Hersh that he had been forced to retire as a result of his report on Abu Ghraib. "Seymour Hersh Reveals Rumsfeld Misled Congress over Abu Ghraib;

How Gen. Taguba was Forced to Retire over his Critical Abu Ghraib Report; and the Site of Another Secret U.S. Prison (Mauritania)," *Democracy Now* [online], 19 June 2007.
37. Judith Butler, *Frames of War: When Is Life Grievable?* (New York: Verso, 2010), 72–73.
38. Azoulay, *Civil Contract*, 269.
39. Ann Gearan, "Military Rape Reports Rise, Prosecution Still Low," *Huffington Post* [online], 17 March 2009. Antiwoman violence is aimed not only at women but discursively at men. Male cadets at the Citadel, for example, report: "They called you a 'pussy' all the time . . . or 'a fucking little girl.'" Howard and Prividera, "The Fallen Woman Archetype," 291.
40. Azoulay, *Civil Contract*, 269–270.
41. Three of these images can be seen at "Rape of Iraqi Women by US Forces as Weapon of War: Photos and Data Emerge," *Asia Tribune* [online], 3 October 2009.
42. Azoulay, *Civil Contract*, 275–276, 280–281.
43. Professor Huda Shaker al-Nuaimi, a political scientist at Baghdad University who interviewed female prisoners as a volunteer for Amnesty International, went to "Noor's" home and was told the family had moved away; she believes that "Noor" was killed by U.S. soldiers to silence her (although women are also threatened with death for bringing dishonor to their families by having been raped). See Kristen McNutt, "Sexualized Violence against Iraqi Women by US Occupying Forces," a briefing paper of International Educational Development presented to the United Nations Commission on Human Rights, 2005, Geneva, available at psychoanalystsopposewar.org/resources_files/SVIW-1.doc.
44. See "Abu Ghraib's Women Prisoners," thinkingpeace.com, 26 May 2004. Francine D'Amico, "The Women of Abu Ghraib," *The Post-Standard*, 23 May 2004, C1; and Annia Ciezadlo, "For Iraqi Women, Abu Ghraib's Taint," csmonitor.com, 28 May 2004.
45. Quoted in Editor, "Rape of Iraqi Women by US Forces as Weapon of War: Photos and Data Emerge," *Asia Tribune* [online], 3 October 2009.
46. Carmine Sarracino and Kevin M. Scott, *The Porning of America: The Rise of Porn Culture, What It Means, and Where We Go from Here* (Boston: Beacon Press, 2008), 144.
47. Ibid., 160, and the entire chapter "The Nexus of Porn and Violence: Abu Ghraib and Beyond."
48. Butler, *Frames of War*, 91.
49. Azoulay, *Civil Contract*, 198–199.
50. Kareem Fahim, "Claims of Wartime Rapes Unsettle and Divide Libyans," *New York Times*, 20 June 2011, A10. Iman al-Obeidi was variously accused by Libyan officials of being drunk, mentally ill, a thief, and a prostitute. She has since been granted asylum in the United States.
51. *Bare Life #1* premiered at VideoBrasil's Fifteenth Festival of Electronic Art and Performance.
52. *A Room of One's Own* was premiered at The Kitchen as part of Performa 05 in New York, and subsequently presented at the Victoria and Albert Museum in London, the Kunstnerneshus in Oslo, PS 122 in New York, the Frost Museum at Florida International University, Yale University, the Philadelphia Fringe Festival, Maidment Theater in Auckland, and the 2008 Whitney Biennial.
53. *Operation Atropos* was premiered at MC Projects in Los Angeles in March 2006 and selected for the 2008 Whitney Biennial.
54. Fusco, *A Field Guide*, 28–29, 31.
55. Ibid., 51, 54.
56. Ibid., 78.
57. Ibid., 82.
58. White Paper by Physicians for Human Rights, "Experiments in Torture: Evidence of Human Subject Research and Experimentation in the 'Enhanced' Interrogation Program," phrtorturepapers.org, June 2010.
59. As Christopher Hitchens observed after agreeing to be waterboarded by SERE soldiers for an article in *Vanity Fair*, waterboarding is not a "simulation" of drowning: "You feel that you are drowning because you *are* drowning." Hitchens noted that his extremely brief experience with waterboarding left him with feelings of shame and nightmares: "I have since woken up trying to push the bedcovers off my face, and if I do anything that makes me short of breath I find myself clawing at the air with a horrible sensation of smothering and claustrophobia." See "Believe Me, It's Torture," *Vanity Fair* [online], August 2008. The video is available on YouTube.
60. Cf. Karen Beckman, "Gender, Power, and Pedagogy in Coco Fusco's *Bare Life Study #1* (2005), *A Room of One's Own* (2005), and *Operation Atropos* (2006)," *Framework* 50, nos. 1 & 2 (Spring 2009): 125–138. Beckman casts doubt on the potential traumatic effect of this exercise and wonders if some of the women were instructed to "act" traumatized.
61. Tanya Zimbardo, "Repetition—Artur Zmijewski," *Shotgun Review* [online], 8 March 2006.
62. Ibid.
63. Ibid.
64. Mya Guarnieri, "Israeli Soldier Mocks Palestinian Prisoners in Facebook Photos," *Mondoweiss* [online], 16 August 2010.
65. David Williams, "Smiling for the Camera, Israeli Soldier Poses with Blindfolded Palestinians . . . and Posts the Humiliating Snaps on Facebook," dailymail.co.uk, 18 August 2010.
66. Guarnieri, "Israeli Soldier Mocks Palestinian Prisoners."
67. Also see Azoulay's various discussions of such photos in *Civil Contract*.
68. Williams, "Smiling for the Camera."
69. Ibid.

70. Marcia Vetrocq, "Rules of Engagement," *Art in America*, June/July 2008, 171.
71. Richard Grusin, *Premediation: Affect and Mediality after 9/11* (New York: Palgrave Macmillan, 2010), 65.
72. Fusco, *A Field Guide*, 24–25.
73. See John Taylor, *Body Horror: Photojournalism, Catastrophe and War* (New York: New York University Press, 1998).
74. See my essay in Apel and Smith, *Lynching Photographs*.
75. Azoulay, *Civil Contract*, 168–169.
76. Robert E. Snyder, "Without Sanctuary: An American Holocaust?" *Southern Quarterly* 39, no. 3 (2001).
77. Jim Auchmutey, "Lynching Exhibit Confronts South's Ugly Past," *Atlanta Journal-Constitution* at ajc.com. 28 April 2002; exhibition press releases, New-York Historical Society, nyhistory.org.
78. For an extended review of the lynching exhibitions in New York, Pittsburgh, and Atlanta, see my *Imagery of Lynching*, chap. 1.
79. "Death Threats against Obama—Racist Atrocities Soar as America Regurgitates Its Soul: Part II," 7 January 2010, *Obama Watch Blog* [online]. Also see my "Just Joking? Chimps, Obama, and Racial Stereotype," *Journal of Visual Culture* 8, no. 2 (August 2009): 134–142.
80. Hilton Als, "GWTW," in *Without Sanctuary: Lynching Photographs in America*, ed. James Allen et al. (Santa Fe: Twin Palms Press, 2000), 38–39.
81. Mark Bauerlein, "History, Horror, Healing: Faculty Deliberations on Lynching Photography Examine Racial and Historical Understanding," *The Academic Exchange: A Place for Scholarly Conversation at Emory*, April/May 2001, 5.
82. Michael Kimmelman, "Photos Return, This Time as Art," *New York Times*, 10 October 2004, B29.
83. Butler, *Precarious Life*.
84. Kimmelman, "Photos Return, This Time as Art."
85. Stephanie Shapiro, "Abu Ghraib Photos Are in Exhibits," baltimoresun.com, 17 September 2004.
86. Mike Crissey, "Vets Groups Decry Warhol Museum Plans for Abu Ghraib Exhibit," AP [online], 10 September 2004.
87. Roger I. Simon, "A Shock to Thought: Curatorial Judgment and the Public Exhibition of 'Difficult Knowledge,'" *Memory Studies*, mss. sagepub.com, 21 February 2011, 1–18.

The Body as Political Corpus

1. Stewart Home, "Regina José Galindo & the Dematerialisation of the Live Artist 1999–2009," stewarthomesociety.org/blog, 2 February 2009. The video is available on YouTube and was shown at the Sydney Biennale in 2010, and the Venice Biennale in 2009, among other exhibitions.
2. Julian Stallabrass, "Performing Torture," preface to *Regina José Galindo, Confesión, Palma de Mallorca*, Courtauld Institute of Art [online].
3. Ibid.
4. Rashid Khalidi, *Resurrecting Empire: Western Footprints and America's Perilous Path in the Middle East* (Boston: Beacon Press, 2005), 21.
5. Robert Parry, "Cheney Exposes Torture Conspiracy," *Consortium News* [online], 14 February 2010. Following the U.S. Navy Seals commando raid on Osama Bin Laden's compound in Abbottabad, Pakistan, in which Bin Laden was killed on 1 May 2011, U.S. Republicans again claimed vindication for the role of torture, including waterboarding, in order to credit the Bush administration with tracking down Bin Laden, while Obama administration officials denied that any important intelligence had been acquired this way. Glenn L. Carle, a retired CIA officer, said that coercive techniques "didn't provide useful, meaningful, trustworthy information" and that "everyone was deeply concerned and most felt it was un-American and did not work." Scott Shane and Charlie Savage, "Harsh Methods of Questioning Debated Again," *New York Times*, 4 May 2011.
6. Home, "Regina José Galindo."
7. Stallabrass, "Performing Torture."
8. Ibid.
9. Her video *Himenoplastia* (Hymenoplasty, 2004) documents in extreme close-up the illegal surgical reconstruction on her hymen, a procedure commonly sought out by women prior to their wedding nights, or performed on girls in sex trafficking rings to serve the demand for "virgins" and to fetch a better price. As is typical, it was a botched operation that landed Galindo in the hospital on the same day. Francisco Goldman, "Regina José Galindo," *BOMB Magazine* 94 (Winter 2006) [online].
10. Home, "Regina José Galindo."
11. Goldman, "Regina José Galindo."
12. La Pocha Nostra, "Thoughts by Gómez-Peña on Corpo/Illicito," *CounterPULSE* [online], 7 September 2009.
13. Charles R. Garoian and Yvonne M. Gaudelius, "Performing Resistance," *Studies in Art Education* 46, no. 1 (2004): 55.
14. Guillermo Gómez-Peña, "Disclaimer," *Drama Review* 50, no. 1 (Spring 2006): 150
15. Ibid., 154–155.
16. Helen Stoilas, "Terrorism Exhibition Cancelled," *Art Newspaper* 196 (November 2008): 14.
17. Arifa Akbar, "Iraqi Artists Denied Entry to Britain for Their Own Exhibition," *The Independent* [online], 3 April 2010.
18. Gómez-Peña, "Disclaimer," 152.
19. Laurietz Seda, "Decolonizing the Body Politic: Guillermo Gómez-Peña's *Mapa/Corpo 2*: Interactive Rituals for the New Millennium," *Drama Revue* 53, no. 1 (Spring 2009): 136–141. Seda notes that "the New Barbarian" is

Gómez-Peña's name for the Other; he has developed a performance titled *The New Barbarian Collection: Design Primitives for the Runway*, which he describes as "engag[ing] the audience with a variety of fashion-inspired highly stylized performance personas stemming from problematic media representations of foreigners, immigrants, refugees and social eccentrics, as both enemies of the state and sexy pop cultural rebels" (137).
20. Guillermo Gómez-Peña, "The New Global Culture: Somewhere between Corporate Multiculturalism and Mainstream Bizarre (a Border Perspective)," *Drama Review* 45, no. 1 (Spring 2001): 26.
21. Conversation with Johnny Evans, Detroit, 27 September 2008.
22. Guillermo Gómez-Peña, "In Defense of Performance Art: A Foremost Practitioner Explains His Métier," *Art Papers* [online] 27, no. 4 (July/August 2003).
23. Phil H. Shook, "Readers Respond to Fallujah Photos," images.google.com, 13 April 2004.
24. Dahr Jamail, "Falluja Revisited," Rense.com, 14 May 2011.
25. Ibid.
26. Khalidi, *Resurrecting Empire*, xi–xiii.
27. Paul Virilio and Sylvère Lotringer, *Pure War: Twenty-Five Years Later*, trans. Mark Polizzotti (Cambridge, Mass.: MIT Press, 2008), 9.
28. Judith Butler, *Precarious Life: The Powers of Mourning and Violence* (New York: Verso, 2004), 37–38.
29. David Cotterrell, "J4MED, Op Herrick 7, 03.11.07–26.11.07," in *War and Medicine* (London: Black Dog Publishing, 2008), 209.
30. Martha Rosler, "Flat Daddy," *Photoworks*, Autumn 2008/Winter 2009, 20–21; also see flatdaddies.com, and flatdaddydocumentary.com. Another photo of a boy on a swing next to a swing holding a Flat Daddy was published on the front page of the *New York Times*, which ran a story inspired by the Maine National Guard's statewide Flat Daddy program. See Katie Zezima, "When Daddies Go to War, Flat Daddies Hold Their Place at Home," 30 September 2006.
31. Dr. Mantador Taher, "Open the Hospital Doors!" in *War and Medicine*, 222–223.
32. Ibid., 223.
33. William Wiesmann, Nicole Draghic, and John A. Parrish, "Advances in Modern Combat Casualty Care with a Vision to the Future," in *War and Medicine*, 227.
34. Ibid., 230–231, 233.
35. Cotterrell, "J4MED," 196, 200, 207.
36. Conversation with David Cotterrell, Miami Beach, 4 December 2008.
37. David Cotterrell, "The Stranger," in *Transmission: HOST* (London: Artwords Press, 2009), 8.
38. See *Purple Hearts: Back from Iraq* (London: Trolley, 2004); *Nina Berman: Purple Hearts: Photographs of Iraq Veterans* at the Jen Bekman Gallery in New York in 2007; Berman's photos are also published online at ninaberman.com.
39. Marcia Vetrocq, "Rules of Engagement," *Art in America*, June/July 2008, 175.
40. Katie Halper, "*Alive Day Memories*: Interview with a Soldier," *Huffington Post* [online], 7 September 2007.
41. Ibid.
42. See Susan Saulny, "Battles over Billboard Space Precede G.O.P. Gathering," *New York Times*, 30 August 2008, A10; for the images, see suzanneopton.com and her blog thesoldiersface.com.
43. Quoted on theunconvention.com.
44. Mark Pitzke, "Images from the Dark Side of War," *Der Spiegel* [online], 30 August 2007.
45. Lindsay Beyerstein, "The Face of War," salon.com, 10 March 2007.
46. In response to the difficulty of socially reintegrating veterans with severe facial wounds, they were treated very differently in World War I, where such German soldiers, known as "men without faces," were hidden away in government institutions and often reported to their families as dead. See my "Cultural Battlegrounds: Weimar Photographic Narratives of War," *New German Critique* 76, Special Issue on Weimar Visual Culture (Winter 1999): 49–84.
47. Robert Hariman and John Louis Lucaites, *No Caption Needed: Iconic Photographs, Public Culture, and Liberal Democracy* (Chicago: University of Chicago Press, 2007), 302–303.
48. See Dora Apel, "Icons of Suffering," in *Ewa Harabasz: Icons*, exhibition catalog in English and Polish, Le Guern Gallery in Warsaw, Galeria Miejska in Poznan, and Galeria Bielska BWA in Bielsko-Biala, 2008, 44–47.
49. Mark Reinhardt, Holly Edwards, and Erina Duganne, eds., *Beautiful Suffering: Photography and the Traffic in Pain* (Chicago: University of Chicago Press, 2007), 7–8.
50. See, for example, Martha Rosler, "In, Around, and Afterthoughts (on Documentary Photography)," in *The Contest of Meaning: Critical Histories of Photography*, ed. Richard Bolton (Cambridge, Mass.: MIT Press, 1989).
51. David Levi Strauss, "Nikons and Icons: Is the Aestheticization-of-Suffering Critique Still Valid?" Bookforum.com, June/July/August 2007.
52. Jesse Hamlin, "His Photos Are Lovely, Erotic, Even a Bit Disturbing. Adi Nes Uses Classical Composition to Portray Israeli Soldiers," articles.sfgate.com, 22 April 2004.
53. Meira Weiss, *The Chosen Body* (Stanford, Calif.: Stanford University Press, 2002), 1.
54. Ibid., 32, 33.
55. Daphne Gottlieb, "Four Photographs by Adi Nes," *Tikkun* [online], November/December 2004.
56. Lisa N. Goldman, "Photographing the Politics of Identity," *Ha'aretz*, 3 December 2004, available at adines.com.

57. Hamlin, "His Photos Are Lovely."
58. Ibid.
59. Catherine Someze, "Meeting with Adi Nes/Biblical Stories," *Eyemazing* 2 (2006), available at adines.com.
60. Richard Meyer, "Home Delivery," *Modern Painters* 20, no. 3 (April 2008): 56.
61. Email from Martha Rosler to author, 21 September 2008.
62. Gómez-Peña, "The New Global Culture," 19–20.

Controlling the Frame

1. J. David Slocum, "Introduction," in *Terrorism, Media, Liberation*, ed. J. David Slocum (New Brunswick, N.J.: Rutgers University Press, 2005), 1–4.
2. Colin Jacobson, "Why Mister, Why?" *Foto8 Magazine* [online], 2005.
3. Thomas N. Gardner, "War as Mediated Narrative: The Sextet of War Rhetoric," in *Constructing America's War Culture: Iraq, Media, and Images at Home*, ed. Thomas Conroy and Jarice Hanson (Lanham, Md.: Lexington Books, 2008), 113.
4. Martha Gellhorn, *The Face of War* (1993), quoted in Greg McLaughlin, *The War Correspondent* (London: Pluto Press, 2002), 100–101.
5. Edward Wyatt, "Now on YouTube: Iraq Videos of U.S. Troops under Attack," *New York Times*, 6 October 2006, front page.
6. Ibid., A19.
7. Erina Duganne, "Photography after the Fact," in *Beautiful Suffering: Photography and the Traffic in Pain*, ed. Mark Reinhardt, Holly Edwards, and Erina Duganne (Chicago: Williams College Museum of Art and University of Chicago Press, 2007).
8. Hal Bernton, "Woman Loses Her Job over Coffins Photo," *Seattle Times* [online], 22 April 2004.
9. Marcia Vetrocq, "Rules of Engagement," *Art in America*, June/July 2008, 169.
10. Michael Hirsh, "Introduction," in Geert van Kesteren, *Why Mister, Why? Iraq 2003–2004* (Amsterdam: Artimo, 2004), n.p.
11. Van Kesteren, "Car Bombs Rock Heart of Baghdad," in *Why Mister, Why?*, n.p.
12. Audio interview with Eric Beauchemin, "*Baghdad Calling: Cell Phone Photographs from Iraq*," baghdadcalling.com, 27 December 2008.
13. Jan Gruiters, on behalf of the Dutch "Iraq Coalition" (Amnesty International, Cordaid, Hivos, IKV Pax Christi and the Netherlands Refugee Foundation), "Introduction," in Geert van Kesteren, *Baghdad Calling: Reports from Turkey, Syria, Jordan, and Iraq* (Rotterdam: Episode Publishers, 2008), n.p.
14. Ariella Azoulay, *The Civil Contract of Photography* (New York: Zone Books, 2008), 192.
15. The organization Reporters without Borders, as of June 2009, reported that 225 journalists and media assistants had been killed, 2 were missing, and 14 had been kidnapped, making it the most dangerous for the media since World War II.
16. Robert Fisk, "Snapshots of Life in Baghdad," independent.co.uk, 18 June 2008.
17. Robert Hariman, "Vernacular Photojournalism in the War Zone," nocaptionneeded.com, 22 October 2008.
18. Roger Hargreaves, "Say It Again, Y'All," *Photoworks*, Autumn 2008/Winter 2009, 75–76.
19. Olivier Laurent, "Bad Connection," *British Journal of Photography* [online], 2 July 2008.
20. Beauchemin, "*Baghdad Calling*."
21. Ghaith Abdul-Ahad, Kael Alford, Thorne Anderson, and Rita Leistner, *Unembedded: Four Independent Photojournalists on the War in Iraq* (White River Junction, Vt.: Chelsea Green Publishing Co., 2005), n.p.
22. Rita Leistner, "Hazardous Terrain," in *Unembedded*, n.p.
23. Kael Alford, "Fall of Baghdad," in *Unembedded*, n.p.
24. Ghaith Abdul-Ahad, "Two Days," in *Unembedded*, n.p.
25. Sabrina Tavernese and Andrew W. Lehren, "Buffeted by Fury and Chaos, Civilians Paid Heaviest Toll," *New York Times*, 23 October 2010, A1.
26. Thorne Anderson, "Crossing Boundaries," in *Unembedded*, n.p.
27. Alan Thomas, "Video Interview with Ashley Gilbertson," wtfiraq.org, n.d.
28. Ibid.
29. Ashley Gilbertson, *Whiskey Tango Foxtrot: A Photographer's Chronicle of the Iraq War* (Chicago: University of Chicago Press, 2007), 120.
30. Nina Berman, "Iraq: When Killing Becomes Personal," alternet.org, 8 November 2007.
31. Thomas, "Video Interview with Ashley Gilbertson."
32. Daryl Lang, "Disembedded: Marines Send a War Photographer Packing," pdnonline.com, 17 July 2008.
33. Dennis Dunleavy, "Do Embedded Photojournalists Actually Work for the Pentagon?" *Black Star Rising* [online], 22 July 2008.
34. Berman, "Iraq: When Killing Becomes Personal."
35. Mark Vallen, "Artists and the Iraq War," art-for-a-change.com, 10 April 2008.
36. James Estrin, "Showcase: The War's Long Shadows," *New York Times*, 11 June 2009, available at lens.blogs.nytimes.com/2009/06/11/showcase-3/.
37. Nina Berman, "Statement: Homeland," Jan Bekman Gallery [online].
38. "Prepare," in *Homeland: Nina Berman*, (London: Trolly Ltd., 2008), n.p.
39. Eric Lipton, "With White House Push, U.S. Arms Sales Jump," *New York Times* [online], 13 September 2008.
40. Lindsay Beyerman, "Theater of War: Portrait

of a Homeland Security State," alternet.org, 22 November 2008.
41. Tony Perry, "Mock Afghan Village at Camp Pendleton Aims to Prepare Troops for Combat," latimesblogs.latimes.com, 16 November 2010.
42. See Christopher Sims, "Theater of War," chrissimsprojects.com.
43. Ibid.
44. See Christopher Sims, "Guantánamo Bay," chrissimsprojects.com.
45. "U.S. Department of Homeland Security," Office of Management and Budget, whitehouse.gov.
46. See, for example, Liliana Segura, "Homeland Security Embarks on Big Brother Programs to Read Our Minds and Emotions," alternet.org, 9 December 2009.
47. Beyerman, "Theater of War."
48. For a thoughtful analysis of how to make the privileged position of witnessing visible, see Jane Blocker, *Seeing Witness: Visuality and the Ethics of Testimony* (Minneapolis: University of Minnesota Press, 2009).
49. Richard Grusin blog, "The Affective Continuity between Modern War and 'Modern Warfare,'" premediation.blogspot.com, 7 April 2010; also see Richard Grusin, *Premediation: Affect and Mediality after 9/11* (New York: Palgrave Macmillan, 2010).
50. Seth Schiesel, "In This Electronic War, Momentum Shifts to the Underdog," *New York Times*, 8 April 2010, C1–2.
51. Richard Grusin blog.
52. Benedict Carey, "Experts Add Conditioning and Heat of Combat to Explain Iraq Airstrike Video," *New York Times*, 8 April 2010, A6.
53. Interview with Peter Singer by Steve Inskeep, "'America's Army' Blurs Virtual War, 'Militainment,'" NPR [online], 2 March 2010.
54. Ibid.
55. Glenn Greenwald, "Iraq Slaughter Not an Aberration," salon.com, 6 April 2010.
56. Glenn Greenwald, "Obama's Support for the New Graham-Lieberman Secrecy Law," salon.com, 1 June 2009.
57. Noam Cohen, "Through Soldiers' Eyes, 'The First YouTube War,'" *New York Times* [online], 23 May 2010.
58. Jennifer Terry, "Killer Entertainments," Author's Statement, *Vectors: Journal of Culture and Technology in a Dynamic Vernacular* 3, no. 1 (Fall 2007) [online].
59. Ibid.
60. Christopher Sims, "Hearts and Mind," chrissimsprojects.com.
61. Terry, "Killer Entertainments."
62. Cohen, "Through Soldiers' Eyes."
63. Dexter Filkins, "Military Report Faults Drone Operators in Deaths of 23 Afghan Civilians," *New York Times*, 30 May 2010, A6.
64. Rohan Sullivan, "Drone Crew Blamed in Allied Civilian Deaths," *Associated Press*, 29 May 2010, available at google.com.
65. See Noah Schactman, "Up to 320 Civilians Killed in Pakistan Drone War: Report," *Wired* [online], 19 October 2009. Also see "Drone Attacks in Pakistan" in *Wikipedia*, which details hundreds of people killed.
66. See youtube.com/watch?v=UdbV5J20mpw.
67. Seth Schiesel, "Whose Side Are You On? It Might Be the Taliban's," *New York Times*, 1 September 2010.
68. Chris Suellentrop, "War Games," *New York Times Magazine*, 12 September 2010, 62–67, quotes on 67.

Israel/Palestine and the Political Imaginary

1. Adam Greenhouse and Nora Barrows-Friedman, "Independent Journalists Dismantling Israel's Hold on Media Narrative," *Electronic Intifada* [online], 15 June 2010.
2. For the Iara Lee video, see Haroon Siddique, "Gaza Flotilla Attack: Activist Releases New Footage," guardian.co.uk, 11 June 2010; for the Israeli video, see "Video: Israeli Navy Troops Storming Gaza Flotilla," Haaretz.com, 31 June 2010.
3. Jeff Halper, *An Israeli in Palestine: Resisting Dispossession, Redeeming Israel* (London: Pluto Press, 2008), 162; Mya Guarnieri, "The Blockade on Gaza Began Long before Hamas Came to Power," 972mag.com, 29 June 2011; Amnesty International [online], "Suffocating: The Gaza Strip under Israeli Blockade," January 2010.
4. Halper, *An Israeli in Palestine*, 191–192; "Understanding the Gaza Blockade," *The Week* [online], 18 June 2010.
5. David Shulman, "Goldstone and Gaza: An Exchange," *New York Review of Books*, 14 July 2011, 60.
6. Svend Erik Larsen, "Landscape, Identity, and War," *New Literary History* 34, no. 3 (Summer 2004): 469–490.
7. The phrase belongs to sociologists Alice and Lincoln Day, who made the 2008 film *Scarred Lands and Wounded Lives: The Environmental Footprint of War*. See "Environment is War's Silent Casualty," voanews.com, 26 March 2008.
8. Larsen, "Landscape, Identity, and War," 470–471.
9. Ibid., 482–483.
10. Ibid., 469–470.
11. Udi Aloni, "As A Jew, I Was Taught It Was Ethically Imperative to Speak Up," Haaretz.com, interview with Judith Butler, 24 February 2010.
12. Larsen, "Landscape, Identity, and War," 480.
13. Eyal Weizman, *Hollow Land: Israel's Architecture of Occupation* (London and New York: Verso, 2007), 134–137.
14. Ibid., 132–133.
15. See btselem.org. Similarly, Syrian activists have circumvented the rolling Internet blackout and efforts to bar foreign journalists from entering Syria during the uprising against the Assad family's forty-year rule through online videos, produced at great risk, that are part of

a patchwork of Facebook groups, such as SyrianRevolution, and YouTube channels, such as Freedom4566, where more than two hundred and fifty videos have been viewed more than 220,000 times. See Liam Stack, "Activists Using Video to Bear Witness in Syria," *New York Times*, 19 June 2011, 11.
16. René Backmann, *A Wall in Palestine* (New York: Picador, 2006), 72–73.
17. Ibid., 139.
18. Halper, *An Israeli in Palestine*, 157–158.
19. Ibid., 100–101.
20. Ibid., 47–53.
21. Naomi Klein, *The Shock Doctrine: The Rise of Disaster Capitalism* (New York: Picador, 2007), 542.
22. Ibid., 544.
23. Ibid., 544–548.
24. Ibid., 552.
25. Ibid., 559.
26. Email from David Tartakover to author, 26 June 2011.
27. The violence has been documented by *Ha'aretz* and the United Nations Office for the Coordination of Humanitarian Affairs, and reported in *Wikipedia* under "Itamar."
28. Email from David Tartakover to author, 26 June 2011; also see James Hider, "West Bank Settlers Use 'Price Tag' Tactic to Punish Palestinians," *Sunday Times* [online], 15 October 2009.
29. Irus Braverman, "'The Tree Is the Enemy Soldier': A Sociological Making of War Landscapes in the Occupied West Bank," *Law & Society Review* 42, no. 3 (September 2008): 450. The Israelis also planted trees in the early years of the state in order to conceal destroyed Palestinian villages, although aforestation also made it difficult to bulldoze the remains of houses in some places, simultaneously obscuring the sites of former villages while preserving evidence of their existence. See Ghazi Falah, "The 1948 Israeli-Palestinian War and Its Aftermath: The Transformation and De-Signification of Palestine's Cultural Landscape," *Annals of the Association of American Geographers* 66, no. 2 (June 1996): 272.
30. Braverman, "'The Tree Is the Enemy Soldier,'" 450.
31. Ibid., 457.
32. Ibid., 459–460.
33. Ted Swedenburg, "The Palestinian Peasant as National Signifier," *Anthropological Quarterly* 63, no. 1 (January 1990): 18–20.
34. Ibid., 27.
35. Quoted in Braverman, "'The Tree Is the Enemy Soldier,'" 464.
36. Elia Zureik, "Constructing Palestine through Surveillance Practices," *British Journal of Middle Eastern Studies* 28, no. 2 (November 2001): 216–217.
37. The U.N.'s Economic Survey Mission, which was known as the Clapp Mission, estimated the number of Palestinians who were expelled at 726,000 in December 1949. Paul McCann, "The Role of UNRWA and the Palestine Refugees," *Palestine–Israel Journal* 15, no. 4, & vol. 16, no. 1 (August 2009) [online]. Ghazi Falah notes that "at least 92 cases of terrorist activities and massacres" also were perpetrated against the Palestinians, including rapes, by the regular Jewish forces (Haganah) and by the Irgun and Stern Gang. The massacre at Deir Yassin, located near the western suburbs of Jerusalem, is the most famous of the massacres. Falah, "The 1948 Israeli-Palestinian War and Its Aftermath," 262.
38. Swedenburg, "The Palestinian Peasant as National Signifier," 20, 22.
39. Conversation with Rana Bishara, Jerusalem, 3 August 2009.
40. See Kamal Boullata, *Palestinian Art: From 1850 to the Present* (London: Saqi Books, 2009), and Gannit Ankori, *Palestinian Art* (London: Reaktion Books, 2006).
41. Moshe Zuckermann, "On Landscapes & Human Beings," in *Shai Kremer: Infected Landscape: Israel, Broken Promised Land* (Stockport, U.K.: Dewi Lewis Publishing, 2008), 7–9; also see Kremer's series *Fallen Empires*, 2011.
42. Tze'elim is also represented in *Chicago: Adam Broomberg and Oliver Chanarin* (Göttingen, Germany: Steidlmack, 2006), with an essay by Eyal Weizman. London-based photographers Broomberg and Chanarin, originally from South Africa, had visited Israel in their youth to join other Jews in planting trees and were shocked, when they returned years later for a film festival, by the conditions of isolation in Ramallah. "It's a reality kept from most Israelis, where everyone's lying on the beach, having a good time, exactly like South Africa in the 1980s," asserted Broomberg in an interview with Hannah Loebel, "Israel Inside Out," *Utne*, June 2007, 62–66.
43. Eyal Weizman, "Frontier Architectures," in *Chicago*, n.p.
44. Weizman, *Hollow Land*, 208–210.
45. Quoted in ibid., 194–195.
46. Susan Buck-Morss, *Dreamworld and Catastrophe: The Passing of Mass Utopia in East and West* (Cambridge, Mass.: MIT Press, 2000).
47. Weizman, *Hollow Land*, 190–191.
48. Ibid., 197.
49. Ibid.
50. Robert Bevan, *The Destruction of Memory: Architecture at War* (London: Reaktion Books, 2006).
51. Quoted in ibid., 23.
52. Ibid., 95.
53. Falah, "The 1948 Israeli-Palestinian War and Its Aftermath," 261.
54. Weizman, *Hollow Land*, 203.
55. See Simon Faulkner, "Land, Landscape and the Wild Zone of Power," in *NurtureNation* (Jerusalem: Museum on the Seam, 2008), 241–254.

56. Shai Kremer, "Shai Kremer," Exhibition brochure, Julie M. Gallery, Tel Aviv/Toronto, 2008.
57. Backmann, *A Wall in Palestine*, 167.
58. Halper, *An Israeli in Palestine*, 174.
59. Ibid., 98–99.
60. Weizman, *Hollow Land*, 107.
61. Ariella Azoulay, "Miki Kratsman," in *Del Revés: Artistes contemporáneos de Israel/Inside-Out: Contemporary Artists from Israel*, ed. Octavio Zaya (Barcelona: ACTAR and MARCO Foundation, Museo de Arte Contemporánea de Vigo, 2006), 64–83. Also see Azoulay's penetrating discussion of Kratsman's photo of the injured Palestinian woman whose relative is present, *Mrs. Abu-Zohir, Balata Refugee Camp* (1988), in *The Civil Contract of Photography* (New York: Zone Books, 2008), 147–150.
62. See chelouchegallery.com.
63. Ibid.
64. Backmann, *A Wall in Palestine* 23.
65. Damien McGuinness, "Out of the Shtetl, into the Brave New World," *SpiegelOnline International*, 20 April 2005.
66. In August 2010, the Israeli military took down the barrier and stored it in a nearby army base, numbering each block so that the barricade could be reassembled in order in one day if necessary. Isabel Kershner, "With Calm at Jerusalem's Edge, a Concrete Barrier Comes Down," *New York Times*, 16 August 2010.
67. Weizman, *Hollow Land*, 46–47, quoting Elisha Efrat, *Geography of Occupation, Judea, Samaria and the Gaza Strip*.
68. Ibid., 50.
69. Sam Jones, "Spray Can Prankster Tackles Israel's Security Barrier," *The Guardian* [online], 5 August 2005.
70. Ibid.
71. William Parry, *Against the Wall: The Art of Resistance in Palestine* (Chicago: Lawrence Hills Books, 2010), 10.
72. Seth Tobocman and Terry Berkowitz, "Susan Greene," in *Three Cities against the Wall: Ramallah, Tel Aviv, New York* (Brooklyn: Voxpop, 2005), 52–53.
73. Parry, *Against the Wall*, 174–175.
74. Ibid., 107–110.
75. Ibid., 51.
76. Minelli himself describes the work as using the informatic command "to underline that something isn't working in the operative system 'Israel/Palestine' and that the only thing to do is to stop everything . . . ," a rather more foggy political view. Zia Krohn and Joce Lagerwij, *Concrete Messages: Street Art on the Israeli-Palestinian Separation Barrier* (Årsta, Sweden: Dokument Press, 2010), 37.
77. Jennifer Allen, "Neo Rauch; Suojiacun's Imminent Destruction; Artists without Walls," artforum.com, 19 June 2011.
78. Ibid.
79. Text and video, "Pippi Longstocking—The Strongest Girl in the World at Abu Dis," digitalartlab.org.
80. Backmann, *A Wall in Palestine*, 21.
81. Gene Ray, "The Trauerspiel in the Age of Its Global Reproducibility: Boaz Arad's Hitler Videos," *Afterimage* 31, no. 2 (September–October 2003): 6.
82. Zuckermann, "On Landscapes & Human Beings," 9.
83. Ilan Pappé, "Israel at a Crossroads between Civic Democracy and Jewish Zealotocracy," *Journal of Palestine Studies* 29, no. 3 (Spring 2000): 34–35.
84. Jasmin Habib, "Memorializing the Holocaust in Israel: Diasporic Encounters," *Anthropologica* 49, no. 2 (2007): 245–256.
85. Meira Weiss, "Bereavement, Commemoration, and Collective Identity in Contemporary Israeli Society," *Anthropological Quarterly* 70 (April 1997): 91.
86. Weizman, *Hollow Land*, 224.
87. Ibid., 225.
88. Simon Faulkner, "Simon's Teaching Blog: Ruins as Political Images," 26 August 2009, available at simonsteachingblog.wordpress.com.
89. Conversation with Yael Bartana, Tel Aviv, 31 July 2006.
90. "Yael Bartana . . . and Europe will be stunned," available at labiennale.art.pl/en under "Exhibition." Bartana was selected to represent Poland at the 54th International Art Exhibition in Venice in 2011 and showed her film trilogy . . . *and Europe will be stunned*.
91. See review by Carol Zemel, "The End(s) of Irony: Yael Bartana and the Venice Biennale, for Poland," *The Forward* [online], 5 July 2011.
92. "Galit Eilat and Charles Esche Talk to Yael Bartana," available at labiennale.art.pl/en, under "Texts." The interview was conducted between November 2009 and March 2010 at the Van Abbemuseum in Eindhoven, Netherlands.
93. *A Cookbook for Political Imagination* is published "under the auspices of the Jewish Renaissance Movement in Poland," and is edited by the curators of the exhibition, Sebastian Cichocki and Galit Eilat, and published by Zachęta National Gallery of Art and Sternberg Press. The introduction is available at Sternberg Press [online].
94. These works were part of an exhibition of Bartana's work at P.S. 1 Contemporary Art Center from October 2008 to May 2009, which also included *Trembling Time* (2001), *Low Relief II* (2004), and *Summer Camp* (2007).
95. For a discussion of the controversy over the exhibition *Mirroring Evil: Nazi Imagery/Recent Art*, see my chapter on "Art" in *The Oxford Handbook of Holocaust Studies*, ed. Peter Hayes and John K. Roth (Oxford: Oxford University Press, 2011), 461–477; for Schech-

ner's works, see his website at dottycommies.com.
96. Ariella Azoulay, *Death's Showcase: The Power of Image in Contemporary Democracy* (Cambridge, Mass.: MIT Press, 2003), 50–53.
97. Guy Ben-Ner, "Synchronization of a Mustache," in *VoozVooz* (Tel Aviv: Center for Contemporary Art, 2007), 54.
98. Gene Ray, chapter on "Working Out and Playing Through: Boaz Arad's Hitler Videos," in *Terror and the Sublime in Art and Critical Theory: From Auschwitz to Hiroshima to September 11* (New York: Palgrave Macmillan, 2005); also see Joanna Lindenbaum, "The Villain Speaks the Victim's Language," in *Mirroring Evil: Nazi Imagery/Recent Art*, ed. Norman L. Kleeblatt (New York and New Brunswick, N.J.: Jewish Museum and Rutgers University Press, 2002), 121–122.
99. Conversation with Boaz Arad, Tel Aviv, 29 July 2009.
100. Sergio Edelszstein, "Sergio Edelszstein in Conversation with Boaz Arad," in *VoozVooz* (Tel Aviv: Center for Contemporary Art, 2007), 64.
101. Slavoj Žižek, **"**Let's Be Realists, Let's Demand the Impossible! Why Pragmatic Politics are Doomed to Fail in the Middle East," *In These Times* [online], 30 August 2006.
102. Former Israeli President Yitzak Ben-Zvi, who assumed office in 1952, claimed that the Palestinians aimed to complete Hitler's project. See Haim Yacobi, "The Architecture of Ethnic Logic: Exploring the Meaning of the Built Environment in the 'Mixed' City of Lod, Israel," *Geografiska Annaler. Series B, Human Geography* 84, no. 3/4 (2002): 173. Still today, Arabs are referred to as "Nazis" and swastikas are sometimes drawn near the front doors of Palestinians in "mixed neighborhoods" in Jerusalem. See Thomas Abowd, "National Boundaries, Colonized Spaces: The Gendered Politics of Residential Life in Contemporary Jerusalem," *Anthropological Quarterly* 80, no. 4 (Fall 2007): 1006.
103. See the exhibition catalog *Wonderyears: New Reflections on the Shoah and Nazism in Israel*, with thirteen essays, including Israeli curator Tali Tamir's "The Shadow of Evil: To the Third and Fourth Generation" (Berlin: Neue Gesellschaft für Bildende Kunst e.V. [NGBK], 2003).
104. Backmann, *A Wall in Palestine*, 107–108.
105. Rafeef Ziadeh, "Palestine and the Cultural Boycott," *Z-Net* [online], 19 April 2009.
106. Another controversy occurred at Brandeis University in 2006, where twenty-seven-year-old Lior Halperin, a Jewish student from Israel and sophomore at Brandeis, curated an exhibit of seventeen paintings by Palestinian youth between eleven and sixteen years of age from the al-Rowwad Cultural Center at Aida refugee camp, near Bethlehem, in the occupied West Bank. The exhibition was called *Voices from Palestine*. But four days into a two-week exhibition, college administrators removed the work, claiming it "confused" and "upset" some students, was one-sided and without context. This is a complaint that is never lodged against exhibitions of Israeli art. Halperin immediately found a new venue for the exhibition at MIT while Brandeis faculty started a petition drive to bring the exhibition back. Halperin explained that she felt "the Palestinian voice has been very marginalized and not as freely expressed and prevalent as the Israeli point of view is on campus." See "Brandeis University Takes Down Palestinian Youth Art Exhibit Mounted by Israeli Jewish Student," interview by Amy Goodman with Lior Halperin and Daniel Terris, democracynow.org, 10 May 2006.
107. Susan Snodgrass, "Controversy at Spertus Museum," *Art in America* 96, no. 8 (September 2008): 34.
108. Menachem Wecker, "Chicago Jewish Museum Cancels Show of Israeli and Palestinian Maps," *Arab American News* [online], 15 August 2008.
109. Ziadeh, "Palestine and the Cultural Boycott."
110. Wecker, "Chicago Jewish Museum Cancels."
111. Snodgrass, "Controversy at Spertus Museum," 34.
112. Rebecca Spence, "Chicago Museum Closes Contentious Exhibit," *Jewish Daily Forward* [online], 26 June 2008.
113. See Jacir's full statement about the work, cited at "The Wall & the Checkpoints," *Darat al Funun* [online].
114. Wecker, "Chicago Jewish Museum Cancels."

Conclusion

1. For literature on humanitarian communication and appeal, see, for example, Lilie Chouliaraki, "Post-humanitarianism: Humanitarian Communication beyond a Politics of Pity," *International Journal of Cultural Studies* 13, no. 2 (2010): 107–126, and Luc Boltanski, *Distant Suffering: Morality, Media and Politics* (Cambridge, U.K.: Cambridge University Press, 1999).
2. Giorgio Agamben, *Homo Sacer: Sovereign Power and Bare Life* (Stanford, Calif.: Stanford University Press, 1998), 133–134.
3. Slavoj Žižek, *Violence* (New York: Picador, 2008), 206.
4. John T. Parry, "Finding a Right to Be Tortured," *Law & Literature* 19, no. 2 (2007): 207–208.
5. Ibid., 209.
6. Ibid., 210.
7. RETORT, Iain Boal, T. J. Clark, Joseph Matthews, Michael Watts, *Afflicted Powers: Capital and Spectacle in a New Age of War* (London and New York: Verso, 2005), 24–29.
8. See, for example, Obama's interview with Steve Kroft for *60 Minutes*, in Brian Montopoli, "Obama: I Won't Release Osama Death Photos," cbsnews.com, 4 May 2011.

9. Yochi Dreazen, Aamer Mahdani, and Marc Ambinder, "The Goal Was Never to Capture Bin Laden," theatlantic.com, 4 May 2011.
10. Ibid.
11. Ibid. Also see Noam Chomsky, "There Is Much More to Say," chomsky.info, May 2011; Glenn Greenwald's series of articles on salon.com, such as "The Osama bin Laden Exception," 6 May 2011; "Bin Laden's Death Doesn't End His Fear-Mongering Value," 9 May 2011; "The Bin Laden Dividend," 12 May 2011; and an interview with Neal Conan for National Public Radio on 9 May 2011. The illegal U.S. entry into Pakistan and the disposal of the body without autopsy were also violations of law, while the burial at sea violated Islamic requirements.
12. Quoted in Chomsky, "There is Much More to Say."
13. Dreazen et al., "The Goal Was Never."
14. CBS News correspondent David Martin said, "I've had it described to me and it does sound very gruesome. Remember, bin Laden was shot twice at close range, once in the chest and once in the head, right above his left eye, and that bullet opened his skull, exposing the brain, and it also blew out his eye"; see "Martin: Bin Laden Pictures Not for the Squeamish," cbsnews.com, 4 May 2011. The description suggests that bin Laden may have been shot in the back of the head. Another reporter notes, "The White House has only confirmed he was shot somewhere above the neck. If bin Laden was shot in the back of the head, the exit wound would likely be so gruesome that a photo of his face may have been barely recognizable." It might also suggest that he was killed execution style, on his knees. Paul Toohey, "Pakistan Unable to Explain How Foreign Operatives Were Able to Work without Detection for Up to Four Months," couriermail.com.au, 8 May 2011.
15. Slavoj Žižek, *The Parallax View* (Cambridge, Mass.: MIT Press, 2006).
16. Ibid., 292.
17. Žižek designates the defeat of the Red Army in Poland in 1920 as the moment of Napoleonic Thermidor—the end of the forward motion of the October Revolution—which then led to the inward thrust of revolutionary energy in the form of the forced collectivization of the *kulaks* (peasants) in 1928, which Žižek characterizes as not only stealing the program of Trotsky and the Left Opposition, but taking it further than the Trotskyists "dared to imagine." The Left Opposition, however, strenuously fought against not only the brutality of this program, but against forced collectivization itself, calling instead for a program based on a system of incentives.
18. Graeme Wood, "Reading Trotsky in Tahrir: What the Russian Revolutionary Can Teach Us about the Arab Spring," *Bookforum* 18, no. 2 (2011): 10.
19. Žižek, *The Parallax View*, 11.
20. Ibid., 321.
21. Terry Eagleton, "On the Contrary: Terry Eagleton on Slavoj Žižek's *The Parallax View*," *Artforum*, Summer 2006, 61–62.
22. Žižek, *Violence*, 2.
23. Gene Ray, "Tactical Media and the End of the End of History," *Linksnet: Für Linke Politik und Wissenschaft* [online], 12 November 2006.
24. Klein, *The Shock Doctrine*, 17.
25. Ibid., 11–12.
26. Ibid., 18–19.

SELECTED BIBLIOGRAPHY

Abdul-Ahad, Ghaith, Kael Alford, Thorne Anderson, and Rita Leistner. *Unembedded: Four Independent Photojournalists on the War in Iraq.* White River Junction, Vt.: Chelsea Green Publishing Co., 2005.

Abowd, Thomas. "National Boundaries, Colonized Spaces: The Gendered Politics of Residential Life in Contemporary Jerusalem." *Anthropological Quarterly* 80, no. 4 (Fall 2007): 997–1034.

Agamben, Giorgio. *Homo Sacer: Sovereign Power and Bare Life.* Stanford, Calif.: Stanford University Press, 1998.

Als, Hilton. "GWTW." In *Without Sanctuary: Lynching Photography in America,* ed. James Allen, Hilton Als, Congressman John Lewis, and Leon Litwack, 38–44. Santa Fe: Twin Palms Press, 2000.

Ankori, Gannit. *Palestinian Art.* London: Reaktion Books, 2006.

Apel, Dora. "Art." In *The Oxford Handbook of Holocaust Studies,* ed. Peter Hayes and John K. Roth, 461–477. Oxford: Oxford University Press, 2011.

———. "Cultural Battlegrounds: Weimar Photographic Narratives of War." *New German Critique* 76, Special Issue on Weimar Visual Culture (Winter 1999): 49–84.

———. "Icons of Suffering." In *Ewa Harabasz: Icons,* 44–47. Exhibition catalog in English and Polish. Le Guern Gallery, Warsaw; Galeria Miejska, Poznan; Galeria Bielska BWA, Bielsko-Biala, 2008.

———. *Imagery of Lynching: Black Men, White Women, and the Mob.* New Brunswick, N.J.: Rutgers University Press, 2004.

———. "Just Joking? Chimps, Obama, and Racial Stereotype." *Journal of Visual Culture* 8, no. 2 (August 2009): 134–142.

———. *Memory Effects: The Holocaust and the Art of Secondary Witnessing.* New Brunswick, N.J.: Rutgers University Press, 2002.

———. "Torture Culture: Lynching Photographs and the Images of Abu Ghraib." *Art Journal* 64, no. 2 (Summer 2005): 88–100.

Apel, Dora, and Shawn Michelle Smith. *Lynching Photographs.* San Francisco: University of California Press, 2004.

Ashford, Doug, Wendy Ewald, Nina Felshin, and Patricia C. Phillips. "A Conversation on Social Collaboration." *Art Journal* 65, no. 2 (Summer 2006): 58–82.

Auslander, Mark. "'Holding on to Those Who Can't Be Held': Reenacting a Lynching at Moore's Ford, Georgia." *Southern Spaces* [online], 8 November 2010.

Azoulay, Ariella. *The Civil Contract of Photography.* New York: Zone Books, 2008.

———. *Death's Showcase: The Power of Image in Contemporary Democracy.* Cambridge, Mass.: MIT Press, 2003.

———. "Miki Kratsman." In *Del Revés: Artistes contemporáneos de Israel/Inside-Out: Contemporary Artists from Israel,* ed. Octavio Zaya, 64–83. Barcelona: ACTAR and MARCO Foundation, Museo de Arte Contemporánea de Vigo, 2006.

Bacevich, Andrew J. *The New American Militarism: How Americans Are Seduced by War.* New York: Oxford University Press, 2005.

Backmann, René. *A Wall in Palestine.* New York: Picador, 2006.

Bal, Mieke. "The Pain of Images." In *Beautiful Suffering: Photography and the Traffic in Pain,* ed. Mark Reinhardt, Holly Edwards, and Erina Duganne, 93–115. Chicago: Williams College Museum of Art and University of Chicago Press, 2007.

Bauer, Stephane, ed. *Wonder Years: New Reflections on the Shoah and Nazism in Israeli Society.* Exhibit catalog. Berlin: Neue Gesellschaft für Bildende Kunst e.V. (NGBK), 2003.

Bauerlein, Mark. "History, Horror, Healing: Faculty Deliberations on Lynching Photography Examine Racial and Historical Understanding." *The Academic Exchange: A Place for Scholarly Conversation at Emory,* April/May 2001, 5.

Beckman, Karen. "Gender, Power, and Pedagogy in Coco Fusco's *Bare Life Study #1*(2005), *A Room of One's Own* (2005), and *Operation Atropos* (2006)." *Framework* 50, nos. 1 & 2 (Spring 2009): 125–138.

Benjamin, Walter. "Theses on the Philosophy of History." In *Illuminations.* New York: Schocken Books, 1968.

Ben-Ner, Guy. "Synchronization of a Mustache." In *Vooz Vooz,* 41–59. Exhibit catalog. Tel Aviv: Center for Contemporary Art, 2007.

Berlant, Lauren. *The Queen of America Goes to Washington City: Essays on Sex and Citizenship.* Durham, N.C.: Duke University Press, 1997.

Berman, Nina. *Purple Hearts: Back from Iraq.* London: Trolley Books, 2004.

———. *Homeland: Nina Berman.* London: Trolley Books, 2008.

Bevan, Robert. *The Destruction of Memory: Architecture at War.* London: Reaktion Books, 2006.

Blackson, Robert. "Once More . . . with Feeling: Reenactment in Contemporary Art and Culture." *Art Journal* 66, no. 1 (Spring 2007): 28–40.

Boullata, Kamal. *Palestinian Art: From 1850 to the Present.* London: Saqi Books, 2009.

Braverman, Irus. "'The Tree Is the Enemy Soldier': A Sociological Making of War Landscapes in the Occupied West Bank." *Law & Society Review* 42, no. 3 (September 2008): 449–482.

Brener, Julie. "Not a Pretty Sight: The Transformative Art of Tamy Ben-Tor." *Tablet* [online], 24 April 2008.

Buck-Morss, Susan. *Dreamworld and Catastrophe: The Passing of Mass Utopia in East and West.* Cambridge, Mass.: MIT Press, 2000.

———. *Thinking Past Terror: Islamicism and Critical Theory on the Left.* New York: W. W. Norton, 2003.

Butler, Judith. *Frames of War: When Is Life Grievable?* New York: Verso, 2010.

———. *Precarious Life: The Powers of Mourning and Violence.* New York: Verso, 2004.

Chichocki, Sebastian, and Galit Eilat, ed. *A Cookbook for Political Imagination.* Exhibit catalog. Berlin: Sternberg Press, 2011.

Chouliaraki, Lilie. "Post-humanitarianism: Humanitarian Communication beyond a Politics of Pity." *International Journal of Cultural Studies* 13, no. 2 (2010): 107–126.

Colomina, Beatriz. *Domesticity at War.* Cambridge, Mass.: MIT Press, 2007.

Conroy, Thomas. "The Packaging of Jessica Lynch." In *Constructing America's War Culture: Iraq, Media and Images at Home,* ed. Thomas Conroy and Jarice Hanson, 61–84. Lanham, Md.: Lexington Books, 2008.

Cook, Alexander. "The Use and Abuse of Reenactment: Thoughts on Recent Trends in Public History." *Criticism* 46, no. 3 (Summer 2004): 487–496.

Correia, Alice. "Interpreting Jeremy Deller's *The Battle of Orgreave.*" *Visual Culture in Britain* 7, no. 2 (2006): 93–112.

Cotterrell, David. "J4MED, Op Herrick 7, 03.11.07—26.11.07." In *War and Medicine,* ed. Wellcome Trust, 192–221. London: Black Dog Publishing, 2008.

———. "The Stranger." In *Transmission: Host,* 5–10. London: Artwords Press, 2009.

Cuir, Raphael. "Krzysztof Wodiczko." *Artpress,* no. 318 (December 2005): 78–79.

Danner, Mark. *Torture and Truth: America, Abu Ghraib, and the War on Terror.* New York: New York Review of Books, 2004.

Delgado, Manuel. "Symbolic Wars: Struggle, Play, Festival." In *At War,* ed. Antonio Monegal and Francesc Torres, 43–54. Barcelona: Centre de Cultura Contemporània de Barcelona, Institut d'Edicions de la Diputació de Barcelona, Forum Barcelona and Actar, 2004.

Der Derian, James. "9/11: Before, After, and In Between." In *Terrorism, Media, Liberation,* ed. J. David Slocum, 321–336. New Brunswick, N.J.: Rutgers University Press, 2005.

Deutsche, Rosalyn. "Krzysztof Wodiczko's *Homeless Projection* and the Site of Urban 'Revitalization.'" In *Evictions: Art and Spatial Politics.* Cambridge, Mass.: MIT Press, 1998.

Downey, Anthony. "Thresholds of a Coming Community: Photography and Human Rights." *Aperture Magazine* [online] 194 (Spring 2009).

———. "Zones of Indistinction: Giorgio Agamben's 'Bare Life' and the Politics of Aesthetics." *Third Text* 23, no. 2 (March 2009): 109–125.

Duganne, Erina. "Photography after the Fact." In *Beautiful Suffering: Photography and the Traffic in Pain,* ed. Mark Reinhardt, Holly Edwards, and Erina Duganne, 57–74. Chicago: Williams College Museum of Art and University of Chicago Press, 2007.

Eagleton, Terry. "On the Contrary: Terry Eagleton on Slavoj Žižek's *The Parallax View.*" *Artforum,* Summer 2006, 61–62.

Eddy, Matthew. "*Nations Have the Right to Kill: Hitler, the Holocaust, and War* by Richard A. Koenigsberg." *Journal for the Scientific Study of Religion* 48, no. 4 (December 2009): 838–840.

Edelstein, Sergio. "Sergio Edelstein in Conversation with Boaz Arad." In *VoozVooz,* 60–78. Exhibit catalog. Tel Aviv: Center for Contemporary Art, 2007.

Eickelman, Dale F. "The Middle East's Democracy Deficit and the Expanding Public Sphere." In *Media, War and Terrorism: Responses from the Middle East and Asia,* ed. Peter van der Veer and Shoma Munshi. New York: Routledge, 2004.

Eisenman, Stephen. *The Abu Ghraib Effect.* London: Reaktion Books, 2007.

Ellsworth, Elizabeth. *Places of Learning: Media, Architecture, Pedagogy.* New York: Routledge, 2004.

Falah, Ghazi. "The 1948 Israeli-Palestinian War and Its Aftermath: The Transformation and De-Signification of Palestine's Cultural Landscape." *Annals of the Association of American Geographers* 66, no. 2 (June 1996): 256–285.

Farmer, James O. "Playing Rebels: Reenactment as Nostalgia and Defense of the Confederacy in the Battle of Aiken." *Southern Cultures* 11, no. 1 (Spring 2005): 46–73.

Faulkner, Simon. "Land, Landscape, and the Wild Zone of Power." In *NurtureNation,* 241–254. Exhibit catalog. Jerusalem: Museum on the Seam, 2008.

Frančišković, Tanja, et al. "Secondary Traumatization of Wives of War Veterans with Posttraumatic Stress Disorder." *Croatian Medical Journal* 48, no. 2 (April 2007): 177–184.

Fusco, Coco. *A Field Guide for Female Interrogators.* New York: Seven Stories Press, 2008.

Gardner, Thomas N. "War as Mediated Narrative: The Sextet of War Rhetoric." In *Constructing America's War Culture: Iraq, Media, and Images at Home,* ed. Thomas Conroy and Jarice Hanson, 107–126. Lanham, Md.: Lexington Books, 2008.

Garoian, Charles R., and Yvonne M. Gaudelius. "Performing Resistance." *Studies in Art Education* 46, no. 1 (2004): 48–60.

Gilbertson, Ashley. *Whiskey Tango Foxtrot: A Photographer's Chronicle of the Iraq War.* Chicago: University of Chicago Press, 2007.

Goldman, Francisco. "Regina José Galindo." *BOMB Magazine* 94 (Winter 2006) [online].

Gómez-Peña, Guillermo. "Disclaimer." *Drama Review* 50, no. 1 (Spring 2006): 149–158.

———. "In Defense of Performance Art: A Foremost Practitioner Explains His Métier." *Art Papers* [online] 27, no. 4 (July–August 2003).

———. "The New Global Culture: Somewhere between Corporate Multiculturalism and the Mainstream Bizarre (a Border Perspective)." *Drama Revue* 45, no. 1 (Spring 2001): 7–30.

Goodman, Susan Tumarkin, Andy Grundberg, and Nissan N. Perez. *Dateline Israel: New Photography and Video Art*. Exhibit catalog. New York: Jewish Museum of New York, 2007.

Gourevitch, Philip, and Errol Morris. *The Ballad of Abu Ghraib*. New York: Penguin Books, 2009.

Green, Rayna. "The Tribe Called Wannabee: Playing Indian in America and Europe." *Folklore* 99 (1988): 30–55.

Greenhouse, Adam, and Nora Barrows-Friedman. "Independent Journalists Dismantling Israel's Hold on Media Narrative." *The Electronic Intifada* [online], 15 June 2010.

Grusin, Richard. *Premediation: Affect and Mediality after 9/11*. New York: Palgrave Macmillan, 2010.

Habib, Jasmin. "Memorializing the Holocaust in Israel: Diasporic Encounters." *Anthropologica* 49, no. 2 (2007): 245–256.

Halper, Jeff. *An Israeli in Palestine: Resisting Dispossession, Redeeming Israel*. London: Pluto Press, 2008.

Handler, Richard. "Overpowered by Realism: Living History and the Simulation of the Past." *Journal of American Folklore* 100, no. 397 (July–September 1987): 337–341.

Hanhardt, John G. "Dé-Collage/Collage: Notes toward a Reexamination of the Origins of Video Art." In *Illuminating Video: An Essential Guide to Video Art*, ed. Doug Hall and Sally Jo Fifer, 71–79. New York: Aperture Foundation Inc., 1990.

Hargreaves, Roger. "Say It Again, Y'all." *Photoworks*, Autumn 2008/Winter 2009, 74–77.

Hariman, Robert, and John Louis Lucaites. *No Caption Needed: Iconic Photographs, Public Culture, and Liberal Democracy*. Chicago: University of Chicago Press, 2007.

Herman, Judith. *Trauma and Recovery: The Aftermath of Violence—from Domestic Abuse to Political Terror*. 2nd ed. New York: Basic Books, 1997.

Horwitz, Tony. *Confederates in the Attic: Dispatches from the Unfinished Civil War*. New York: Pantheon, 1998.

Howard, John W. III, and Laura C. Prividera. "The Fallen Woman Archetype: Media Representations of Lynndie England, Gender, and the (Ab)Uses of U.S. Female Soldiers." *Women's Studies in Communication* 31, no. 3 (Fall 2008): 287–311.

Hromack, Sarah. "What It Is: A Conversation with Jeremy Deller." *Art in America* [online], 4 March 2009.

Jacobson, Colin. "Why Mister, Why?" *Foto8 Magazine* [online], 2005.

Kester, Grant. *Conversation Pieces: Community and Communication in Modern Art*. Berkeley: University of California Press, 2004.

Khalidi, Rashid. *Resurrecting Empire: Western Footprints and America's Perilous Path in the Middle East*. Boston: Beacon Press, 2005.

Kitamura, Katie. "'Recreating Chaos': Jeremy Deller's *The Battle of Orgreave*." In *Historical Reenactment: From Realism to the Affective Turn*, ed. Iain McCalman and Paul A. Pickering, 39–49. Houndmills, U.K.: Palgrave Macmillan 2010.

Klein, Naomi. *The Shock Doctrine: The Rise of Disaster Capitalism*. New York: Picador, 2007.

Krohn, Zia, and Joce Lagerwij. *Concrete Messages: Street Art on the Israeli-Palestinian Separation Barrier*. Årsta, Sweden: Dokument Press, 2010.

Krstich, Vesna. "On the Road Again with Jeremy Deller: Conversations about Iraq." *Art Papers* 33, no. 4 (July–August 2009): 18–21.

Kwon, Miwon. *One Place after Another: Site-Specific Art and Locational Identity*. Cambridge, Mass.: MIT Press, 2002.

Lane, Guy. "Jorge Ribalta on Documentary and Democracy," *Foto8 Magazine* [online], 2 July 2009.

Larsen, Svend Erik. "Landscape, Identity, and War." *New Literary History* 34, no. 3 (Summer 2004): 469–490.

Laurent, Olivier. "Bad Connection." *British Journal of Photography* [online], 2 July 2008.

Lewin, Rebecca. "Venice Biennale: Yael Bartana." *This Is Tomorrow: Contemporary Art Magazine* [online], 20 June 2011.

Lind, Maria, and Hito Steyerl, eds. *The Greenroom: Reconsidering the Documentary and Contemporary Art*. Berlin: Sternberg Press and the Center for Curatorial Studies, Bard College, 2008.

Lindenbaum, Joanna. "The Villain Speaks the Victim's Language." In *Mirroring Evil: Nazi Imagery/Recent Art*, ed. Norman L. Kleeblatt, 121–122. New York and New Brunswick, N.J.: Jewish Museum and Rutgers University Press, 2002.

Lott, Eric. *Love and Theft: Blackface Minstrelsy and the American Working Class*. New York: Oxford University Press, 1995.

Lowenstein, Roger. "The Immigration Equation." *New York Times Magazine*, 9 July 2006.

Lütticken, Sven. "An Arena in Which to Reenact." In *Life, Once More: Forms of Reenactment in Contemporary Art*, ed. Sven Lütticken, 17–60. Rotterdam: Witte de With, Center for Contemporary Art, 2005.

Maass, Peter. "The Toppling: How the Media Inflated a Minor Moment in a Long War." *New Yorker* [online], 10 January 2011.

Mason, Carol. "The Hillbilly Defense: Culturally Mediating U.S. Terror at Home and Abroad." *NWSA Journal* 17, no. 3 (Fall 2005): 39–63.

McCann, Paul. "The Role of UNRWA and the Palestine Refugees." *Palestine-Israel Journal* [online] 15, no.4 & vol. 16, no. 1 (August 2009).

McCorquodale, Duncan, ed. *Krzysztof Wodiczko*. London: Black Dog Publishing, 2011.

McLaughlin, Greg. *The War Correspondent*. London: Pluto, 2002.

Meyer, Richard. "Home Delivery." *Modern Painters* 20, no. 3 (April 2008): 56, 58.

Mitchell, W.J.T. *Cloning Terror: The War of Im-

ages, 9/11 to the Present. Chicago: University of Chicago Press, 2011.
Nickel, Douglas R. "History of Photography: The State of Research," *Art Bulletin* 83, no. 3 (2001): 548–558.
Pappé, Ilan. "Israel at a Crossroads between Civic Democracy and Jewish Zealotocracy." *Journal of Palestine Studies* 29, no.3 (Spring 2000): 33–44.
Parekh, Serena. "Resisting 'Dull and Torpid' Assent: Returning to the Debate over the Foundations of Human Rights." *Human Rights Quarterly* 29, no. 3 (2007): 754–778.
Parry, John T. "Finding a Right to Be Tortured." *Law & Literature* 19, no. 2 (2007): 207–227.
Parry, William. *Against the Wall: The Art of Resistance in Palestine*. Chicago: Lawrence Hills Books, 2010.
Petro, Patrice, and Andrew Martin. "Introduction." In *Rethinking Global Security: Media, Popular Culture, and the "War on Terror,"* ed. Patrice Petro and Andrew Martin. New Brunswick, N.J.: Rutgers University Press, 2006.
Phelan, Peggy. "Hinckley and Ronald Reagan: Reenactment and the Ethics of the Real." In *Life, Once More: Forms of Reenactment in Contemporary Art,* ed. Sven Lütticken, 147–168. Rotterdam: Witte de With, Center for Contemporary Art 2005.
Phillips, Patricia. "Creating Democracy: A Dialogue with Krzysztof Wodiczko." *Art Journal* 62, no. 4 (Winter 2003): 32–47.
———. "(Inter)Disciplinary Actions." *Public Art Review* 15, no. 1 (Fall/Winter 2003): 11–15.
Puar, Jasbir K. "Abu Ghraib: Arguing against Exceptionalism." *Feminist Studies* 30, no. 2 (Summer 2004): 522–534.
———. *Terrorist Assemblages: Homonationalism in Queer Times*. Durham, N.C.: Duke University Press, 2007.
Rancière, Jacques. *Dissensus: On Politics and Aesthetics,* ed. and trans. Steven Corcoran. New York: Continuum International Publishing Group, 2010.
Ray, Gene. "Tactical Media and the End of the End of History." *Linksnet: Für Linke Politik und Wissenschaft* [online], 12 November 2006.
———. "The Trauerspiel in the Age of Its Global Reproducibility: Boaz Arad's Hitler Videos." *Afterimage* 31, no. 2 (September–October 2003): 6–8.
———. "Working Out and Playing Through: Boaz Arad's Hitler Videos." In *Terror and the Sublime in Art and Critical Theory: From Auschwitz to Hiroshima to September 11,* 121–134. New York: Palgrave Macmillan, 2005.
Reinhardt, Mark. "Introduction." In *Beautiful Suffering: Photography and the Traffic in Pain,* ed. Mark Reinhardt, Holly Edwards, and Erina Duganne. Chicago: Williams College Museum of Art and University of Chicago Press, 2007.
Reinhardt, Mark, Holly Edwards, and Erina Duganne, eds. *Beautiful Suffering: Photography and the Traffic in Pain*. Exhibit catalog. Chicago: University of Chicago Press, 2007.
RETORT, Iain Boal, T. J. Clark, Joseph Matthews, and Michael Watts. *Afflicted Powers: Capital and Spectacle in a New Age of War*. New York: Verso, 2005.
Ribalta, Jorge, ed. "Introduction." In *Public Photographic Spaces: Exhibitions of Propaganda, from Pressa to the Family of Man, 1928–55*. Barcelona: Museu d'Art Contemporani de Barcelona, 2008.
Ricigliano, Robert, and Mike Allen. "Cold War Redux." In *Rethinking Global Security: Media, Popular Culture, and the "War on Terror,"* ed. Andrew Martin and Patrice Petro, 85–103. New Brunswick, N.J.: Rutgers University Press, 2006.
Roeder, Jr., George H. *The Censored War: American Visual Experience during World War Two*. New Haven: Yale University Press, 1993.
Rosler, Martha. "Flat Daddy." *Photoworks* 11 (Autumn 2008/Winter 2009): 20–21.
———. "In, Around, and Afterthoughts (on Documentary Photography)." In *The Contest of Meaning: Critical Histories of Photography,* ed. Richard Bolton, 303–342. Cambridge, Mass.: MIT Press, 1989.
———. "Video: Shedding the Utopian Moment." In *Illuminating Video: An Essential Guide to Video Art,* ed. Doug Hall and Sally Jo Fifer, 31–50. New York: Aperture Foundation, Inc., 1990.
Rosler, Martha, and Iwona Blazwick. "Taking Responsibility: Martha Rosler Interviewed by Iwona Blazwick." *Art Monthly* 3 (2008): 1–7.
Saltzman, Lisa. "When Memory Speaks: A Monument Bears Witness." In *Trauma and Visuality in Modernity,* ed. Lisa Saltzman and Eric Rosenberg, 82–102. Hanover, N.H: University Press of New England, 2006.
Sarracino, Carmine, and Kevin M. Scott. *The Porning of America: The Rise of Porn Culture, What It Means, and Where We Go from Here*. Boston: Beacon Press, 2008.
Seda, Laurietz. "Decolonizing the Body Politic: Guillermo Gómez-Peña's *Mapa/Corpo 2*: Interactive Rituals for the New Millennium." *Drama Revue* 53, no. 1 (Spring 2009): 136–141.
Segal, Rafi, and Eyal Weizman, eds. *A Civilian Occupation: The Politics of Israeli Architecture*. Exhibit catalog. Tel-Aviv: Babel; London: Verso, 2003.
Simon, Roger I. "A Shock to Thought: Curatorial Judgment and the Public Exhibition of 'Difficult Knowledge.'" *Memory Studies* [online], 21 February 2011, 1–18.
Slocum, J. David. "Introduction." In *Terrorism, Media, Liberation,* ed. J. David Slocum. New Brunswick, N.J.: Rutgers University Press, 2005.
Smith, Shawn Michelle. "Afterimages: White Womanhood, Lynching, and the War in Iraq." *Nka: Journal of Contemporary African Art,* Special Issue: "Strange Fruit: Lynching, Visuality, and Empire" 20 (Fall 2006): 72–87.
Snodgrass, Susan. "Controversy at Spertus Museum." *Art in America* 96, no. 8 (September 2008): 34.

Snyder, Robert E. "Without Sanctuary: An American Holocaust?" *Southern Quarterly* 39, no. 3 (2001): 162–171.

Someze, Catherine. "Meeting with Adi Nes/Biblical Stories." *Eyemazing* 2 (2006). Available at adines.com.

Sontag, Susan. *Regarding the Pain of Others*. New York: Farrar, Straus and Giroux, 2003.

Stallabrass, Julian. "Performing Torture," preface to *Regina José Galindo, Confesión, Palma de Mallorca*. The Courtauld Institute of Art [online].

Stoilas, Helen. "Terrorism Exhibition Cancelled." *Art Newspaper* 196 (November 2008): 14.

Strauss, David Levi. "Nikons and Icons: Is the Aestheticization-of-Suffering Critique Still Valid?" Bookforum.com [online], June/July/August 2007.

Suellentrop, Chris. "War Games." *New York Times Magazine*, 12 September 2010, 62–67.

Swedenburg, Ted. "The Palestinian Peasant as National Signifier." *Anthropological Quarterly* 63, no. 1 (January 1990): 18–30.

Tagg, John. *The Disciplinary Frame: Photographic Truths and the Capture of Meaning*. Minneapolis: University of Minnesota Press, 2009.

Taher, Dr. Mantador. "Open the Hospital Doors!" In *War and Medicine*, ed. Wellcome Trust, 222–225. London: Black Dog Publishing, 2008.

Tanelian, Terri L. *Invisible Wounds of War: Psychological and Cognitive Injuries, Their Consequences, and Services to Assist Recovery*. Santa Monica, Calif.: RAND Corporation, 2008 [online].

Taylor, John. *Body Horror: Photojournalism, Catastrophe, and War*. New York: New York University Press, 1998.

Terry, Jennifer. "Killer Entertainments." *Vectors: Journal of Culture and Technology in a Dynamic Vernacular* [online] 3, no. 1 (Fall 2007).

Thompson, Jenny. *War Games: Inside the World of 20th-Century War Reenactment*. Washington, D.C.: Smithsonian Books, 2004.

Tobocman, Seth, and Terry Berkowitz. *Three Cities against the Wall: Ramallah, Tel Aviv, New York*. Exhibit catalog. Brooklyn: Voxpop, 2005.

Turner, Rory. "Bloodless Battles: The Civil War Reenacted." *Drama Review* 34, no. 4 (Winter 1990): 123–136.

Van der Veer, Peter. "War Propaganda and the Liberal Public Sphere." In *Media, War and Terrorism: Responses from the Middle East and Asia*, ed. Peter van der Veer and Shoma Munshi, 9–21. New York: Routledge, 2004.

Van Kesteren, Geert. *Baghdad Calling: Reports from Turkey, Syria, Jordan, and Iraq*. Rotterdam: Episode Publishers, 2008.

———. *Why Mister, Why? Iraq 2003–2004*. Amsterdam: Artimo, 2004.

Vetrocq, Marcia. "Rules of Engagement." *Art in America*, June/July 2008, 168–175.

Virilio, Paul, and Sylvère Lotringer. *Pure War: Twenty-Five Years Later*, trans. Mark Polizzotti. Cambridge, Mass.: MIT Press, 2008.

Walsh, Kevin. *The Representation of the Past: Museums and Heritage in the Post-Modern World*. London: Routledge, 1992.

Weiss, Meira. "Bereavement, Commemoration, and Collective Identity in Contemporary Israeli Society." *Anthropological Quarterly* 70 (April 1997): 91–101.

———. *The Chosen Body*. Stanford, Calif.: Stanford University Press, 2002.

Weizman, Eyal. "Frontier Architectures." In *Chicago: Adam Broomberg and Oliver Chanarin*. Göttingen, Germany: Steidlmack, 2006.

———. *Hollow Land: Israel's Architecture of Occupation*. London and New York: Verso, 2007.

Wexler, Laura. *Fire in a Canebrake: The Last Mass Lynching in America*. New York: Scribner, 2003.

White Paper by Physicians for Human Rights. "Experiments in Torture: Evidence of Human Subject Research and Experimentation in the 'Enhanced' Interrogation Program," June 2010, phrtorturepapers.org.

Wiesmann, William, Nicole Draghic, and John A. Parrish. "Advances in Modern Combat Casualty Care with a Vision to the Future." In *War and Medicine*, ed. Wellcome Trust, 226–241. London: Black Dog Publishing, 2008.

Wodiczko, Krzysztof. *Critical Vehicles: Writings, Projects, Interviews*. Cambridge, Mass.: MIT Press, 1999.

Wood, Graeme. "Reading Trotsky in Tahrir: What the Russian Revolutionary Can Teach Us about the Arab Spring." *Bookforum* 18, no. 2 (2011): 10.

Woodward, Richard B., Hilton Als, and An-My Lê. *An-My Lê: Small Wars*. New York: Aperture, 2008.

Yacobi, Haim. "The Architecture of Ethnic Logic: Exploring the Meaning of the Built Environment in the 'Mixed' City of Lod, Israel." *Geografiska Annaler. Series B, Human Geography* 84, nos. 3 & 4 (2002): 171–187.

Ziadeh, Rafeef. "Palestine and the Cultural Boycott." *Z-Net* [online], 19 April 2009.

Zimbardo, Tanya. "Repetition—Artur Zmijewski." *Shotgun Review* [online], 8 March 2006.

Žižek, Slavoj. "Let's Be Realists, Let's Demand the Impossible! Why Pragmatic Politics Are Doomed to Fail in the Middle East." *In These Times* [online], 30 August 2006.

———. *The Parallax View*. Cambridge, Mass.: MIT Press, 2006.

———. *Violence*. New York: Picador, 2008.

Zuckermann, Moshe. "On Landscapes & Human Beings." In *Shai Kremer: Infected Landscape: Israel, Broken Promised Land*. Exhibit catalog. Stockport, England: Dewi Lewis Publishing, 2008.

Zureik, Elia. "Constructing Palestine through Surveillance Practices." *British Journal of Middle Eastern Studies* 28, no. 2 (November 2001): 205–227.

INDEX

Aamer, Hani, 210
Abbas, Ali Ismail, 169–170
Abdelhade Palace, 203
Abdul-Ahad, Ghaith, *Unembedded,* 161–164
Abergil, Eden, 102, 103
Abu Faloos, 162
Abu Ghraib, 13, 79–111, 152, 179; and Bush administration, 4, 32, 88, 104, 154; crimes of, 108; and democracy, 81, 106; and Galindo, 114; hooded prisoners of, 120; and imagination of violence, 99; pornography at, 94; and rape images, 89–89; and Rosler, 145; and sex and class, 81–89; sexual torture at, 96; testimony from prisoners in, 89; torturers at, 104; and Wodiczko, 24; and women's capacity for violence, 95–103; and Zimbardo, 100; and zones of indistinction, 7. *See also* interrogation; torture and abuse
Abu Ghraib photographs: banned, 71; and Bush administration, 4, 82; and cell phones, 161; critique of as "art," 108–109; dismissal of, 179; eroticized choreography of, 104; and Fallujah, 124; free circulation of, 19; government suppression of, 82; of Hooded Man, 21, 79–81, 103, 115, 139, 235; and Internet, 104, 105, 109, 110; and killing of Reuters journalists, 178; of man on leash, 120; mediality of, 161; memory of, 154; and Obama administration, 179; and pornography, 92; public display of, 103–111; and public understanding, 155; reception of, 13; staging of, 3
Activision, 176
Adams, Eddie, 151
aesthetics/aestheticization, 5, 10, 11, 140–141, 155
Afghanis, 32, 108, 177, 179, 181
Afghanistan, 135
Afghanistan, war in: and Cotterrell, 129; deaths in, 32; and Lê, 68; and *Mapa/Corpo,* 122; and military recruitment, 56, 57; occupation of, 44; and Rivera Court, 122; and Rosler, 145, 146; soldiers' filming of, 180; and video games, 176, 182; and Wodiczko, 31, 46
African Americans: death threats and attacks against, 107; equality for, 51; government murder of, 24; and lynching photos, 106, 124; in military, 88; and reenactment, 48, 49, 57–59, 61, 73, 74, 75, 76
African American veterans, 73
Agamben, Giorgio, 6, 7, 28, 75–76, 232
Agnew, Vanessa, 60
AIZ (magazine), 5
Alford, Kael, *Unembedded,* 161–164
"Alive Day Memories: Home from Iraq" (HBO documentary), 133, 135
Allen, James, 107

al-Naser Mosque, 203
al-Qaeda, 17
Als, Hilton, *Without Sanctuary,* 107–108
amateurs. *See under* photography
Ambuhl, Megan, 85
American Civil Liberties Union, 25
American Civil War, 2; end of, 72; and medical advancements, 128; memorialization of, 49; photographs of, 67; reenactment of, 49, 57, 58, 60, 61, 76; revisionist approach to, 59
American Photo League, 5
American Revolution, 49
American West, 195
"America's Army" (video game), 177–178
America's Road Home, 35
amputees, 128, 134–135, 173
Anarchists Against the Wall, 210
Anasta, Ayreen, 228
Anderson, Thorne, 162, 164; *Unembedded,* 161–164
. . . and Europe will be stunned exhibition, 221
Andy Warhol Museum, 13, 105, 107, 108, 110
Anthony, Michael, *Mass Casualties,* 43
antisemitism, 216
Aqraba, 193
Arabic, 40, 146, 172, 195, 196
Arabs: and Abu Ghraib, 13, 81, 83, 87, 89, 90, 92, 108, 253n102; and Fort Polk, 172; hostility against, 27; and Israel-Palestinian conflict, 185, 189, 190, 191, 195, 196, 198, 205, 216, 230, 231; and Marxism, 84; and Wodiczko, 30, 40; working masses of, 231
Arab Spring, 236, 237
Arad, Boaz, 224–226; *Hebrew Lesson,* 225; *Immense Inner Peace,* 224; *Marcel Marcel,* 225; *100 Beats,* 224; *Safam (Mustache),* 224–226
Arbeiter Fotograf, Der (magazine), 5
Arendt, Hannah, 7, 121; *The Origins of Totalitarianism,* 6
Argentina, 237
Artists without Walls, 213
Ashkenazi, 142, 144–145
Association for Uniformed Services, 109
Australia, 24
Awlaki, Anwar al-, 7
Azoulay, Ariella, 6, 9, 90, 91, 92–93, 94, 151, 159, 206, 224; *The Civil Contract of Photography,* 8
Azzarella, Josh, 117

Bacevich, Andrew, 18
Backmann, René, 189
Baghdad, 162, 163; July 2007 American helicopter attack in, 175, 178, 179
Bal, Mieke, 34
Balata, 203
Balata Refugee Camp, 202
Banksy, 14, 210–212
Bannerman, Stacy, 37–38
Barbican Gallery, 158
bare life: and Galindo, 112; and Hooded Man, 80; and human rights, 6, 232; and Iraq Veterans against the War, 72; and *Mapa/Corpo,* 121, 122; and Palestinians, 200; as politicized, 9; and Rancière's dissensus, 8; and reenactment of lynching, 75; and U.S. government, 81; and zones of indistinction, 7

Bartana, Yael, 219–222, 226, 228; *Kings of the Hill*, 222; *Mary Koszmary (Nightmares)*, 220; *Mur i wieża (Wall and Tower)*, 220; *Wild Seeds*, 222; *Zamach (Assassination)*, 221–222
Barthes, Roland, 6
Bataille, Georges, 199
"Battlefield: Bad Company" (video game), 176
Battle of Gettysburg, reenactment of, 47
Battle of the Bulge Living History Commemoration, 55
Bauerlein, Mark, 108
Bearing Witness: Photos of the Iraq War in April–May 2008 exhibition, 169
Beautiful Suffering exhibition, 140–141
Bedouins, 205, 206
beheadings, 17, 108
Beit Jalla, 208
Bellini, Giovanni, *Pietà*, 143
Ben-Ami, Shlomo, 190
Benjamin, Walter, 80
Ben-Tor, Tamy, 223, 224, 226; *Women Talk about Adolf Hitler*, 223
Berg, Nick, 125
Berlin, 125
Berlin Wall, 205, 237
Berman, Nina, 13, 14, 136–138, 166, 169, 174; *Homeland*, 170–172; *Human Target Practice, All America Day, Ft. Bragg, North Carolina*, 172; *Marine Wedding*, 136–139; *Purple Hearts: Back from Iraq*, 131–132
Beslan school hostage crisis of 2004, 140
Bethlehem, 208, 211
Bevan, Robert, 202, 203
Beyerman, Lindsey, 174
Bible, 187, 195, 204, 216
Biddia, 210
bilingualism, 25
bin Laden, Osama, 17, 233–235
Bishara, Rana, 195, 208; *Homage to Palestine*, 196
blackface minstrelsy, 73
Black Panthers, 24
Black Power movements, 49
Blackson, Robert, 49–50, 62
Blackwater mercenaries, 122–125
Blu, 212
bodies, 13; of American dead, 79; control over, 92; as decolonized, 116–122; and Deller, 64; and Galindo, 112, 113, 116; gay, 142; and global community of viewers, 111; grievable, 108, 122–125; iconic, 139–147; and images of rape, 89; images of tortured, 106, 111; impact of war on, 129; and Kratsman, 206; and land, 186; and Landau, 230; and Lê, 66; missing, 19, 64, 125–131; of others, 111; Palestinian, 193; privileged viewing of, 106; public mutilation of American, 123, 124; and reenactments, 74; reification of black, 108; and Rosler, 145; surveillance of, 17, 28; and Wodiczko, 21, 33, 34; wounded, 131–139
Borriaud, Nicolas, 63
Boston, 23
Boston Tea Party, 62
Bourke-White, Margaret, 154
Boy Scouts of America, 52, 54, 180
Bradbury, Ray, *Fahrenheit 451*, 25

Brady, Matthew, 67
Brazil, 118
Break the Silence Mural Project, 210
Bremer, L. Paul III, 156
British Mandate Palestine, 203
Brooklyn Museum, 96
Brooks, Jo, 210
Brown, Bridget, 126
B'Tselem, 188, 201
Buck-Morss, Susan, 39, 200
Burrows, Larry, 67, 154
Bush, George H. W., 33, 152
Bush, George W., 53, 106, 114, 123, 152, 166; and global war on terror, 95; loss of faith in, 156; "Top Gun" landing of, 2–3
Bush (George W.) administration, 118; and Abu Ghraib, 4, 32, 82, 88, 104, 154; and Berman, 172; and congressional oversight, 24; and denial of rights, 233; and electroshock, 115; and funding for arts, 117; and Hirsh, 156; and Hooded Man, 81; and image-defeat, 233–234; and National Guard, 57; and Physicians for Human Rights, 99; and police state, 22; and policy of secrecy and suppression, 90; as redefining torture, 25; and terrorists, 7; and unlawful enemy combatants, 7; and waterboarding, 113, 114
Butler, Ben, 109
Butler, Charles, 58
Butler, Judith, 1, 8–9, 81, 91, 94, 108, 125; *Ha'aretz* interview, 24 February 2010, 183, 186

cactus, 195–196
Calley, William, 32–33
Call of Duty (video game series), 176
Camp Bread Basket, 245n25
Camp LeJeune, 172
Camp Pendleton, 172
Cana'an soap factory, 203
Canada, 118
Candice, Tolman, 123
Capa, Robert, 67, 154; *Falling Republican Soldier*, 68
capitalism, 27, 39, 114, 151; and culture of war, 1; disaster, 190–191; and documentary practice, 4; and human rights, 232; and Israeli/Palestinian conflict, 230; and liberalism, 237; radical critique of, 235–236; and Rosler, 145, 146, 147; and state, 8; and violence, 237; virtual, 146; and Žižek, 236
Caravaggio, Michelangelo Merisi da, 139, 142
Carey, Benedict, 177
Carney, Jay, 234
Catholic Church, 33
Cavenaugh, Charles, 123
cell phones, 13, 153, 154, 158, 159, 161. See also photography
censorship, 19, 117, 118, 151, 152, 154, 228
Central American immigrants, 26
Cessna, Brian, 54
Chaney, James, 72
Chapman, Dinos, 117
Chapman, Jake, 117
Chechen rebels, 140
Cheney, Dick, 33, 113–114

Chicago, 23
Chicago School, 237
children, 20; and Banksy, 211; and Berman, 170, 171; and DeRidder reenactment, 58; and Flat Daddy, 126; and Harabasz, 140; Iraqi, 44–45, 98, 145, 159, 162, 175, 181; Israeli, 213; Palestinian, 188, 189, 200, 210, 213; rape of, 44, 90, 93; and Schechner, 222–223; and Wodiczko, 38, 40, 41, 42, 45
China, 237
Chinese workers, 144
Chmagh, Saeed, 175
Chomsky, Noam, 234
Christ, 79, 143; Christological imagery, 79, 80
CIA, 112, 115, 156
Cichocki, Sebastian, *A Cookbook for Political Imagination*, 212
Cienfuegos, Ernesto, 93
citizens, 71, 81; and human rights, 6–7; photographs as endangering, 179; of photography, 159; and rape victims, 91; viewers as, 151
citizenship, 29, 46, 80; and Palestinians, 7, 189–190, 196; and photography, 9; of photography, 151; and state, 233; universal, 3
"Citizen Soldier," 55
civilian contractors, 122–125
civil rights era, 49, 75
Clinton, Bill, 27
Cold War, 5, 18
"Collateral Murder" video, 154, 163, 175, 177, 179
Colomina, Beatriz, 21
colonialism, 46, 51, 89, 125, 233; and dehumanization, 90; in Iraq, 113; and Israel, 194, 201, 218
Colonial Williamsburg, 51
Columbus, Christopher, 116–117
communism, 236
Communist International, 5
community: and *homo sacer*, 80; and Internet, 18; and public viewing of torture photos, 106, 111; and rights, 7; and state, 26; and Suskind, 53; and Wodiczko, 30, 32, 35, 43
Confederacy, 58
Confederate flag, 57–58, 121
Confederate History Month, 58
Congress, oversight by, 24
conscientious objectors, 69
Constitution of the United States, 25, 76
consumer culture, 145
Contemporary Art Iraq exhibition, Cornerhouse Art Gallery, Manchester, 118
contractors, American, 13
Cook, Alexander, 60–61, 62
Cook, Greg, 44
Cook, James, 60
corporate America, 28
corporate elite, 146, 147
Cotterrell, David, 13, 125–126, 128–131; *Serial Loop*, 130; *Theater*, 130
counterhegemony, 2, 8, 154, 232
counter-memory, 62–65, 69, 72, 76. *See also* memory
cowboys and Indians, 62
Creative Time, 63

Crewdson, Gregory, 130
Crimean War, 152
Cronenberg, David, 120
Cross of Iron (film), 52
Cuir, Raphael, 20, 28
cultural property, destruction of, 202–203
Cultures of Resistance (film), 184

Darby, Joseph, 86
David, James, 70
David and Goliath, 216
Dead Ringers (film), 120
Debord, Guy, 199
Delahaye, Luc, 10, 154
Deleuze, Gilles, 199
Delgado, Manuel, 33
Deller, Jeremy: *The Battle of Orgreave*, 63; *It Is What It Is: Conversations about Iraq*, 63–64
democracy: and Abdul-Ahad, 151; and Abu Ghraib, 81, 106; and Azoulay, 9; as criminal occupation, 33; and documentary, 2–5; and Gaza, 185; and Gómez-Peña, 121; and Greenfield-Sanders, 139; and homeland security, 23; and human rights, 232; ideals of, 151; and Israeli/Palestinian conflict, 215, 222, 227, 230; and lynching photographs, 108; and Nes, 143; and 9/11 attacks, 235, 238; and photography, 10; and protection of freedoms, 12; and Ray, 237; and reenactment, 48; and state-run hegemony of television, 18; and Wodiczko, 23, 30, 35, 46
Democratic National Convention, August 2008, 69
Democratic Party, 27, 28
Denver, 35
DeRidder, Louisiana, reenactment, 57, 58
desegregation, 73
desert, and Israeli-Palestinian conflict, 204–205
Detroit Institute of Arts, 119
dialectical materialism, 236
Dialectics of Terror, The, exhibition, Chelsea Art Museum, 117–118
Doctors without Borders, 182
Documenta 11, 239n30
documentary image: critically deployed, 8; and state, 8
documentary photography, 155; civil contract of, 8; and politically engaged art, 2; and revolutionary transformation, 5; and state, 10. *See also* photography
documentary practice, 43; and art, 2, 9–11; and democracy, 2–5; as emancipatory representation, 5; imaginative, 46; oppositional, 6; and Wodiczko, 23
domestic sphere/space, 26, 28, 32, 46, 183, 199, 201; militarization of, 12; and Rosler, 147; and war trauma, 37; and Wodiczko, 21, 22
domestic violence, 20, 37–38, 44
Dorsey, George, 72, 73
Dorsey, Mae Murray, 72
Downey, Anthony, 6–7
Downie, Leonard Jr., 90
Dreazen, Yochi, 234, 235
Dred Scott decision, 76
drone porn, 182

Drooker, Eric, 210
Drowning Pool (band), "Bodies," 181
Duchamp, Marcel, 225
due process, 81
Dugan, Joseph, 109
Duganne, Erina, 10, 140, 154
Dunleavy, Dennis, 169

Eagleton, Terry, 237
Eakins, Thomas, *The Gross Clinic*, 130
Earnhardt, Dale Jr., 55
Eastern Side/Abu Dis (video project), 213
East Jerusalem, 188, 205
Edomim, Ma'ale, 205
Edwards, Holly, 140
Egypt, 238
Eilat, Galit, *A Cookbook for Political Imagination*, 222
Eisenman, Stephen, *The Abu Ghraib Effect*, 139, 244n6
enemy combatants, 6, 7, 24, 81
England, Lynndie, 84, 85–87, 89, 101–102
English, Ron, 212
Enhanced Interrogation Techniques (EITs), 99
Enwezor, Okwei, 239–240n30
equality, 46, 73, 233
Eretz Israel, 187
eroticism, 102, 104. See also sexuality
ethnic cleansing, 189, 216
ethnicity, 143. See also Israel
eugenics, 142–143
Exum, Andrew, 182

Facebook, 3, 159
Fahrenheit 9/11 (film), 121
Faile, 212
Faleh, Abdou Hussain Saad, 79
Falklands conflict, 152
Fallujah, 13, 165, 167, 169; and photo of burned Blackwater mercenaries, 122–125
Farmer, James, 58
Fasa'a, Burhan, 123
fashion, 143, 145, 146
Fast, Barbara, 83
Faulkner, Simon, 219
FBI, 191; COINTELPRO, 24
Fein, Clinton, 103–104
feminism, 18, 83, 84, 95, 96, 97, 99, 120. See also women
Fenton, Roger, 152
Fifth Zionist Congress, 193
Filkins, Dexter, 165, 169
Flat Daddies, 126–127
Flat Mommies, 126
Fleischer, Ari, 24
Ford, Henry, 51
Foreign Press Association (FPA), 184
Fort Polk, 172
Foucault, Michel, 7
frame, 132, 174, 232; alternative, 5, 6; as made apparent, 6; official, 151, 152; and production of meaning, 5; and radical critique, 2; and state, 6; structuring of, 1; and war, 1
Free Gaza Movement, 184
French Revolution, 65

Fried, Michael, *Why Photography Matters as Art as Never Before*, 10
Friedman, Milton, 190–191
fruit trees, 195, 205
Fukushima Daiichi, 238
Fulana, "If You Fear Something, You'll See Something," 25
Full Metal Jacket (film), 52
Fusco, Coco, 13, 83, 84, 85, 95–100, 105, 117; *Bare Life Study #1*, 95, 99; *A Field Guide for Female Interrogators*, 96–99; *Operation Atropos*, 95, 99–100; "Our Feminist Future," 96; *A Room of One's Own*, 95, 99; *Two Undiscovered Amerindians Visit . . .*, 116–117

Galerie Lelong, 23
Galindo, Regina José, 13, 112, 247n9; *America's Family Prison*, 116; *Confesión (Confession)*, 112–113, 114–115; *(279) Golpes ([279] Blows)*, 115; *Himenoplastia (Hymenoplasty)*, 247n9; *150,000 Volts*, 116; *Social Cleansing*, 116; *We Don't Lose Anything by Being Born*, 116; *Who Can Erase the Traces?*, 115; *Why Are They Still Free?*, 116
Gandolfini, James, 133, 135
Garcia, René, 119, 121
Gardner, Alexander, 67
Gates, Bill, 233
gays, 24, 49, 142
Gaza, 125, 188, 217, 218; conditions in, 185; and Holocaust, 226; Israeli assault on, 185, 196; Israeli blockade of, 183, 184, 185; as militarized ghetto, 191
Gellhorn, Martha, 152
Geneva Conventions, 80, 81, 156, 203
genocide, 33, 110
Georgia Association of Black Elected Officials, 72
German Social Democrats, 236
Germany, 110; artistic avant garde in, 10
ghost detainees, 6, 81
Gilad Farm settlement, 222
Gilbertson, Ashley, 164–169; *Bedrooms of the Fallen*, 169; *Whiskey Tango Foxtrot*, 165
Gilo, 207, 208
global blogosphere, 18
global community of viewers, 111
Global Feminisms exhibition, 96
global financial collapse of 2008, 238
globalization, 120, 190, 237
global media, 107
Goldman, Francisco, 116
Gómez-Peña, Guillermo, 13, 118, 119, 120, 122, 146; *Corpo/Illicito*, 116; *The Cruci-fiction Project*, 117; *Mapa/Corpo* series, 116; *The Temple of Confessions*, 117; *Two Undiscovered Amerindians Visit . . .*, 116–117
Gone with the Wind (film), 121
Gonzales, Alberto, 24
Goodman, Andrew, 72
Goodrich, Greg, 182
Google Video, 153
Gordon, Philip, 228
Gourevitch, Philip, 79, 86
graffiti, 14, 210–213
Graham, Lindsey, 179

Graner, Charles, 82, 85, 86, 87, 88
Great Depression, 122
Greek sculpture, 142
Greek tragedy, 140
Greene, Susan, 210
Greenfield-Sanders, Timothy, 13, 139; *Dawn Halfaker, First Lt., U.S. Army*, 132–135
Greenfield Village, 51
Greenwald, Glenn, 179, 234
Grimonprez, Johan, 117
Gruiters, Jan, 159
Grusin, Richard, 104–105, 175–176, 177
Guantánamo Bay, 7, 13, 24, 29, 84, 114, 173–174, 241n21
Guatemala, 115
Guatemala City, 115
Guatemalan army, 115, 116
Guatemalans, 26, 115
Guattari, Félix, 199
Guernica, 33–34, 110, 125
guerrilla theater, 69–72
Gulf War (1991), 19, 33, 79, 152, 179
Gush Katif, 217

Haber, John, 20, 29
Haditha, 32, 33
Hague Convention for the Protection of Cultural Property in the Event of Armed Conflict, 202–203
Hague Convention of 1977, 203
Halfaker, Dawn, 132–135
Hall, Ed, 63
Halper, Jeff, 189, 205
Halperin, Lior, 253n106
Hamas, 184
Hamza, Abeer, 93, 245n29
Harabasz, Ewa, 139–140; *Untitled*, 140
Hargreaves, Roger, 161
Hariman, Robert, 34, 160, 239n23; *No Caption Needed*, 139
Harmon, Sabrina, 79, 82, 84, 87–88
Harrison, Loy, 73
Hatoum, Mona, 228
Hawajri, Mohammed al-, 195; *Cactus Borders*, 196
Heartfield, John, 145
Heller, Eytan, 213–214
Helmand Province, 128
heritage museums, 51
Herman, Judith, 36; *Trauma and Recovery*, 35
heroes/heroism, 52, 54, 81; and Berman, 132, 136; fantasies of, 36; and foundational crimes, 226; and Halfaker, 133, 134, 135; as staged, 2
Heroes on a Stick, 126
Hersh, Seymour, 32, 90
Herzl, Theodor, 225–226
heterosexuality, 59, 142
Hewitt, Hayden, 180
Hicks, Tyler, 67
high-resolution quality, 104, 105
hillbilly defense, 87
Hinckley, John, 52–53
Hippocrates, 128
Hiroshima, 125
Hirsh, Michael, 156
Hitchens, Christopher, 246n59

Hitler, Adolf, 121, 220, 223–226, 253n102
Holder, Eric, 234
Holocaust, 14, 142, 215, 216–227
Holocaust Remembrance Day, 224
Holzer, Jenny, 117
homeland security, 23, 174, 183, 190, 191. See also under United States
homelessness, 35, 36, 39, 44
homoeroticism, 50, 142, 143
homo sacer, 6, 75–76, 80, 120, 235
homosexuality, 142
Hooded Man, 79–81
Horwitz, Tony, *Confederates in the Attic*, 57
Howard, John, 59, 86
human rights, 6–7, 120, 161, 188, 232–238. See also rights
Human Rights Watch, 201
Human Subjects Committee, 100
Hurricane Katrina, 155
Hussein, Saddam, 2, 39, 108, 145, 156, 161, 162, 165, 234

Ickowicz, Gaston Zvi, 222; *Settlement* series, 217–219
Idea Generation Gallery, London, 169
IKV Pax Christi (organization), 159
il Cane, Erica, 212
illegal combatant, 233
Imaginary Coordinates exhibition, 228
immigrants, 17, 19, 24, 117, 120, 121, 122; deportation of, 27, 29; from Iraq and Afghanistan, 172; and law, 25–26, 27; Middle Eastern, 28; and Nes, 144; remittances of, 27; South American, 27; and war on terror, 19–23; and Wodiczko, 21, 22, 23, 25–30; as workers, 28–29
imperialism, 46, 89, 99, 145, 233
imperial presidency, 28
Inconvenient Evidence exhibition, 105, 108, 109, 110
Indians, 61–62
Insect, Paul, 212
Institute of Contemporary Art, Boston, 39
International Center of Photography (ICP), 13, 105, 108, 109, 110
International Committee of the Red Cross, 164
International Gothic style, 139
International Style, 23
International Women's Peace Service, 210
Internet, 17, 97, 103, 107, 186, 188; Abu Ghraib images on, 104, 105, 109, 110; and "America's Army," 177; and censorship, 3, 4, 250n15; and "Collateral Murder," 179; global blogosphere of, 18; Israelis assaulting Palestinians on, 103; and *Mavi Marmara* incident, 183; military videos on, 180, 182; pornographic sites on, 13, 90, 93; and Wodiczko, 31, 35. See also social networking websites; YouTube
internment camps, 7
interrogation, 84, 85, 95–96, 114, 156. See also Abu Ghraib
interrogation courses, 97–98
Iraq: American occupation of, 111, 124; and Deller, 63; and embedded photographers, 13–14, 152, 164–170; invasion of, 112, 118;

Iraq (*continued*)
  kidnappers and coroners in, 161; and Lê, 68; and military recruitment, 56, 57; occupation of, 32, 44, 125; psychiatric hospitals in, 162; and Rosler, 146; survival of wounded in, 128; and unembedded photographers, 154–158, 161–164; and Wodiczko, 31, 33, 40, 42, 44, 46
Iraqi artists, 118
Iraqi insurgency, 124, 154, 156, 165, 167
Iraqi military, deaths of, 44
Iraqi prisoners, 89, 96; considered other, 104; families and community of, 82; sexual assaults on, 89–95, 96; torture and abuse of, 3; and van Kesteren, 157. *See also* Abu Ghraib
Iraqi refugees, 158, 159, 161
Iraqis/Iraqi civilians, 63, 98–99, 154, 156, 177; brutalization of, 156; and cell phones, 158, 161; and chat groups, 159; and corpses in Fallujah, 123–124; deaths of, 44, 79, 125, 128, 155; experiences of, 71; helicopter strafing of, 163–164; and July 2007 American helicopter attack, 175, 178, 179; orphaned, 145; revolt against British, 125; senseless slaughter of, 19; and unembedded journalists, 154; unnamed bodies of, 108; and van Kesteren, 156–157, 159; vernacular photographs by, 14, 158–159; and Wodiczko, 12, 42, 44, 46
Iraqi women, 89, 156, 163; assaults on, 13, 82, 89, 92, 93; and Wodiczko, 40, 41
Iraq Veterans against the War (IVAW), 12, 13, 69–72, 244n63
Iraq war, 17, 31, 44, 46, 64, 69, 72, 112–113, 118, 121, 122, 145, 152, 155; and Abu Ghraib, 79; American press coverage of, 64; count of wounded American soldiers in, 135; soldiers' filming of, 180; staging for camera in, 2; and video games, 176, 182
Israel, 27, 39, 125, 203, 204; as apartheid state, 190; attack on Gaza, 185; blockade of Gaza, 183, 184, 185; and counterterrorism, 191; and cult of fallen, 216; as democracy and occupying power, 222; destruction of buildings by, 199–201, 202–203; economy of, 190, 191; founding of, 223; and Green Line, 205, 207, 216; Jewish ethnic minorities within, 142; as Jewish ethnocracy, 185, 189, 215, 227, 230; and Jewish identity, 194; and Jewish victimization, 216; and landscape of war, 186–188; and macho sabra stereotype, 142; and *Mapa/Corpo*, 121; national borders of, 187; and Nes, 142–144; and Palestinian artists, 227–228; policy of dispossession and transfer, 189, 205; as prison, 143–144; and rocket fire into, 184; and security and surveillance systems, 191; security in, 205–206; and Separation or Barrier Wall, 14, 188–189, 191, 194, 196, 205–216, 217; and strike on *Mavi Marmara*, 183–185; transfer of Palestinians out of, 216; and two-state solution, 230; and war of 1948, 186, 194, 195, 201, 203, 216; and war of 1967, 216; and West Bank settlements, 187, 188. *See also* post-Zionism
Israeli artists, 187
Israeli Committee Against House Demolitions (ICAHD), 189, 205

Israeli Defense Forces (IDF), 183–184, 199, 202, 205, 206, 217
Israeli government, 183
Israeli military, 13, 102–103, 203; and Banksy, 212; and Holocaust, 226; and Kremer, 196, 198; and Nes, 142–143; and swarming strategy, 200–201; training camps of, 203–205; and wall holes, 199–201, 202
Israeli-Palestinian conflict: and Holocaust, 222; and land, 186–190; and land as metaphor for people, 186; and Nes, 143–144; and Separation or Barrier Wall, 14, 188–189, 191, 194, 196, 205–216, 217; and trees, 192–196, 205. *See also* Palestinians
Israeli settlements, 187–188, 189, 190, 191, 193, 194, 205, 210, 217–218
Israel/Palestine, 14, 102, 122, 183–231

Jaar, Alfredo, 10
Jacir, Emily, 228, 229–230, 231; *Crossing Surda (A Record of Going to and from Work)*, 229–230
Jackson, Robert, 235
Jacobson, Colin, 152, 153
Jakary, Susan, 119
Jamadi, Manadel al-, 81–82
Jefferson, Thomas, 40
Jerusalem, 190, 193, 207, 208, 209, 210, 211, 214
Jewish diaspora, 142
Jewish Federation of Metropolitan Chicago, 228
Jewish Museum, New York, 142, 223
Jewish National Fund, 193
Jewish settlements, 190
Jewish United Fund, 228
Jews: as persecuted victims and exiles, 226; and Poland, 220–221; Soviet, 191. *See also* Israel
Jirza, Jassin, 158
Johnson, Shoshana, 88
journalists, 63; aboard *Mavi Marmara*, 184; controlled movement of, 19; embedded, 151, 152, 155; Gonzales's intimidation of, 24; as government spies, 162; neutrality of, 152; in Palestine Hotel, 170. *See also* photojournalism
Judea, 186

Kafri, Nir, *Balata Refugee Camp*, 202
Kahlo, Frida, 120
Karpinski, Janis, 83
Keane, John, 11
Keeser, Dorothea, 118
Kelly's Heroes (film), 52
Khalid Mohammed, 122
Khatib, Ghassan, 103
Kheiber, Faleh, 169–170
Khmer Rouge, 110
Khudairi, Tala, 43
Killen, Edgar Ray, 72
Kimmelman, Michael, "Photos Return, This Time As Art," 108
King, Rodney, 4, 110
Kirshenblatt-Gimblett, Barbara, 228–229
Klein, Naomi, 190, 191–192, 237; *The Shock Doctrine*, 115
Kline, Renee, 136–138
Kochavi, Aviv, 201, 202
Korean War, 49, 79, 151; No Gun Ri massacre, 32

Koster, Samuel, 32
Kotzen, Michael, 228
Kratsman, Miki, 206–208, 222, 226; *Abu Dis*, 214–215; *Displaced*, 206; *Gilo 1*, 207–208; *Gilo 2*, 208; *Nablus #2*, 200, 203; *Panoramas of Occupation*, 206, 207; *Road 443 #9*, 206; *Road 443 #12*, 206; *Targeted Killing*, 206; *Territory* series, 217
Kremer, Shai, 215; *Infected Landscape* series, 196, 198–199, 204–205; *Interior, Urban Warfare Training Center, Tze'elim*, 199–200, 203; *Separation Wall, Jerusalem*, 196
Krytyka Polityczna (magazine), 220
Kubrick, Stanley, 52
Ku Klux Klan, 73, 75, 121
Kuper, Roi, *Necropolis*, 203–204
Kurdish refugees, 165

La Caja Blanca, 114
Lacan, Jacques, 225
Lady Gaga, "Telephone," 181
Landau, Sigalit, 228, 230, 231; *Barbed Hula*, 230; *Day Done*, 230; *DeadSee*, 230
Latin America, 115
Lê, An-My, 12–13, 65–69, 172, 244n56; *Small Wars*, 66–68; *29 Palms*, 68–69, 244n56; *Việt Nam*, 66
League of Palestinian Artists, 227–228
Lee, Iara, 184
Leistner, Rita, 162–163; *Unembedded*, 161–164
Lemon Tree (film), 194–195
Lenin, V. I., 236
Leonardo da Vinci, 142
lesbianism, 88
Levac, Alex, 193
Levin, Meyer, 243n47
Levin, Mikael, 243n47
liberal capitalist state, 132, 235
liberals/liberalism, 34, 82, 233, 237
liberal state, 14, 80
Libya, war in, 95
Lieberman, Joe, 179
Littlefield, John, 107
Liveleaks.com, 180
Liverpool, England, 36–37
Lives of Others, The (film), 22
Livestream, 184
living history, 47, 51, 62, 64
London, 24; bombings, 23, 26
Looking at Life exhibition, 109
Lott, Eric, 73
Love Sum Game (film), 213–214
Lucaites, John Louis, 34, 239n23; *No Caption Needed*, 139
Luftwaffe, 110
Luna, Violeta, 119–120, 121
Lütticken, Sven, 62, 65
Lynch, Jessica, 87
lynching photographs, 105, 106, 124; exhibition of, 107–108, 109–110
lynchings, 80, 106; and Abu Ghraib photos, 111; reenactment of, 72–76

Madonna figure, 139, 140
Madrid train bombing, 23
Malcolm, Dorothy, 72

Malcolm, Roger, 72, 73
Mann, Sally, 10
Mansour, Suleiman, 212
Mapa/Corpo 3: Interactive Rituals for the New Millennium performance, 118–122
Marine Air Ground Combat Center, 29 Palms, California, 68
Martin Luther King Jr. National Historic Site, 107
Marxism, 84
Masada, 216
masculinity/manliness, 12; as ideal of soldier, 88; and identity, 72; and male bonding, 50; and military culture, 86; and military recruitment, 56, 57, 59; and Nes, 142, 143; and war experience, 36; and war reenactment, 50, 52, 53, 54
Mas'ha, 210
Mason, Carol, 87
Mass, celebration of, 80
Matta-Clark, Gordon, 199
Mavi Marmara (ship), 183–185
Maya groups, 26
McCarthy era, 24, 29
McDonnell, Robert, 58–59
McVeigh, Timothy, 25–26, 59
"Medal of Honor" (video game), 182
media, 17; and Abu Ghraib photos, 109; and artistic images, 154; attempts to control, 19; and blacking out coverage of American atrocities, 19; digital, 2, 82, 89, 104, 114, 153, 163, 175; and failure to control visual field, 153; and Fusco, 95; and Harabasz, 140; and Iraq Veterans against the War, 71, 72; and Jessica Lynch, 87; and Johnson, 88; and Lê, 68, 69; and Lynndie England, 85–87; mass, 18, 21; and military control, 169; and ongoing effects of Iraq war, 125; and private and public, 18; and rape images, 82; and Sergewa, 95; and technology, 18, 29; television, 18, 21, 183; and tortured body images, 106, 107; and war experience, 151; and Wodiczko, 17, 19, 21, 22, 23, 29, 34, 35, 39. *See also* technology
mediality, 13, 104–105, 161, 175, 177
Meiselas, Susan, 154
Melinn, Lisa, 119
memory, 69, 75, 202; American, 68; collective, 62; and Cotterrell, 130; destruction of cultural, 203; and Galindo, 114; of Holocaust, 226; and Israel, 142; and Lê, 66, 68; official, 62–63, 215; public, 106; and reenactment, 49, 51, 52, 64, 75; social and political, 114; and Wodiczko, 44. *See also* counter-memory; nostalgia
Menuhin, Yishai, 103
Mercy Housing Colorado, 35
Metropolitan Transit Authority. *See* New York City
Mexicans, 26–27
Mexico, 118
Michelangelo, 142
Middle Ages, 139
middle class, 21, 57
migrant laborers, 6
Milgram Experiment, 100
militarism, 3, 51, 54, 55, 132, 152, 180

militarization, 29, 151; and Berman, 170; of campus life, 83; of civil society, 30; of domestic society, 51; of domestic space, 12, 18, 39; of homefront, 183; of homeland, 12, 21; and Rosler, 145; of society, 12, 30; of U.S./Mexican border, 27; and van Kesteren, 157; and Wodiczko, 21, 22

military: conquest by, 94; and damage to cultural property, 203; history of, 51; institutions of, 103; medical staff of, 125–126; systemic problems in, 85; women in, 13, 82, 83, 88, 96, 99, 100

military, U.S., 59, 177; and Abu Ghraib photographs, 4, 82; as archetypal, 81; and Berman, 172; and civil community, 32; culpability of, 88, 111; internalized prevailing ethos of, 102; and July 2007 American helicopter attack in Baghdad, 175, 178, 179; and killing of civilians, 32–33; and Kremer, 196, 198; medical personnel of, 127–128; patriarchal ethos of, 87; and predator drones, 181–182; and Rosler, 147; service in, 45; videos by, 180; videos of operations of, 3–4; women in, 97, 99, 100. *See also* Israeli military; soldiers; United States

military families, 35, 36, 38, 126–127, 136, 138–139
military recruitment, 13, 36, 55–57, 72, 81, 83, 171, 177–178, 180, 181
military reserves, 38
military technology, 13, 21
military training camps, 172–173, 196, 198, 203–205
military wives, 37–38
Miller, Lee, 154
Miller, Zoriah, 168
Milliard, Geoff, 70
Minelli, Filippo, 212
Mirroring Evil exhibition, 223
Mitchell, W.J.T., 79; *Cloning Terror*, 139
Mizrahim, 142, 216
"Modern Warfare" (video game), 176, 177
"Modern Warfare 2" (video game), 182
Mohammed, 80
Moore, Bret A., 177
Moore's Ford, Quadruple Lynching Reenactment at, 72–76
morality/ethics, 30, 32, 67, 100, 101, 105, 106, 108, 117
Mormons, as interrogators, 97
Morris, Errol, 85, 87; *Standard Operating Procedure*, 101
Moses, 79
Mosse, George, 52
Mosul, 165
Museum of Contemporary Art (Los Angeles), 96
Museum of Modern Art (MoMA) (New York), 5, 110
Museum of the History of Polish Jews (Warsaw), 220
Muslims, 21, 24; constructed as "aliens," 27; constructed as "terrorists," 90; and grievable crimes, 90; torture of, 13, 81, 83, 89; and Violeta Luna, 119; and Wodiczko, 40
Muthaffar, Enas, 228, 231; *A World Apart within 15 Minutes*, 229

My Lai massacre, 32–33, 66, 109

NAACP, 57, 58
Nablus, 200, 202, 203; Kasbah, 201
Nachtwey, James, 67, 154
NAFTA, 26
Nagasaki, 125
Najaf, 161, 162
Nakba (catastrophe), 186, 195
Nakhoul, Samia, 169–170
NASCAR, 56, 180
national cohesion, 133
national community, 151
National Guard, 38, 54, 55–57, 69, 81
national identity, 1, 12, 44, 91, 208
nationalism, 46, 56, 111, 143, 152, 230
national mythologies, 226
NATO, 181
Nazis, 7, 50, 110, 121, 145, 221, 236
neocolonialism, 118, 147, 190
neoconservatism, 89, 237
neoliberalism, 115, 237
neo-Zionism, 216
Nes, Adi, 13, 141–145; *Untitled* (1996), 142–143; *Untitled* (2003), from series *Prisoners*, 143
Neshat, Shirin, 120
Neuen Gesellschaft fuer Bildende Kunst, 226
New Barbarian, 120
New Museum, 63
New York City, Metropolitan Transit Authority (MTA), 23, 24, 25, 240–241n20
New-York Historical Society, 107
New York Post, "Fight Terror, Speak English," 25
9/11 attacks, 11, 69, 238; and dead bin Laden image, 233, 234, 235; and Fusco, 83; and global war on terrorism, 17, 18; and Homeland Security, 170; patriotic fervor after, 83; and photography, 155; and La Pocha Nostra, 116; and surveillance, 39; and Wodiczko, 23, 29
1948 war, Israel/Palestine, 194, 195, 201, 203, 216
1967 war, Israel/Palestine, 207, 216
No Gun Ri massacre, 32
"Noor" (pseud.), 93
Noor-Eldeen, Namir, 175
nostalgia, 47, 49, 51, 64, 139, 198. *See also* memory
Nuaimi, Huda Shaker al-, 246n43

Obama, Barack, 59, 91, 107, 234
Obama administration, 24, 28, 79, 82, 90–91, 179, 233
Obeidi, Iman al-, 95
O'Brien, Conan, 178
Occupied Territories, 191, 216, 217. *See also* Palestinians
Ohio Department of Homeland Security, 23
Oklahoma City bombing, 25–26
olive trees, 193, 194, 195, 205
Olujimi, Kambui, 96
O'Neill, Jim, 42
On the Subject of War exhibition, 158
Operational Theory Research Institute (OTRI), 199
"Operation First Casualty" (OFC), 70
Operation Rapid American Withdrawal, 70

Ophir, Gilad, 215; *Necropolis*, 203–204
Opton, Suzanne: *Soldier*, 135–136; *Soldier Billboard Project*, 135–136
Orthodox Church (Nablus), 203
Orwell, George, *1984*, 25
Oslo Accords of 1993, 190
O'Sullivan, Timothy, 67
Ottoman Caravanserai, of al-Wakalh al-Farroukkyyeh, 203
Ottoman Land Code, Article 78, 193–194

Pacbot, 178
Paik, Nam June, 18
Pakistani civilians, 182
Palestine, Occupation of, 183, 190, 195, 198, 206, 215, 230
Palestine Hotel, 170
Palestinian artists, 14, 227–229
Palestinian Intifadas, 191, 202, 207, 215, 217, 227
Palestinian labor, 191
Palestinian land: and Separation or Barrier Wall, 188–189; and West Bank settlements, 187–188
Palestinian prisoners, 102, 143
Palestinian refugees, 185, 190, 202, 216
Palestinians, 103, 177, 185, 253n102; agriculture of, 189, 193, 194, 205; attacks on innocent Israeli civilians by, 216; and B'Tselem, 188; and Butler, 186; and citizenship, 7, 189–190, 196; destruction of buildings of, 199–201, 202–203; destruction of homes of, 190, 200, 201, 205, 217; destruction of orchards of, 217; economic life of, 191; as foreign intruders, 195; general exit permit of, 184; and Green Line, 207, 216; and Holocaust, 217, 226; identity of, 194; industry and infrastructure of, 205; and Israeli residency status, 209; and Kremer, 196, 198; and landscape of war, 187; mass dispossession and displacement of, 189, 195; medical assistance for, 215; objectification of, 102; peasant or *fellahin*, 194; as persecuted victims and exiles, 226; and right of return, 190, 220, 222; and rights, 7; self-determination of, 190; and Separation or Barrier Wall, 14, 188–189, 191, 194, 196, 205–216, 217; as shepherds, 193; statelessness of, 7; and trade, 191; and transfer out of Israel, 216; and two-state solution, 230; video cameras for, 188; violence against, 188, 189, 193; and wall holes, 199–201, 202; and war of 1948, 186, 194, 201, 216; and West Bank settlements, 187–188. *See also* Israeli-Palestinian conflict
Palestinian workers, 192, 194
Palma de Mallorca, "Night of Art," 112, 114
Pappé, Ilan, 215–216
Paradox (production company), 158
Paris World's Fair of 1939, 110
Parry, John T., 46, 233
Parry, William, 211
Pasolini, Pier Paolo, 142
past, 13, 52, 75, 80, 81
Patai, Raphael, *The Arab Mind*, 89
Paths of Glory (film), 52
Patriot, The (film), 243n24

patriotism, 12, 36, 47, 50, 51, 54, 83, 132, 151
Pearl, Daniel, 125
Peloponnesian War, 128
Peres, Shimon, 190
Peress, Gilles, 67, 154
performance/the performative: and Berman, 170; and documentary practice, 2, 232; and Fusco, 13, 95, 96, 99; and Galindo, 13, 112–113, 114, 115, 116; and Gómez-Peña, 116, 117, 118, 119–122; and Israel, 14, 214; and Iraq Veterans against the War, 13, 70, 71, and lynching reenactment, 73; and Wodiczko, 22, 34
Phelan, Peggy, 52–53
photographers: embedded, 13–14, 164–170; identification with soldiers, 152; independent, 154; perspective of, 155
photographic realism, 5
photographic objectivity, 6, 154, 155, 167, 174; transparency, 155
Photographs from S-21: 1975–1979 exhibition, 110
photography, 66, 67, 68; amateur, 104, 109, 114, 153, 155, 161; of atrocities, 110; and citizenship, 9, 151; and democracy, 10, 108; and documentary, 2, 9–11; as endangering soldiers or civilians, 179; fine art, 10, 154; of flag-draped coffins, 79; of homefront, 170–175; by Iraqis, 14; low resolution, 13, 103, 104, 161; as mediated and framed, 174; and 9/11 attacks, 155; potential violence of, 9; by soldiers, civilians, insurgents, and refugees, 153, 161; staging for, 2; and state, 10, 154; and technology, 153; trophy, 82; and universal citizenship, 9; and violence, 9; and vulnerability of photographed persons, 9; war, 127, 152–153. *See also* Abu Ghraib photographs; cell phones; documentary photography; lynching photographs
photojournalism, 13, 139, 151–152, 154, 155, 239n23. *See also* journalists
photomontage, 145, 146
Physicians for Human Rights, 99
Picasso, Pablo, *Guernica*, 33–34, 110
pietà, 139, 143
pine trees, 193, 194
Pippi Longstocking (fictional character), 214
Platoon (film), 52
PlayStation, 178
Plimouth Plantation, 51
Pocha Nostra, La, 13, 116, 118
Poland, 220–221
pope, image of, 80
pornography, 13, 81, 90, 92, 93, 94, 104. *See also* sexuality
poststructuralism, 199
posttraumatic stress disorder (PTSD), 34, 36, 37, 44–45, 128, 169
post-Zionism, 215–216, 223, 226–227
Prisoner of War Interrogation Resistance Program, 96
private space, 17, 18, 183
Prividera, Laura, 59, 86
Puar, Jasbir K., 89, 245n31
public images, 139
public institutions, 111
public opinion, 151

public sphere, 8, 17, 18, 39, 46, 154, 183, 232; acknowledgment of racial violence in, 108; counterhegemonic, 2, 8, 154; defined, 18, 151; display of photos in, 111; expansion of, 4–5; grieving in, 106, 111; Levinasian, 8–9; transnational, 27; and universal citizen, 3; and van Kesteren, 157, 159; and Wodiczko, 21, 22, 23; working-class, 5
public testimony, 29
public viewing, 106

Qaddafi, Muammar el-, 95
Qalandia checkpoint, 211
Qalqilia, 206–207

Rabin, Yitzhak, 190
race, 57–62, 73, 76, 83, 88
racism, 21, 58, 61, 76
Rancière, Jacques, 7–8
rape, 36, 105, 116, 245n29; of American women in military, 91–92; and Fusco, 96; images of, 105; of Iraqi children, 44, 90, 93; of Iraqi women, 13, 92; suppressed image of, 13, 81, 82, 85, 89–95. *See also* torture and abuse; violence; women
Rashad Psychiatric Hospital, Baghdad, 162
Ray, Gene, 215, 237
Reagan, Ronald, 52–53
Red Cross, 81
reenactments, 66; authenticity of, 48, 59–61; and connection with past, 64; fallacy of, 104; and film and life, 53; individual experience of, 50; and lack of death, 54; and Lê, 65–68; as loosely scripted or unscripted, 49–50; of lynchings, 72–76; motivations for, 47; political, 47; and self-reflexivity, 62; and simulated atrocities, 52; of Stanford Prison Experiment, 100; of torture, 112; of war, 12–13, 47–72, 180
refugee camps, 7, 188, 198, 201, 202, 217
refugees, 6, 44, 155
Reinhardt, Mark, 11, 140, 141
religion, 80
religious images, 139, 141
Rembrandt, *The Anatomy Lecture of Dr. Tulp*, 130
rendition, 24, 28, 112, 114
Reno, Janet, 103
Republican National Convention (2008), 136
Republican Party, 27, 28
Reuters news agency, 13, 175, 178, 179
Revolutionary War, 55
Ribalta, Jorge, 3, 4, 5, 10
Rice, Condoleezza, 83
Richards, Eugene, 154
Riefenstahl, Leni, 220, 224
rights: and bin Laden, 235; and civil rights movement, 73; and community, 7; democratic, 5, 23, 30, 46, 238; denial of, 81, 233; and Gaza, 185; and *homo sacer*, 76, 80; and Hooded Man, 83; of immigrant workers, 27; and Iraq Veterans against the War, 71; to look, 106–107; and Palestinians, 7; and political invisibility, 46; and public sphere of documentary practices, 151, 232; as restricting and liberating, 233; and Wodiczko, 21. *See also* human rights
Riklis, Eran, 194–195

Ríos Montt, José Efraín, 115
Rivera, Diego, *Detroit Industry* murals in Rivera Court, 121, 122
Road to Guantánamo, The (film), 121
Robertson, Geoffrey, 235
Rockefeller, John D., 51
Rosen, Rhoda, 228
Rosen, Roee, 226; *Live and Die as Eva Braun* installation, 223–224
Rosler, Martha, 8, 71, 145–147; *Bringing the War Back Home: House Beautiful*, 145; *Bringing the War Back Home* series, 145; *Invasion*, 146–147; *Photo Op*, 146; *Saddam's Palace (Febreze)*, 145–146
Roth Horowitz art gallery, 107
Rotterdam Fotomuseum, 158
Rovner, Michal, 228
Rumsfeld, Donald, 33, 82, 90, 91, 165, 166
Russia, 238; artistic avant garde of, 10
Russian Revolution, 65, 236–237

sabr (cactus), 196
sabra (Israeli Jew), 142, 145, 196
sacred life, 80, 140
sacred space, 119
sadism, 94, 96, 100
Sagiv, Oren, 213
Salem witch trials, 24
Salgado, Sebastião, 154
Salsaa, Wissam, 212
Sam3, 212
Samaria, 186
San Francisco, "See Something? Say Something!" program, 23
Santa's Ghetto, 210
Sarracino, Carmine, 93, 94
Saving Private Ryan (film), 243n24
Schapiro, Meyer, 80
Schechner, Alan, 222–223, 226; *Bar Code to Concentration Camp Morph*, 223; *The Legacy of Abused Children*, 222–223; *Self-Portrait at Buchenwald: It's the Real Thing*, 223
Schiesel, Seth, 176, 182
Schlander, Tanja, 214
Schmidt, Helmut, 234
Schwab, Eric, 243n47
Schwerner, Michael, 72
Scott, Kevin, 93, 94
Sekula, Allan, 8
Sephardic Jews, 216
SERE (Survival, Evasion, Resistance, Escape), 96, 99
Sergewa, Seham, 95
Serra, Richard: Hooded Man lithographs, 110–111; *Stop Bush and Stop B S*, 111
Serrano, Andres, 10
sexual assault, 89–95, 96. *See also* rape; torture and abuse
sexuality, 13, 73, 84. *See also* eroticism; pornography
sexual pathology, 104
sexual sadism, 104
Sfard, Michael, 227
Shalit, Gilad, 184
Sharon, Ariel, 207, 226

Ship, The (BBC historical reenactment), 60
Shor, Shirley, 228
Shulman, David, 185
Siegel, Ty, 136–138
Sierakowski, Slawomir, 220
Sifuentes, Roberto, 119, 120, 121; *The Cruci-fiction Project*, 117; *The Temple of Confessions*, 117
Silas, Susan, 243n47
Silicio, Tami, 155
Simon, Roger, 110
Sims, Christopher, 14, 172; *Guantánamo Bay*, 173–174; *Hearts and Minds*, 180, 181; *Jihad Lamp, Fort Polk, Louisiana*, 173; *Mosque, Camp Mackall, Louisiana*, 173; *Mother with Babies, Fort Polk, Louisiana*, 173; *Theater of War*, 173; *Village Residence, Fort Polk, Louisiana*, 173
Singer, Peter, 177–178
slavery, 58–59, 61, 76, 157
Slocum, David, 151
Slome, Manon, 118
Smith, W. Eugene, 154
Snodgrass, Susan, 228
social class, 84, 114, 145, 236, 237
social networking websites, 3, 158. *See also* YouTube
Sokol, Brett, 54
soldiers, U.S., 106; and Abu Ghraib photos, 82, 89, 109, 154; and Berman, 171; and death in Iraq, 32; and Gilbertson, 166; injured and traumatized, 44, 46; in Iraq, 71; Iraqi women raped by, 13; and Iraq Veterans against the War, 69; mental condition of, 104; in Mogadishu, 123; multiple redeployments of older, 38; official count of wounded in Iraq, 135; and Opton, 135–136; photographers' identification with, 152; photographs as endangering, 179; photos by, 153; and rape, 245n29; and reenactment, 50, 56; and Rosler, 145; tombs of unknown, 33; torture and abuse by, 84; and van Kesteren, 156–157; and video games, 177; videos of, 3–4, 153, 180, 181; and Wodiczko, 31–32, 33, 34, 43; women as, 13, 82, 83. *See also* military, U.S.; United States; warrior
soldiers, British, 37–38, 113, 245n25
Sontag, Susan, 90, 105; *Regarding the Pain of Others*, 11
Soros, George, 233
South African Bantustans, 191–192
South Carolina, 58
Southerners, 73
Spanish Civil War, 33–34
Spanish Inquisition, 113
Spertus Museum (Chicago), 228
Spyropoulos, Theodore, 38
Stalinism, 29, 45, 236
Stallabrass, Julian, 113, 114, 115
Stanford Prison Experiment, 100
state: arbitrary and violent power of, 200; and Azoulay, 159; bureaucratic, 23; and capitalism, 8, 232; and citizenship, 233; and community, 26; construction of subject by, 30; control by, 17; criticism of, 232; democratic, 23; and derealization of war's effects, 46; discourse of responsibility of, 132; and documentary image, 8; and documentary photography, 10; documentary practice of, 4; efforts to control images of war, 79, 106; and embedded journalists, 152; as framing meaning, 6; and Greenfield-Sanders, 139; and *homo sacer*, 80; and human rights, 232; and images, 1; images as serving interests of, 232; injunction to spy on behalf of, 24; liberal, 14, 80; liberal capitalist, 132, 235; and morality in warfare, 110; and New Deal era, 4; people as eyes and ears of repressive apparatus of, 30; police, 8, 28, 29; and political invisibility, 46; prohibition and control of photographic technologies by, 154; repression by, 45; and Rosler, 145; security of, 8; and television, 18; as valorizing Israeli dominance, 103; veterans abandoned by, 34; violence of paternalistic, 232; and warrior archetype, 59; and Weizman, 203; and Wodiczko, 21, 22, 24
state of exception, 6, 7, 71, 200
states, and homeland security industry, 174
States' Rights Party (Dixiecrats), 73
Stone, Geoffrey, 24
Storming of the Bastille reenactment, 65
Storming of the Winter Palace in Petrograd reenactment, 65
Strauss, David Levi, 141
Suellentrop, Chris, 182
suicide, 44
suicide bombers, 190, 210
Supreme Court, 76
surveillance, 17, 21, 22, 26, 27, 28, 39; technology of, 12, 17–18, 29, 183
Suskind, Ron, 53
Swoon, 212

tableaux vivants, 13, 119, 122
Tagg, John, 4, 8, 132, 133
Taguba, Antonio, 91; Taguba Report, 91
Taher, Mantador, 127–128
Taliban, 182
Talmadge, Eugene, 73, 74
Tamari, Vera, 227–228
Tartakover, David, "Season Greetings from the Middle East," 192–193
Taxi Driver (film), 52
Taylor, John, 11
Team Delta, 95, 96
Tea Party movement, 59
technology, 39, 161; counterterrorism, 191; digital, 5, 79, 146, 153–154, 175, 180–181; and media, 18, 21, 29; military, 13, 21, 180–181; portable and nomadic, 39; and Rosler, 145, 146, 147; surveillance, 12, 17–18, 29, 183; video, 22, 183; of war, 21, 29, 35; and war photography, 153; and Wodiczko, 21. *See also* media
Tel-Hai, legend of, 216
terrorism: Arabs and Muslims constructed as practitioners of, 90; and Bush administration, 7; and *Dialectics of Terror* exhibition, 117–118; global war on, 17; and homeland security industry, 174; and Hooded Man, 80; and immigrants, 27, 28, 29; and Israel, 191; and rights, 233; and Rosler, 145; as tactic and not enemy, 27, 29; war on, 21, 22, 26, 29, 183, 186, 238; and Wodiczko, 27, 28, 29, 30, 33

Terry, Jennifer, 180, 181
Thatcher, Margaret, 152
Thomas, Alan, 167, 169
Thompson, Jenny, 51, 52, 55; *War Games*, 47–48
3 Doors Down (band), 55
Three Cities against the Wall exhibition, 213
Tiananmen Square massacre, 237
torture and abuse: acceptance and normalization of, 96; of Arabs and Muslims as terrorists, 90, 90; banned visual documentation of, 82; and bin Laden killing, 247n5; Bush administration justification of, 25, 114; and citizen's human rights, 6; and Democrats and Republicans, 28; and Fallujah, 125; and Fein, 104; and Fusco, 84, 85, 97; and Galindo, 13, 112, 113, 114, 115; and Geneva Convention, 81; and Hitchens, 246n59; images of, 105, 106, 111; of Iraqi children, 44; and *Mapa/Corpo*, 122; and military prison environment, 100; by Nazis, 110; nonaccountability for, 84, 91; as part of government policy, 32; and pornography, 81, 92; of power, 29; punishment for, 84; as redefined, 25; sexual, 89, 96; U.S. government redefinition of, 82; in videos on Internet, 3; and waterboarding, 97, 112, 113–114, 246n59, 247n5; by women soldiers, 13, 82–83; and zones of indistinction, 7. *See also* Abu Ghraib; violence
training camps. *See* military training camps
trauma, 39, 66; and Cotterrell, 126, 128; and counter-memory, 62; and domestic sphere, 37; and Fusco, 96, 99, 100; and Iraq Veterans against the War, 70, 71; and landscape of war, 186, 187; and military medical personnel, 127; and Opton, 135–136; and reenactment, 47, 51, 55, 64, 75, 76; and Rosler, 145; and Wodiczko, 21, 32, 34, 35–36, 37, 38, 39, 42, 43, 44, 45, 46
Trotsky, Leon, 236
Trotskyism, 236
Truman, Harry S., 235
Tulkarem, 206–207
Tuol Sleng death camp, 110
Turkey, 185
Turner, Dan, 97
Turner, Rory, 58, 59
Tze'elim training camp, 196, 198

United Kingdom/Great Britain, 28, 51, 113, 118, 121, 245n25
United Nations, 120–121, 156, 210, 218
United Nations Security Council, 185
United States, 17, 33, 44, 71, 80, 118, 120–121, 151; anti-immigrant law of 1996, 25–26; as arrogant and repressive, 30; and Berman, 170; Constitution, 121; Department of Defense, 182; Department of Homeland Security, 118, 170, 171, 174; Department of Justice, 114; "Detainee Photographic Records Protection Act of 2009," 179; Freedom of Information Act, 155, 179; funding from, 117, 174; and Fusco, 96; Intelligence Agency, 96; and Iraq Veterans against the War, 71; and July 2007 American helicopter attack, 178; memo on standards of conduct, January 2004, 82; nationalist ideology in Middle East, 111; occupation of Iraq, 69, 155; Patriot Act, 27, 83; Pentagon, 94, 155, 169; Prevention of Terrorism Act, 28; and Rosler, 145; Sedition Act of 1918, 24; and Wodiczko, 23; as world's greatest military power, 113. *See also* military, U.S.; state
unlawful combatant, 6, 7, 80, 81, 112
Ut, Nick, 151; photograph of napalmed girl, 139

Vakfi, Insani Yardim, 184
van der Veer, Peter, 18, 151
van Kesteren, Geert: *Baghdad Calling*, 158–161; *Why Mister, Why?*, 155–158
veterans, U.S., 13, 44, 51, 54, 55, 63, 69, 180; and "Collateral Murder" video, 177; Denver-based, 35; disabled, 128; families of, 52; homeless, 35, 36; maimed, 131; and memories and images of war, 38; traumatized disabled, 138; of Vietnam War, 66; and Wodiczko, 12, 34, 35–39
veterans, British, 36–37
veterans' groups, 109
Vetrocq, Marcia, 104, 132, 154–155
video artists, 213
video games, 13, 51, 175–178, 179, 180, 181, 182
video-sharing sites, 3, 153, 180
video/videos, 17, 18, 22, 31, 35, 38, 39–40, 153, 183; from Apache helicopters, 175, 177, 178, 179–180; and *Mavi Marmara* incident, 183–184; of military operations, 3–4; for Palestinians, 188; rock, 56; and Wodiczko, 19, 21, 22
Vietnamese, 90
Vietnam War, 19, 36, 83, 105, 115, 128, 139, 151; movement against, 49; My Lai massacre, 32–33, 66, 109; reenactment of, 12, 49, 52, 64, 65–68; and Rosler, 145
violence, 59, 67, 100, 120, 151, 204; aestheticization of, 10; against civilians, 115; domestic, 20, 37–38, 44; experience of traumatic, 71; and human rights claims, 233; imagination of, 99; legitimacy of picturing, 10; of meaning, 132; objective, 237; and Occupation of Palestine, 215; and photography, 9; and pornography, 94; and reenactment, 47, 52, 54; and Rosler, 145; sexual, 85, 89, 90, 96; of state, 46, 232; and veterans, 34; and Žižek, 237. *See also* rape; torture and abuse; women
Virginia, 59
virgin/whore dichotomy, 87
"Virtual Army Experience," 180
Vogue Hommes (magazine), 143
von Donnersmarck, Florian Henckel, 22

Wack! Art and the Feminist Revolution exhibition, 96
"walking through walls," 199–201, 202
Wallis, Brian, 105
Wall of Separation. *See* Israeli-Palestinian conflict
Walsh, Kevin, *The Representation of the Past*, 50–51
war, 66, 68, 69; and Berman, 170–171; and cell phones, 161; construction of meaning of, 154; domestic presentation vs. actual experience of, 130; experience of, 3, 42, 151; fact and fiction in, 69; fantasies of, 171; and foreign claim on landscape, 186; and frame, 1; as

fun, 170; ideology of, 30; in Israel/Palestine, 185; landscape of, 13–14, 185–231; media representations of, 151; normalization of, 1; official framing of, 151, 152; perpetual, 2, 11, 18, 29, 46, 183, 190; resisters of, 69; romance of, 12, 13, 34, 47, 51, 54, 64, 69, 72, 130, 134; and Rosler, 145, 146–147; as staged for camera, 2; technology of, 21, 35; and truth, 70; and video games, 176, 178, 179

War and Medicine exhibition, 126

war crimes, 52, 113, 179

war culture: and American landscape, 170; and capitalism, 1; and national identity, 12; opposition to, 2, 11–12; and reenactment, 47, 51; and Wodiczko, 21

Warhol, Andy, 109; *Race Riot* series, 109

Warhol Museum, 109, 110

War of Annihilation, The, exhibition, 110

warrior, 59, 76, 86, 88, 142. *See also* soldiers, U.S.

Warsaw Ghetto, 215, 220, 223

Washington Metro, 23

waterboarding. *See* torture and abuse

Watson, Paul, 123

weapons of mass destruction (WMD), 156

Webb, Alex, 154

Weiss, Meira, 142, 217

Weizman, Eyal, 187, 188, 198, 200, 203, 208, 209–210, 217

Wellcome Trust, 126, 129

West Bank, 27, 190, 194, 206, 209, 217, 222; economy of, 189; and Holocaust, 226; Israeli state land on, 194; as militarized ghetto, 191; Palestinian artists in, 227; and Separation or Barrier Wall, 14, 188–189, 205; settlements in, 187–188, 189, 191, 205

whiteness, 59, 73, 106

whites, 49, 58, 74, 75, 76

white supremacists, 49, 57, 59, 73, 74, 106, 111

Whitney Biennial (2010), 136

Whitney Museum, 110

Wikileaks, 13, 175, 177

Will, George, 18

Williams, Serena, 178

Without Sanctuary exhibition, 105, 107

Wodiczko, Krzysztof, 12, 17, 19–46, 241n34; *Aegis: Equipment for a City of Strangers*, 22; *Alien Staff*, 22; background of, 45; *Bunker Hill Monument Projection*, 20; *Dis-Armor*, 22; *Hiroshima Projection*, 20; *If You See Something . . .* , 19–25, 27, 30, 46; *1991 Poliscar*, 39; *. . . OUT OF HERE: The Veterans Project*, 39–45, 46; *Porte-Parole (The Mouthpiece)*, 22; *Speaking Flames*, 30–32, 46; *Voices of Krakow City Hall Projection*, 20; *War Veterans Vehicle Projects*, 35–39, 46; *Xenology* project, 21–22

women, 37–38, 48, 69, 106, 113, 114; African American, 88; capacity for violence of, 95–103; in Congress, 83; discrimination against, 13; and fallen woman archetype, 87; as immigrants, 24; as interrogators, 84, 85, 95–96; Iranian, 120; Iraqi, 13, 40, 41, 82, 89, 92, 93, 156, 163; in Iraqi psychiatric hospitals, 162; in military, 13, 82, 83, 88, 96, 99, 100; Muslim, 119; rights of, 49; and Rosler, 146; of ruling class, 84; and state interests, 99; subordination of, 87; voting rights for, 84; as wives of British soldiers, 37–38; working class, 84. *See also* feminism; rape; torture and abuse; violence

Wonderyears: New Reflections on the Shoah and Nazism in Israel exhibition, 226

Wood, Graeme, "Reading Trotsky in Tahrir," 236–237

workers, 24, 25; Chinese, 144; immigrant, 28–29; imported, 144; and labor rights, 238; Palestinian, 192, 194

working class, 5, 56, 57, 84, 88, 122

World Bank, 218

World Trade Center, 23, 233, 235. *See also* 9/11 attacks

World War I, 3, 36, 49, 52, 84, 113, 128, 164, 236

World War II, 5, 18, 23, 24, 36, 49, 51, 56, 60, 73, 79, 110, 125, 151

Xbox, 178
Xbox Live, 182

Yad Vashem, 216–217, 226
Yamasaki, Minoru, 23
Yefman, Rona, 214; *Pippi at Abu-Dis*, 214
YouTube, 3, 17, 153, 175, 181

Zapruder, Abraham, film of Kennedy's assassination, 109, 110
Zimbardo, Philip, 100
Zimbardo, Tanya, 100, 101
Zionism, 142, 193, 215–216, 221, 225, 231
Žižek, Slavoj, 28–29, 226, 232–233, 236–237; *The Parallax View*, 236
Zmijewski, Artur, *Repetition*, 100–101
zone of exception, 75
zone of indistinction, 6, 7, 12
Zuckermann, Moshe, 215

ABOUT THE AUTHOR

Dora Apel is the author of *Imagery of Lynching: Black Men, White Women, and the Mob*; *Memory Effects: The Holocaust and the Art of Secondary Witnessing*; and *Lynching Photographs*, coauthored with Shawn Michelle Smith. She has written articles and essays for journals such as *The Art Bulletin, Art Journal, Oxford Art Journal, New German Critique, American Quarterly, Dissent, Journal of Visual Culture, Mississippi Quarterly,* and *Left History*; for the online journals *OpenDemocracy* and *Other Voices*; and has contributed chapters to the edited volumes *What Is Radical Politics Today?*, *The Oxford Handbook of Holocaust Studies*, and *Visual Culture and the Holocaust*. Her articles have been translated into Polish and Hungarian and reprinted in the edited volumes *The Uncertain States of America Reader* and *Krzysztof Wodiczko*. She teaches modern and contemporary art history and visual culture at Wayne State University in Detroit.